PENGUIN BOOKS

HILAIRE BELLOC

A. N. Wilson was born in Staffordshire and grew up in Wales. His first novel, *The Sweets of Pimlico*, was awarded the John Llewelyn Rhys Memorial Prize for 1978. He has written six other novels: *Unguarded Hours*, *Kindly Light*, *The Healing Art* (Penguin, 1982), which won the Somerset Maugham Prize for 1980, the Southern Arts Literature Prize for 1980 and the Arts Council National Book Award for 1981, *Who Was Oswald Fish?* (Penguin, 1983), *Wise Virgin* (Penguin, 1984), which received the W. H. Smith Annual Literary Award for 1983 and *Scandal* (Penguin, 1984). He has also written a study of Sir Walter Scott, *The Laird of Abbotsford*, which won the John Llewelyn Rhys Memorial Prize for 1981, and a biography of John Milton. He has edited Sir Walter Scott's *Ivanhoe* for the Penguin English Library. He is a Fellow of the Royal Society of Literature.

D0994516

HILAIRE BELLOC

A. N. WILSON

I pray – for fashion's word is out
And prayer comes round again –
That I may seem, though I die old,
A foolish, passionate man.

W. B. Yeats

PENGUIN BOOKS

Penguin Books Ltd, Harmondsworth, Middlesex, England
Viking Penguin Inc., 40 West 23rd Street, New York, New York 10010, U.S.A.
Penguin Books Australia Ltd, Ringwood, Victoria, Australia
Penguin Books Canada Limited, 2801 John Street, Markham, Ontario, Canada L3R 1B4
Penguin Books (N.Z.) Ltd, 182–190 Wairau Road, Auckland 10, New Zealand

First published by Hamish Hamilton 1984
Published in Penguin Books 1986

Reproduced, printed and bound in Great Britain by
Hazell Watson & Viney Limited,
Member of the BPCC Group,
Aylesbury, Bucks
Typeset in Bembo

CONTENTS

CONTENTS

ILLUSTRATIONS

ACKNOWLEDGEMENTS

Biography is an intrusive exercise, but in the course of writing this book, my inquisitiveness has been greeted with nothing but courtesy and eager co-operation. Although I have unearthed a good many letters and papers which were thought to have been destroyed during the 1950s, no member of Hilaire Belloc's family or circle has made any attempt to impede their publication. Indeed, from the very start of the enterprise, I have enjoyed the very warmest encouragement, hospitality and friendship from all concerned.

The manuscript sources of this book are chiefly located in the library of Boston College, Massachusetts, where I enjoyed the warm hospitality of the Society of Jesus, and the students, during the fall of 1981. I have also quoted from manuscripts in the Library of Congress, Princeton University Library and the British Library, and I am grateful to these foundations for permission to quote from their material.

I am also deeply indebted to the Earl of Oxford and Asquith, to Mrs John Bennett, to Mr and Mrs Philip Jebb and to Mrs Hoffman Nickerson who have made available manuscripts in their possession and allowed me to quote from them. All quotations from Belloc are reproduced with the kind permission of the Belloc estate.

In the course of my work, I have also consulted books or manuscripts in other places, and I am grateful to the staff of the Bodleian Library, the library of Marquette University, Milwaukee, the Oxford Union Library and the New York Public Library for their various acts of kindness. Special mention must be made of Mr Matthews and the staff of the London Library for their particular helpfulness.

The conversational recollections of those who knew Hilaire Belloc have been almost more valuable to me than any published word. In particular, I am grateful to his surviving family who have been so generous with their time and hospitality: to Belloc's nieces, the Dowager Countess of Iddesleigh and Mrs Lowndes Marques; to Mrs Eustace; to Mr and Mrs Philip Jebb, to Dom Philip Jebb OSB; and to

Mr Julian Jebb. Mr Charles Eustace, a great-grandson of Belloc, welcomed me at King's Land, which is now his home. Mrs Hoffman Nickerson not only entertained me on both sides of the Atlantic but provided me with many invaluable insights into Belloc's thought and character. Miss Stephens, the last person in the office of A. D. Peters Ltd to remember Belloc, shared her recollections with me, as did the Rt Revd Abbot Aelred Watkin. And I am very grateful for the hospitality and conversations of the Earl of Oxford and Asquith, Lady Helen Asquith, Lady Diana Cooper, Mr Malcolm Muggeridge, Lady Phipps, Mrs Renee Tickell and the Hon. Mrs Mia Woodruff.

I am also indebted to the following who helped me in various ways: Lady Clare Asquith; Mr Peter Ackroyd; Miss Suzanne Baboneau; Mrs Ursula Baily; Mrs Julian Barnes; the Rt Revd Monsignor Francis Bartlett; Mr Alan Bell; Professor Bernard Bergonzi; the Revd Ian Brayley SJ; Mr David Butler; Mr Raymond Carr; Mr Jeremy Catto; the Revd Philip Caraman, S.J.; Mr John Stewart Collis; the Hon. Artemis Cooper; Mr Alan Cowle; Mr Felix Crowder; Miss Dawnay; Miss Duncan-Jones; Lord Egremont; Sir Rupert Hart-Davis; Mr Richard Ingrams; Mr Louis Jebb; Mr Matthew Jebb; the Hon. John Jolliffe; Mrs Lucy Judd; Mr William LeFanu; Mr Kenneth Lindsay; Miss Marion Lochhead; Professor John McCarthy; Mrs Susan Marlowe; Dr Thomas O'Connell; Mr Anthony Powell; Mr Peter Quennell; Dr A. L. Rowse; Mr Frank Seegraber; the Revd Brocard Sewell, Order of Carmelites; Mr Christopher Sinclair-Stevenson; Miss Anna Somers-Cocks; Mrs Anthony Storr; the Revd Francis Sweeney SJ; Mr F. H. C. Tatham; Mr Auberon Waugh; Miss Harriet Waugh and Mr Terence de Vere White.

PART ONE

Old Thunder

ONE

OLD THUNDER
1870–1890

Hilaire Belloc was born during a thunder-storm on July 27, 1870, nine days after Pius IX had declared the doctrine of papal infallibility, and two days before the outbreak of the Franco-Prussian war.

Both these events shaped the pattern and texture of his life. But neither would have done so – indeed, he might never have existed at all – had not the Archdeacon of Chichester, Henry Edward Manning, become a Roman Catholic, in 1851. The conversion of Manning is the most crucial event in Belloc's pre-history, and one of the most important events in the history of the English church. The friend of Gladstone, the brother-in-law of the Bishop of Oxford, Archdeacon Manning was at the very core of the Anglican establishment. He was destined for an important career in the Church of England; many already spoke of him as a future Archbishop of Canterbury. After his secession, he did not merely, like John Henry Newman, attract an enormous number of converts to his point of view. He also possessed the political acumen, the high personal reputation and the excellence of mind necessary to organise what had been little more than a sect – 'the Italian mission' – into a grand and serious rival to the Established Church from which he sprang.

The conversion was not without heroism and personal sacrifice. Within a few months, he had exchanged his handsome rectory at Lavington, and his Archdeacon's stall in Chichester Cathedral, for mean lodgings in Bayswater, where he founded a small religious group, devoted to pastoral work among the poor, called the oblates of St Charles Borromeo. It was the greatest mortification to him to be obliged to wear the Roman collar in the streets of London. This item of attire, now universally regarded as normal clerical wear even by the most protestant clergymen, was, in the 1850s, bizarre, foreign and outlandish. It was not something which would be seen on the neck of a gentleman.

When visitors came to Manning's handsome Gothic presbytery in Moorhouse Road (since despoiled by modernist priests), the former archdeacon would apologise for his collar. It was the only thing in the way of smalltalk which he offered Belloc's mother, for instance, when she visited him there in the early 1860s.

At that date, she was a young woman called Bessie Parkes. Her father, Joseph Parkes, had been a Birmingham solicitor. He was a leading figure in the Liberal Party. Since Bessie's girlhood, he had been living in London. He was one of the founders of the Reform Club. And her memories of his house in Savile Row were studded with the names of great writers and politicians. There was none that she admired more than George Eliot. 'My father was much attached to her, and whenever any special celebrity was invited to dinner, such as Thackeray, Grote the historian or old Mr Warburton (one of the principal founders of London University) he was never content unless he had also secured his young countrywoman Marian Evans, for he himself was a Warwickshire man'.[1]

Bessie remembered George Eliot coming down the great staircase of the house which later became the Stafford Club. 'She would talk and laugh softly, and look up into my father's face respectfully, while the light of the bright hall lamp shone on the waving masses of her hair, and the black velvet fell in folds about her feet.'[2]

Bessie was swift to point out that at this date 'not a soul suspected her of a tinge of imaginative power'. They admired George Eliot as a woman of ideas. In politics, Bessie learnt to be a radical and a feminist, positions from which she never wavered throughout a long life. In religion, her parents were fairly unenthusiastic Unitarians; and the circle in which they moved was doubtless influenced by the agnosticism of George Eliot. It was she, while tearfully translating Strauss's *Life of Jesus* in 1848, who had lost her simple nonconformist faith; and she was also largely responsible for introducing the English intelligentsia to the atheistical writings of the French 'positivist', Auguste Comte.

Something in all this must have been spiritually unnourishing, as far as Bessie Parkes was concerned, else we should not find her calling on 'Dr Manning of Bayswater', as the Archdeacon of Chichester had now become. Although 'he was not severe in later years', she found him so on this occasion. 'He was perfectly polite, but I thought that he disliked speaking to a woman who had taken an active part in a public movement. This may have been a morbid impression on my part, but it caused me to be frightened.'[3]

[1] Bessie Rayner Belloc: *In a Walled Garden*, p. 17.
[2] Ibid.
[3] p. 209.

The interview did not last long, and Manning 'spoke with the most measured chilly calmness'.

> He spoke as if perfectly conscious of the Comtist influence then taking possession of English society. It was just at the time when George Henry Lewes and George Eliot were beginning to reign supreme. If one so peculiarly impersonal as Dr Manning could stoop to a personal revelation, the words and the accent he used may be held to have conveyed his inner meaning: 'Though I am well aware of the length to which the controversy has been carried, still I have never had to concern myself with it. Doubt never touched me in that direction. I have always had an entire faith in a Personal God'.[1]

In spite of this revelation, the interview was in no sense concerned with spiritual direction. He merely wrote down the titles of a number of books to do with the History of the Reformation, on a sheet of paper, and passed them over the table to her.

> His look seemed to say, 'You are an unpleasant young woman, one of the stiff old Presbyterian stock; but I will tell you faithfully what I think, and let it take its chance'. I do not think he had any suspicion that I was so impressed and overpowered by his intellect, that when I left the room and the house I ran nearly all the way home, with the sense that I was fleeing from an overmastering brain, and that I dreaded it.[2]

If this chilly little conversation had not taken place, between a gaunt and grief-stricken convert priest, and a rich young woman of advanced radical views, the story which follows would be very different. Indeed, it is quite possible that there would be no story at all. Bessie went off and joined the Roman Church, but she did not see Manning again for many years, 'till he was Archbishop of Westminster and I a married woman with a young child, whom I took to him for his blessing one day when I had to call upon him about the subscriptions got up for poorer French exiles in 1870–1. How good and kind he was about it.'[3]

Five years later, the young infant who had received the cardinal's benediction heard him preach, and his little voice was heard echoing round the Brompton Oratory, 'Is it a man or a woman?'[4] Later on,

[1] Ibid.
[2] *In a Walled Garden*, p. 209.
[3] Ibid.
[4] Marie Belloc-Lowndes: *The Young Hilaire Belloc* (New York 1956), p. 35.

when he had settled that matter to his satisfaction, the little boy grew into a man on whom Cardinal Manning was a lasting and important influence. The boy was Hilaire Belloc.

* * *

Belloc liked to aver that you belonged to the flower of the bourgeoisie if you knew the maiden names of your four great grandmothers. He belonged to the flower of the bourgeoisie. Of the four females who confirmed him in this impression, one was Irish, two were English, and one was French.

His mother Bessie was thirty-eight before she married. In 1867, her friend Barbara Bodichon, a doughty fellow-campaigner for female emancipation, had suffered a collapse of health, and Bessie had accompanied her on holiday to recuperate. When they met in Paris, Barbara having come from Algiers, Bessie was so struck by her friend's frail appearance, that she decided they should eschew a city holiday, and go for refreshment to a village in the country. The village they chose was La Celle Saint Cloud, twelve miles outside Paris, where they took a chalet, belonging to a recently-widowed woman called Louise Swanton Belloc. Madame Belloc's father, an Irishman called Colonel Swanton, had been an officer in the Berwick Brigade in Napoleon's army, having previously fought on the royalist side at the time of the Revolution. Her husband, Hilaire Belloc, had been a portrait painter. She was now left alone in the house at La Celle; or, not quite alone. For, after only a few days in the chalet, Barbara Bodichon and Bessie Parkes were visited by an ill-looking young man who turned out to be Madame Belloc's son Louis. He said that his mother would like them to come to luncheon.

Bessie did not immediately fall in love with Louis Belloc, but she very quickly decided that she wanted to marry him. She made the proposal to Madame Belloc, who was initially inclined to reject it. For Louis Belloc, as well as being younger than Bessie, was a hopeless invalid. He had qualified as a barrister, but been unable to practise his profession because of ill health. Indeed, he seems to have been too ill to do anything much, and his mother felt that, however kindly meant, Miss Parkes's suggestion would have involved burdens which it was not fair to impose upon a strange young woman. However, displaying the brisk insistence with which she took up so many other works of charity, Bessie insisted, and, when the matter was put to Louis, he accepted and was glad of it.

As their daughter, Mrs Belloc-Lowndes, tells the tale in her delightful memoirs, it sounds like an inauspicious beginning for nuptial happiness; but they were happy. Louis Belloc, who was so totally silent and withdrawn in almost all other society, blossomed with Bessie. They were not only very fond of each other. They fell in love; and thus it was that Bessie Parkes, having passed the age when most Victorian ladies would have considered marriage, found herself a new home, and a new name, and a French family. Her attachment to her mother-in-law was, if anything, as deep as her love for Louis, and she determined that she would, for the rest of her life, go on thinking of La Celle Saint Cloud as her home. They returned to London to marry, however, a ceremony which took place at the Catholic Church in Old Spanish Place.[1] They did not lack for money. Her father, Joseph Parkes, had had three houses, in Great George Street, Westminster, Wimpole Street and Savile Row. His collection of Italian paintings was enormous. Seventeen of them now hang in the National Gallery. He possessed two Guardis, a Parmigianino, and many others. He had died in 1865. When she married, Bessie and Louis divided the year between La Celle Saint Cloud, and Mrs Parkes's house in Wimpole Street, living alternately with their mothers. The lease on the Savile Row house was allowed to lapse but, on the demise of her uncle Josiah Parkes, Bessie and Louis moved into the Westminster house and inherited from him a fortune of £20,000. They were not merely flowers of the bourgeoisie; they were costly blooms.

When the idea of their marriage had been suggested, it had probably crossed no one's mind that there would be children. But, within three months of the wedding, Bessie was pregnant, giving birth to her first child, a daughter, in the summer of 1868. This was Marie, who was to become Mrs Belloc-Lowndes, in her day famous as the author of over forty exciting crime novels. It was extremely unusual by the French standards of the day for a woman to have her first child when she was nearly forty. But Louis very much wanted a son. Bessie became pregnant again the next year, but had a miscarriage. Undeterred, she was with child again by the end of 1869.

Marie Belloc had been born in London. When the time of Bessie's second confinement drew near, she was in France, much terrified by the prospects of what she would suffer at the hands of French midwives. Mercy Baker, the Quaker maid who had presided at Marie's birth, was therefore despatched to France. It was a torrid, hot July. She found Bessie lying in a large First Empire bed in the *grand salon* of La Celle Saint Cloud. The drawing-room furniture had been moved out. There was something almost theatrical about this lying

---

[1] Demolished in 1885 and replaced by Goldie's St James's Spanish Place.

in, a bourgeois re-enactment of some scene in the memoirs of Saint-Simon. As the sweltering day, the twenty-seventh of July 1870, wore on, everyone felt thunder in the air. By afternoon, it broke, the most stupendously noisy storm which had been known in the district for more than half a century. As the thunder-claps burst, Bessie went into labour. The next day, Mercy Baker wrote back to England.'I was here alone and brought the baby in to the world, as Mme Louis was so short a time in labour, the doctor could not arrive until the event was quite finished & baby nearly washed and dressed. The little fellow has done nothing but sleep since his advent – & his Mamma has been reading the news all the afternoon, so you will judge that she is first class.'[1] It was an appropriately loud and independent arrival into the world for Hilaire Belloc. As a child, whenever he screamed or made scenes, his mother would call him 'old thunder' in memory of the storm which had heralded his birth.[2]

*   *   *

What Bessie was reading in the newspapers the day after her son was born was something more alarming than thunder. The Franco-Prussian war broke out a few days later. Louis's mother had already left the country, and, at her insistence, Bessie and the young family followed in August; first, to the Isle of Wight, and then on to London where they all stayed with Mrs Parkes in Wimpole Street.

In the year which followed, the first year of Hilaire Belloc's life, the news which came from France was violently alarming. A number of their family were stuck in Paris during the siege, and in the spring of 1871 they began to receive accounts of the Prussian occupation of La Celle Saint Cloud. The Paris Commune, adding to the wreckage of war, made it impossible for Bessie and her family to return to France until June. The devastation, according to a letter of Bessie's, defied description. In the little chalet where she had first stayed with Barbara Bodichon, only the outer walls survived. Floor-boards and staircase had been wrenched out, and windows smashed. In the bigger house, the spoliation was heart-breaking. All their china had been wantonly smashed. Paintings had been used for target practice. Family portraits had been adorned with moustaches and beards. Furniture and carpets had been defiled or destroyed. Doors had been wrenched off their hinges, and in many rooms the hinges themselves had been gouged out and stolen. 'Both the gardens of the house and of the chalet are still heaped up with indescribable mounds of rubbish and – forgive me the

[1] Letter in the possession of Lady Iddesleigh.
[2] Marie Belloc-Lowndes: *I too have lived in Arcadia* (1941), p. 114.

word – filth. You know the word *fumier*? Well, each mound looks as if it was a *fumier*! Indeed, an ordinary English farm dunghill is sweet-smelling and clean, in comparison.'[1]

This horrifying experience left an indelible impression on Bessie, which she was to communicate to her children. It took a team of hard-working men four weeks to clear up the sodden mess on the ground floor of the house alone. The place was not habitable for months, and many of their most precious belongings were gone forever. So, too, more importantly, was the France that Bessie had first known and loved. 'You will find another France,'. Louis's sister had warned her, 'a bitter, miserable, unhappy France.' And that was true.

It was not until the next summer that they all came back to La Celle Saint Cloud, Madame Belloc, Louis, Bessie and the two children. At the beginning of August, Louis and Bessie left the children with their grandmother and went off for a holiday in the Auvergne. The heat was intense, and Louis wilted under it. After less than a fortnight, they decided to come home, and by the time he reached his mother's house, Louis was clearly very ill. On Monday, August 19, 1872, he felt too weak to rise from his bed and slept through the day. As the afternoon passed, they realised that he was suffering from more than simple fatigue and they sent for the priest and the doctor. But he died shortly before midnight without regaining consciousness, aged only forty-two.

He was buried on the following Thursday in the cemetery at La Celle Saint Cloud. Hilaire Belloc, aged two, was the chief mourner, stumbling along behind the coffin holding his mother's hand. Madame Belloc followed them, leading Marie who was aged six. A huddle of aunts brought up the rear in the intense August sunshine. There was Requiem Mass in the village church. Then, when they reached the open grave, Bessie knelt down with her back to it, and put an arm round each of her children, so that they should not see the coffin being lowered into the ground.

Louis had seemed a very frail creature to everyone else, but Bessie had learnt to love him and to respect him. 'I try and think of my little children, and I suppose a day will come when I shall care to bring them up. But their father was so entirely the foundation of my own life, that I don't seem to realise that the children, after all, are his children, and so should mean very much to me.'

Thus, from his earliest years, Hilaire Belloc was to grow up

[1] *I too have lived in Arcadia*, p. 192.

without any men in his immediate family. All the women close to him, moreover, his mother and his two grandmothers, were widows. When they returned to London, Bessie called on the Cardinal, who had himself suffered the loss of a spouse while Archdeacon of Chichester. (In later years Belloc was to say that he admired Manning because he had 'more in him than the rest of the Oxford converts put together – a great love affair and a great death'.[1]) Manning, who doubtless spoke from his own experience, told Bessie that 'grief is a luxury which, like all luxuries, if too much indulged in, becomes injurious to the character'.[2] But it was a thing, in Manning's case as well as Bessie's, which it was easier to say than to put into practice. To the end of her life, Bessie was unable to refer to Louis without her eyes filling with tears.

Belloc, then, grew up with an in-built domestic mythology of Paradise Lost, of mourning-dresses and handkerchieves dabbed to the corner of eyes, of bittersweet memories of a France which had vanished forever, destroyed by the armies of Prussia.

*   *   *

The double life, however, in France and England, continued. The little family were always on the move between La Celle St Cloud and Wimpole Street. From three years old, he had a Methodist nurse called Sarah Mew, who taught him Moody and Sankey hymns and read to him from *Pilgrim's Progress*. But, unlike most purely English children of his generation, Belloc also saw a lot of his mother. It was the French custom for children, however young, to sit up at luncheon and dinner, with the grown-ups, and for servants to share their work, rather than being divided strictly into 'nursery staff' and the rest. Sarah Mew disliked this casualness and said 'you never knew where you were' in the household at La Celle Saint Cloud. She doted on little 'Master Hilary' as she called him, who was perfectly happy to be left alone with her, imbibing her strong, bad-tempered opinions and chanting the pious ditties which she taught him, while his mother was away. Marie disliked Sarah Mew very much however. Left briefly with Sarah Mew at La Celle in the spring of 1874, Marie wrote with the impassioned urgency of a seven-year old: '*Maman, – When are you coming back? I kiss you with all my heart.*' Old Thunder, in his first piece of recorded writing, had this to say:

[1] Letter to Duff Cooper March 22, 1938, q. Robert Speaight, *The Life of Hilaire Belloc* (Hollis & Carter 1957), p. 10, hereafter 'Speaight'.
[2] *I too have lived in Arcadia*, p. 243.

Maman, – I am four years old. I've been given a drum, but I'm not allowed to beat it in the house, only in the garden, or out in the road. I have also been given some little wooden animals. I kiss you.
H. Belloc.[1]

It is striking in many particulars. It shows him to be indulged, and to be noisy. It also shows him, from the first, to have had a tendency towards historical inaccuracy and boasting, since, at the time of writing, he was only three.

He was happy, in this early phase of childhood; and petted by his nurse and his mother who were justifiably amused by his puckish belligerence. Years later, delighting in a baby grandson[2], he exclaimed, 'His face is most fascinating, and has the same effect upon me as the serpent on the bird. He thinks life a really amusing place, which is a way all Belloc children have. It takes years to make them understand what a silly mistake they are making.'[3] Too much, perhaps, can be read back of what we know of the man into his infancy. But this 'silly mistake' that life is really an amusing place was something never wholly eradicated from Belloc's nature and, like a child, he never fully grasped that what he considered amusing did not match everyone else's sense of humour. The very qualities which made some people dislike him were ones with which he had learnt to charm the grown-ups when he was a little boy, the strutting certainties, the rumbustious combativeness, the banging of the drum. When he was six, his mother recorded, 'Hilary asked me today how I knew him to have been a little boy and not a little girl, and he asked, "Is my mouth larger and my teeth more carnivorous?"'[4]

From the first, Bessie, like everyone else who had to do with Belloc, was overwhelmed by his prodigious energy of mind and body. From a very early age, he was reading, and a letter survives which he wrote when he was five, describing himself learning by heart, for pleasure, *The Lays of Ancient Rome*. When he was not out in the garden banging a drum, he was constructing miniature landscapes, and designing canal-systems in the lawn. 'I am most anxious that the vivid fire of his little mind should not burn itself out,' Bessie confided to a friend. For, when he was not reading, he was writing poetry, clipped, metrical and usually elegiac in character. While the Jesuit Father Hopkins was writing a lament for the loss of H.M.S. *Eurydice* in March 1878, the seven-year old Belloc was doing the same:

[1] *I too have lived in Arcadia*, p. 257.
[2] Now Dom Philip Jebb O.S.B.
[3] The Belloc Archive at Boston College (hereafter BC), February 9, 1933.
[4] *The Young Hilaire Belloc*, p. 29.

> While prayers were being offered from the deck
> On came that cruel cloud to wreck
>   The Frigate Eurydice.

Nor was this his earliest effort. For, two years before, he had produced a perfect and morbid little ditty which ran:

> I had a little Fly
> I called it Silver Wing
> And over little bits of thread
> This little Fly would spring.
>
> I made it little hedges
> Of little bits of thread;
> And I made a stick memorial
> When this little Fly was dead![1]

Like all clever children, he besieged his mother with questions. Walking down Whitehall one day, again at the age of six, he stopped and said, 'Mamma, I know that you are extremely old. I suppose you didn't know Charles the First, as he was a king, Mamma? But you must often have seen him, if he lived in St James's Palace before his head was cut off?'[2]

The question shows how full his head was with the past. Nor was it a wholly absurd thing to ask, when one considers how old some of the first-hand historical memories were which he heard in his mother's drawing-rooms. Grandmother Parkes could clearly remember her husband starting from the hearth where the young Belloc played, and setting off for Birmingham when they heard of the passing of the Reform Bill in 1832. But this was a recent memory compared with the ones he heard in France. One of his French grandmother's closest friends, the daughter of the man who invented the hot-air balloon, was Adelaide de Montgolfier, a figure of almost pre-revolutionary antiquity. He recalled her in *The Cruise of the Nona*:

> That woman as a child of four was present in Paris when the mob poured up the Faubourg of St Antoine to the capture of the Bastille in 1789, and I, as a child of seven, eight and onwards, was brought to her time and again to hear her tell the story. I am now in my fifty-fifth year, and the stretch of time is already remarkable. Were I in extreme old age, and told a child of this incident, that child himself, living to a similar old age, would be able to say that he had

[1] *The Young Hilaire Belloc*, p. 36.
[2] Lady Iddesleigh to the author.

spoken to one who had heard of the fall of the Bastille from an eye-witness; and that would be as though some very old person today were to tell one that he had spoken to one who had known a page at Charles II's court, and had seen as a child the funeral of General Monk; or again, it is as though some very old person to-day were to remember having met in childhood a person who had seen John Milton.[1]

'History,' he said, much later in life, 'is a matter of flair rather than of facts.'[2] Certainly, historians have not been slow to point out the inaccuracy of much that Belloc wrote. But the best of his historical writing, such as *Marie Antoinette*, or his little book of imagined historical scenes, entitled *The Eye Witness*, or his *British Battles* series is illuminated by true *flair*, an acute power to feel himself into the past. It was a faculty which was developed very early in his childhood.

★　　★　　★

Belloc was in France, aged seven years old, when the news came that his English grandmother, Mrs Parkes, had died in Wimpole Street. Presumably the Methodistical Sarah Mew sat by him as he wrote: 'My darling Mama, I am very sorry Grandmama is dead and that I shall never see her again. I send you a text, God is love.'[3]

From now onwards, his life was to undergo a change almost more important than all the other chances of fortune to which he had been subject in a short life. For his mother was now left in charge of her own finances. Bessie was always 'hopeless' with money. She was certainly not enriched by her mother's death, since the trustees, after Joseph Parkes's death, had tied up the money in an annuity because of Bessie's religion; for it was feared that, if she were to inherit her mother's capital, she might become a nun or hand over the inheritance to the papists.

Nevertheless, she had no reason to feel poor. Her income was already double that of her mother's (from her Josiah Parkes inheritance) and there was nothing to make her suppose that she would not continue in the prosperity to which she had been accustomed since girlhood.

But, although she did not inherit any money from her mother, Bessie did inherit her lodgers, one of whom was a Catholic spinster of advanced years, the other a young stockbroker. These persons had

[1] *The Cruise of the Nona* (1928), p. 213.
[2] Arnold Lunn: *Yet so new* (1958), p. 64.
[3] *The Young Hilaire Belloc*, p. 23.

been taken in, not because Mrs Parkes had needed the rent, but in order to provide her with companionship when Bessie and the children were in France. But, when the young family settled into 17, Wimpole Street for the winter, the lodgers remained.

Somehow, throughout the winter of 1877–8, Bessie found that life was infinitely more expensive than she had hitherto found it. The Catholic spinster ate a lot. So did the young stockbroker. The Catholic spinster was also drinking her way through the wine–cellar. There was a staff of servants to pay and organise; whereas hitherto, in her Westminster establishment, Bessie had only kept one French maid. She was bewildered to discover that the weekly bills amounted to twice what they had been when her mother was alive.

Confiding her troubles in the young stockbroker, and trusting to his financial expertise, was Bessie's undoing. He persuaded her that she would make more out of her capital if she went in for a scheme of 'shifting investments'. Believing that he knew what he was talking about, Bessie put her affairs in his hands. There were enough distractions, without having money to think about. Both Hilaire and Marie were upset by yet another new way of life having been thrust upon them. They had grown used to dividing their time between La Celle St Cloud and Westminster. They were now in their grandmother's house in Wimpole Street once more, and having to put up with the bad-tempered complaints of the Catholic spinster (kindly unnamed in Marie's recollections of those times). 'It takes all my energies, everything there is in me, to keep this household going well, and, I trust, happy,' Bessie said. 'I have nine human beings to think of, and care for, all of them younger than I am, excepting the poor old lady, who is an invalid, and Nurse. Thank God no one has quarrelled with anyone else, but it has not always been easy.'

Hilaire was fractious and unhappy in 17, Wimpole Street. The servants were not used to him and he was puzzled by their lack of affection. He went on strike over meals, and refused to eat unless he was paid a penny.

In the spring of 1878, Bessie went down to Sussex for a few days of much needed rest. When she returned, she found a note from her young stockbroker lodger to say that he had been called urgently abroad. He also added that his speculative investments of Bessie's inheritance had gone very badly wrong, and that he was sorry to say that he had lost her £12,000.

It was a shattering blow, and one from which Bessie's finances never recovered. In despair, she turned to her old friend and mentor, George Eliot. By this date, the famous novelist was a very rich woman, and, for that reason, a prey to spongers of all kinds. On April 20, 1879, she had a begging letter from George Lewes's nephew Vivian, asking for £100, which she paid up. But by the same post came a letter from Bessie, 'asking me to lend her £500'.

The request was deeply embarrassing. It was a large sum of money. Bessie was by now notoriously unreliable, and there would be no chance that George Eliot would ever see it again. Unable to discuss it with her immediate household, she wrote off to Johnny Cross (whom she was subsequently to marry), signing her letter 'Your much worried Aunt'. Cross's advice, clearly, was to hold on to her £500. She took the advice and 'wrote a letter to Mme Belloc declining'.[1]

For the rest of her life, Bessie was to live in a state of financial chaos, requiring constantly to be bailed out by family and friends. But she did not tell the children of the calamity. Belloc grew up under the pathetic delusion that he was a rich man. It was yet another Paradise Lost, but he was not to know of it yet. To his childish eyes, what happened next seemed more like Paradise Regained.

Feeling that she could no longer retain a London establishment, Bessie tried to let 17, Wimpole Street, but failed. As Marie bitterly remembered, 'In the 'seventies, Wimpole Street and Harley Street were each simply regarded as "a long unlovely street"'.[2] Failing to get a tenant, Bessie hastily and unwisely sold the lease. She had made up her mind to go to Slindon, in Sussex. Slindon House had been, in the Middle Ages, one of the rest-houses of the Archbishops of Canterbury. At the time of the Reformation, the village had remained loyal to the old religion, and mass was still said in The House, as it was called until the nineteenth century, when a small Roman Catholic church had been built. It was therefore a place where Bessie could get (not universally easy to this day) the advantages of rural seclusion allied to the proximity of Catholic privileges.

'Listen, Barbara,' she wrote excitedly to Mrs Bodichon, 'and I will try and picture Slindon, without a labyrinth of sentences.

'Picture a village set on the edge of a glorious down, filled with old grey cottages, and gardens bordered with yew hedges, within which are vigorous fruit trees and lovely spring flowers. The views of the strip of silver sea from east to west are splendid, under certain effects of light. . .'

Bessie took the dower house, called Slindon Cottage, but in fact a substantial residence which could easily accommodate all her things. 'I am in tremendous chaos! All the household gods – by which I mean

[1] Gordon S. Haight: *George Eliot: A Biography* (1968), p. 526.
[2] *I too have lived in Arcadia*, p. 363.

Dr Priestley, Burke, Fox, Jeremy Bentham – are whirling in a saturnalia about the rooms. Thousands of books lie in a great heap on the floor of what I intend shall be called the library; and with *Rasselas* in my hand, I cry, "Enough!"'[1]

While Bessie vaguely swept about the new house in a state of excited muddle, her young daughter Marie, gloomily missing London, sat down, thinking what a mistake they had made. There was only one member of the family who immediately felt a sense of peace and homecoming on their arrival in Sussex, and that was Hilaire Belloc, who was just eight years old.

> In this place, when I was a boy, I pushed through a fringe of beeches that made a complete screen between me and the world, and I came to a glade called No Man's Land. I climbed beyond it, and I was surprised and glad, because from the ridge of that glade I saw the sea.[2]

He had hated London in latter months. He had hated the atmosphere of unhappiness, the unsympathetic servants, the intrusive lodgers, and the constant dashing hither and thither. At last, he felt free and he felt stable. In all the wanderings and turmoil which lay ahead, Sussex was to be more than the place where he sometimes lived. It was to be an emblem of innocent solidity, of the permanence which forever eluded him.

> I never get between the pines
>   But I smell the Sussex air;
> Nor I never come on a belt of sand
>   But my home is there.
> And along the sky the line of the Downs
>   So noble and so bare.
>
> A lost thing could I never find,
>   Nor a broken thing mend:
> And I fear I shall be all alone
>   When I get towards the end.
> Who will be there to comfort me
>   Or who will be my friend?

The answer to this question, in terms of Belloc's life, was his mother, Bessie. She was to outlive his wife and his elder son, and to remain a constant figure in his adult life, only dying (aged ninety-five)

---

[1] Ibid., p. 367.
[2] *Hills and the Sea* (1906) p. 148, 'The Mowing of a Field'.

when Belloc himself was fifty-five. Slindon and Bessie, and the link with childhood which they represented, provided a very stable rampart against the slings and arrows of outrageous fortune which lay ahead.

Of course, 'settling down' was something of which she and Belloc were both incapable. The arrival at Slindon did not mean that she abandoned her life at La Celle St Cloud; nor did it mean leaving London. For she had his education to think about.

Almost as soon as she had unpacked her things at Slindon, Bessie let the house, and took lodgings in Hampstead so that Hilaire could attend a prep school called Heath Brow, and be given solid Catholic instruction at the Dominican Priory on Haverstock Hill. She had no doubts about his future schooling. At Heath Brow, his reports said that he was 'clever, but rather idle'; and his mother must have been pleased to see that he came second in French until she realised that he was being taught in a set which contained only two boys.[1] This did not prevent her from writing to Cardinal Newman in Birmingham to ask if her son could enter his school there at the Oratory.

> Your Eminence, I desire to place my little son under your care at the approaching term. His name is Joseph Hilaire Belloc and he is just ten years old. He is great grandson, on the maternal side, of Doctor Joseph Priestley, and he has a pronounced taste for all natural science. His religious instruction has been commenced by Father Arden of the Dominican Priory, Haverstock Hill. He is a good little boy and he has hitherto never been separated from me. I write from Paris, but my home is at Slindon, near Arundel.

Belloc was to spend the next seven years of his life at the Oratory School. He was ten years old when he arrived and Newman (who had been a Cardinal for less than a year) was seventy-nine, so it is not surprising that no particular intimacy grew up between the pugnacious, beefy little boy and that ethereal and remote Victorian sage. The boys, who nicknamed the old man 'Jack', very rarely saw him. From time to time he would sweep into a classroom and disconcert them, first by making them recite some favourite passage from Virgil, and then by bursting into a flood of tears at its poetic poignancy. Once a year, he directed a Latin play, usually Terence. Newman adapted the comedies himself, with all the earthier jokes excised.

It would seem as though they regarded him as something of a joke;

[1] *The Young Hilaire Belloc*, p. 50.

schoolboys find it hard to idolize grown-ups, particularly when they take themselves as seriously as Newman did. Nowadays, Newman's reputation is higher than it has ever been. He is loved and admired by Christians both within and without the Catholic Church. In his own day, however, this was not so. Liberal converts such as Bessie Belloc held him in high esteem, and he was rightly, and universally, admired as a stylist. But within the Catholic Church, there were many who distrusted him. His time in Dublin, as Rector of the newly-founded Catholic University there, attracted the obloquy of the Irish hierarchy, who regarded him not only as a dangerous liberal but also (quite understandably) as an almost impossible man to deal with. 'Poor Newman is a great hater,' Manning used to say. As the tale is told now, since Lytton Strachey's *Eminent Victorians*, we are asked to believe that Manning was a devious ecclesiastical politician who deliberately thwarted Newman's career by persuading the Vatican that he should not be offered a Cardinal's hat. Seen from the point of view of English Roman Catholicism, Manning's position is entirely reasonable. Newman had a gift for close intimacy and affection with a few trusted friends; but he was also touchy and neurotic and made many enemies. He liked to think people were ganging up against him, and would record, year after year in his diaries, the exact date when he stopped speaking to various contemporaries. There was one young Oratorian at Birmingham with whom Newman lived and ate for twenty years without a single word passing between them.[1] Words, not always of an agreeable nature, *did* pass with other Oratorians. It was his unreasonable beastliness to the (admittedly florid and histrionic) Father Faber which led to the founding of the London Oratory, Faber's associates being only too glad to get away from all the tears and sharp intakes of breath which were part of the daily routine in Newman's company.

Manning and his ultramontane supporters (in those days the majority of English Catholics) had serious reason to doubt Newman's loyalty to the Catholic cause. When the First Vatican Council was summoned in 1870, and the doctrine of Papal Infallibility mooted, Newman wrote voluminous letters to his many correspondents saying that it would never be unambiguously defined; and then, when it was, saying that it was 'most unfortunate and ill-advised'.[2] When the Council decided that the Pope was, in spite of Newman's doubts on the matter, infallible, he characteristically decided that it was 'safer to accept it', but he was not slow to point out that the doctrine had

[1] Told to the author by Fr Humphrey Crookenden, Cong.Orat.
[2] Wilfrid Ward, *The Life of John Henry Cardinal Newman* (1912), Vol. II, p. 299.

been decreed with 'a very large number of dissentient voices' in the Council itself. 'It looks as if our Great Lord were in some way displeased with us'.[1]

Such talk undermined, as Manning saw, the whole *raison d'être* of Roman Catholicism in England. Belloc was always a firm admirer of Manning, and a keen ultramontane in his view of theology and Church politics. It is hardly likely that he had come to these views when he first, at the age of ten, confronted the frail lachrymose figure of Cardinal Newman. But, from the perspective of adult life, there can be no doubt that he did not, like so many English Catholic intellectuals, idolize Newman. He liked to see him as an essentially parochial figure. In 1924, Bede Jarrett, the great Dominican, asked him to contribute a preface to a book on Newman and he refused on the very peculiar grounds 'that quite honestly I do not know anything about him. . . You see Newman's whole position turned upon the difference between the Anglican and the Catholic, and that is a subject which has never come across my life, and interests me but little. I am only interested in the difference between the sceptic and the Catholic. . .'[2]

The misreading of Newman which this dismissal implies is grotesque. Nobody interested in the difference between the sceptic and the Catholic could fail to be interested in *The Grammar of Assent*. And when one considers the output and range of Newman's mind – from his work on the *Development of Christian Doctrine* to his great book on *The Idea of a University* – it seems rather hard to dismiss him as a writer whose only interest is to Anglican converts. Yet, the charm of this silvery-toned and suffering figure failed to enchant the young Belloc. 'Newman was a don,' he used to say in later life; and, in the Bellocian scale of abuse, you could not get much lower than that.[3]

Newman, in any case, played very little part in the lives of the boys. The headmaster was Father Norris. There were twelve other masters and about a hundred boys. When he first arrived, Belloc hated the place. He was terrified by the older boys of seventeen or eighteen who 'looked to me like enormous giants. It was fearfully rough and I suffered heavily. . . They. . . gave us uneatable food and there was bad bullying and as for the attitude towards the outside world, it was that of the Old Catholic clique'.

When he was himself the father of boys, Belloc chose for them to be educated by the Benedictines of Downside, and he would always do

[1] Ibid., p. 308.
[2] BC, February 7, 1924.
[3] Speaight, p. 31.

his best to dissuade Catholic friends from sending their children to the Oratory. The parochialism, the narrowness of outlook, the insular snobbery of what he called the 'Old Catholic clique' always repelled him. Belloc's Catholicism, like Manning's, was of a broadly European base. The older Catholic families in England had happily settled down as though they belonged to some minor and esoteric sect; and you would not have known, from their attitude, that they actually belonged to what the majority of Christians throughout the world regarded as the one and universal church. This was an attitude which Belloc, taught by Manning, found despicably narrow.

Independence of mind in any case makes it impossible to enjoy school. Belloc did quite well at the Oratory. He won prizes, and he was indebted to his teachers for giving him a thorough grounding in the classics. Virgil, Horace, Catullus and Sophocles were all early loves; authors he did not merely read, but knew and absorbed thoroughly so that, throughout life, he had large quantities of them by heart. Above all, he loved Homer, and in particular the *Iliad*; he used repeatedly to read the great combat between Hector and Achilles in the twenty-second book. 'As a boy it was my delight to fashion English to express the glory of that suffering.'[1] He also grew to love, as a schoolboy, the plays of Molière and Racine. And the delight he took in these books more than outweighed any initial discomfort he felt at the Oratory.

Besides, he became quite popular there, and he made at least two friendships, with Arthur Pollen and Charles Somers Cocks, which were to last until death. With Pollen, Belloc shared many literary interests and they were to make their first essays at journalism together. Somers Cocks was to remain a correspondent and travelling companion into old age. A career in the Foreign Office lay ahead, though a promise of high preferment was disappointed by a regrettable scandal. This was certainly not the only descent, before or since, by a member of the British Foreign Office into the Cities of the Plain. Belloc can not have liked this aspect of Somers Cocks. He was perfectly sincere when he wrote:

> The world is full of double beds
> And sweet young things with maidenheads.
> This being so, there's no excuse
> For sodomy or self-abuse.

[1] MS. Letters in possession of Lord Oxford and Asquith at Mells (hereafter Mells), 9. ix. 33.

But Somers Cocks's débâcle did nothing to undermine their friendship.

As school drew to an end all these sorrows lay in the invisible future. Somers Cocks was going into the Foreign Office. Of his other class mates, Hugh Pope was to become a Dominican friar, and James Hope a politician (eventually Deputy Speaker of the House of Commons).

Belloc himself left the Oratory at the age of seventeen, eager to see the world, but with no sure idea of his place in it. Throughout the summer of 1887, while the unfortunate truth was brought home to him that he was not actually the heir to a huge fortune, he thrashed about for ideas, wildly veering from one extreme to another in his notion of who he was and what he ought to be.

The choices were far wider for him than for most boys of his age. He had to make up his mind, for instance, about his nationality. He was still technically a French subject. But, in July, when he left school, he was perfectly certain that he wanted to be an Englishman.

'I love my country,' he wrote, meaning France, 'but I cannot bear the cosmopolitan folly which is destroying the Frank and the Gaul in our class. I dislike the life of a Paris student. My desire is to make a name in literature and as I can write in English, I choose England if it be possible.'[1]

'The cosmopolitan folly' was something which was to be an over-riding obsession in Belloc's mind for the next sixty-five years. The choice of literature as a career, given his background, is not surprising. Not only had his mother written books and grown up in a deeply literary atmosphere (from her earliest years she had known, as well as George Eliot, Thackeray, Trollope, the Brownings; her father had even taken her to Haworth to meet Emily Brontë). But also, on his French side, Belloc had a strong literary inheritance. Mademoiselle de Montgolfier, in effect his great aunt, had had a deep devotion to English writers. She had enjoyed the conversation of Byron. Dickens was her favourite author (though meeting him in Paris had been a disappointment) and she had translated several English novels into French, including *The Cricket on the Hearth*.[2] Belloc's French grandmother, Louise Swanton Belloc, likewise, was an unstoppably prolific author. Lamartine, Victor Hugo and Stendhal all praised her work.[3] Except on Sunday, his grandmother wrote for three hours every morning of her grown-up life, a huge output of biographies and

[1] *The Young Hilaire Belloc*, p. 86.
[2] *I too have lived in Arcadia*, p. 15.
[3] Ibid., p. 20.

of children's stories. She never *spoke* about her work to Belloc or his sister, but the example remained as one to follow.[1]

But, at the age of seventeen, nothing is certain. He had no sooner declared his distaste for being French, and his passionate desire to be an English writer, than he had changed his mind and decided that he would like to prepare to enter the French navy. His mother was rather disconcerted by this *volte-face*. But it was arranged for him to enter the Naval Class of the Collège Stanislas, in Paris, in October 1887.

Belloc had discovered a passion for sailing in the course of the summer holidays, which was to remain with him for the rest of his days. 'It has made a great difference to my life that I went out to sea quite young and sailed alone almost before I was allowed to do anything in the way of other travel alone,' he was to write when he was nearly fifty.[2] But solitarily tacking out of Chichester Harbour, while confirming a taste for the sea, did not prepare him for the rebarbative disciplines of the Collège Stanislas.

It was a curious institution, unlike anything in England at the time, or anything at all nowadays. It was in part an ordinary academic college and in part a sort of prep-school for military training-colleges. It was run by the Marist fathers with a strict pettiness that Belloc had not bargained for. The boys were taught to regard their schoolmaster as the 'délégué de Dieu'. All Paris was outside the walls, but the cadets were not allowed out unless accompanied by a 'grown-up'. Even these outings could only be bought by a trivial system of 'points' collected for virtuous conduct or good class work. Belloc never settled happily to institutional life and he disliked taking orders. It can not have been much surprise to his mother and sister to open the door of their house in London early in December and see the disgruntled figure of H.B. standing there in the uniform of a French naval cadet. That, as far as his naval career goes, was that.

*   *   *

The next three years of Belloc's life were punctuated by a series of false starts. He could not settle to anything; and the reason given, when he tried to explain the matter, was put down to his shock on discovering that his mother had lost all the family fortune.

But poor men settle down to their careers in life as simply as rich men. It has very little to do with money. There was a deep, adventurous restlessness in Belloc's heart. It was tinged with melancholy, and infuses his most poignant poetry; and yet it was not all sad. The world

[1] Ibid., p. 194.
[2] Speaight, p. 34.

was spread out before him, like a meal so delicious that he did not know what to eat first.

His mother, who could not really afford to keep him, got him a job on the Duke of Norfolk's estate in the Arundel Gap with the idea that he would learn to be a land agent. He rode a good deal, and he bought himself a gun, 'but the only thing human I ever shot was a farmer called Halkett. It was his fault, he got out of place in a line on the edge of the wood and came out suddenly from cover without warning'.[1] He was rather a trial to his employer, a farmer whose name does not survive. Time not spent riding on the Downs or taking pot-shots at the neighbours was devoted to lolling in a cornfield reading Milton, and perfecting his own sonnets. The agricultural life did not really answer any more than the Collège Stanislas. Belloc wrote to a friend in Paris giving a satirically hostile account of the farmer and his wife, which his employer opened and read. The wife knew French and Belloc was promptly dismissed.

That was in the summer of 1888. In October he went for an extended tour of Ireland, where he rowed up and down rivers and read poems. By the winter he had returned to London, and his mother noted that 'Hilary is radiantly happy'.

> Kings live in Palaces, and Pigs in sties,
> And youth in Expectation. Youth is wise.

as he was to doodle in much later years. Neither a French naval officer nor an English farmer, he was apprenticed to an architect's office in Bloomsbury. 'My work is now draughtsmanship,' he wrote doggedly to a friend.[2] None of these professions was a wholly absurd idea. His love of France and his love of the sea never deserted him; there was nothing improbable about the notion of Belloc the French sailor. Similarly, though he had failed to get on with his employer at Manor Farm, it was always part of his ambition to own and farm his own little patch of Sussex. G. K. Chesterton wrote in his *Autobiography*, 'I remember drinking a pot of beer with a publican not far from Horsham and mentioning my friend's name; and the publican, who had obviously never heard of books or such bosh, merely said, "Farms a bit, doesn't he?" and I thought how hugely flattered Belloc would be.'[3] Nor should we be surprised that Belloc thought of being a draughtsman. He had a most accurately delicate eye and hand, as his

[1] Quoted Speaight, p. 36.
[2] *The Young Hilaire Belloc*, p. 93.
[3] G. K. Chesterton, *Autobiography*, p. 291.

many surviving sketches show. While he traipsed about Europe and America in later life, he was a compulsive sketcher.

But, of course, the main business of his life was to be literature, as he had known in his heart since childhood. And with his blossoming songs and sonnets there coexisted (as befitted an admirer of Milton, his favourite English poet) a passionate interest in contemporary politics.

*　　*　　*

Belloc tells us in *The Cruise of the Nona* that

> It was my custom during my first days in London, as a very young man, before I went to Oxford, to call upon the Cardinal as regularly as he would receive me; and during those brief interviews I heard from him many things which I have had later occasions to test by the experience of human life. I was, it may be said, too young to judge things so deep as sanctity and wisdom; but, on the other hand, youth has vision, especially upon elemental things; and Manning did seem to me (and still seems to me) much the greatest Englishman of his time... He never admitted the possibility of compromise between Catholic and non-Catholic society. He perceived the necessary conflict and gloried in it.[1]

This was to be the biggest, and most abiding, influence in Belloc's political career. It was his dogged adherence to principles which he learnt from Manning which led him into so many politically heterodox positions in later life. As a disciple of Manning's he became passionately committed to the idea of a 'Catholic society'.

In social and political terms, Manning's Catholicism liberated him from a slavish attachment to either of the mainstream parties; in fact, he saw little distinction between them, and was free to see, what was manifestly true, that they were both governed by greed and self-interest. During the year in which Belloc called on him so often, the Cardinal noted down that 'Whig and Tory are names without equivalents. The Revolution of 1688 wiped them both out. The parliamentary title of the Crown equalises both. They survive as two forms of class selfishness. The aristocratic selfishness and the well-to-do selfishness. Liberal and Conservative are still more unmeaning. The law and constitution of England excludes all such political sections'.[2]

This was to be Belloc's position exactly. The odd thing is that he took some time (as his phrase suggests in *The Cruise of the Nona*) 'to

[1] p. 54.
[2] Edmund Sheridan Purcell: *Life of Cardinal Manning* (1896), Vol. II, p. 630.

test by the experience of human life' the truth of Manning's words. Until his mid-thirties, Belloc tried manfully to believe in the English Liberal party. Piety to his mother, and to his Parkes ancestry, doubtless had something to do with this. But he would always try to marry the English radical tradition to the principles of the French Revolution, to Rousseau and Danton and Robespierre.

Manning's view of 'Catholic society' had an equally hybrid pedigree, but it was based on experience rather than ideology. He had been born into a high Tory protestant household and learnt his social radicalism, by which he meant 'going down to the roots of the sufferings of the people'[1] in the gradual way which such an upbringing allowed. It had begun by feeling pain as a boy, 'when servants or poor people were roughly spoken to'. Later, as a boy at Harrow, he felt that 'the public-school life. . . in which all are equal and dukes are fags, is a great leveller'.[2] His reading of the Bible and of the classics impressed him, on the one hand with the equality of all men before the law in the commonwealth of Israel and on the other with the sympathy for 'the people' to be discerned (rather fancifully one cannot help noting) in Aristotle's *Ethics* and the ancient histories of Greece and Rome. At Oxford, he read Lord Somers's *Defence of the Revolution of 1688* and Burke's *Appeal from the New to the Old Whigs*, and was convinced, on these grounds, of the rightness of the Reforms of 1833, of Catholic Emancipation and Free Trade. In this, he had quite departed from other Tractarians like Newman, Pusey and Keble, all of whom thought that it was almost tantamount to religious apostasy not to be High Tory in politics. When, after his conversion to Catholicism, Manning read Thomas Aquinas, he found set out there principles of social justice which he was to apply rigorously to contemporary Victorian society. *Reges propter regna, non regna propter reges.*[3]

In all this, Manning differed markedly – and taught Belloc so to differ – from the political stance of the old Catholic families of England, who had retained their religion ever since the Reformation, and through the penal times. 'The Catholics of England,' Manning wrote, 'seem to me to be in their policies like the Seven Sleepers. If anything they are Charles the First Royalists. But there is no Charles the First left.'[4]

[1] Purcell, p. 633.
[2] Ibid., p. 629. 'Fags' are/were younger boys at English boarding schools who perform menial tasks such as cleaning shoes for the older ones. The word has no sexual connotation east of Nova Scotia.
[3] The rulers for the realm, not the realm for the ruler's convenience.
[4] Purcell, p. 631.

What was there left? On what did Manning take his stand?

At home, there was poverty on a scale which it is hard for a modern Englishman to believe actually existed. It is humiliating to record that children were dying of starvation on the streets of London in the year that Belloc left school, a year in which the industrial wealth of England had never been greater, her imperial power in the world never more stupendous. It was the grossness of this inequality which fired Manning's radical zeal. in the autumn of 1889, for instance, when the London Dockers went on strike, Manning was the only public figure who was brave enough to take the side of the poor. In the first round of the strike, the Dockers appeared to be victorious. It was a major achievement. For as long as they were on strike, coal, railroads and gas supplies were interrupted. The Directors of the London Docks tried to bluster and bully the men into accepting an increase of pay which would bring up a man's average hourly earnings to sixpence. In this, they had the full support of the Home Secretary and the Bishop of London. When the offer was rejected, there were angry scenes, meetings in Hyde Park, and near-riots in the poorer districts of the East End of London. Manning, almost single-handedly, mediated in the dispute. His own austerity of life, and the fact that he had worked tirelessly among the London poor, gave him an authority with the Dockers which the Directors of the Docks entirely lacked. He pleaded with them not to resort to violence and to go back to work rather than cause worse misery to their half-starved wives and children. He also pleaded with the Directors to show clemency to their underpaid subordinates. 'I never in my life preached to so impenitent a congregation.'[1]

When the strike ended, it was known generally as 'the Cardinal's Peace'. Labour relations in England were never to be the same. A blow had been struck, a point had been made. The English working-class had begun to recognise some of its power, and Manning had been strongly instrumental in tempering the violence of this power and preventing an armed revolution.

It was of this Dock Strike of 1889 that Belloc was thinking, and of the ravaged faces of the poor he had seen on the London streets, which prompted him to write his poignant poem on the poor of London.

> The poor of Jesus Christ whom no man hears
> Have waited on your vengeance much too long.

The socialism of the strike leaders and their supporters impressed Belloc. 'It was before the socialist creed had been captured for the

[1] Purcell, p. 662.

sham battle at Westminster. The leaders *did* desire and *did* think they could achieve an England in which the poor should be poor no longer.'[1]

The sort of William Morris socialism which saw the progress of the rights of man as going hand in hand with a return to Medievalism in matters of craft, taste and faith might, one suppose, have had a great appeal to Belloc. Indeed, this was the case, as he admitted years later.[2] But, once again, Belloc had Manning to thank for the fact that he was not a socialist. The Papal Encyclical *Rerum Novarum* of 1891 though nominally composed by Leo XIII was really written by Manning. It castigated the evils of capitalism quite categorically. It assailed 'the callousness of employers and the greed of unrestrained competition' and exposed the manifest injustice of 'a small number of very rich men' being 'able to lay upon the masses of the poor a yoke little better than slavery itself'. And it clearly enunciated the view that the state has a duty to prevent injustice and to protect 'the poor and the helpless'.

Nevertheless, *Rerum Novarum* is quite as fiercely anti-socialist as it is opposed to capitalism. The basis of society was, it insisted, the family; and the encyclical views 'the stable and permanent possession' of *property* as the essential ingredient of human freedom. The danger of capitalist society was not, as socialists diagnosed, that of ownership. It was that too few people owned too much. Socialism sought to deprive individuals of the power of ownership by absorbing all property into the arms of the State. *Rerum Novarum* sought, rather, a fairer distribution of property, a society in which no one was too poor to own their own house or little bit of land. This encyclical is deeply important to the development of Belloc's political thought, and lies at the bottom of nearly all his economic and political beliefs. Although unpublished in the year he spent most time in Manning's company, the views it contains must have been aired in conversation between them, and when the encyclical appeared in 1891, Belloc must have recognised the drift of Manning's thought behind its turgid Vatican-bureaucratic Latin.

Neither a farmer nor a draughtsman for long, Belloc wanted to be absorbed in the Great World, the world of ideas, of contemporary politics and journalism. It was at this time that he started, in collaboration with his school-friend Arthur Hungerford Pollen, a monthly magazine called the *Paternoster Review*. It doubtless took this name because Paternoster Row, at the top of Ludgate Hill, looks down upon Fleet Street and was, in those pre-Blitz days, at the very centre of

[1] *The Cruise of the Nona*, p. 153.
[2] Wilfrid Scawen Blunt, *My Diaries 1888–1914* (1932), p. 423.

London's newspaper world. But there is also an obvious appropriateness about the name, for the *Paternoster* is the great prayer of Christendom.

Like most attempts to launch journals on little capital, it was unsuccessful. It only ran for six months. But these six issues are an impressive testimony, both to the flair of its young editors, and to the wide amount of 'pull' which they and their families exerted in the literary world. The first issue had a poem by George Meredith; a frontispiece drawn by the Earl of Carlisle; an extraordinarily vivid photograph of Cardinal Newman (the last ever taken; he looks like the spry inmate of a female geriatric ward); and a leading article by Manning called *Darkest England*.

It appeared in the summer of 1890. It being a bright May, Belloc appointed himself 'cycling correspondent in France' and disappeared to Brittany where he was nominally 'covering' the French general election. Thus, from the beginning of his journalistic career, Belloc manifested a great flair for attracting good articles and interesting material; and at the same time an extraordinary inability to settle down to any kind of office routine without leaving, capriciously, for sorties in France. Years later, Mrs Cecil Chesterton recalled dining with her husband and Belloc in the Gambrinus, 'a jolly German beer-house just behind the Café Royal'. After the steak and Volnay were consumed, Belloc suggested that he and Cecil should run over to France – if they started immediately they could catch the night train and arrive in the early morning. Luggage was quite immaterial, they could buy as they went. Cecil turned down the suggestion that evening, but I have known them on occasions set off at a moment's notice, without so much as a toothbrush and disappear into the void, *en route*, perhaps, for some interesting trees whose acquaintance Belloc had made the previous summer in Brittany or the Pyrenees'.[1]

From Brittany, on this adolescent trip, he made his way down to the Auvergne. At the age of forty-two, he made the same journey, and wrote this letter to his wife.

> I went, yesterday, my life's darling, all along the road which I went 24 years ago on my way round France in '89, on my way to *you*, though I knew it not. I was 19. I went through the Torèze mountains which were full of clouds as they were then, and very magnificent.[2]

---

[1] Mrs Cecil Chesterton, *The Chestertons* (1941), p. 55.
[2] BC, May 13, 1913. He remembered the year as 1889 but it was in fact 1890.

TWO

ELODIE
1890–1891

Belloc's sister Marie developed a happy friendship with Henry James towards the close of the great novelist's life. Their meetings usually took the form of tête-à-têtes over supper or tea and they would discuss books, and life, and London gossip. She once exclaimed, '"Of course I know why you are so kind to me". He answered at once, in French, "Surely the reason is because you are you and I am I?" I exclaimed, "There is a much better reason than that! The real reason is surely because I am the only writer of your acquaintance who has never sent you one of his or her books. How you must groan as the parcels come in". He observed, in a shamefaced voice, "You are the only human being who has ever guessed – shall I say, ah me, what the coming of those parcels – those kind, those generous, those gracious gifts – means to their grateful, their often embarrassed, their sometimes perplexed, recipient" – and then his voice died away'.[1]

All this was in 1911 or 1912. Two decades earlier, in 1890, a highly Jamesian situation had arisen in the Bellocs' house in Great College Street. An American widow, from Napa, near San Francisco, was passing through London at the conclusion of a European tour. Her name was Mrs Hogan, and she was accompanied by two of her daughters, Elizabeth and Elodie. Their chief reason for pausing in the metropolis was to see their friend W. T. Stead, the editor of the *Pall Mall Gazette*. Elizabeth Hogan had aspirations to journalism, which were shared to a lesser extent by her sister Elodie. Stead, who was generous in his encouragement of young writers, had been introduced to the Bellocs by Cardinal Manning, and had paid Marie Belloc what seemed to her the enormous sum of ten pounds to cover the Paris Exhibition in the previous year.[2]

It was in June 1890 that the Hogans came to see Stead, and he arranged rooms for them in Cecil Street off the Strand.[3] Their plans

[1] Marie Belloc-Lowndes, *The Merry Wives of Westminster* (1946), p. 187.
[2] Marie Belloc-Lowndes, *Where Love and Friendship Dwelt* (1943), p. 147.
[3] Speaight, p. 54.

were decidedly unfixed. Elizabeth Hogan was anxious not to return to California, intending rather to try her hand at journalism in London. Mrs Hogan, on the other hand, wanted to go home, and Elodie was torn between the desire to please her parent, and the wish to enjoy herself.

Elodie Hogan at this date was twenty-two years old. She was 'of medium height, and she had a graceful figure; but her principal beauty was a mass of red-gold hair, and she had the translucent-looking white skin which occasionally accompanies red-gold hair. The varying expressions on her face always betrayed what she was thinking, and she possessed a strong, at times, an exuberant, sense of humour.'[1] But a cloud of indecision hung over the girl's future. A young man was pressing his not particularly welcome suit back in California. Her spiritual adviser, a Polish priest encountered in Rome, was urging her to become a nun. She felt torn between these two not wholly palatable alternatives. London provided a very happy, if temporary, respite.

The Hogans were an Irish family, only first generation Americans. Both Elodie's parents had been born in Ireland; and Elodie was one of seven children, three girls and four sons. Their Catholic piety was deep, and in the bone. They had not reached the faith, as Bessie Parkes had done, as a result of intellectual conviction. It had been bred in them for generations, intensely strong, simple and, in the best as well as the worst sense, peasanty. Bessie, it is true, had felt overwhelmed by Manning's intellect and personality, to the point where she wanted to join the Catholic Church. But this gesture itself, involving, as it did, a loss of fortune, showed extreme independence of mind. She was not a woman to be brow-beaten. She had grown up in a radical, liberal atmosphere in which Women's Rights and the Feminist cause were being aired for the first time in history.

Elodie Hogan, a generation later, was in a very different position. Spirited and clever as she may have been, she had not been brought up to value freedom and independence of mind more highly than obedience to the dictates of religion. It was a Catholicism which some would consider priest-ridden. The pressure which was being put upon her to become a nun (for Mrs Hogan undoubtedly backed up their Polish acquaintance in his view) was something which could not be shrugged off lightly. The Polish priest had been their guide in Rome. He had escorted them through the catacombs; he had taken them to St Peter's to see the beatification of Jean Giovenal Ancina; he

[1] *The Merry Wives of Westminster*, p. 28.

had even secured them an audience with the Pope. And when they left him behind in Rome, pursuing a leisurely journey through Switzerland and France, he bombarded them with letters, urging Elodie all the time to 'try her vocation'.[1]

Too much can be, and has been, made of the matter. Elodie's little diary,[2] which she kept in the earlier part of her continental tour, reveals only a strong disinclination to become a nun. Perversely, it is her very unwillingness to take the veil which, she believes, would, make such a gesture all the finer. 'If one has a strong revulsion or disinclination to anything, this is simply another opportunity to overcome oneself, and thus render greater Glory to God. When one has resigned oneself to God,' she adds optimistically, 'God gives perfect rest and peace.'

Given her background and upbringing, it is inevitable that she would take the notion of the religious life seriously. While doing so, she had every intention of enjoying herself in London, in spite of the fact that the Polish priest urged her not to stay there, but to return forthwith to California and enter a convent. Unfortunately, we cannot follow her thoughts on the matter from day to day because, after her arrival in London, the diary entries peter out. Keeping a journal of a sporadic kind is more usually a consolation in melancholy than an outlet of exuberant happiness. The fact that she stopped jotting down meditations on Christ's passion in her little notebook is probably a sign that she had more enjoyable things to do.

Whatever the thoughts which were churning in her brain, her time in the rooms at Cecil Street came to an end. W. T. Stead had evidently introduced the Hogans to Marie Belloc, and she brought them back to tea in Great College Street.

While the women sat over their cups and plates, the door of Bessie Belloc's drawing-room opened and Hilaire Belloc, intensely preoccupied with the *Paternoster Review*, hair awry and brow furrowed, burst into the room. It was his first meeting with his future wife.

Henry James, all those years later, talking of Turgenev's life and loves to Mrs Belloc-Lowndes, said that the only thing which causes a *liaison* between a man and woman to endure is if she has taken a hold of his imagination.[3] Elodie unquestionably took a hold of Belloc's imagination; and he, equally, of hers. 'I loved you for your sad face,' she confided to him a few years later.[4]

[1] Speaight, pp. 53–4.
[2] Preserved at Boston College.
[3] *The Merry Wives of Westminster*, p. 184.
[4] BC March 10, 1894.

Belloc often liked to give the impression that he was a bit of a dog. 'His conversation was kinda raunchy,' one of his American hosts remarked in later life.[1] In fact, his love for Elodie was marked by intense fastidiousness and shyness.

The ground floor of Great College Street was temporarily vacant, and Bessie Belloc, ever hospitable, suggested that the young Hogan sisters occupy these rooms after their mother returned to California. This plan was adopted, and for the next six weeks Elodie was free to explore the great city with her hosts. Unchaperoned, she and Belloc went about together.[2] There could not be much doubt, on either side, that they were falling in love. But it is here that the pen and imagination of Henry James could alone untangle the complicated emotions and motives of the situation. London was, for Elodie, a revelation. She had, moreover, stumbled upon a young man of genius; twenty years later, looking back, she could say that 'I plainly foresaw all his power and realised the greatness of his soul'. Yet, as Henry James would have noticed had he observed the budding passions of the young pair, there were other ways of looking at the situation. Elodie was a young woman of simple Irish stock with very little money and no background. Belloc, on both his mother's and his father's side, was a person of distinguished intellectual stock and, she might wrongly have guessed, some substance. He was trying his hand at journalism, the profession which Elodie, two years older, wished to follow. The worldly attractions of this young man were, though it would be paradoxical to stress them, unquestionably strong when compared with the allurements of a return to her widowed mother in Napa, where the only choices which apparently lay before her were the unwelcome attentions of a man and the austerities of the religious life.

Elodie wrestled with herself, and tried to act for the best. But they were heady weeks, and for all Belloc's shy courtliness, their *liaison* made no progress. He talked endlessly of politics, of modern literature, of the *Paternoster*. But the rest was told in looks and glances and smiles and blushes.

One day, as their taxi-cab paused outside the Houses of Parliament, Elodie plucked up the courage to seize his hand and kiss it. '"What an awful girl" the prudes and propers would say and with some justice. Now weren't you shocked that a young woman's democratic enthusiasm should run so away with her? I think you must have nearly fainted, Honey-bun. And very probably Mr Cabby up above was

[1] A Jesuit of Fordham University in conversation with the author.
[2] Speaight, p. 55.

highly edified and if he knew I was an American, the Lord help the name he will give to others of my country.'[1]

The truth, at last, was out. She loved him, and the affection was reciprocated. Belloc, nevertheless, was emotionally incapable of making any of the 'running'. He made a few bluff comments to the effect that, at twenty-two, she was a little old for him, and that he certainly would not consider courting a girl any older.[2] But his diffidence, shyness, and chastity were deep and hard to shake. The chaste nature – and Belloc's was preternaturally chaste – feels sexual passion more, and not less, strongly than those of more promiscuous habits. Belloc's feeling for Elodie was *une grande passion*, something which ossified and became mythologised as he thundered through life. As Chesterton once wisely observed, 'the superficial impression of the world is by far the deepest'; and what Belloc felt to be true about his early passion for Elodie probably was, in a sense, true; though there were innumerable vicissitudes of feeling and fortune before he married her.

One can hardly doubt that he had his own life in mind when, in old age, he was penning his book about Louis XIV:

> There falls upon some very few human lives an experience transcending every other. They that receive it stand separate from all their fellows. It has no name.
>
> To call it exalted love or love inspired means nothing. The word 'love' is used in every tongue and by all mankind to mean things so different, so varying in degree and quality, that to use it here is meaningless. It has no name.
>
> The thing has no name. For names attach only to things generally known and *this* thing, a revelation, is known to very few and is incommunicable. The only parallel to it is the experience of the mystics, their momentary union with the Divine. This, those who have been so transfigured can never later describe.
>
> But – though what Mary Mancini awoke in him has no name – we can call it flame of fire. It seized his whole being as from without and from above. It is not of mortality; and in one great English line it has been justly saluted 'the ultimate outpost of Eternity'. Such a Visitor met Louis in his twentieth year.[3]

And, we may believe, such a visitation took place in Belloc's twentieth year also. The romantic egotism of the theory that the thing

[1] BC. Undated, but evidently of 1890.
[2] BC. Remembered Good Friday 1896.
[3] *Monarchy* (1938), p. 66.

with no name has been experienced by very few men cannot, of course, be tested. Looking back at his courtship towards the close of his life, Belloc could see it in clearer outlines than it appeared at the time.

But of one thing we can be certain. He and Elodie, in the summer of 1890, were deeply in love. The six weeks that the Hogan girls stayed in Great College Street passed rapidly. At the end of August, she and Elizabeth were summoned back to California by their mother.

*　　*　　*

By the end of August, Belloc had told his mother that he intended to marry Elodie Hogan. Bessie, who had been twice his age when she married his father, viewed the notion rather cautiously. She advised the young people not to become engaged. The future, after all, was very uncertain. Belloc was just twenty years old, and scarcely in a position to marry. The *Paternoster Review* was on its last legs. (It was to come to an end that year.) He had no 'career' in prospect beyond an undirected, if intense desire to 'write'. His intended bride lived thousands of miles away, and there was no reason to suppose that her mother would approve the match.

Reluctantly, the young people agreed to accept Bessie's advice. But Elodie's boat had scarcely left Southampton before she was writing a stream of unhappy letters to the young man she had left behind her. Once home in Napa, her pen flowed no less freely. And it would seem, in correspondence, as in life, as if she 'made the running'.

> My darling, To begin with you are very bad, rather you have been very bad. Why do you not write often? Do you know that more than a fortnight ago you wrote me a dear letter, and very humble because you did not write? Well, you have been horrid again, and left me, oh so long without a line – you are bad, bad, bad!
> There now! I will not say anything more.

Already out of date with his London life, she continues,

> What a success you are making of the Paternoster! Didn't I tell you so, Honeybun? And when you were beginning it and you were neglecting it, I did not keep my engagements how furious you used to be! (*sic*) Elizabeth will write you concerning it – I cannot write– there is a girl here talking and talking and I wish she would keep still.[1]

---

[1] BC, undated letter, evidently of 1890.

It is unfortunate that a chief source of information concerning this period in the life of Belloc and Elodie is in the *Adventures of a Novelist* by Gertrude Atherton (1932). Ten years Elodie's senior, Gertrude Atherton was a fellow-Californian with literary pretensions, brought up, as she put it, 'with a Prayer Book in one hand and the *Atlantic Monthly* in the other'.[1] At this date, she had not published anything. In her day, however, she became a popular, slightly trashy novelist, now confined to oblivion. When her memoirs appeared in 1932, Belloc did not have much to say about them, but he always cautioned people to take them with a pinch of salt in so far as they related to himself.[2] In the light of documentary evidence, this caution would seem to be justified.

Mrs Atherton, for instance, describes Elodie when she got back to California crying into her cocoa and saying that she wanted to become a nun.[3] At this distance in time, one is not in a position absolutely to deny this vignette. But, although the idea of her religious vocation had not been altogether dismissed, Elodie's letters do not suggest an overwhelming longing to take the veil. When she confessed her lingering doubts about the idea of trying her vocation, Belloc was horrified and accused her of lack of frankness:

'Darling', she replied.

Do not ask me to be frank with you – it looks so as if you thought I am not. I could not bear to tell you sooner and believe me darling I was not conscious that I put so much sorrow in my letters to you. Don't tell me I'm morbid; I am not. I love you dear and I am so afraid of the future. And I have suffered so much on your account. I am not blind – you see I am an unhappy girl, and I keep putting my misery on you, Honey Bun. If we were only near to each other, there is so much that we could say and ink and paper are of so little worth.[4]

It seems from this effusion as if Belloc's charge of morbidity was perfectly justified. Elodie was probably too miserable to be able to see that, in so far as she was still toying with the idea of the religious life, it was as a spur to encourage her suitor. Doubtless, in her wretchedness, she thought that if he did not marry her, she would become a nun. But, in those autumn months of 1890, there was still very strong hope, on both sides, that something would come of their attachment.

[1] *Notable American Women* (1973), Vol. I, p. 64.
[2] Mrs Hoffman Nickerson to the author.
[3] Quoted Speaight, p. 57.
[4] BC, 1890.

Her plea that they should be near to each other was, however, an unnecessary prompting. Belloc had already announced to his mother that he thought of looking up some Priestley cousins in Philadelphia.

Bessie Belloc was too wise a parent to suggest that she perceived any connection between Elodie's crossing the Atlantic, and her son's sudden desire to look up American relations in whom he had hitherto taken no interest. There was no money available for such an adventure, but love will find a way. Belloc borrowed twenty pounds from one of his mother's friends and sold all his prize books from the Oratory: the calf-bound poets, the single volume of *Chambers Encyclopaedia* and the complete edition of Newman, signed by the Cardinal himself. Since 'Jack' had just died, on August 11 of that year,[1] there was no danger of his hobbling down Oxford Street and seeing what the ungrateful Oratory boy had done with his benefaction. But Madame Belloc was still alive, and when she saw the volumes in the shop window a few days later, she went in and bought them back.

Belloc by then was in the steerage of a transatlantic liner, his heart high with a sense of romance and adventure. It was his passion for Elodie which led him on. But, in the pursuit of it, he was about to discover another, if a lesser, love: his feeling for America, which was always strong and deep.

> After I had journeyed on the ocean many days in no great comfort, for I did not travel as the rich travel, I came to a part of the sea where all things changed.
>
> It was in crossing the Grand Banks that I discovered this new air; I was appalled and vastly intrigued. I was coming to unknown things. It was in what I breathed and in the quality of the wind...
>
> The first ship twinkling upon the horizon was like a herald. I wondered at the coming world; and when I passed through the Narrows into New York Harbour, I saw grass and trees, contours of low hills, the houses of men, and all was utterly strange.

He wrote those words long afterwards, when the Manhattan skyline had begun to spring up to the world's amazement, destroying the last of those trees and contours. The book in which the reflections appear, *The Contrast*, remains one of the best accounts of the differences between England and America.

He made his way first down to Philadelphia to stay with his cousins the Priestleys. But he was still only half-way to Napa. Nowadays, one can arrive at an airport, pick up a shuttle-flight and by waving a plastic

[1] Ward, p. 537.

banker's card, secure one's arrival in any part of the United States within a matter of hours. It was not like that ninety years ago. The journey from east to west was enormous and expensive. Belloc's funds had almost run out when he set out for California. He made a little by gambling in saloons along his way, down the Ohio river to Cincinnati. But that method of raising cash soon ensured that Belloc became penniless. From then on, he had only his wits, and his hand and his eye, to get him the next meal, as he set out to tramp his way across the United States of America. Much of the journey had to be accomplished 'on foot for lack of a railway ticket along the Denver and Rio Grande, through the deserts and threading odd and deep canyons by way of the railway embankment, seeing trains go by with people in them and sleeping out and trudging on next morning and marvelling at the rocks and the new sights and sleeping in unexpected houses and so on, with no end but getting somehow to Denver and selling pictures on the way and wondering about things that don't matter and writing verse in one's head and losing money at cards on the Cimarron and then having none and so limping into Canyon City and then getting money again and walking over the shoulder of Pike's Peak down on to the Florente and landing up at night in a goods wagon – and so on to the end!'[1]

All this was recalled to his friend George Wyndham, when he thought of the journey as emblematic of his life's work. 'Theology calls it a task. I call it a bloody ramble. But I am glad it is still possible to find a companion.'

The journey felt, as in a very different way did the letter to Wyndham twenty years later, like a quest for companionship. In his poetry of 'bloody ramble', too, he asks, 'Who will be there to comfort me/And who will be my friend?' But, for all his compulsive gregariousness, his combative and hilarious companionability, there was a profound solitariness about Belloc. In his best poetry and travel-writing, he is a man on his own. Even in his works of apologetics and political theory, he sounds, more often than not, like a man talking to himself. He would never have believed, with Leonard Woolf, that 'the journey not the arrival matters'. But it was the bloody ramble with which he was to be perpetually preoccupied for as long as his legs were active. 'This world is made,' he continued in the same letter to Wyndham, 'as the Physical Universe is. It is full, yet empty. It is full of some tenuous stuff which transmits and permits mere living and the forces that permit life, but . . . the bodies of which one can say

[1] BC February 5 1910.

"I am I", "you are you" are little points in an illimitable void – or void that seems void compared with their stuff and reality. So are the specks of planets in the immensity, yet they are worlds: and so are men.'

To his American lecture audiences, twenty-five years later, he would say, 'When I first crossed the ocean to the New World it was in an adventure of boyhood: I was not yet of age. Discovery tempted me and the hunger of new things.'[1] He did not make public, of course, his boyish passion for Elodie. Every step that he tramped westwards took him nearer to her. When begging and borrowing failed to find him a meal or somewhere to stay the night, he would turn his facile pen to making sketches of the passing landscape which he sold in exchange for bed and board.

'I would make a good little sketch in sepia of some peak, and this a lonely fellow on a ranch was very glad to have, giving me in exchange my supper, my breakfast and my bed; and I would go on next day to another and draw another picture and sell it for another lodging.'

One wonders how many of these little sketches survive, to this day, in farm-houses of the mid-west.

The landscape of the Eastern sea-board had been unattractive to him; later in life he was to describe the country round Philadelphia as the ugliest in the world. The Rio Grande and the Rockies had frightened him by their crude immensity. But, once they were passed, he was able to look down upon 'the cascade of dense forests' which descended into California.

> But now such busy work of battle past
> I am like one whose barque at bar at last
> Comes hardly heeling down the adventurous breeze;
> And entering calmer seas,
> I am like one that brings his merchandise
> To Californian skies.

The actual land-journey brought no less peace and pleasure than the imagined sea-voyage: the peace, that is, which Pacific sunshine, and fertile lands, and sea air could always bring. California was, for him, 'a vision of Europe glorified'. He would always be grateful for having seen it before it was 'spoilt': it had for him, with its vineyards and its blue sea, a purely European flavour; the flavour of a Europe still innocent and unsullied by commerce, protestantism or over-population.

[1] *The Contract* (1923), p. 27.

The object of his journey was, of course, to woo Elodie. Throughout the previous months, until he took to the road, she had been as good as her promise when she wrote, 'I am going to flood you with letters.' This was because her mother had been away. Mrs Hogan had got home by December 20, 1890 and, after that, the correspondence ceased.

Belloc reached San Francisco on March 10, 1891. The Hogans had moved in to the city from Napa so that the younger sons could attend Santa Clara College as day-scholars. The arrival of Belloc was obviously a surprise to them all, even to Elodie herself.

It was Gertrude Atherton's first glimpse of him. 'He was not an impressive figure in those days. His hair was long and dusty, his hands and linen were never clean, and his clothes looked as if they had been slept in, which no doubt they had.' Since he had just spent three months on the road, this was hardly surprising. As I have stressed, Mrs Atherton is not the most reliable witness, but she is the only one that we have. Clearly, to Elodie and Belloc she was something of a joke, and they nicknamed her 'the widow'. Mr Atherton had first tried to woo her mother (he would have been her mother's third husband) before persuading Gertrude to marry him. It had not been a happy union and she had not much grieved for him when he had died of a kidney haemorrhage while sailing as a guest on a Chilean warship in 1887. When Belloc met 'the widow' she was 'a striking blonde of middle height with blue eyes and a classical profile'.[1] She was thirty-four; he was 'not yet of age', and had already hinted that a woman of twenty-two was too old for his tastes. The friendship which grew up between him and Mrs Atherton was therefore a safe enough topic to joke about with Elodie.

Gertrude, for her part, did not take Belloc too seriously either. 'He is in love with a friend and protégée of mine, a very pretty little Irish girl, and I am post office, as her family violently oppose the match. He would wear me out in about three interviews,' she wrote at the time.[2] Later, she would recall:

He was a 'dynamic personality' and his mind was so active and blazing that I was always expecting it to explode and burst through his skull. One evening he came to call on me alone, and remained until four in the morning. He sat huddled over the fire, his hands hanging between his knees, his shoulders above his ears, and talked and talked and talked. Such a flow of words I have never listened to,

[1] *Notable American Women*, Vol. I, p. 64.
[2] Library of Congress. Lippincott MSS.

and every one of them sparkled. From his passion for Elodie and his determination to marry despite the Church, Mothers, Youth and Poverty, he passed on to affairs of the world, and never before or since have I heard anyone discourse so brilliantly. I sat in fascinated silence, regardless of time or of possible Grundys across the street. I still wondered how Elodie could have fallen in love with him, but when he turned on that extraordinary mind of his at full blast, I could have listened to him for ever. He convinced me that he knew more than any statesman in Europe.[1]

'Dear me!' Elodie urged. 'Do be good to the widow. I am sure you are quite safe no matter how potent her charms.'

What was Elodie feeling all this while? Her mother's opposition to her marrying Belloc was absolute. If she disobeyed, she had to face the prospect of being cut off from her family, to whom she felt closely attached, in order to throw in her lot with a young man whom she had known for six weeks.

Gertrude Atherton was, of course, quite wrong to think that 'the Church' would have put up any opposition to the match. Both the young people were Catholics; Elodie extremely pious, Belloc at this date sitting rather light to it all. There would have been no ecclesiastical objection.

Belloc always regretted not having married Elodie in that Californian spring of 1891.[2] He bowed, instead, to the wishes of her family. There was still talk of her religious vocation, and with the prospect of separation in view, Elodie perhaps felt it was the only alternative for her. But there can be little doubt that she, too, wanted to marry Belloc at this date. Another four years were to pass before she actually went into a convent. It was Mrs Hogan, and not the call of the cloister, which made the young people hold back. Disconsolately, Belloc made his way east once more. Nothing as yet was certain. Mrs Hogan had obviously persuaded him to go away and leave Elodie time to make up her mind 'on her own'. But at the end of April, when he was in New Jersey, he wrote back to England, 'My dearest Mother, Elodie's refusal came today.'[3]

If she had not been persuaded to write this letter, Belloc's 'bloody ramble' would certainly have taken a different course. He had no career to draw him back to London. He would almost certainly

[1] Speaight, p. 60.
[2] Ibid, p. 61.
[3] *The Young Hilaire Belloc*, p. 102.

have returned to California and settled down, as one of his sons was to do thirty years later, as an American citizen.

When he had gone, Elodie collapsed. 'I cried myself blind and ill and almost insane,' she confessed to him later. And, with a most revealing misquotation, she said, 'Do you remember Marianna (*sic*) in the moated grange?

> He cometh not, she said,
> I would that I were wed!

(Lord Tennyson's Mariana actually exclaimed, 'I would that I were dead.') 'I was nearly being Marianna. But no one saw me,' she dolefully confided.[1]

All this was in the following winter, of 1891, 'the winter that I was in Berkeley and you in France'.

Belloc, in spite of a wholly English upbringing and a strong temptation to become an American, was still legally a French citizen; and, if he wished to continue to hold French citizenship, he was obliged to do French military service.

Joining the army is a conventional distraction from the pangs of despised love. Bessie was opposed to the notion of her son joining the French army, however. She said that it would make his life difficult if he wished to pursue a career in England since, ever afterwards, he would be branded as a foreigner. In this, he afterwards admitted her judgement to have been correct. But at the time he was in need of a completely new experience. As the only son of a widow, he would not be required to serve more than ten or twelve months in the army. He crossed to Paris in November 1891, and on the 9th he received his *feuille d'appel*. He opted for the Artillery and he joined the 10th Battery of the 8th Regiment of Artillery at Toul.

Because Alsace and Lorraine had been annexed after the Franco-Prussian war, Toul was a frontier town. It is situated at a junction of the Meurthe and the Moselle in an open plain bounded by deep woods on the western side, which divide it from the valley of the Meuse, and on the eastern by the Forêt de Haye.[2] In later years, Belloc would say that, because of his military experiences there, it was the part of France which meant the most to him.[3]

Thus the great hills that border the Moselle, the distant frontier, the vast plain which is (they say) to be a battlefield, and which lay

[1] BC July 19, 1894.
[2] Speaight, p. 63.
[3] BC, July 4, 1926.

> five hundred feet sheer below me, the far guns when they were practising at Metz, the awful strength of columns on the march moved me. The sky also grew more wonderful, and I noticed living things. The Middle Ages, of which till then I had had but troubling visions, rose up and took flesh in the old town, on the rare winter evenings when I had purchased leisure to leave quarters by some excessive toil. A man could feel France going by.[1]

The military exercises themselves were arduous and dull. Artillery regiments were, of course, equestrian in those days. (The Royal Artillery remained so until the Second World War.) Driving a gun was a complicated operation, in which three men had to take charge of six horses. Belloc never saw action, and when he was discharged at the end of a year he was only deemed a *conducteur médiocre*. But the year in the army deepened his feeling not only for military history, in which he always took an intense interest, but also for France.

At first, in the regiment, he was '*l'anglais*', and he felt excluded by the language barrier.

> I had come into the regiment faulty in my grammar and doubtful in accent, ignorant especially of those things which in civilisation are taken for granted but never explained in full; I was ignorant therefore of the key which alone can open that civilisation to a stranger. Things irksome or a heavy burden to the young men of my age, born and brought up in the French air, were to me, odious and bewildering. Orders that I but half comprehended; simple phrases that seemed charged with menace; boasting (a habit of which I knew little) coupled with a fierce and, as it were, expected courage that seemed ill suited to boasting – and certainly unknown outside this army; enormous powers of endurance in men whose stature my English training taught me to despise; a habit of fighting with the fists, coupled with a curious contempt for the accident of individual superiority – all these things amazed me and put me into a topsy-turvy world where I was weeks in finding my feet.[2]

All his life, curiously enough, Belloc was unsure of his competence in the French language which he learnt from an English mother. Like his sister, he had a French pronunciation of the letter 'r' which was to be a characteristic of his speech for the rest of his life. But he never felt confident about writing letters in French; and his conversational idioms in that language were coarse. Years later, as an honoured guest

[1] *Hills and the Sea*, p. 84.
[2] Ibid.

of the British Ambassador in Paris, he would horrify the table by lapsing into what his hostess called 'soldier's French'; and look up at the startled faces of his company entirely oblivious of any offence that might have derived from his choice of expressions.[1]

There developed, moreover, habits of thought and opinion which were not going to be entirely palatable to all ears in the future. Belloc was only one quarter French, his paternal grandmother, Madame Swanton Belloc, being of Irish descent. His French ancestry stemmed from a seventeeth-century Nantes wine-merchant whose name was Moses Belloc or Bloch, scarcely the most gentile of names. In his old age, Belloc would laugh about his forefather Moses and dismiss any notion that he might have been Jewish with raucous contempt. But this would have been harder to do when he first arrived in the regiment and was not fluent in the language. He was lucky to escape with the appellation '*l'anglais*'. Bloch, it may be remembered, is the name that Proust chose to label Marcel's boring young companion unambiguously as a Jew in his great novel.

Belloc was doing his military service just two years before the discovery of the notorious *bordereau*, the flimsy piece of paper which appeared to be a disclosure of French military secrets to the German attaché. The *bordereau*, as was later confirmed, was a fake. But, at the time, the blame for the supposed espionage was placed firmly on an officer named Alfred Dreyfus, who was court-martialled and sentenced to exile on Devil's Island, a leper settlement off the Guiana coast.

L'Affaire, which began as an ill-considered blunder on the part of a few intelligence officers, in 1894 erupted into a tempest which shook France for over a decade, revealing the extraordinary divisions between Republican and Royalist, Catholic and Free-thinker, Right and Left which existed in the Third Republic. But the first and most obvious thing it showed was the extent to which the Jews were detested and feared in all ranks of French society.

'It was the Dreyfus case that opened my eyes to the Jew question,' Belloc was to remark in old age.[2] Some would think it truer to say that it was his year in the French army which closed his mind to the 'Jew question' before the Dreyfus affair had ever happened.

Since his attitude to the Jews caused such deep offence to so many of his contemporaries, his biographer is inevitably faced with a serious technical difficulty. Belloc had not come from an anti-semitic home. His mother, as an English liberal, had many Jewish friends; and probably, to a certain extent, romanticised the Jews in the way that

[1] Mrs Hoffman Nickerson and Lady Phipps in conversation with the author.
[2] Hesketh Pearson and Hugh Kingsmill: *Talking of Dick Whittington* (1947), p. 212.

her mentor George Eliot had done in *Daniel Deronda*. She always expressed extreme shock, as did his sister Marie, when Belloc let fall vigorously anti-Jewish sentiments.[1]

The biographer, is forced to speculate where Belloc's undoubted antipathy to the Jews came from. He must try to explain it. He is forced to chronicle it. Equally, he has a duty to point out what Belloc's views on various aspects of the Jewish question were when circumstances prompted him to make comments upon it. In fairness to Belloc, it is also the biographer's task to point out when he was factually correct in his analysis of this question.

But I do not intend to weary the reader, on each occasion that the matter arises, with apologies or excuses, or references to *The Protocols of the Elders of Zion* or to the slaughter of Jews by the Nazis and the Stalinists. I shall let Belloc's words, on this, as on other political and religious matters, speak for themselves. In writing the life of a Jew-baiter or a Jew-persecutor, it might be necessary to inject a note of moral indignation with one's subject. Belloc was neither. In common with all his generation, Jews, pro-Jews and anti-Jews, he spoke with a vigour of language on the subject which, after the horrors of the mid-twentieth century, will seem hideously distasteful to the huge majority of readers. That is the only note of apology which I want to sound. Belloc's deep interest in the Jews, amounting at times to an obsession – and one need interrupt the narrative no further than to say this – began during his year of military service in France. It was almost certainly (but here I speculate) provoked by the company of rough soldiers who thought his name semitic. When, a decade later, he applied for British citizenship, his name was misspelled on the papers: BLOC.

This was very far from being his only preoccupation during that year in France. The winter was bitterly cold.

> The undefeated enemy, the chill
> That shall benumb the voiceful earth at last,
> Is master of our moment, and has bound
> The viewless wind itself. There is no sound.
> It freezes. Every friendly stream is fast.
> It freezes, and the graven twigs are still.

Throughout the winter, the soldiers had done nothing. Seven times they had been mobilized, four times in the middle of the night, only to be marched back to barracks 'to undo all that serious packing and to

---

[1] Lady Iddesleigh to the author.

return to routine'. Undoubtedly, when he said his comrades openly spoke of 'those things which in civilisation are taken for granted but never explained in full', he had in mind their talk of women. His heart was still too full of Elodie to be distracted by it.

> You came without a human sound,
>   You came and brought my soul to me;
> I only woke, and all around
> They slumbered on the firelit ground,
>   Beside the guns in Burgundy.
>
> I felt the gesture of your hands,
>   You signed my forehead with the Cross;
> The gesture of your holy hands
> Was bounteous – like the misty lands
>   Along the Hills in Calvados. . .

But, though he dreamed of her, he heard no news. '*If anything comes from America*, pray send it on at once,' he wrote desperately to his mother. 'Do not keep anything back. I have lost here a little photograph which I had kept sixteen months and it gives me great pain.'[1] That had been in December 1891. Elodie's mother was dead by now, and there could be no obstacle in the way of their marriage. Bessie, knowing of this, wrote to Elodie and asked her to come to Slindon, but of this Belloc knew nothing. It was just as well, for it would have been intolerably agitating to possess such knowledge while he was still marooned in France.

The coming of Spring, after such a very hard winter, brought joy to the whole Battery. And, at last, they got the news that they were going to march. The story is told in one of Belloc's most brilliant pieces of short prose, 'The First Day's March'[2], which describes his column making their way through the valley of the Meuse. As they marched through Commercy. 'the boys looked at us with pride, not knowing how hateful they would find the service when once they were in for its grind and hopelessness. But then, for that matter, I did not know myself, with what pleasure I should look back upon it ten years after'.

* * *

Meanwhile, as Belloc got through his year in the Artillery, his mother was wondering what to do with him when he came out of it.

[1] Quoted Speaight p. 65.
[2] *Hills and the Sea.*

All her advisers, including her trustees, were agreed in the ludicrously inappropriate notion that he should take a job in a bank. It shows, merely, that they had not noticed what he was like. When he grew up, he had a great interest in economic theory. But he was even more 'hopeless with money' than his mother.

Perhaps she still nursed the idea that he might develop as a natural scientist. Perhaps she hoped that he would follow his father's profession of the law. In either case, he would need to study at the University; and, for so devout a protégé of Manning and Newman, that could only mean Oxford. Was such a thing possible? She had no idea how to go about it, and there was no money to pay for such a scheme. Her trustee was appalled, and did his best to dissuade her. Bessie was not a woman that it was easy to dissuade.

She turned to Marie, by now a comely, plump twenty-three-year old, who knew the ways of the world. Marie was walking out with a young *Times* journalist called Freddie Lowndes. She had refused to marry him, but he still continued, in spite of Bessie's disapproval, to see his beloved. Recognising it as a way to the heart of the woman he hoped to make his future mother-in-law, he set about investigating the possibilities of getting Belloc into Oxford. He discovered the procedure for taking the College Entrance Examination, and he drafted letters to the heads of several colleges.[1] The response was lukewarm. Meanwhile, Bessie, a friend of the Dean of Westminster, attended a party at the Deanery where she bumped into the great Master of Balliol, Benjamin Jowett. The eccentricities and conceit of 'the Jowler', as he was known on home territory, have passed into legend. But, like many social climbers and snobs in the academic world, Jowett had a passion for excellence and had collected about him at Balliol generations of young men not merely of good breeding but of good brain.

> This is Balliol, I am Jowett
> All there is to know I know it;
> What I don't know isn't knowledge;
> I am Master of this College.

To 'nobble' Jowett was to put oneself in the way of belonging to the most distinguished academic society in late-nineteenth-century England. This Bessie boldly proceeded to do. There would still be an examination to pass; but the biggest hurdle was over, for Jowett, impressed by the Bellocs' literary connections, agreed to consider the boy's case.

[1] *Where Love and Friendship Dwelt*, p. 236.

There remained the problem of how to pay for Belloc to go to University. Here Marie was able to help. In the terms of her maternal grandfather's will, she had interest in the Parkes Trust Fund. This she was prepared to sell for £800 to donate to her brother's needs. It was an act of generosity which was misunderstood on both sides. She hoped, if she did not assume, that when he came to earn his living, he would pay her the money back. And this expectation was to sow the seeds of misunderstanding and estrangement between them.

Belloc, in France, was kept informed of his family's plans. They had made their applications too late to get him into Oxford at the start of the academic year in October. He would have to postpone his entry until January.

Discharged from the Artillery, he returned to the grind of preparing for an academic life. After four years away from school, it was difficult to settle, and the tutor they had engaged for the purpose, A. M. Bell, found him 'clever and clear-minded; but *very* unequal in his work from day to day'.[1]

He cannot have been easy to teach. He gloried in having had experience of the world. He was never to regret the years he had spent on his 'bloody ramble' before settling down to his serious studies.

'When one is quite young then is the time to see the world. One never learns it later. I have always been glad that I left school at 17, learnt to plow, reap and sow, shot a lot, went off to America from east to west, walked all over California and Colorado, went into the French Artillery and got into Balliol all before I was 22.'[2]

He got into Balliol in December 1892. His examiners were chiefly impressed by his essay on poetry. In January 1893, he took up residence as an undergraduate, a few days before the beginning of the Hilary Term. It was a propitious time of year, the term taking its name from Saint Hilary, Belloc's patron saint, whose feast day falls on January 13.

---

[1] Quoted Speaight, p. 77.
[2] Letter to Juliet Duff, quoted Speaight, p. 33.

THREE

OXFORD
1893–1896

When Belloc went up to Oxford, in January 1893, the place was full of new buildings, designed to cope with the swelling undergraduate numbers. The monstrous Gothic hall at Balliol (designed by Waterhouse) was just thirteen years old. The re-built Master's Lodgings and the façade of the college on the Broad Street side had been built by the same architect not much before. Sir George Gilbert Scott's new range at New College was being added to by Basil Champneys during Belloc's time. But it was, above all, the era of Sir Thomas Jackson whose buildings had sprouted up all over Oxford in the previous decade, in the neo-Jacobean style which inevitably came to be known as Anglo-Jackson. When Belloc arrived as a Freshman, Jackson's Examination Schools were only a decade old. The Town Hall was being built (in the Anglo-Jackson manner but designed by Henry Hare). Brasenose, Trinity, Hertford, Christ Church and Magdalen, to name only a handful of the colleges, all erected new buildings close to the time when Belloc arrived there.[1]

In the knowledge of what was to come, in the twentieth century, when the Morris motor-works destroyed the town and committees of dons (building hideous lumps in every available green space) destroyed the University, we can look at the late-Victorian buildings of Oxford with some nostalgia. At the time, they must have appeared incongruous, threatening a beauty which to the eye surveying modern Oxford is almost unimaginable.

It was a meadowy, rustic town. Cattle still grazed on the Oxpens. The roads leading north out of the town quickly dwindled into open fields. Summertown, now a suburb, was a remote village. So were Wolvercote and North and South Hinksey. Even a walker less vigorous than Belloc could reckon on a perambulation in the country each afternoon.

For all its expansions, the University remained a tiny place when

[1] Jennifer Sherwood and Nikolaus Pevsner: *Oxfordshire* (1971), p. 98.

Belloc arrived there. 170 undergraduates made up the total of his own college of Balliol. Any form of eccentricity became fast conspicuous; and Belloc was a 'famous' undergraduate by the end of his first term.

Those were the days when undergraduates almost invariably came to the University aged seventeen or eighteen direct from school. Even the number of schools which sent men to Oxford were limited. For instance, although the University had changed its statutes in order to admit Roman Catholics, Cardinal Manning (who had died in the previous year) had doggedly forbidden them to avail themselves of this opportunity. Not everyone obeyed, but Catholic undergraduates were few. The presence of a twenty-two-year old Roman Catholic in their midst would, therefore, have been noted, even if he had not chosen to drink wildly, to shout at the top of his voice, and to dress in a large dark cloak and soft hat.

Most of his contemporaries found him, initially, a rather alarming figure. They were baffled by his age. At twenty-three, he seemed strikingly old, and his experiences had been extraordinarily exotic, an impression increased by his French 'r's.[1]

It was in the Oxford Union, that nursery of famous politicians and statesmen, that Belloc first came to prominence. He made his maiden speech there in his first term. For those who do not know it, one should explain that the Oxford Union Society is something between a Debating Club and a Students' Union. Fortnightly debates are organised during term. The chamber in Belloc's day had recently been built to accommodate larger undergraduate numbers (debates previously having happened in the library). The new hall was arranged like a toy version of the House of Commons in Westminster, and any undergraduate with political ambitions would aim to make a showing there. A high proportion of British statesmen, advocates and prelates – Gladstone, Curzon, Asquith, Cosmo Gordon Lang, Harold Macmillan – first stretched their wings in this handsome Victorian room. But, from the first, Belloc stood out as one of the most remarkable speakers that the Oxford Union had ever known. Frequent references in the undergraduate magazine *The Isis* pay tribute to Belloc's forceful eloquence: 'A consistent view of almost every subject, based on intelligent and broad principles; an elaboration of forcible and easily comprehended argument; an appropriateness of phraseology adorned by an appositeness of analogy and delivered with an irresistible vehemence of utterance –

[1] David Butler to the author, based on his father's memories.

each of these Mr Belloc has in greater abundance than any other member of the Society.'[1]

In particular, they were struck by the confidence with which he spoke about 'his favourite and peculiar subject – war and foreign policy'.[2] Most undergraduates arrived at the Union with their opinions unformed. Belloc seemed to know what he thought about everything. In the course of his life, inevitably, some of his views shifted. But it is striking how few of them did. Reading the *Isis* accounts of Belloc in 'Union Jottings' one might be reading an account of Belloc aged forty or sixty or seventy. In October 1893, we read, 'Mr Belloc, Balliol, who had already taken a fair share in the conversational rhetoric of the debate, spoke as a Roman Catholic, a Frenchman and a Democrat. He abused the aristocracy, of whom he has quite primitive ideas, he abused the Church [of England, presumably] and he abused the preceding speaker. He cannot help being eloquent and whatever he says must always be listened to, for it is always interesting and well said. But it is a pity he does not always confine himself to the question at issue'.[3] For a time there was a tendency 'to regard Mr Belloc as a windy rhetorician with one speech';[4] and they complained '*toujours la patrie* is as tiring to us as everlasting partridge was to the king'.[5]

Belloc 'abused the aristocracy' on democratic French Revolutionary principles. He was yet to evolve his informed sense of their irresponsibility as landlords, or his hardened belief that they had sold 'their daughters, their land, and even their bodies to the Jews'. But this creed was not to prevent him from having friendship with both Jews and aristocrats. One of his closest friends in his first year was Hubert Howard, second son of the ninth Earl of Carlisle, who was to die from a sniper's bullet in 1898 at Omdurman.[6] Arthur Stanley (fifth Baron Stanley of Alderley) was an acquaintance before he came up to Balliol, and they became friends. The most important Balliol friendship from this date, perhaps, from the point of view of the literary historian, was that with Lord Basil Blackwood. Belloc had little in common politically with this handsome, slightly lethargic and cynical High Tory young man. Blackwood believed in the British Empire. And, as Belloc would so often reiterate, 'My dear old mother used to say of the

---

[1] *The Isis* November 1894
[2] Ibid., January 19 1895.
[3] Ibid., October 28 1893.
[4] Ibid., January 19 1895.
[5] Ibid., June 10 1893.
[6] Speaight, p. 84.

British Empire: I hate the name and I hate the thing'. Belloc was a radical, Catholic republican; Blackwood a scarcely-believing Protestant of the Established Church. Only in a distaste for the Jews did their opinions much overlap. But they became firm friends. They drank Burgundy together, they went canoeing and walking together for prodigious distances (Belloc, like many undergraduates of this date, thought nothing of walking the fifty-four miles from Oxford to London; but he broke all records when he did it in eleven and a half hours). Above all, they shared the same sense of the ridiculous. It was Basil Blackwood's drawings (as B.T.B) which so perfectly were to complement and illustrate Belloc's first published rhymes for children.

In his own most famous verses, Belloc has immortalised those idyllic rambles by road and waterway in the countryside near Oxford.

> The quiet evening kept her tryst:
>   Beneath an open sky we rode,
> And passed into a wandering mist
>   Along the perfect Evenlode.
>
> The tender Evenlode that makes
>   Her meadows hush to hear the sound
> Of waters mingling in the brakes,
>   And binds my heart to English ground.
>
> A lovely river, all alone,
>   She lingers in the hills and holds
> A hundred little towns of stone,
>   Forgotten in the western wolds.

Belloc was drunk with happiness in his first year at Oxford. He found there, for the first time in his life, congenial male companionship. He had been brought up in a family entirely composed of females. School, the Collège Stanislas and the French Artillery had all been constricting, and, in the range of intelligent comradeship which they offered, distinctly limited. Belloc always enjoyed the company of both sexes. But he was a man who deeply needed the talk and the drink and the shared exertions of walks and rambles which male companionship provided.

> Here is a House that armours a man
>   With the eyes of a boy and the heart of a ranger,
> And a laughing way in the teeth of the world
>   And a holy hunger and thirst for danger:
> Balliol made me, Balliol fed me,

> Whatever I had she gave me again:
> And the best of Balliol loved and led me.
> God be with you, Balliol men.

Belloc was never taught by Balliol's great Master, but there were few enough undergraduates for Jowett to be able to take notice of them and befriend the more remarkable. Freshmen would be invited to 'take wine' with the Master, not always the smoothest of social occasions. Archbishop Lang, up at Balliol a decade before Belloc, recalled,

> We were all so shy that, as often happened, our *gaucherie* irritated the Master and he gave up any effort to talk. Result – very soon a deadlock in conversation. The silence was oppressive. At last, a scholar from Christ's Hospital, accustomed to independence in the London streets, boldly broke it. 'Master', he said, 'I like the painting in the Chapel awfully'. The Master looked at him and said in his direst crispest tone: 'Don't say "awfully". This isn't a girl's school; and it isn't paint: it's alabaster'.[1]

Belloc at least would not allow any embarrassing pauses in the conversation. But Jowett's cold, incisive wisdom succeeded in knocking even him off his stroke:

> Jowett ... asked me the political question which was always uppermost in his mind, and which, he believed all young men should consider. It was, 'Under what form of government is the state of man at its best?' I answered, as all young men should answer, 'A Republic', to which he answered gently in his turn, 'You cannot have a Republic without Republicans'. Now that, for terseness and truth and a certain quality of *revelation* was worthy of Aristotle.[2] . .

It was to take twenty years, however, for the revelation, properly, to sink in.

Belloc had hoped to read 'Greats', that is, a combination of classical literature, history and philosophy. Greats is still the pre-eminent school at Oxford, and to do well in it requires a remarkable range, depth and application. When the wife of a Warden of All Souls' College met Lindemann (later Lord Cherwell) who had recently been appointed to a scientific professorship at the University, he expressed to her his misgivings about the status of science at Oxford. "You need not worry," she assured him, "a man with a first in Greats could get

[1] J. G. Lockhart: *Cosmo Gordon Lang* (1949), p. 26.
[2] *The Cruise of the Nona*, p. 56.

up science in a fortnight". Lindemann is alleged to have replied, "What a pity it is that your husband has never had a fortnight to spare".[1]

Certainly, had Belloc read Greats, and done well in it, he would have stood a stronger chance later of getting an academic job. But he had been persuaded by the man who prepared him for College Entrance that his Latin and Greek were too rusty; he opted, therefore, to read Modern History. His tutor was A. L. Smith, said by some to be a 'tutor of genius', an expert on college finance and cricket. Certainly, he recognised the range and forcefulness of Belloc's brain, and watched him sail through all the necessary preliminary examinations – 'Divvers', Logic and Responsions, which had to be passed before undergraduates settled down to the fascinating study of Anglo-Saxon Land Law, and the Wars of the Roses.

In work, then, and at the Union, Belloc made a striking début in his first year at Balliol. He established himself as an eccentric, and he made many friends, in his own and in other colleges. There was only one cloud, and that a heavy one, in his otherwise sunny sky.

While he triumphed and enjoyed himself in Oxford, letters continued to stream in from California from Elodie. Since her mother's death, she had declined into a religious melancholy, verging, by her own accounts, on insanity. Belloc could not but be disturbed, as he prepared for his first examinations, by her emotional outpourings. She was still dithering with the idea of joining a convent, but nothing seemed to come of it; and her letters betray a desperate desire not to lose touch with her beloved.

'Oh! I am so glad, darling, that you have succeeded,' she wrote to him after the Michaelmas Term of 1893,

> Tell me a fable, love, and say I helped you to it. (I know I didn't, but that's immaterial) – tell me anyway because you know I was sick of fright that if you failed that awful logic 'they' would say I was to blame. I know all that Francesca and Paolo said in Dante and in my torn-up letter I said that I wished that I had the heart and courage . . . of Francesca. That was before I knew you had succeeded.

'They', of course, are not the college authorities, who would have known nothing of Elodie, but Belloc's family, who could not fail to be troubled by the persistent emotional drain which this correspondence caused him.

> Whatever they say of me, do not you believe but that I have loved you and held to you and believed in you and hoped for you all the

[1] R. F. Harrod *The Prof* (1959) p. 53.

time? And I as well as you have learnt something of the realities. . .
Shall I tell you a wonderful secret? Well it's this. In despair I
determined to do something for the sake of study. So I began
singing lessons and now I sing quite wonderfully! And there's a
song I sing all the time and the people who hear me love it, and I
sing it across the hills and waters and fields to *you*. *You* are in my
heart and they say: 'How wonderful'.[1]

*   *   *

With this secret gnawing at his heart, Belloc returned to Oxford for
the Hilary Term of 1894. He was elected to the inner circle of the
Union as Librarian on February 24, the first step on the ladder which
would lead him to the Presidential Chair. The books proposed by the
Library Committee in that term reflect a characteristic taste of the
Librarian: Hutton's *Life of Cardinal Manning* – 6/–; Stephen's *European
History 1789–1815* – 4/6; Sabatier's *Vie de S. François d'Assise* – 5/– and
de Goncourt's *Italie d'hier* – 6/3.[2]

Friendship, history, debates and country rambles formed the substance of that busy term. His friends knew nothing of the passionate
correspondence which he still kept up with Napa. He was too young
and too stubborn to be able to put Elodie out of his heart. But,
whether he liked it or not, she was fading from his memories. He
wrote asking her for a photograph, and produced an hysterical
response:

Look, darling, you have understood me – and you love me? No?
Well, if you do not it must be that my portrait has shattered your
memory of me. Unhappy portrait to do that! Pray love me better
for my portrait. I have loved you for yourself – for your dear head
and heart – and then I loved you for your sad face.[3]

Of course, he loved her. But the uncertainty of the future, and the
unhappiness of their separation, seemed insoluble while his successful
undergraduate life continued.

By the end of that Hilary Term, 1894, the third anniversary of his
visit to her in San Francisco had passed. Elodie was desperate with
self-reproach for having turned down his proposal of marriage on that
occasion, and wrote to him in impassioned terms:

Dear love: It is three years ago today since you arrived in San
Francisco, while I was in Napa sick to hear from you. Hilaire,

[1] BC New Year's Day 1894.
[2] Minutes of the Oxford Union Society.
[3] BC March 10, 1894.

darling, do not think that I forget or can forget. During these long days that have gone by without letters from you. . . I have been so near you, so with you all the time. And then, dear heart, it is the time and season of our meeting. I do want to write to you today. But my heart is so full of memory, of you and of all that I hardly know what to say. Only this – I love you and I hope for you and I pray for you and I remember you. And I care for you so much. I know all those griefs of your dear soul and I love you for them. And also, darling, all these years and all the dark and all the misery have not touched you where you rest sweet, secure and known in my heart. But I cannot bear to think of all I have caused you to suffer. Do not, for our loves' sake, believe that I have been only selfish. There are time[s], dear, when I would sit and write you to come to me. And I would go with you forever. Do you believe this? Of course you know it. How else could it be that I love you – if I never wish to be near you, to be with you, to help you and to be helped by you. Then, I am frightened by so many things and I almost persuade myself that it is for your happiness and final good that I go away. And yet I know you love me – tell me, Honey, – dear friend of my heart, why do I vacillate and change so? O, if we meet and are one some day, it will all be nothing. Meanwhile, darling brave Hilary, do be patient with me. There – I shall stop this raving and shall take your dear head and kiss it 'sweet and twenty'.[1]

Belloc found her wild changes of mood deeply upsetting. By one post she declared her undying love for him. By the next, she spoke of her plans of going east – Baltimore – to join the Sisters of Charity. Since there were plenty of religious orders in California, this gesture in itself shows how much Elodie was fooling herself. On the eastern seaboard, she was infinitely more easily reached from England.

Things drag so that nothing ever seems to come to an end. But I shall never neglect you again. I shall tell you as soon as I know anything definite. Meanwhile, I shall write you all the time, and it shall be only when I am dust that I shall forget you.

I have tried to count the time when I should hear from you. No letter has come, yet.[2]

No letters came, perhaps because he did not have anything to say to her, and because he had other things on his mind.

At Oxford, he had formed a group called the Republican Club. It

[1] Ibid.
[2] BC March 10, 1894.

had four members: Malcolm Seton, F. Y. Eccles, J. S. Phillimore and Belloc. Eccles's memories of those days are not of a lovesick boy.

> On the contrary, he was the gayest of companions . . . we laughed together a great deal; our conversation was extremely free; we ragged each other; and we sang at the tops of our voices. We feasted and smoked together, we went out for walks and excursions, and nothing could have been happier or more high-spirited. Belloc was never attracted by organised games but he was indefatigable on foot, on horseback, or in the water. He was especially keen on sailing and canoe-ing up the river – waiting until he could have a little yacht of his own. . . Those were good times.[1]

The four were to lodge together in their last year at number 6, St Aldate's, a house they called 'Austerlitz'. It was with them that Belloc was to conclude:

> From quiet homes and first beginning.
> Out to the undiscovered ends,
> There's nothing worth the wear of winning,
> But laughter and the love of friends.

In later years, he disliked the popularity of the lines because he said they were not true. But, at the time, it must have *felt* as if they were true, and the joy of his undergraduate life breathes through every line of his famous poem.

> Where on their banks of light they lie,
> The happy hills of Heaven between,
> The Gods that rule the morning sky
> Are not more young or more serene
>
> Than were the intrepid Four that stand,
> The first that dared to live their dream.
> And on this uncongenial land
> To found the Abbey of Theleme.
>
> We kept the Rabelaisian plan:
> We dignified the dainty cloisters
> With Natural Law, the Rights of Man,
> Song, Stoicism, Wine and Oysters. . .

At the time, his reputation in the Union went from strength to strength. At the end of the year, he was elected its President. *The Isis* published a long 'Profile' of him to mark his term of office.

[1] F. Y. Eccles, quoted Speaight, p. 81.

The modest 'H. Belloc, Balliol, President,' which we shall see at the foot of the Union's notices this term is symbol for much. Beneath that unpretending abbreviation lurks Joseph Hilaire Pierre Sébastien Réné Swanton Belloc – Catholic, artilleryman, journalist, draughtsman, poet, sailing-master, &c. &c. &c. If you meet him, you will learn that he likes women to stick to their petticoats . . . and that he is not a teetotaller nor a friend to teetotallers. . .

His English is better than his French, and he means to practise at the English Bar, where strong indeed will be the British Jury which shall refuse to hear the voice of the charmer. . . Only one college turns out a school of men whose brains are not turned to muscle, nor their thews to flap-doodle; but even Balliol has seldom before numbered among her trophies such a combination as the familiar figure with the big dark cloak, soft hat and bludgeon, known to its friends as 'Peter'.[1]

This account shows how early the great elephantine, rumbling Belloc 'persona' had been developed. He was never called 'Peter' by his intimates in grown-up life. Otherwise, the portrait could very easily have described Belloc in old or middle age.

Of one thing, there could be no doubt: his brilliance. At the Union, he had occupied the Presidential chair from which men had gone on to hold the highest office in the land. His notion of reading for the Bar would be merely another step along the same road. As his final year wore on, he applied himself with increased diligence to his books. In the previous summer, letters from Elodie had made it manifest that she still regarded him as her 'intended'.

You have no idea what a small town is for gossip. And so when July 14 came along I hardly dared to write you because, forsooth, the postmistress had already forwarded three letters to that unknown name and far-off address. One of my dear friends in Napa came to console with me because of your desertion.[2]

While her own flirtation with the religious life continued, she began to worry about the effect their correspondence was having on Belloc.

Darling, why must you run risks of loss? And you must have wonderful visions of what they call a career. Have you not? Well, however great your duty to your love you owe something to your mother and something to yourself and something to the world. Be good to your mother. Some day the world will be very black and

[1] *The Isis*, January 19, 1895.
[2] BC July 19, 1894.

the only bright light will be the memory of what good you blessed her with.[1]

It is perfectly true that Belloc's success at Oxford was a source of pride to Bessie. Marie afterwards believed that 'my brother having done well at Oxford . . . shed a light on our mother which lasted until the end of her life'.[2] But Elodie was playing with fire. If she had really wanted Belloc to forget her and pursue his career, she would have brought the correspondence to a close. She was dabbling instead with the heady courtship of suffering, the notion that if you suffer enough in a religious cause, some good will come of it. She wanted, not merely to embrace suffering, but to involve Belloc in it.

> Oh, Honey bun, I see so much foolish selfishness in women that is due to an insane desire for happiness. Where there is no happiness, Blessedness and Companionship and Peace are to be found. And if after all this time we meet again those are the things we shall look for. But how can we even hope for them if we get the habit of despair – but has ever woman seen such hope? I know your grief, but I know too your laughter and your cheerfulness. A few days ago I received a letter from you and in it was the unkindest word you ever said to me. I did not mind it, but it grieved me. You told me that I had no right to speak to you of hope and energy and success and hope in life. Well, I have a right to speak of those things to you. You say I do not love you, that I do not remember you. I only laugh at that. You cannot see me. You cannot be with me now. But you *have* seen me and you have *been* with me and if you do not know me now, judge me by your memories of me while we were together. . .[3]

Elodie was someone who throve on emotional drama. She wanted the best for Belloc with one part of herself. But, with another, she could not bear to be out of the picture. And when she felt herself fading from that picture, she felt all the more strongly the need to draw attention to herself by becoming a nun. This is not to say that she was being deliberately manipulative, still less that the affectionate correspondence was entirely one-sided. In November 1894, he wrote her a beautiful (almost too beautiful, and finished) epistle from the flooded Kirtlington Park, near Oxford:

[1] Ibid.
[2] *Where Love and Friendship Dwelt*, p. 235.
[3] BC July 19, 1894.

There is a great *big* house and here one may hunt beasts or ride about on horses or walk in an immense park and generally be an oligarch.

Also it floods. The rains have come over the Thames valley in a way that rains have never come before – and Oxford is almost an island. The line from London is washed away. The country is all water like a big lake and it was all I could do to get out here today – the train was anyway late and I saw water away and away on both sides of the rails. If this goes on much longer I shall build an ark and put into it all manner of living beasts for fear the race should fail.

And you my Bee? Are there pleasant cloudy skies and drifts before the wind in California?... Suddenly I remember that we have a thing in common even over the misty edge of the world – and that is the old Moon which we spoke of, if you will notice how she looks just now [at] nine or ten o'clock at night you will find her beautiful. But oh! so beautiful also I forget the fortnight! And when you get this the old moon will be new – & will have no nine or ten o'clock & though it is great news it is hardly worth a telegram, so wait and write a sweet line.[1]

This is, to be sure, very lovely doodling. But, even in its romantic fantasizing, the beloved pen-pal has become a creation of Belloc's poetic imaginings. There is nothing in his letters either of the violent mood-change or of the quotidian tedium of poor Elodie's effusions. 'Quietly I take you in my arms & I kiss you quietly,' he concluded soothingly. Elodie did not feel happy with this quietness. There is no reason to doubt that, to her, it felt as though she was being tugged between a great love and a religious vocation. But one cannot help noticing that her great religious crisis came upon her just at the moment when Belloc, too, was on the verge of choosing a career. While he tried to concentrate for his final examinations in the Schools, he received the following letter, in April 1895:

... My own and best friend... The superior of the American branch of the Sisters of Charity is in San Francisco. I shall probably go to Baltimore with her where I shall go into the Mount Hope Hospital. At least, that is where I am to postulate. Elizabeth begs me to stay a month longer – that would allow me to hear from you again. But I think I shall have gone before a month. I shall see the superior either today or to-morrow and then I shall know definitely. I shall write to you then, another letter, to tell you.

I realise now, darling Hilary, that I have done you a grave wrong

---

[1] BC November 17, 1894.

in asking you to wait. Mrs Atherton gave me no details but she said you had grave decisions to make within the next six months. So listen, Hun. I have no right to attempt to legislate for an uncertain future. It is all that I can do to manage (and that badly) this present. In addition to all the pain that I have given you I have no possible right to jeopardise your welfare in the world. I know all that dearest old Hun. So I leave you absolutely free. Let me go. Whistle me down the wind and if things go wrong with me I shall face them as well as I can – my one consolation to be that I have tried in the dark to do that which seemed the best for us both. If I should come back and if you be free I shall write you to Great College Street or Slindon, either of which will be a safe address to find you.

Dearest Hun, do not believe that I am as heartless as this reads. I have suffered so much and so have you that it seems rather good to be getting down to certainties – even such certainties as these.

I shall write you again – either tomorrow or Thursday, and then I shall be able to give you the definite date of my departure.

Meanwhile, goodbye, darling.

God be good to you all the time – better to you than I have been. Lovingly, Elodie.[1]

It is impossible to doubt Elodie's sincerity in this letter. She genuinely wanted to try her religious vocation. But nor can there be any doubt that she was in love with Belloc, and this letter, and the visit to Baltimore, constituted a challenge. In emotional terms, she was calling his bluff. Busy with exams, and caught up in his own love affair with Oxford, Belloc allowed his bluff to be called, and Elodie to go her way.

He sat Schools in June, and, to no one's surprise, he was placed in the First Class. The following month, he sat for a Prize Fellowship at All Souls' College.

All Souls' is a unique academic institution. It does not have an undergraduate body, and only a proportion of its Fellows reside in Oxford. A Prize Fellow is elected for a period of seven years; and, during the 1890s, he would have been expected to reside in college and remain a bachelor for that period. But he would not have to use that time for purely academic research. He would, for instance, have been at liberty to join an Inn of Court in London and read for the Bar; and it would seem that this was one of Belloc's ambitions. From Friday to Monday, he would have spent in the company of his fellows, who would have included not merely dons, but also judges, noble lords

[1] BC April 6, 1895.

and parliamentarians among their number. No more perfect stepping-stone could be imagined for a career in the great world. And the fact that he contemplated it shows that he had put any thought of marrying Elodie out of his mind.

The method by which a Prize Fellow is chosen is famously whimsical. Each candidate is required to write a number of essays in subjects of his choice, and to show an aptitude for languages. But much, too, depends, on his social demeanour. Each candidate is invited to dinner and assessed; for it is a private society, and the fellows might feel entitled to decide, however clever a man may be, that they do not want him as a member of what was, and is, a rather intellectual gentleman's club.

For every distinguished man who has succeeded in obtaining an All Souls' Fellowship, there must be a hundred who have failed. Belloc, as is notorious, failed. It was almost certainly of Belloc that one of his examiners, Sir Charles Oman, was thinking in his somewhat acid recollections:

> Far the most interesting kind of examination in which I have ever taken part was the annual competition for the All Souls' Fellowships in October. The number of candidates was never very great, and all (with few exceptions) were picked men – there were only a few whose judgement of their own capacity was hopelessly optimistic, and rested on 'Union' oratory, or popularity among their own particular literary or political clique, won by persistent self-assertion. These candidates gave little trouble when pinned down to the rather searching questions set before them – though I have known one or two who did give the fellows some little annoyance in the smoking-room, where they tried to sparkle, or to demonstrate that they were men of the world or epigrammists.[1]

It is sometimes said that Belloc failed to get a Fellowship at All Souls' because of his strident belief in the guilt of Alfred Dreyfus, a belief not shared by his hosts and examiners. This is nonsense. It is very doubtful at this date whether many of the Fellows had even heard of Dreyfus, who had been condemned for espionage in February on what seemed reasonably good evidence. It was not until 1898, at the time of Esterhazy's court martial, and Zola's famous letter, *J'Accuse*, that the world became alerted to the injustice which had been perpetrated.

Anti-Catholicism did, however, contribute to Belloc's downfall at

[1] Charles Oman: *Memories of Victorian Oxford*, p. 74.

All Souls'. He had a statue of Our Lady on his desk while he was writing his examination papers, and one can imagine a few eyebrows being raised at that. As for his trial-dinner: if he had behaved with politeness, and not shouted, nor drunk too much, nor tried to hog the conversation, it would have been the only meal in his life at which he adopted such unnatural behaviour. The sad truth is that they did not like him much, and did not want him to join their club.

F. E. Smith, Belloc's great sparring partner in the Union, was present on the fateful evening when Belloc was 'dined' after the Fellowship examination at All Souls'. Belloc allowed no one to speak except himself, and harangued the Fellows on the French military manoeuvres in which he had taken part in the winter of 1891–2. He walked away from the evening with Smith, buoyant in the moonlight and confident that everyone had been impressed by the brilliance of his conversation. 'And do you think,' Smith asked him, 'that you have improved your chances in that ancient house of learning?' Belloc turned to him, and his facial expression changed to one of horror. It had never occurred to him that he would be rejected by All Souls'.[1]

Smarting from the blow, he went on holiday to Scandinavia with Basil Blackwood. They went hunting, where presumably they encountered no baboons, marmosets or tigers, but where they began to amuse each other with the rhymes which were to become *The Bad Child's Book of Beasts.*

> The Whale that wanders round the Pole
>> Is not a table fish.
> You cannot bake or boil him whole
>> Nor serve him in a dish;
> But you may cut his blubber up
>> And melt it down for oil.
> And so replace the colza bean
>> (A product of the soil).
> These facts should all be noted down
>> And ruminated on,
> By every boy in Oxford town
>> Who wants to be a Don.

Belloc, having failed at All Souls', now wanted to be a Don very much indeed. Without the support of an All Souls' Fellowship, he could not afford to read for the Bar. He was, moreover, besottedly in love with Oxford, and with his old college of Balliol in particular. It must have

---

[1] Oral tradition passed from F. E. Smith to A. L. Rowse to the author.

seemed inconceivable to him at this date that he would fail to get some academic preferment somewhere. His failure to do so was something from which he never recovered. Indeed, as the years progressed, he minded more, not less, and would treat total strangers, in his old age, to accounts of how All Souls' and the other colleges failed to see his genius. Nearly fifty years later, at the beginning of the Second World War, he described a recent visit to Oxford:

> It always revives my youth to see the bloody dons shuffling along the pavement of that town and stammering and yammering and talking to themselves as they go. Maurice Baring always says that it was God's Providence the Dons would not let me become a Don. But I deny this! If they had taken me in I should have turned them inside out and given them such Hell that they would have had to invent a post to get rid of me. Also, once I had the Hall mark, I should have been able to expose their measly pretensions with authority. Writing, for instance, on the monstrous Elizabethan myth, leaving it a smouldering heap and signing the work Hilaire Belloc, MA sometime Fellow of All Souls', Senior Historical Scholar of Balliol Coll: Oxon. . .[1]

It was not to be.

He held out hopes that his own old college of Balliol would elect him to a Fellowship. Their failure to do so caused deep pain. In his dining room at King's Land, he had a panel which came from the old door of Balliol hall before Waterhouse's reconstruction replaced the medieval building. Pinned to the blackened wood was a post-card for all to read: 'This panel comes from the door of the Great Hall of my old college, Balliol, which fed me, nurtured me, and rejected me.'

Once again, he could console himself with the thought that the Dons were anti-Catholic. But, in the following year, 1896, they elected to a Fellowship a slightly younger contemporary of Belloc's, F. F. Urquhart. 'Sligger', as Urquhart was universally known, during his long career as a don, had been educated at Stonyhurst. He was the first Catholic to be appointed to a Fellowship at an Oxford college since the days of James II. Belloc's only refuge was to dismiss Sligger as a 'tame' Catholic.[2] That was in 1896. Gallantry would never allow him to suggest, by so much as a syllable, that he might have had a chance of being elected in Urquhart's place had he not been distracted by his love for Elodie.

Her attempt to become a nun had been disastrous. In October 1895,

[1] Letter to J. S. Nickerson (née Soames) October 17, 1940.
[2] Speaight, p. 119.

she entered St Joseph's Central House of the Sisters of Charity at Emmitsburg in Maryland. After a month, she could stand no more of it. The chaplain seems to have been a kind man, and when she showed him some of Belloc's letters, he is said to have remarked that any man capable of writing such letters must indeed be in love with her.[1]

Probably, the letters she was treasuring were fairly old. Belloc did not write to her during the winter, which she spent in loneliness, on the verge of complete emotional collapse, in New York. With great shame, she returned to her family in California.

The Hogans were quickly running out of what little money they had. Elodie's nerves were in shreds. It was Mrs Atherton who appears to have written to Belloc informing him that his beloved had come out of her convent, and now awaited him, in a state of psychological and financial helplessness.

Belloc, still desperately uncertain about his future at Oxford, was shocked by the news, and wired to her, on January 24, 1896, 'Elodie write plans won't wait.' It was precisely at the moment in his career when a further self-application to scholarship, and his mere physical presence in Oxford, would have helped him with his career. But his old love tugged at his heart-strings; and honour, too, had to be satisfied. He and Elodie had, after all, become childishly and secretly betrothed, and when she declared that she needed him, he knew that he had to go. Once returned from New York to California, she wrote to him on February 1:

Darling,
Ever since I wrote you at the beginning of the week I have been thinking of our future. And it seems to me if I can help you in any way it is clearly my duty to do so. Things have been so vague and indefinite between us, dearest, that I really know little of your affairs. It may be difficult for you to come to California without incurring debt or jeopardising your place in Oxford. If either thing be probable, would it be any comfort to you, darling, if I offered to go to England to you, in order to save you the expense and time of so long a trip? I make the proposition with much diffidence for many reasons: since my latest trip I have a horror of ever being alone again; it is most unconventional; it might do you an injustice in the eyes of the world. All this, though, could easily be waived if it would be of material benefit to you for me to go to you. On the other hand, you may be in need of the rest and the change and

[1] Speaight, p. 101.

certainly it would be a joy for us to be together once more in California.

In money matters, things have gone from bad to worse with us. One loss after another, until nearly everything is involved. It is too long a story of continued disaster to give you the details. If I had much means of my own, I would not suggest this plan, but under the circumstances I am sure I owe it to you and to your great loyalty to make things as easy for you as I can. You will not misunderstand, dearest Hilary? I should be much happier to meet you here, but if it will be for our good I shall gladly go. Think about it, dear, and let me hear from you and give me your plans. You will be perfectly open with me, darling? And you will feel free to accept or reject as your best judgment and desires dictate?

Oh dear heart, God give me the light and strength to be only a help and comfort to you, forever, and in all things. I take good care of myself and avoid all colds. The weather is bad and I am so susceptible to cold since I came home. But I got such a heroic freezing in New York that I had hoped it would make me proof against our make-believe Winter.

I shall wait anxiously to hear from you. I shall be so glad to see your dear writing again.

Goodbye, darling. God bless you and keep you safe.

With my love, your Elodie.

P.S. I thought something of this plan while I was in New York. But I was too utterly useless and ill and miserable to face the sea alone. I should have been only a burden to you. God be good to you, Elodie.[1]

It was the crucial turning point in his life. Elodie's letter did not, in fact, outline any 'plans' at all. It said that she wanted them to be together again, but that she could not afford, nor would her nerves stand, a transatlantic crossing. The letter put Belloc in a position where he could only do one thing.

With extraordinary rashness, but an admirable romanticism, he and his mother set sail, in March, for New York.

[1] BC February 1, 1896.

FOUR

EARLY MARRIED LIFE
1896–1899

The Purple Wig, one of G. K. Chesterton's short stories, tells of an aristocratic family said to be descended from a mad peer who sold his soul to the devil during the seventeenth century and in consequence to have grown diabolical ears. The present Duke of Exmoor, a terrifyingly belligerent and supposedly Satanic figure, wears a purple wig, beneath which these monstrous protuberances are believed to lurk. The climax of the story comes when Father Brown leans forward and grasps the purple locks. 'Then the silence was snapped by the librarian exclaiming: "What can it mean? Why, the man had nothing to hide. His ears are just like everybody else's." "Yes," said Father Brown, "that is what he had to hide."'

Belloc had such a profound desire to mythologise his own marriage, that his biographer necessarily feels timid about snatching away the purple wig, for fear that some monstrous misery will be concealed beneath the surface of the idyllic legend. The whole story is coloured, moreover, by the fact of Belloc's long widowhood, and the wretchedness of his domestic existence after Elodie died in 1914. Elodie was canonised by Belloc after her death, and his circle of friends accepted the picture of his marriage as a seventeen-year sojourn in the Garden of Eden before the gate was shut.

The happiness of other people is much harder to penetrate than their sorrow; and an uncloudedly happy marriage is so nebulous a rarity that one approaches it cautiously. The truth is that Belloc and Elodie *were* well-suited, and were happy. But their marriage was not wholly serene. It was punctuated by poverty, anxiety and bad temper; and by long periods of enforced separation. Belloc's ears were just like everybody else's; and that is what he had to hide.

Bessie, as she accompanied her son across the Atlantic, tried to talk him out of marrying Elodie. It was of no use. When they got to New York, she wrote back to Marie, 'He behaved very kindly to me on the voyage but his mind is unchanged. Gertrude Atherton spoke to him; but he told her he could not care for anyone but Elodie.'[1]

[1] *The Young Hilaire Belloc*, p. 135.

Belloc could do nothing by halves. To his mother's eye, it must have seemed that he was behaving with an alarming recklessness, born of innocence. He had spent, five years before, a harmlessly happy six weeks showing the sights of London to a pretty young woman. Their love had been perpetuated, and formalised, in a constant correspondence ever since. But they actually knew nothing about each other, and if Belloc had been more versed in the ways of the world, he would not have allowed himself to be trapped by something which (however innocently begun and continued) was really a form of emotional blackmail. To Belloc, the matter appeared quite differently. It was partly a matter of honour: he had declared, persistently for five years, a chivalric ardour for Elodie, and now she had at last given her consent, there could have been no question of backing out, even had he felt so disposed. But there was much more to it than that. He was burning with the sense of himself as a great lover, Dante in pursuit of Beatrice, or one of the wandering troubadours of old Provence.

It is striking, in this, as in so many other areas, how much he was at variance with the ethos of his contemporaries. It was 1896. Zola, who had befriended Marie and Bessie during his exile in England, was writing frank chronicles of sexual passion. Oscar Wilde was about to leave Reading Gaol. H. G. Wells had begun his literary career and Arnold Bennett was about to descend on London. Wilfrid Scawen Blunt, who was to become a friend and neighbour of Belloc's, was pursuing a life of happy debauchery, as were a high proportion of the male population of England from the Prince of Wales downwards. Belloc's courtship of Elodie seems worlds and aeons away from his lecherous contemporaries. We can now see – and say – that he did not have a very active sexual life. He was sufficiently a modern to attribute his periodic short temper and black moods to his habits of chastity. But he was temperamentally unwilling to allow his emotional energies a sexual outlet. In this, he strongly resembled his friend G. K. Chesterton, for whom Mr Toots, in *Dombey and Son*, was the archetypal lover, 'when he goes up to the door and rings the bell and then has not the courage to ask for his lady'.[1] But, whereas one feels GKC to have been a wholly asexual figure, Belloc was a man to whom sex was visibly important, but who nevertheless could not be doing with it. Whether one attributes this to a conventional Catholic anti-sexual education; or to an egotism which fears anything which involves the absurd self-abandonment of sex; or to some other cause, makes no

[1] Quoted Maisie Ward: *Return to Chesterton*, p. 23.

difference. What drew him to Elodie in 1896 was not sexual passion but the excitement of a spiritual idea.

On Good Friday, she wrote to him in New York, 'Beloved, beloved, poor martyr, you shall take unto yourself (by God's grace) a woman 27 years old. And do you remember what you said about a woman older than 22? Oh Hun, you must have changed your tune.'[1]

Elodie concealed from him the full extent to which she had collapsed, during the previous winter, under a series of emotional and psychosomatic illnesses. But her relieved delight in his final arrival in America, and her amusement at the high courtliness of his marriage proposal, scarcely conceals a realistic fear that they do not actually know one another.

> When will you stop loving me? Well, I shall never stop being good to you, beloved. Because love of you means to me to help you and comfort you and do your will, to keep eternally near you. And I love you. And you must not call this analysis, because it is not. It is a mere commonplace expression of a very old story. Won't we have a time 'getting acquainted'? It is quite wonderful to think of. It is like the old Kings and princesses who had to woo by proxy. Our proxy has been the post man alas! Well I have planned some wonderful walks for you and me. That's how I know I am well. I love to walk again. Incidentally I laugh to myself and most of the time I am happy.[2]

Shortly after he received this letter, Belloc set out for California on the train. Even those close to Belloc in after years received a quite distorted impression of what that journey down to San Francisco entailed. 'The most romantic stories were extant about the Belloc marriage. It was said that Hilaire had seen her – as a girl – at her home in California but her image always remained, and when he heard she was going to become a novice, he worked his way out to San Francisco and plucked her from the convent doors.[3] Those words were written by the widow of one of Belloc's closest friends, Cecil Chesterton. He never much liked the woman. But it is striking that, in 1941, this was the considered belief among Belloc's friends, of how he came to marry Elodie. In the course of writing this book, I have tried to converse with as many of Belloc's surviving family and friends as possible. It has astonished me how many of them believe that Belloc snatched Elodie from the cloister; that she was a nun when he arrived in San Francisco in 1896. And this legend persists, in spite of Robert

[1] BC Good Friday 1896.
[2] Ibid.
[3] Mrs Cecil Chesterton: *The Chestertons*, p. 77.

Speaight's biography, and the memoirs of Belloc's sister, which tell the story as fully as it was then possible to do.

When Belloc arrived in San Francisco, he did not go directly to Napa. Elodie was away, having been taken by her brother and sister to the funeral of an old friend further up the coast. 'As our train trailed along our side of the bay in sight of Tamalpais I thought of you and wondered where you were,' she wrote, not knowing that he was already within a few miles of her home.[1]

Three days later, they met. Elodie had envisaged them having 'a time' getting acquainted. But this encounter, after five years of separation, five years of frenetic and impassioned correspondence, was a moment of terror and shock. Elodie looked desperately ill. She was, as Belloc wrote to his mother, 'at death's door while you and I were in New York'.[2] But he was hardly in a position to notice. For he himself now underwent a total collapse.

He wrote about it that night to his Oxford friend J. S. Phillimore; confessing that, when he met Elodie, he 'went to pieces. I suppose every man does that once or twice in his life, but I hope never again to suffer from a collapse of the kind. It is worse than drink – one is afraid of delirium'.[3]

Belloc was terrified of emotional exposure, and had a perpetual habit of concealing the deeper emotions under an exterior of noise and jollity. 'He was a man of robust health and strong will who, when trapped into exposing his deeper feelings, regained his balance, as it were, before you had noticed what had happened. He enjoyed the good things of life in the heartiest manner, and was far too sane to allow personal grievances or misfortunes to interfere with good company. I remember a man saying to him: "So your old friend Philip Kershaw is dead." He said "Yes", and was silent for a moment. Then he burst into song, and everyone joined in. That was, I think, the first time that I was not deceived.'[4]

Morton's anecdote is a very perceptive account of the tricks which Belloc played to keep his chaotic emotions in check. 'Laughter and the love of friends' were an essential antidote to his pessimistic and fundamental loneliness.

> I said to heart, 'How goes it?' Heart replied,
> 'Right as a ribstone pippin'. But it lied.

[1] BC May 25, 1896.
[2] *The Young Hilaire Belloc*, p. 136.
[3] Quoted Speaight, p. 102.
[4] J. B. Morton: *Hilaire Belloc, a Memoir* (1953), p. 45.

But, alone on the long journey from New York to California; alone, when the journey was done; alone, when he finally came face to face with Elodie, this essential safety-valve was closed to him. Mr Toots was finally confronted with his lady whether he had the courage to be there or not. It had been easy enough to write all the letters of the previous five years. But, now, there they were, face to face with each other. Belloc spoke to Phillimore of his 'intense loneliness here – the shock of readjustment after all the wreck of these five years'.[1]

The tension was relieved, not by sex, but by religion. Belloc had never 'lost his faith', in the sense of being an atheist. But, although belligerently happy to argue the Roman Catholic point of view, and glad to be at one with the great church which was the mother of European civilisation, he had not been a pious young man. In temperament and politics, he was a devotee of Rousseau, Danton and the anti-clerical heroes of the French Revolution. In later life he was to enjoy showing that there was nothing incompatible in the revolutionary ideal with the essence of Catholicism and he was to be a hearty champion and apologist for religion. But, in that late May of 1896, we see only an uncharacteristically fragile, humble Belloc. 'I feel as though I had not understood the Mother Rome until these days,' he confessed. 'The Mass and the Sacraments are the same: and I tell you it is like home to me to hear the Mumbo-Jumbo of the young priests and the venerable common sense of the old Fathers: and to able to pray at Our Lady's Altar and to find my childhood again. I had no conception till I got here of what these five years had been. My soul had frozen – a little more and I should have done nothing with my life'.[2] In the years to come, as he did battle for his religion with violent pugnacity against sceptical foes like H. G. Wells or G. G. Coulton, he seems such a frighteningly certain individual that it will be easy to forget this moment of truth in the Irish church at Napa, where it was not the cerebral neatness of Thomist logic which brought him to his knees, but 'Mumbo-Jumbo' which helped him regain his lost childhood. Having regained it, he would never let it go, and it was for that reason that he defended it with such trenchancy. His intellectual adversaries could not know the degree to which they were assailing the very core of Belloc's emotional life, the one element of stability in all the geographical and emotional vicissitudes of his early childhood.

Elodie's piety, which had caused Belloc so much distress when it appeared to be leading her in the direction of the religious life, was also the characteristic which most deeply attracted him. 'You must not

[1] Quoted Speaight, p. 103.
[2] Ibid.

think my intellect permanently injured because the Church looms over me here,' he reassured Phillimore. On the contrary, it was 'an unforgettable oasis of Discipline, and duty and right feeling and home'.[1]

Only a fortnight later, on June 15, 1896, the ceremony took place in the Church of St John the Baptist, Napa, a pleasing building of neo-Gothic simplicities, now demolished. He wrote to his mother that they had been married, 'in as Catholic a way as could be. With a nuptial mass and Communion and all sorts of rites and benedictions by an old priest called Slattery'. Elodie, he added, 'made me go to confession twice before risking the Sacrament'.[2]

They must have felt like the babes in the wood. Three of their parents were dead. Bessie remained anxiously with the Priestleys in Philadelphia. A huddle of Irish friends and relations of Elodie provided a wedding-breakfast, but none of Belloc's friends or family were there. That evening, they set out together to Geysers in Sonoma County. The fastidious impulses which had made Elodie think she would like to be a nun, and which had kept Belloc chaste throughout his young manhood, were not disturbed by their new-found marital status. As they began their lives together, they were less like lovers than orphans who, in each other's company, were setting out to find their childhood again.

* * *

Marie Belloc had married Frederic Lowndes in January 1896 and had taken over the lease of the house in Great College Street from her mother. She remembered her brother's return from America with his bride as happening in the spring of that year, though it must have been late summer.

> There are certain moments in life that remain immortal. Such a moment was that when, looking out of the middle window of my drawing-room, I saw a hansom cab draw up before the door and my brother and Elodie leap – for leap was the word – out of it.[3]

Henceforward, Marie was to be very fond of Elodie, even though relations with her brother were to cool over the years. Belloc used to mock at her calling herself Mrs Belloc-Lowndes – 'as though the great estates of the Bellocs had been allied to those of the Lowndeses', and there were to be, as we shall see, quarrels between the siblings over

---

[1] Ibid.
[2] *The Young Hilaire Belloc*, p. 136.
[3] *The Merry Wives of Westminster*, p. 28.

money. These feelings of coldness, however, were entirely on Belloc's side; and, from the first, Mrs Belloc-Lowndes befriended her new sister-in-law. She took her to her dressmaker (a grand-daughter of Dickens) and gave her, as a wedding-present, a white satin evening-gown.[1]

For Elodie, the neurotic sorrows of the previous five years had melted away on her wedding-journey across the Atlantic. Belloc had feared that 'opposition which has been so bitter will translate itself into active rudeness when I bring my wife home', but the fears were largely groundless. Elodie was beautiful, very far from being a fool, and quickly loved by Belloc's family and friends. There were no snubs. Belloc was anxious that she should not be regarded as a bumpkin and trained her to speak with an English accent. From the first, she was happy to take a completely subservient role. When G. K. Chesterton's wife Frances imposed a ban on his Fleet Street friends, and insisted on his staying at home in Beaconsfield, they all felt outraged and wondered why he stood it. 'He loves her,' said Elodie with eloquent simplicity. 'But really he should beat her. Hilary would beat me if I behaved like that.[2] She never once questioned Belloc's right to lead a completely independent life after his marriage, spending long periods away from home, and making no concessions to her happiness or convenience. Her marriage was to be a martyrdom beside which incarceration with the Sisters of Charity in Baltimore would have seemed sybaritic and luxurious. But it made her happy.

Uncertainty hung over their future, for Belloc had no professional prospects, and Elodie had no money of her own. It had not yet fully sunk into Belloc's head that he had no hope of an academic career. His friend Phillimore had become a don at Glasgow University, and before he left the United States, Belloc was writing to him, asking for news of academic vacancies. During a rainy August, he packed his wife off to stay with his mother ('Madame', as Elodie always called her) in Slindon while he hung about with his cronies in London. She wrote to him 'the first letter I have written to my dear husband' on August 24, asking him to buy her 'a half yard of black velveteen cut on the bias. I don't think it will be more than two shillings'.[3]

In September they had a short holiday in Normandy and went to Lisieux. Thérèse Martin was still alive there, enclosed in her Carmelite convent. She died the following year aged twenty-four and Elodie always retained a deep veneration for 'the Little Flower'; even

[1] Ibid., p. 29.
[2] *The Chestertons*, p. 77.
[3] BC August 24, 1896.

though she was not canonised until after Elodie's death, there was always a photograph of Thérèse of Lisieux in the chapel at King's Land. In part, it was Thérèse's simplicity of heart which endeared itself to Elodie, a sentimental piety which would not be to everyone's taste. ('Je vais faire tomber un torrent de roses'). But it was also the tender memories of their short stay in Lisieux which increased Thérèse's attraction, even though of course the Bellocs could not have set eyes on the saint, who was locked away even from the gaze of her own father.

On their return they went back to Oxford. Belloc had taken rooms at 5, Bath Place, a tiny house perched beneath the old city walls and the tower of New College. The only source of income at this date came from what Belloc could get as a hack 'extension' lecturer; an unrewarding task to which he would be bound for the next decade. At the end of September, he was in Cheltenham, and complained of the 'middle-class faddists' with whom he was obliged to mix, women who were 'as rude as the blackest Protestant could be. Charming people'.[1] A month later he was in Lancashire, and then in Derby.[2]

Belloc was very far from even-tempered when he was at home, and those early months of married life were alarming for them both. Their innocence in sexual matters was absolute. Elodie was wise enough to be patient, confident that they would eventually come to terms with that side of life. But for Belloc the matter was shaming, and he compensated by eruptions of fury with her when he was at home. From Derby, he wrote in abject apology:

> My Hunny-bunny,
>
> I love you so much that I am writing this with freezing fingers in a jolting cart to let you have a word. The man can probably read all I am writing, so there is glory for you! All Derby will know how much you are loved!
>
> You must excuse my very cross-ness. I am very sorry indeed, sweetheart, but it comes from little physical matters in which we will both grow wiser.
>
> You are my own and dear good wife, the best and only possible wife, and my life is active and happy now because of your help, Darling.[3]

There is no need to speculate about the exact nature of these 'little physical matters', except in so far as they show the extreme fas-

[1] BC September 29, 1896.
[2] Speaight, p. 109.
[3] BC November 1896.

tidiousness of both the Bellocs at this date. On his return from Derby, however, things were evidently set to rights, and by Christmas Elodie was with child.

They were still no nearer, however, to having a regular source of income, and Oxford was not a particularly good place to be from that point of view. A man who had finished his degree and was not going to become a don had no place there, in those days before 'research students' were heard of. Belloc worked in energetic spurts at a life of Danton. He was offered some teaching of undergraduates. In this year, he acted as a tutor to Auberon Herbert (afterwards 6th Baron Lucas and Dingwall), whose family were to become Belloc's life-long friends. His cousin Aubrey Herbert was to be another close friend. Another Balliol undergraduate who fell under Belloc's spell at this time, and would remain a lifelong friend, was E. S. P. Haynes. Old friends, like John Phillimore, dropped in from time to time, and so did Basil Blackwood, who supplied the drawings for Belloc's nonsense rhymes for children composed at this date.

> O stands for Oxford. Hail! salubrious seat
> Of learning! Academical Retreat!
> Home of my Middle Age! Malarial Spot
> Which People call Medeeval (though it's not).
> The marshes in the neighbourhood can vie
> With Cambridge, but the town itself is dry,
> And serves to be a kind of fold or Pen
> Wherein to herd a lot of Learned Men.
> Were I to write but half of what they know,
> It would exhaust the space reserved for "O";
> And, as my book must not be over big,
> I turn at once to "P", which stands for Pig.

> ### MORAL
> Be taught by this to speak with moderation
> Of places where, with decent application,
> One gets a good, sound, middle-class education.

It was not a lesson which he ever took to heart. In 1896, he applied for a College Lecturership at New College. Lecturerships in Oxford are the humblest form of employment, College lecturers being several rungs lower than scouts and porters in the hierarchy of things. They are merely hack teachers, ushers, with no 'tenure', no status, and very little money. Very occasionally, a college lecturer might turn himself into a fellow. But, more usually, they are a lower order of creation altogether. The 'lecturers' teach the undergraduates for whom the fellows and tutors are actually responsible. Belloc, anyway, failed to get even a lectureship.

Even Belloc's friends, like the young New College don H. A. L. Fisher, were unable to do anything to help him. Belloc's cultivation of Fisher was not without self-interest. He wrote to Elodie in January 1898, 'Ask Mr Fisher a long time ahead to meet Mamma and Phillimore. I want to keep up my acquaintance with him very thickly. I think he is of great value.'[1] But it was a friendship which Belloc maintained long after it ceased to be 'useful' to him. Fisher was the only non-Catholic historian (unless one counts the lapsed Catholic Gibbon) whom Belloc respected. 'He was the one man in England who was allowed to write although he knew History, in so far as it can be known by a man cut off from Catholic Europe.'[2] Fisher, for his part, was amused by Belloc even when he spoke or wrote nonsense. In early days, he esteemed his intellect. And, to the end of his life, Fisher retained the very warm affection which Belloc inspired in such a wide range of differing characters.[3]

Affection, however, could not pay Belloc's bills or feed his dependents, in those early struggling years of married life. Since Elodie was now pregnant, matters were serious. By the time this news was confirmed, they were already in America again, in search of work.

The days have vanished now in which European men of letters could accumulate large sums of money simply by going about the United States on lecture tours. Dickens was perhaps the first Victorian to exploit this gold mine; Wilde was not slow to reap its rewards. In more recent times, Dylan Thomas died a martyr to it and the last triumphant survivor of it is Dr A. L. Rowse. Belloc's life was to be punctuated by visits to America whenever he needed spare cash. But, in these early tours, he was not, of course, a famous man who could ask large sums of money for his reflections on Danton and the French Revolution. Nor was he, by any means, quite certain that his future remained in England. He had married an American wife. He had no prospect of employment in Oxford. There was every pressure on them, at this stage in their marriage, to emigrate; every pressure, that is to say, except personal inclination. California would continue to delight them both as a dream-place, never revisited in the flesh, constantly dwelt upon in the mind. The East Coast bored them.

[1] BC January 17, 1898.
[2] J. S. Nickerson, April 6, 1940.
[3] Mrs John Bennett (H. A. L. Fisher's daughter) to the author.

Elodie stayed with his Priestley relations in Philadelphia, while he traipsed about the country in trains giving his lectures.

'Honey, this train is a cheap palace,' he complained, as he rattled towards New York, 'and I don't like to see all the fake-luxury and not have you to enjoy it. I always want you to have good things and will do without them to give them to you. In spite of this virtuous attitude of mind my body has rebelled and I have indulged in 50c. worth of Riesling...'

A sketch follows, jolted by the movement of the train, of himself before and after consuming the wine. Then he continues,

> Oh Honey! I wish you were with me on this nice train looking out of the window and smoking cigars. There is all the commercial traveller can wish for on this imitation luxury caravan. But when I am a rich man I shall have a train to myself in which all the luxury shall be real and you shall go with me and be my sweet Honey. I love you very much.[1]

If the fake-luxury of the commercial traveller seemed unpalatable to his European taste, he liked even less the Puritanism of restricted drinking hours. (This was before the Liberal Parliament of which he was a member brought in the Licensing Laws in England.) 'The damnable Sunday closing prevented my having a *drop* to drink yesterday. I wonder a nation can last that plays the fool in this fashion,' he complained.[2] Nevertheless, money is money. He was not earning enough to enable them both to travel together. But he was earning, and, as he went, rather wallowing in the 'fake luxury' and 'eating and drinking like a pig-hog'.[3]

The letters from this date, and from now onwards, until Elodie's death, survive in enormous profusion, an eloquent testimony both to the Bellocs' fondness for each other, and to the small amount of time they spent in one another's company. All Belloc's letters to Elodie from Pittsburgh in January 1897 are directed to 1206, Arch Street, Philadelphia, where the Priestleys lived. But when, in late February, Belloc returned to Philadelphia, to teach a course of evening-classes there, we find that Elodie has moved to Brooklyn to stay with her friend Mrs Kellogg. At the end of March, he could write to her,

> How relieved I am when each course is *over*. Now the Philadelphia evening course is – thank God – Done. It was a good proposition

---

[1] BC January 16, 1897.
[2] BC January 11, 1897.
[3] BC undated, from Pittsburgh, 'Monday evening'.

that I should write to you and I do it but oh! Honey! I dare not sacrifice my tum. I had an EXCELLENT dinner – the best I have had in America. & I felt so good after it. 75c. & a bottle of wine at the Club. (i.e. The Art Club of Philadelphia)[1]

The pattern of the Bellocs' marriage had been oddly formed by their courtship. You would think, after such an agonisingly long betrothal, they would, once married, never have wished to be separated. In fact, they had grown rather used to separation; their affection, perhaps, actually demanded it. When the marriage was all over, this was to fill Belloc with profound guilt from which he never recovered. He felt, not without cause, that he had 'neglected' Elodie. Once the children had been born, there were always reasons for this. Not only was childbirth in itself exhausting, but you could not take babies on walking-holidays and lecture-tours, and there was always a limit to the amount of nursing and housekeeping which the Bellocs could afford to pay for. But, in these early months of their marriage, one would have expected them to spend more time in each other's company than they did. One of the reasons that they gave the impression to the world that they were so happily married was that they were so able to respect each other's solitude. Another of the reasons why it was never, in fact, an entirely happy arrangement, was that neither of them could wholly assuage the other's loneliness. This is not to say that they deceived each other by their expressions of passionate love; on the contrary, by living so very much apart, they remained in a state of excited adoration which would be most unusual in couples living together all the time.

They returned to Oxford in the spring of 1897, and moved to a cottage in Littlemore, the small village where, in his Anglican days, Newman had been vicar, built a church, and established a religious community. From Littlemore, so many letters from Elodie survive that it is evident that Belloc spent most of the summer apart from her. An undated letter, evidently from this period[2], speaks of 'how I missed you last night after our whole week together', as though a whole week in the company of one's husband was something of a luxury.

On July 15, she wrote anxiously, 'I am so glad, dear heart, that you are going to be home so much in the Winter. You *must not* begin planning work for those days – you must use them to rest and be

---

[1] BC March 30, 1897.
[2] BC. The Bellocs were only in Littlemore from April to October 1897, so anything written from Littlemore must automatically be assigned to this date.

happy in preparation for the Inferno beyond seas in the Spring. And then you can do a lot of writing perhaps and polish up your verse'.[1]

In the event, however, Belloc did not spend much of that winter with Elodie, and the 'inferno beyond seas' swallowed him up sooner than she had feared. In September, they left Littlemore because it was an impractical and lonely house in which to have a baby. Belloc found them poky rooms on the upper floor of 36, Holywell, whose only advantages were that they were in the centre of Oxford and they had pretty views overlooking the gardens of Wadham College. It was here, on September 23, 1897, that Elodie gave birth to their first son, Louis John. As soon as she was able to move, Belloc took her on a reading party with Phillimore in Norfolk, where the men could sail together on the Broads.[2] But, by Christmas, he was off again to the United States, and this time, alone.[3]

Writing to her on Christmas Day, while his ship the U.S.M.S. *St Louis* was still in Southampton Water, Belloc was distraught:

> My little Honey,
>   I stayed looking at you till you went away and I cried a great deal. It makes me intolerably sad to go away, but I am sincerely glad that you will be in Sussex a few days to pick up. I love you. You are my little honey, all I have and all I want & I will write to you allee-timee. Give the Pick-Pack a kiss from me and keep up your heart seeing that you are such a nice girl. Look Honey I am only going to earn a heap of money then I come back to Angel in a boat. Please God all will be well with you whom I love more than all the world. . . *Have friends to stay with you, dear Heart*, mind you do & see how soon I come back, 105 days: tomorrow it will be 104.[4]

Bessie Belloc had, of course, been very devoted to her husband; but she found her son's marriage, with its endless baby-talk ('allee-timee') and its strange combination of long separations with very emotional language, rather hard to understand. 'I think Grandmama thinks it disedifying and humiliating to the sex to see a woman so in love with her husband – even though that husband has the honour to be her own son,'[5] Elodie wrote, failing to see how troubling, from a mother's point of view, the marriage must have seemed.

[1] BC July 15, 1897.
[2] Speaight, p. 119.
[3] Speaight, p. 114, speaks of 'the Bellocs' having made this tour of 1898 together but the letters at BC show that she was at home looking after the baby.
[4] BC Christmas Day, 1897.
[5] BC February 26, 1898.

While Belloc steamed towards America, Elodie was worrying about little Louis's baby-illnesses, sacking the nurse and hiring another.[1] There was a great shortage of money. Nurse Owen, the new employee, charged £2-2-0 per week... 'I try as hard as I can to save on my household and grocers and butcher, but I do not seem to make much headway at it,' poor Elodie confided, feeling obliged to confess that she had just spent two guineas on 'a large photograph of one of Raphael's sweetest madonnas... – it is over his cradle now and is to be in the Nursery in perpetuity'.[2]

Although the baby (the 'pick-pack') was bottle-fed, by the nurse, Elodie was deeply exhausted and sleepless. American friends and relations came to stay – her sister Julia, and Mrs Atherton. And Elodie had many Oxford friends. The wife of Belloc's old tutor, for instance, Mrs A. L. Smith, is described as having been 'most awfully good to me since you went away. She *is* a kind woman & she reminds me of Julia – she has about as much tact as a kicking bronco – & she deliberately puts people's backs up – but "tis not my freshness" – she is always kind and good to me.'[3]

One of the most touching letters she wrote to Belloc during this period of separation described an evening out in Oxford when

> I saw a lot of lantern slide pictures in Balliol Hall of the hills about Bashan & Gilead. There were the great flaming blue sky, the shaggy hills of golden earth, the patches of purple shrubs, the black shadows and white sunlight that I have seen so often in the more desert parts of home. And it tore my soul not for the desire of the light & sun & heat of California but with the need of you – who are my sun and light and heat beyond all the magnets set in the earth of the Californian hills.[4]

Belloc, for his part, slogging about America, felt 'very overworked and miserable'.[5] From Harrisburg, Pennsylvania, he complained,

> This place is ugly. God made it the night after a debauch when His ideas were neither many nor interesting (you see I judge the Creator by myself like other theologians). Here I lecture to horrible people, kindly, of the middle class (as I am) yet, oddly enough,

[1] BC January 21, 1898.
[2] BC January 7, 1898.
[3] BC January 21, 1898.
[4] BC February, 1898.
[5] Princeton, March 11, 1898.

not congenial to me. I am bored and lonely. Also, the wine is dear and bad.[1]

As he always tended to do, Belloc overworked on this tour and found that 'fatigue greatly interferes with my efficiency'.[2] He befriended a bluestocking called Maria Lansdale who was writing an historical guide to Paris. She enlisted his help – and paid him for it – but it turned out to be a big job; whole chapters had to be rewritten. She had transcribed most French names wrong, and he had to retranslate many of her sources for her. He thanked her fulsomely, saying, 'for the first time in my life I have been overpaid',[3] but to have undertaken this job for Miss Lansdale on top of his other work – lecturing, touring and writing – was more than even his frame could stand. He was collapsed and ill when he got back to England, and the two months after he came home were 'little better than convalescence, and you know how in such cases there are periods almost worse than illness'.[4]

Such periods of collapse were the inevitable outcome of the burdens which he (so unnecessarily) placed upon his system. Having failed to get the All Souls' Fellowship, or any other sort of Fellowship, Belloc, had he been planning a 'career' for himself, should have settled on two or three possible areas of action. His mother (Elodie, too) still hoped that he would try to read for the Bar, scraping the money from somewhere. Alternatively, he could have sought regular employment in Fleet Street. Instead, he chose to dash about under the mistaken impression that this would make him 'a rich man' and a 'heap of money'. At the same time, most characteristically, he was unable to cut the umbilical cord which held him to Oxford, and to Balliol. Edward Thomas remembers his first summer as an undergraduate, that summer Belloc got back exhausted from America, standing with a friend at the foot of Boars Hill and hearing a high tenor voice lifted on the air:

> 'S'ils tombent, nos jeunes héros,
> La France en produit de nouveaux,
> Contre vous tous prêts à se battre
> Aux armes, citoyens!'

A bicycle swept by, down a steep hill, guided, so far as it was guided at all, by the spirit of the Spring, winged by the south wind,

[1] Quoted Speaight, p. 115.
[2] Princeton, February 21, 1898.
[3] Quoted Speaight, p. 115.
[4] Princeton, July 4, 1898.

crowned with superb white clouds, and singing that song in a whirl of golden dust. 'That was Belloc', said my companion, as he lay by the roadside trembling from the shock of that wild career.[1]

In any generation in Oxford, there is the slightly embarrassing ghost-like figure of the man who won't go down. Often – more often than not, perhaps – such a person has been an unusually successful undergraduate; so successful, in fact, that nothing in grown-up life is ever going to earn or provide the reassurance of such parochial laurels and accolades as a First in the Schools and Presidency of the Union.

Belloc, by hovering about in Oxford long after the chance of employment had passed him by, became this embarrassing figure. It did lasting damage to him, for it made his disappointment over the All Souls' Fellowship into a lasting, festering wound. But the mistake brought its compensations. Belloc had very few friends in his life who were older than himself. He liked, as he openly confessed, to be the senior partner in a friendship; and his two or three years of married life in Oxford brought him into touch with some of the friends who were to mean the most to him in the years to come.

Above all, perhaps, in those years, one should mention Maurice Baring, who lodged with Bron Herbert in King Edward Street in 1897, but did not make friends with Belloc until the summer. ('I had met him once before with Basil Blackwood, but all he had said to me was that I would most certainly go to hell, and so I had not thought it likely that we should ever make friends.'[2]) This free advice about Baring's chances in the after-life was prompted, no doubt, by the young man's connexion with the famous banking family, and by the assumption (probably, as it happens, a false one) of Jewish blood. Years afterwards, when they had become firm friends, Belloc would attribute any 'unsound' opinion of Baring's to the fact that 'Maurice is, never let it be forgotten, a quarter Jew'.[3] At the supper parties in King Edward Street when he and Maurice Baring (together with Donald Tovey, Auberon Herbert and others) first got to know one another, Belloc 'discoursed of the Jewish Peril, the Catholic Church, the *Chanson de Roland*, Ronsard, and the Pyrenees with indescribable gusto and vehemence'.[4] It sounds fairly uncongenial to the modern ear; but one must set down, in loyalty to Belloc's memory, that a high

[1] Quoted Speaight p. 182, who tells the story of Belloc's undergraduate career. Edward Thomas in fact came up to the University when Belloc was aged twenty-eight.

[2] Maurice Baring: *The Puppet Show of Memory* (1922), p. 171.

[3] JSN to the author.

[4] *The Puppet Show of Memory*, p. 171.

proportion of those who met him, loved him; and that those who loved him, went on loving him. Maurice Baring was only one of hundreds who would rather spend an evening with Belloc than with anyone else. He made his friends laugh until they ached.[1] He was ebulliently well-informed, spontaneously hilarious, mischievous and, at the same time, tough. And any picture of Belloc which fails to take account of this is a distorted picture. He was publicly, and in print, a belligerent and controversial figure. He has been much vilified, by people who did not know him, for the strength or wrongness of his views. Nowadays, it perhaps sounds unattractive to have 'discoursed of the Jewish Peril . . . with indescribable gusto and vehemence'. It is only fair to record that fun was had at the time; and, more than that, his huge and wide variety of friends loved him deeply. Baring was such a friend, one of Belloc's closest. A brilliant generation of undergraduates were coming up to the University at this time. Raymond Asquith (son of H. H. Asquith, the future Prime Minister) was acknowledged to be the most brilliant of them all. Coming up to Balliol in 1897, he observed that 'the College is for the most part composed of niggers and Scotchmen: and the prevailing dialect is a compound of Gaelic and Hindustani which is not easily acquired by the average Londoner'.[2] H. T. Baker ('Bluetooth'), Conrad Russell and John Buchan were friends of these days. Asquith's career was a glowing succession of honours, including Presidency of the Union, and a Fellowship at All Souls'. His friends were less lucky. Buchan failed to get an All Souls' Fellowship in 1899. Raymond Asquith noted, 'Most people are very indignant at John Buchan being passed over: he is certainly a much more brilliant man than either of the others. . .'[3] His friend Baker failed to get a much-coveted University Prize. 'I must say I thought Bluetooth would get the thing, as he did well in the most important papers. But as you say there is no fighting the Jews; they ought to institute some form of Varsity competition for which the prize would be a slice of York ham . . . then perhaps we poor Gentiles should have a chance. . .'[4]

I quote these two extracts from Raymond Asquith's letters to make the point that Belloc was not alone either in his failure to get a Fellowship at All Souls' or in his fondness for strong talk about the Jews. The editor of these letters, a grandson of Raymond Asquith, notes that 'it should not – but just conceivably may – be necessary to

[1] Daphne Pollen to the author.
[2] Raymond Asquith: *Life and Letters*, ed. John Jolliffe (1980), p. 33.
[3] Ibid., p. 62.
[4] Ibid., p. 64.

mention that he is not speaking of the victims of any kind of persecution. His Jews were not the refugees from Russia or Poland, struggling for existence in Whitechapel or Kilburn; they were a handful of Lawsons, Sassoons and Rothschilds, triumphant in their intelligent prosperity'.[1]

Into this clever, sharp-spoken, somewhat aristocratic undergraduate set Belloc and his wife happily moved.

> People would come in through the window, and syphons would sometimes be hurled across the room; but nobody was ever wounded. The ham would be slapped and butter thrown to the ceiling, where it stuck. Piles of chairs would be placed in a pinnacle, one on top of the other, over Arthur Stanley, and someone would climb to the top of this airy Babel and drop ink down on him through the seats of the chairs. Songs were sung; port was drunk and thrown about the room. Indeed, we had a special brand of port which was called *throwing port* for the purpose. . .[2]

For quieter evenings, the young sparks would come and sit with Elodie in the tiny little flat in Holywell, where Belloc's pupils might be discussing French literature. One of Baring's sonnets was so highly approved that Belloc hung it up on the back of one of his pictures in his room, and it was clearly as a poet that they all, at this date, regarded him.

The first book which Belloc published was a small collection entitled *Verses and Sonnets* in 1896. 'I do not think that this book excited a ripple of attention at the time, and yet some of the poems in it have lived, and are now found in many anthologies, whereas the verse which at this time was received with a clamour of applause is nearly all of it not only dead but buried and completely forgotten.'[3] That was Maurice Baring's judgment in 1922. Since that time, Belloc's reputation as a poet has declined to the point where his serious verse is only known or appreciated by a small band of enthusiasts. At the best of times, he is a very uneven poet. And the things he was good at have never been less admired by critics than now: lyric facility, metrical fluency, and the self-consciously 'beautiful' effects which have made 'Georgian' almost a term of abuse. At times, in this 1896 volume, he approaches (though never here achieves) the technical virtuosity of A. E. Housman or Yeats, only to cascade into rhymes which seem too easy, or effects which seem mannered rather than meant.

---

[1] Ibid., p. 31.
[2] *The Puppet Show of Memory*, p. 171.
[3] *The Puppet Show of Memory*, p. 171.

The Moon is dead. I saw her die.
She in a drifting cloud was drest,
She lay along the uncertain west,
A dream to see.
And very low she spake to me:
'I go where none may understand,
I fade into the nameless land,
And there must lie perpetually.'
And therefore I,
And therefore, loudly, loudly I
And high
And very piteously make cry:
'The Moon is dead. I saw her die'.

This could be any reasonably competent Nineties poet, steeped in the rhythms of Swinburne and the lethargic postures of *la Décadence*. Its 'spake' and 'drest' make it embarrassing now. Yet, in the same volume, there are poems which display three very distinctive qualities of Belloc's best verse: three qualities which were all part of his personality and which create the most authentically Bellocian *sound* when read aloud: bombast, lyricism and satire.

The first is bombast. It is a quality little esteemed in poets nowadays, but which is not wholly to be despised. One sees it in some of his sonnets on the twelve months of the year, mingled with an elegiac tone which is completely Belloc's; as in his 'November' poem in which he likens the month to Napoleon.

November is that historied Emperor
    Conquered in age but foot to foot with fate
Who from his refuge high has heard the roar
    Of squadrons in pursuit, and now, too late,
Stirrups the storm and calls the winds to war,
    And arms the garrison of his last heirloom,
And shakes the sky to its extremest shore
    With battle against irrevocable doom.
Till, driven and hurled from his strong citadels,
    He flies in hurrying cloud and spurs him on,
Empty of lingerings, empty of farewells
    And final benedictions and is gone.
But in my garden all the trees have shed
Their legacies of light and all the flowers are dead.

The effect of the poignant last couplet, after all the swirling and bombastic storm of the previous lines, shows that Belloc had a wholly distinctive poetic voice, and that had he only 'polished up' his verse, as Elodie urged him to do, he might have achieved great things.

Simple lyricism is the second quality which was apparent in Belloc's poetry from the beginning, lyrics as simple as the best medieval songs, lyrics which reflect his essential simplicity of heart but which are so technically accomplished that in poems like 'Auvergnat' or 'On a winter's night long time ago' one could easily take the perfect rhythms for artlessness. 'The Early Morning' is another such poem, which has some of the smiling simplicity which was always a part of Belloc's nature:

> The moon on the one hand, the dawn on the other:
> The moon is my sister, the dawn is my brother.
> The moon on my left and the dawn on my right.
> My brother, good morning: my sister, good night.

But there is a third, and quite different category of poem in his *Verses and Sonnets* of 1896. Technically as accomplished as the other sorts of poem in the volume, it has the satirical edge which one thinks, perhaps wrongly, to be Belloc at his most distinctive.

On Torture, a Public Singer

> Torture will give a dozen pence or more
> To keep a drab from bawling at his door.
> The public taste is quite a different thing –
> Torture is positively paid to sing.

And, appropriately, it was his savage gifts as a comic poet which made his verses for children so abidingly successful. In much of his later prose, as in his conversation, Belloc's delight in strong speech won him many enemies. Some of the same qualities which made him such an impassioned controversialist, when channelled into manifest nonsense, produced pages in which generations of children have revelled.

> A Python I should not advise,
> It needs a doctor for its eyes,
> And has the measles yearly.
> However, if you feel inclined
> To get one (to improve your mind,
> And not from fashion merely),
> Allow no music near its cage;
> And when it flies into a rage
> Chastise it most severely.

> I had an aunt in Yucatan
> Who bought a Python from a man
> And kept it for a pet.
> She died, because she never knew
> These simple little rules and few; –
> The Snake is living yet.

In the forty-five years after the publication of *The Bad Child's Book of Beasts*, he wrote over a hundred and fifty prose works of history, of political and economic theory, and of religious apologetics. Almost none of these works is in print, and the general opinion even (or especially) among Catholics is that he spent his life talking and writing nonsense; violent, vitriolic, and, the general opinion would be, frequently dangerous nonsense. This huge output of books never sold very well, and it is now almost completely neglected. But his early doodlings, when he was deliberately writing violent nonsense, remain in print and are the possession of every literate, English-speaking child. The paradox is positively Chestertonian. Belloc had a keen desire to make his readers see Sense, about Economics, Politics, History and Religion. But, when he encapsulated all this Common Sense in lucid prose, it was dismissed for two or three generations as Nonsense. But Nonsense, so very undesirable in prose, was apparently an excellent thing in verse. Even today, when many of Belloc's political and social prophecies have been proved to be luminously common-sensical, the paradox remains. Parents who would shudder to read *The Servile State* or *The Jews* urge their children to recite the unhappy end of Rebecca Offendort, flattened by a marble bust of Abraham in her banker-father's Bayswater residence.

The Bad Child's Book of Beasts sold 4,000 copies within three months of publication,[1] and has been in print ever since. *More Beasts for Worse Children* followed it in 1897 and was equally successful. In 1898, he published *The Modern Traveller*, illustrated, as were the previous two volumes, with ludicrously apposite drawings by Basil Blackwood. It tells the story of two explorers called Commander Sin and William Blood. As Arthur Quiller Couch noted in his review of the book, it specifically satirises the British Press and the Imperialist ideal: 'The exploration business, the "Anglo-Saxon" *entente* – can a journalist who has been watering these plants with emotion for months past be expected to welcome a book which hints that some recent and practical applications of

[1] Speaight, p. 115.

his creed have been absurd and others more than a little base?"[1]
William Blood is

> A sort of modern Buccaneer,
> Commercial and refined.
> Like all great men, his chief affairs
> Were buying stocks and selling shares.
> He occupied his mind
> In buying them by day from men
> Who needed ready cash, and then
> At evening selling them again
> To those with whom he dined.

But, although the 'satirical' elements in the tale reflect Belloc's
perennial political preoccupations, the glory of it is in the inven-
tiveness of its rhymes, the absurdity of its plot, and the wonderful
arbitrariness of its general observations:

> And yet I really must complain
> About the Company's Champagne!
>   This most expensive kind of wine
> In England is a matter
> Of pride or habit when we dine
>   (Presumably the latter).
> Beneath an equatorial sky
> You must consume it or you die;
> And stern indomitable men
> Have told me, time and time again,
>   'The nuisance of the tropics is
>   The sheer necessity of fizz'.

The extraordinary magic of Belloc's light verse, as anyone who
enjoyed it in childhood can testify – is that one can revel in this, and
know it by heart before one has even seen a bottle of champagne. The
parts of the poem which relate to 'grown-up' life are not distinguished, in the minds of the children who read it, from the rumbusti-
ously absurd pace of those parts of the narrative which are not
remotely 'satirical'.

> On June the 7th after dark
> A young and very hungry shark
>   Came climbing up the side.
> It ate the Chaplain and the Mate –
> But why these incidents relate?

[1] Speaight, p. 116.

> The public must decide
> That nothing in the voyage out
> Was worth their bothering about,
> Until we saw the coast, which looks
> Exactly as it does in books.
> Oh! Africa, mysterious land!
> Surrounded by a lot of sand
>   And full of grass and trees...

A man who was capable of writing those lines need not have striven to capture the attention of posterity.

But, of course, Belloc, at that date, if he had an eye on posterity at all, was pursuing fame of an altogether different kind; and his children's verses were only the most minimal interlude, as far as he was concerned, in a life dominated by his two over-riding concerns, of history and politics.

★   ★   ★

Throughout 1897, and 1898, in the intervals when he was neither crossing the Atlantic, lecturing to the middle-classes about St Joan of Arc, sailing or drinking with his friends, Belloc was at work on the *Life of Danton*, a substantial piece of prose 'by Hilaire Belloc B. A., late Brackenbury Scholar of Balliol College Oxford', and published by James Nisbet and Co in 1899. It is a book which reflects many of Belloc's familiar preoccupations, notions which anyone who has read the entire Belloc *corpus* will find reiterated to the point of tedium in later books. Above all, it proclaims that the French Revolution was 'a reversion to the normal – a sudden and violent return to those conditions which are the necessary bases of health in any political community, which are clearly apparent in every primitive society, and from which Europe had been estranged by an increasing complexity and a spirit of routine,.[1] Those necessary bases were 'the Roman idea' – 'absolute sovereignty in the case of the State, absolute ownership in the case of the Individual'. This, in essence, was to be his political *Credo* for the rest of his life, and it is interesting that he should have taken so long in discovering that the first basis of the Roman idea was incompatible with any existent British political system or ideal. Throughout his active political life, Belloc struck attitudes which were deliberately, self-consciously, un-English. There was in England at that time, as there still is, a smug belief that the system of parliamentary democracy, the House of Commons and the House of

---

[1] *Danton* (1899), p. 1.

Lords, were the most perfect political institutions devised by man, and the most conducive to liberty and justice. Belloc frequently saw reason to question this; and, by the middle of his life, he had come to doubt it altogether. His doubts all sprang from a scepticism which was fed by comparing Great Britain with Europe. To his eye, the commercial muddled values of English parliamentarians did not always represent the highest summit of human achievement. He paid dearly for pointing this out.

And his enemies could point, in their turn, to Belloc's disastrous habit of backing the wrong horse, in political terms. This may be true. But it must also be conceded that, when he backed the wrong horse, he did so with unfailing loyalty and gusto, never wavering in his support, when more faint-hearted or rational men would have changed their allegiance.

The first symptom of this tendency in Belloc can be seen at the close of 1898, when he left Elodie on her own for Christmas, and went over to Paris to acquaint himself more fully with the details of the Dreyfus case. By then, it was becoming apparent to most reasonable people that Captain Dreyfus had been sentenced to exile for an offence of which he was completely innocent. Colonel Henry, the officer responsible for his condemnation, had been so sincere in his belief that Dreyfus was guilty, that he had forged the evidence against him. The notorious *bordereau*, giving a list of secret documents which its author was willing to sell to the Germans, had been penned not by Dreyfus but by Major Esterhazy, who was initially acquitted of the offence by a more than biassed court martial. These events came to light in the course of 1898, largely because of the publicity given to the case by Zola's famous '*J'Accuse*' letter in *L'Aurore*. Zola, who was sued for defamation, was obliged to leave France and, in his exile, he had been well-received both by Belloc's mother and sister.

Belloc's prejudices, after a year in the French army, were very different from his mother's. In spite of the fact that both Marie and Bessie befriended the French writer, Belloc would always maintain that Zola 'was hardly received in polite society',[1] and that his word could not be trusted.

The Dreyfus case dragged on for years. The full facts of it will never be known, but crucially important details of it were still being revealed as late as 1906. Its importance went far beyond the initial question of who had written the *bordereau*. It completely split French society. The pro-Dreyfusards were far more interested in under-

[1] Speaight, p. 98.

mining the authority of the Church, the Army and the Right Wing, than they were in defending the innocence of one unfortunate man. The anti-Dreyfusards felt threatened. They believed, correctly in many ways, that the fabric of society was undermined by the dispute. Belloc was not alone in his belief that the vindication of Dreyfus had been gained at the expense of destroying the French Intelligence Bureau, which permitted the German surprise on Mons and Charleroi in 1914. In this view, he was probably right.

But he would never admit that he had been wrong about Dreyfus himself. He conceded that the majority of those who knew most about the subject believed in the Captain's innocence. For himself, he could pretend to 'no certain conclusion in the matter'. Far more important than the trivial details of forgery and personal innocence was the furore which the case aroused. People took sides and betrayed their allegiances. When Dean Inge accused Belloc of being the only man in England who did not take Dreyfus's side, it was just more evidence, as far as Belloc viewed things, of the existence of an 'Anglo-Judaic alliance'. Most English people *thought* they took Dreyfus's side because he was a wronged man, falsely accused. In fact, they were instinctively on his side because he was Jewish. This 'fact' opened Belloc's eyes to 'the Jew question'. It made him see – and it was clear enough for all to see – that the Jews were bitterly feared and hated in wide sections of French society. After the Dreyfus *affaire*, you could not shut your eyes to the fact that there was a 'problem'. But Belloc of course meant more than that. He meant that the affair showed up the existence of the Jewish power, their control of European commercial interests, their capacity for influencing public opinion. Here Belloc entered deeper, and muddier, waters, where it is difficult to prove anything, and where prejudice flourishes more freely than sober fact.

* * *

The dons had evidently seen through Belloc's bluster during his dinner conversation at All Souls'. When you argued him into a corner, he started to shout things which he knew, and you knew, were untrue. Dr A. L. Rowse, an historian who *was* elected to an All Souls' Fellowship, believed that they were right to reject him 'on his qualifications and eventual showing as an historian'. But he adds, 'I have never doubted that he was something rarer: a man of genius.'[1]

Men of genius have rarely flourished in Oxford. As the nineteenth

[1] A. L. Rowse, *Portraits and Views* (1979), p. 72.

century tottered to its close, Belloc began to realise that he did not have a hope of a Fellowship. His friends there were tending to drift towards London, and that was the obvious direction for him to go himself. In the winter of 1899–1900, he and Elodie took a lease on 104, Cheyne Walk, and they went to live in Chelsea. He was to miss Oxford bitterly for the rest of his life, and to mind about his failure there. Like the loss of his family fortune, the failure became myth-ologised in his mind; another Paradise had been lost. 'Financiers' were the bogey-men who had deprived his mother of her holdings on the Stock Market. 'Dons' were the men who had deprived his wife and children of a regular income, a cheap, substantial house and an orderly domestic life. Both categories of person were to receive the most scathing Bellocian abuse for the next half-century.

FIVE

'EUROPE AND ALL OUR PAST'
1900–1901

The move to 104, Cheyne Walk was an adventure. But it did not immediately solve the problem of what Belloc was to do with his life. It was an elegant little eighteenth-century house, in which they 'fixed up a scratch bedroom' and installed a telephone, the first in Cheyne Walk.[1] It was an early symptom of Belloc's passion for this instrument, the most infallible method devised by modern science for intruding upon other people's lives.

Elodie, with no money, began to make the place a home. She made friends with her sister-in-law Marie,[2] and soon had a wide London acquaintanceship. She was still worn out by her baby, Eleanor, now six months old; and by Louis, a boisterous three-year-old. Much of her time was spent recumbent in the 'scratched-up' bedroom, and alone.

Belloc had been commissioned by Edward Arnold to write a history of Paris, and, three weeks after establishing his young family in Chelsea, he crossed the Channel in order to do the necessary research at the Bibliothèque Nationale. He went with misgivings, and feelings of guilt.

> My dearest wife, our marriage has put heavy burdens on you. I pray God that my work may lighten them in time & whereas I once desired success for the sake of fame I now desire it almost entirely for your sake. Do not be down-hearted my own love. There have been many struggles like ours & so long as the man keeps at it they usually end in time. You shall have no such future troubles my Elodie in so far as it depends on me.[3]

Initially, he stayed at the Hôtel St Romain in the Rue St Roch, where he was pursued by rather melancholy accounts of how poor and ill

---

[1] Speaight, pp. 146–7.
[2] *The Merry Wives of Westminster*, p. 28.
[3] BC undated.

Elodie felt. 'I am so sorry for you I do not know what to do,'[1] he wrote back, promising that he would cancel his French sojourn and be back with her in seven or eight hours if she needed him. But, of course, she insisted that he remained in Paris, and got on with the book. He moved in to stay with friends at 41, Rue des Ecoles, was 'treated like a God' at the National Library, and was delighted that they had heard of him there, having read his *Danton*; that he had a reputation.[2] The book went well. 'It is a good, good, book, explanatory of the City as is none other', as he himself modestly averred.[3] Belloc is never better, as an historical writer, than when he is telling the story of a *place*. His *Paris* is not a guide book. Reading it is to receive something of the pleasure people had who were lucky enough to be his travelling companions. Other books have been more painstakingly accurate as to exact dates and nomenclature. Few can have made a stronger appeal to the faculty of the historical imagination, nor made it in a more elegant prose. A typical example of this is the passage in which he tells the story of the Hôtel St Paul.

> It was in this palace that the young Charles VI grew up, amiable, ill-balanced, into his unhappy manhood; here he brought home Isabella, and here that she bore him the child for whom Joan of Arc was to recover the kingdom. Here, in the same year, the recurrent curse of the Valois fell upon him, and he came home mad from the armed ride. All the tragedy of the long reign passed in that palace. Its walls kept the echo of the poor king calling out to be saved from himself, looking with blank eyes at his children, and giving them the names of strangers.

From thence, in a short page, Belloc traces the gradual collapse of the palace towards the close of the Middle Ages, its sale and partial rebuilding in the time of Catherine de Médicis, its gradual dissolution, so that all we see now (or saw in 1900) are 'the tall gloomy houses that have filled up the old gardens and courts of the nobles'.[4]

Every page of the book breathes not only the sense that 'all the streets are noisy with an infinite past'[5] but also the sense that Paris embodied all that Belloc believed in and considered good. He wrote back to Elodie when he had been there a few weeks: 'It is horrible to be here and *realise* what a stench surrounds Protestantism & what a

[1] Ibid.
[2] Ibid.
[3] Princeton, August 9, 1900.
[4] *Paris* (1900), p. 252.
[5] Ibid., p. 419.

decaying corpse the society of England has become.' He determined that her nostrils should not be polluted by the Protestant stench for much longer in Chelsea.

> Listen, my heart, you shall come over this year – somehow we will manage it – it is like getting health again. Especially I wanted you in St Sulpice at Benediction; the service was most glorious & they had paid a man to sing solos who sang them better than an angel. St Sulpice is a very large church and there were about a million candles and the church was packed like the Cathedral at Rouen when we went there together. A man had with him a little boy like Ruck-a-buck & the little boy felt his father's neck with his fingers as my son does mine, so that I was filled with divine charity. Indeed this country is the chosen instrument of God & without it the Devil would rule the world.[1]

One thing was certain. Belloc was sick of England. With his hopes of an academic career in ruins, there seemed no future there. What he did not know when he wrote to her from Paris, was that Elodie had conceived another child shortly before he left Cheyne Walk. There would be no chances of her seeing the Continent with him that summer.

Impulsively, and despondently, he put it to her, when his work on the Paris book was done, that they should emigrate. London was expensive, and the English climate was temperamentally disagreeable to Elodie. Her health was being worn down by poverty and child-birth. They should return to her native California. It is not clear how he thought this would improve their financial situation. Perhaps he imagined that he would farm in the wine-growing country there, and write verse while she sat, and his children gambolled, in the Pacific sunshine.

It must have been a very tempting prospect, but she saw that it would not do. Elodie had married Belloc partly in order to escape California. If, for the moment, her life would have been easier in Napa than in London, and if she missed the company of her remaining family there, she was wise enough, and big-hearted enough, to recognise that Belloc's future must be made in England. 'Yes, darling,' she wrote, 'we must think carefully over the Californian matter. If it can be avoided I do not want to bring Louis up as an American. . . Have you thought seriously of being called to the Bar in the Fall, if by hook or by crook we could get the fees?'[2]

---

[1] BC Ruck-a-buck (like Pick-a-pack) was one of the many whimsical nicknames for Louis Belloc.
[2] BC undated, spring 1900.

He had *thought* about it. But thinking was not enough. The idea of forcing Belloc to use his considerable rhetorical powers at the English Bar had been floating about since his undergraduate days. His sparring partner at the Oxford Union, F. E. Smith, was already making a great career at the Bar. Belloc could have done so, no doubt, had he possessed either the money or the inclination. He could not knuckle down to mastering the law of Tort any more than he could have flown. Once back in England, he became passionately involved in journalism, in social life, and in political activity. His mother's family had 'known everyone' in the London of the 1860s and 1870s, and entertained them lavishly in their palatial residence in Savile Row. Now, the Bellocs were poor. But they kept their friends of an earlier generation; and to these had been added friends made in Oxford. Via Raymond Asquith, for instance, Belloc came into touch, though not, at this date, any intimacy, with that exalted circle of people (Lord Curzon, George Wyndham, Lady Desborough, Margot Asquith, Arthur Balfour) who were known as the Souls. There was never any shortage of invitation cards on the chimney-piece at 104, Cheyne Walk.

Moreover, 'literary London', which at this date intermingled with 'high society', did so to a great extent in *public*. In the bars and restaurants of Fleet Street, and in the Café Royal, and in the clubs, writers liked to meet one another, and talk and shout much more than their modern equivalents. George Bernard Shaw and H. G. Wells befriended Belloc in these days, while he made money writing articles for the *Daily News* and *The Speaker*.

The Boer War was much discussed. Fabians like Wells and Shaw were in favour of the war. Liberals of the *Speaker* group were not. Belloc saw the war as a blatant attack by commercial imperialism on small private landowners; a category of person, regardless of race, with whom he was always in sympathy. His mother always said of the British Empire that she hated the name and she hated the thing. Belloc inherited, and elaborated, this hatred. He supported the small Boer farmers against the Imperial aggressors, and in this he had the full support of his friends on *The Speaker* such as J. L. Hammond and Lucian Oldershaw. *The Speaker*'s attitude enraged rabid Imperialists, and a peer rose in the House of Lords to complain that 'those who opposed the South African adventure confused soldiers with money-grubbers'. This wonderfully absurd observation inspired Belloc to verse. It was the whole essence of the Liberal case that the 'Imperial' ideal in South Africa was the purest humbug. The war was being fought, as he never tired of saying, in order to preserve the commer-

cial interests of international speculators and investors in the mines of
the Transvaal. It was the Boers who had farmed this land and
husbanded it. No one at this date appeared to think it should simply be
handed back to the Africans, though Belloc's *Modern Traveller* makes
fairly clear that he did not consider European intrusion into Africa in a
wholly sympathetic light. Since then, the blatant commercialism of
the South African war had become more and more apparent, and
there was a grotesque absurdity about the so-called British Empire
going to war to defend the interests of financiers, many of whom had
nothing to do with Great Britain.

> You thought because we held, my lord,
>   An ancient cause and strong,
> That therefore we maligned the sword:
>   My lord, you did us wrong.
>
> We also know the sacred height
>   Up on Tugela side,
> Where those three hundred fought with Beit
>   And fair young Wernher died.
>
> The daybreak on the failing force,
>   The final sabres drawn:
> Tall Goltman, silent on his horse,
>   Superb against the dawn.
>
> The little mound where Eckstein stood,
>   And gallant Albu fell,
> And Oppenheim, half blind with blood
> Went fording through the rising flood –
>   My Lord, we knew them well.
>
> The little empty homes forlorn,
> The ruined synagogues that mourn,
>   In Frankfort and Berlin;
> We knew them when the peace was torn –
> We of a nobler lineage born –
> And now by all the gods of scorn
>   We mean to rub them in.

This brilliantly vitriolic poem will not seem needlessly offensive to
anyone acquainted with the true history of South Africa. It also
encapsulates the essence of Belloc's controversial method. He was
obsessive. He would take up a cause and worry it, like a dog with a rat.
As a child, he had assumed that men were distinguished from women

because their mouths were larger and their teeth more carnivorous. Once he was certain that he had uncovered dirt, he rubbed it in for all that he was worth. He, and his friends on *The Speaker*, saw perfectly clearly that no one was absolutely 'entitled' to the Transvaal; but that, if any Europeans had claimed a moral right to the place, it was the Dutch farmers who had settled there. They were not men that he knew very much about; and what he heard of them did not make them sound very sympathetic. He who in Paris felt refreshed because the stench of Protestantism had faded from his nostrils would not have enjoyed the company of those puritanical Calvinists. But he could see that their position had something doggedly honourable about it. whereas the 'British' position was based on the purest hypocrisy.

The mention of synagogues in Frankfurt and Berlin was not gratuitous. The essence of the Pro-Boer argument was that the farmers of the Transvaal should be allowed their autonomy rather than being forced, or bought, out by financial speculators from Europe. A high proportion of those who stood to gain by mining the gold and the diamonds in Boer farming country happened to be Jews.

Feelings ran high on the subject, and the Boer War was debated hotly and frequently in the course of that spring of 1900. One such meeting was held at the studio of Archie Macgregor, the painter, in Bedford Park. Macgregor (friend of W. B. Yeats) was, unlike most of the 'Bedford Park atheists', an opponent of the war,[1] and his studio was a meeting place of like-minded radicals and liberals. He became a friend of Belloc's, who came to his studio to speak at a debate there held in April, along with E. C. (Clerihew) Bentley, J. L. Hammond and others. Among those who heard Belloc's speech was a young pro-Boer called Gilbert Keith Chesterton. He wrote to his fiancée, Frances Blogg,

> You hate political speeches: therefore you would not have hated Belloc's. The moment he began to speak one felt lifted out of the stuffy fumes of forty-times repeated arguments into really thoughtful and noble and original reflections on history and character. When I tell you that he talked about (1) the English aristocracy (2) the effects of agricultural depression on their morality (3) his dog (4) the Battle of Sadowa (5) the Puritan Revolution in England (6) the luxury of the Roman Antonines (7) a particular friend of his who had by an infamous job received a political post he was utterly unfit for (8) the comic papers of Australia (9) the mortal sins in the Roman Catholic Church – you may have some concep-

[1] *Return to Chesterton*, p. 26.

tion of the amount of his space that was left for the motion before the house. It lasted half-an-hour and I thought it was five minutes.[1]

G. K. Chesterton was at this date a little less than twenty-six years old, and Belloc was nearly thirty. Chesterton's background was very different from Belloc's. His father was a Kensington house-agent (one still sees the family name on FOR SALE notices in houses and flats all over London). He had been educated at St Paul's School and then gone to the Slade School of Art, intending to become a painter. But he also wrote poetry, and had desultory journalistic ambitions. In politics, he was uncomplicatedly Liberal, with leanings towards Christian Socialism. One of the worst poems he ever wrote (from a technical point of view) was entitled 'To a Certain Nation'; he penned it in a fit of enthusiasm for the cause of Dreyfus. France, the nation addressed, has betrayed its own great ideals by the shabby treatment of Dreyfus, and

> we
> Who knew thee once, we have a right to weep.[2]

There is a great difference here from the things that Belloc believed about *L'Affaire*.

In religious background, once again, there were striking divergences. Belloc's upbringing had been wholly Roman Catholic. He would often admit to having no understanding of, no interest in, the Church of England. He was interested in the differences between Catholicism and scepticism. G. K. Chesterton, on the other hand, had been brought up by free-thinking parents who owed nominal allegiance to the Established Church. He had gone through a period of unbelief, and then been attracted by the intellectual position, and by the ritual exuberance, of Anglo-Catholicism. Through his fiancée, Frances Blogg, he had met that enthusiastic socialist in a biretta, Conrad Noel; and much of his time was spent gossiping in Anglican clergy-houses.

He seemed an altogether more unformed character than Belloc. He had not much travelled and, in spite of his enthusiasm for many of the ideas which happened to be in the air during the late 1890s, he was not, at this date, characterised by any notable intellectual rigour. He had gone through aesthetic, sub-Swinburnian phases; he had dabbled with, and been shocked by, the pseudo-occultism of persons like Yeats, Madame Blavatsky and other charlatan hangers-on of the

---

[1] Ibid., p. 52.
[2] G. K. Chesterton: *Collected Poems* (1958), p. 356.

Order of the Golden Dawn. An almost saint-like innocence had made these dabblings with ouija boards and Rosicrucianism repulsive to him; and he was redeemed by a delightful, somewhat fey, sense of humour.

Edmund Clerihew Bentley, who was at school with him, always remarked in Chesterton a bump of veneration, and a desire to be rather clinging. In later years, he found these qualities vexing, and attributed them to a wholly suppressed homosexual tinge to Chesterton's make-up.[1] Any such suggestion, if made explicit, would have horrified Chesterton, and perhaps there was nothing in it. Incontrovertibly, however, he was a hero-worshipper, as his account of Belloc's speech in the Macgregor studio makes abundantly clear.

The meeting of the two famous friends was therefore infinitely more momentous for Chesterton than it was for Belloc. Belloc merely gained yet another friend with whom he could drink and laugh and talk. Chesterton gained a mentor who was to sharpen, and largely reshape, his whole outlook on life, literature, politics and, ultimately, religion.

They appear to have first met in the company of F. Y. Eccles, E. C. Bentley, and Lucian Oldershaw at the Mont Blanc restaurant in Gerrard Street, Soho. From the fact that Belloc was wearing a straw hat, we may infer that it was some time after Chesterton heard him speak at Macgregor's studio, perhaps in May 1900.

> When I first met Belloc he remarked to a friend who introduced us that he was in low spirits. His low spirits were and are much more uproarious and enlivening than anybody else's high spirits. He talked into the night, and left behind in it a glowing track of good things. When I have said that I mean things that are good, and certainly not merely *bon mots*. I have said all that can be said in the most serious aspect about the man who has made the greatest fight for good things of all the men of my time.[2]

This again, like his letter to his future wife, is the language of hero-worship. Chesterton was a malleable, soft-centred man who, whether he knew it or not, was looking about for someone to convert him. He was one of nature's converts, just as Belloc was one of nature's most stubbornly controversial individualists.

> We met between a little Soho paper shop and a little Soho restaurant; his arms and pockets were stuffed with French Nationalist

[1] Malcolm Muggeridge to the author.
[2] Quoted Maisie Ward: *Gilbert Keith Chesterton*, p. 113.

and French Atheist newspapers. He wore a straw hat shading his eyes, which are like a sailor's, and emphasising his Napoleonic chin. . .[1]

Chesterton himself at this date was a soft-faced, slightly pouting young man, six foot two in height, who had not yet developed the grotesque obesity for which he is famous. Like almost everyone who ever met Chesterton, Belloc was charmed by his puckish good nature and by his wit, and the two men soon became friends. Elodie, too, was delighted by Chesterton, and when, in the following year, he eventually married Frances Blogg and went to live in Battersea, the four of them frequently spent evenings together.

Chesterton's younger brother Cecil (younger by five years) should also be mentioned at this point. 'We really devoted all our boyhood to one long argument, unfortunately interrupted by meal-times, by school-times, by work hours and many such irritating and irrelevant frivolities,'[2] Gilbert remembered in his *Autobiography*, in which he described Cecil as 'supremely pugnacious and provocative'.[3] Cecil lacked Gilbert Chesterton's high imaginative gifts, his romanticism, his poetry, or his charm. But, in so far as he was pugnaciously devoted to argument and opinion, he happily became addicted, as Gilbert was, to Belloc's friendship.

It must not be supposed, however, that, after Belloc met G. K. Chesterton, he had no time for anyone else. 'It was from that dingy little Soho café,' Chesterton wrote in his *Autobiography*, 'that there emerged the quadruped, the twiformed monster Mr Shaw has nick-named the Chesterbelloc.'[4] It may have been true, but the twiformed monster was quite quickly dissected, since the two men can hardly have met again until the autumn. Finding himself without money, Belloc nipped off to the provinces to give some lectures. From the Bolton Reform Club, he wrote, 'OH! the good dinner I am going to get! Ha! Ha! I see it in my mind's eye. I have just given a lecture to the oligarchs of Bolton with pretty pictures on a screen and tonight full of wine I shall talk Republicanism to the Demons.' Pocketing his fee, he then made plans for getting away to the Continent as soon as possible. Since Elodie was five months pregnant, they had to abandon the idea of rambling about France together. Belloc went off instead to stay

[1] Ibid.
[2] G. K. Chesterton *Autobiography* (1937), p. 165.
[3] Ibid., p. 42.
[4] Ibid., p. 114.

with their friends the Herberts at Portofino, leaving in abeyance the notion, still urged by his mother, of reading for the Bar. He missed the wedding of his friend John Phillimore, on July 26, which Elodie attended, in the Henry VII Chapel in Westminster Abbey.[1]

Belloc had bought his wife a motor-car, and arranged for her to spend a fortnight at the Sea View Hotel, at the Marina near Bournemouth, with the nurse, Clara, and the two children. In order to pay for this enterprise, Elodie found that she had to pawn her diamond cross for £4. Belloc sent her a cheque for a further £8, but this had to cover £4/14/6 for the hotel bill exclusive of drink, and three lots of Clara's overdue 10/- weekly wage. In addition, Elodie found herself being hounded by the revenue office for failing to license their little dog (Tip). The licence was 7/6, and the penalty for failure to pay it in the first place was 5/-.[2]

Stuck in Bournemouth, Elodie felt depressed, and her melancholy was not diminished by losing the purse which contained her last 10/6, as well as her stamps 'and my little silver elephant that you brought me home as a souvenir of The Bad Child's Book of Beasts! And worse still my beloved old rosary beads that a Spanish friend brought me from Gethsemane and a crucifix blessed by the Pope for *me*!'[3] Moreover, they were still quite uncertain about the future. Belloc evidently had not abandoned the idea of emigrating to California, and Elodie said, 'About California, darling, we shall talk it over carefully and as I always do, my heart, I shall take your judgment.'[4]

Men of a different temperament would have felt that they had to spend the summer holiday in the company of their wives. But it is hard to picture Belloc sitting in a boarding-house in Bournemouth for a fortnight. Elodie saw perfectly clearly that 'I should think you would enjoy time on the Continent more than here', and that was that. From Portofino, where he only stayed briefly, he wandered about northern Italy with his old friend Charles Somers Cocks, and then headed north again to spend a few days in Paris, where he worked on his Robespierre biography in the Bibliothèque Nationale. He also encountered Maria Lansdale, the American travel-writer, who had done him a good turn by employing his services as a research assistant some years before in Philadelphia.[5]

Whether he read for the Bar or not, Elodie longed for him to be

[1] BC July 26, 1900.
[2] BC August 7, 1900.
[3] BC Ibid.
[4] BC August 12, 1900.
[5] Princeton, August 9, 1900.

settled, and 'I hope darling that you *really* will have some kind of rest before September'.[1] Rest, of course, did not refresh Belloc, it merely depressed him, which is what made him such an exhausting person to live with. Had Elodie accompanied him on all his ramblings, it is doubtful whether her short life would have lasted as long as it did. And, had he given up his 'bloody ramble', he would unquestionably have gone mad.

As they settled down to life together in Cheyne Walk at the end of the summer, the future looked no less uncertain. The *Paris* book did not bring him in much money. He worked solidly at his *Robespierre*, which was finished by the end of the year. In November, Elodie gave birth to their third child, Elizabeth, and, in that cold and underheated house, prepared for another English winter.

Belloc had his mind on other things. His brief jaunt in Italy, during the summer, had fired him with an idea, and after Christmas spent, for once, in the company of his family, he wrote about it to Maria Lansdale, to see if she could use her influence in the American journalistic scene:

Dear Miss Lansdale,
May I put in this informal way on a rough scrap of paper the idea I was speaking to you of the other day. I am going to walk on a kind of pilgrimage from *Toul* (which is my old garrison town) to Rome next Easter & on my way I shall write down whatever occurs to me to write – what proportion will deal with landscape, what with architecture, what with people & what with general subjects I can't yet tell – it will be as the spirit moves me. I shall take sketches and *in my book* I shall use them but whether they would be up to the standard of the American Illustrated magazines I very much doubt. It would be perfectly easy however to send Photographs from which drawings could be made as I hear is sometimes done. You see in my book there will be no pretence at art, the drawings will be there for fun, but in a magazine I can understand that Art is first thought of. I don't know if the subject would attract anyone, it will be full of what I think and that's recondite, peculiar and often unsympathetic. Also it will be 'décousu' and written anyhow of its essence. I should be glad if it could get a serial public in America before I publish it here in October.

On the face of things, it seemed an odd scheme from the point of view of those, like his mother, who considered that Belloc should be

[1] BC August 9, 1900.

making his way in the world. But, once the idea was fixed in his head, it became immovable, and the only concession he would make was to delay his journey by three months in order to raise cash. He did 'an enormous amount of work for the *Daily News*',[1] gave University extension lectures, and collected £65 for his finished life of Robespierre. It was his most extended period of solid domestic life since getting married.

For all his hard work, there would not have been enough money if it had not been for his mother helping out. Bessie called on the young people in Chelsea at the end of May and, when she got back to Slindon, she wrote,

> My dearest Hilary – I suppose you are not gone. I wrote to W. Pennington [trustee of the Parkes estate] & told him that after my midsummer Dividends are paid the step you wish can be taken. I am *very* anxious about your Baby. When I saw it I had an instant impression which I concealed at the moment, not wishing to make a sudden scene –
> But, my darling, if you do not give it country air and country milk *at once* you are running a terrible risk, and I should be wrong not to say so to you quite plainly.
> Do listen to your old mother for once.[2]

He did not listen. The baby – Elizabeth Belloc – *did* survive. And, by the time Belloc read the letter, he was on the train for the Continent, and Elodie was pregnant again.

In extreme old age, he was to say, 'I hate writing. I wouldn't have written a word if I could have helped it. I only wrote for money. *The Path to Rome* is the only book I ever wrote for love.'[3] Belloc was such a compulsive pen-pusher, that it would be foolish to miss the irony of the remark. But there is something pleasing about the claim. His voluminous outpourings cover yards on the bookshelf: history, topography, verse and controversy, apologetics and economic theory streamed from his pen. And yet, if there is one prose work by which he is remembered, it is *The Path to Rome*. It was undertaken in defiance of common sense. It is a work of pure self-indulgence and caprice. Rambling, elegant, mannered and chatty, it was by far the most 'successful' book, in financial terms, that he ever wrote.

And its scheme is very bold. It tells the story of his journey by foot,

[1] Quoted Speaight, p. 157.
[2] BC May 30, 1901.
[3] *Talking of Dick Whittington*, p. 213.

in little less than a month, from Toul, where he had done military
service, along the Moselle, over the Alps and down through
Tuscany to the holy city itself, but it is not exactly a travel book.
He writes of places which take his fancy, and he skips past places
which do not. He devotes ten pages to the comparatively obscure
town of Flavigny, its Roman remains, its hay-making nuns, its jolly
baker; but in rather less space, towards the end of his pilgrimage, he
races through the towns and hills of Tuscany with hardly an
allusion to the fact that they contain some of the most magnificent
architecture, paintings and sculpture, the bones of some of the most
illustrious saints, and associations with some of the greatest poets
and statesmen that the world has ever known. This, being entirely
typical of Belloc's outlook and method, is a symptom of what kind
of book *The Path to Rome* is. It is very far from being an autobiography. 'No gentleman writes about his private life.'[1] (No
gentleman, he could have added, *has* a private life). But it is a
self-portrait. It is more than that. It is a celebration of himself, and
all that he exemplified. It is a picture of Belloc on the march; and,
by his casual asides, we know, not only where he is marching *to*,
but what he is marching for. It is a proclamation of his delight in
Europe, his addiction to its past, and his happy acquiescence in its
Faith.

Among its almost Shandean devices, Belloc allows the reader –
who is an Englishman of the middle class – to interrupt his narrative
at various points, protesting that he is bored, confused or distracted. And outside Lodi Vecchio, the reader proposes that they
should tell one another stories:

AUCTOR: With all my heart. And since you are such a good
judge of literary poignancy, do you begin.
LECTOR: I will, I will draw my inspiration from your style.
     Once upon a time there was a man who was born in Croydon,
and whose name was Charles Amieson Blake. He went to Rugby
at twelve and left it at seventeen. He fell in love twice and then
went to Cambridge till he was twenty-three. Having left Cambridge he fell in love more mildly, and was put by his father into
a government office, where he began at £180 a year. At thirty-
five he was earning £500 a year, and perquisites made £750 a
year. He met a pleasant lady and fell in love quite a little compared with the other times. She had £250 a year. That made
£1000 a year. They married and had three children – Richard,

[1] Ibid., p. 213.

Amy and Cornelia. He rose to a high government position, was knighted, retired at sixty-three and died at sixty-seven. He is buried at Kensal Green.

AUCTOR: Thank you, Lector, that is a very good story. It is simple and full of plain human touches.[1]

The Path to Rome is not a direct assault on Charles Amieson Blake and his kind, who, then as now, inherited the earth. It is a proclamation of why Belloc is different, and why he is glad to be different.

LECTOR: Pray dwell less on your religion, and –
AUCTOR: Pray take books as you find them, and treat travel as travel. . .[2]

Readers in the past have tended to praise the book for its 'set' passages, often of great beauty, as when the sun rises over the Alps, or when 'youth is borne up the valley on the evening air'. But if this is all that the book was – 'lovely' prose, interlarded with arch jokes – it would not have deserved to survive. Nine years before, Oxford had been startled by the arrival in its midst of a loud, wine-swilling young man, in a soft hat and a cape, who sang Napoleonic songs, and argued with a forcefulness which earned him the nickname of 'the Balliol Demosthenes'; who judged all English institutions and manners by the standards of the Continent. By the standards of Charles Amieson Blake, this figure had failed to 'get on' in the world. It could even be said that he had already hardened into a caricature of himself.

In *The Path to Rome*, he boldly trundles this exaggerated piece of self-portraiture out on to the public stage. But this supreme act of literary exhibitionism was also a true pilgrimage in the religious sense of the word. He was taking stock; not so much of his own character, which he took as given, like a rock jutting out against the sky; but of his own position and purpose in the world. 'It is a good thing,' he writes, 'to have loved one woman from a child, and it is a good thing not to have to return to the Faith.'[3] He had never wholly apostasized from the Faith. But his pilgrimage marks a new commitment to it, a refreshed sense of its importance. Its import dawns most forcefully and movingly in the Alpine village of Undervelier, where he buys a cigar, and, leaning over a low wall to smoke it, he watches the population of the entire village stream into the church for Vespers.

[1] *The Path to Rome*, p. 260.
[2] Ibid., p. 98.
[3] Ibid., p. 144.

At this I was very much surprised, not having been used at any time in my life to the unanimous devotion of an entire population, but having always thought of the Faith as something fighting odds, and having seen unanimity only in places where some sham religion or other glazed over our tragedies and excused our sins. Certainly to see all the men, women and children of a place taking Catholicism for granted was a new sight, and so I put my cigar carefully down under a stone on the top of the wall and went in with them. I then saw that what they were at was vespers.

All the village sang, knowing the psalms very well, and I noticed that their Latin was nearer German than French; but what was most pleasing of all was to hear from all the men and women together that very noble good-night and salutation to God which begins –
'Te lucis ante terminum'.

My whole mind was taken up and transfigured by this collective act, and I saw for a moment the Catholic Church quite plain, and I remembered Europe and the centuries. Then there left me altogether that attitude of difficulty and combat which, for us others, is always associated with the Faith. The cities dwindled in my imagination, and I took less heed of the modern noise. I went out with them into the clear evening and the cool. I found my cigar and lit it again, and musing much more deeply than before, not without tears, I considered the nature of Belief.

This was a very momentous evening in Belloc's life. By temperament and nature, he was a Voltairean, never happier, intellectually, than when deflating the absurdity of other people's beliefs. He was a natural sceptic. And his mind, throughout youth and young manhood, had been forced to hold in check a knowledge that, for every elaborate intellectual justification for the Faith, there was an equally sound argument for atheism. Such conflict had never come out into the open before; and, in marrying Elodie, he had gone most of the way towards resolving it. But the vision of the Alpine village at prayer had brought before his eyes, as it were, a whole and unanimous community of Elodies. She held to her religion, like all Catholics practising their faith in late Victorian England, as a member of a very distinct minority. But, in bigger, European terms, the Faith was the religion of the *majority*; indeed, it was the natural religion of European man. And, in that majority, one includes not merely the arithmetical fact that there are more baptised Roman Catholics in Italy, France and Spain than there are Protestants or agnostics; one recognises the numberless dead. They, like the Alpine villagers, were united in the collective rituals, belief and language of the great and undivided Latin Church. The present generation will look askance at Belloc's religion: none more than modern Catholics, brought up on lengthy, polyglot liturgies, on modern translations of the Bible, and on an ecumenical attitude to Protestantism. 'The Mass was low and short – they are a Christian people,' he recorded one morning in a village on the Moselle. Now, he would be lucky to find a morning mass at all. In many French villages, it is offered only weekly, and in the evening, often to the accompaniment of song, and an extempore commentary on the latest world news. Devotion to Our Lady, likewise, plays a much smaller part in modern Catholic piety than Belloc would have dreamed imaginable. In *The Path to Rome*, She is always referred to with a capital S, whereas God, if he is mentioned, always remains in a lower-case *h*. Modern Christianity has taken on the character of a sect. The Mass, with some ancient precedent, is once more the exclusive meeting-place of the reborn. There is talk of committed Christians and uncommitted Christians.

Commitment, too, was in the air, when Belloc walked to Rome, but of a different order. It was in the closing years of the pontificate of Leo XIII who, in 1900, had dedicated the whole human race to the Sacred Heart of Jesus. In 1899, he had condemned the heresy of Americanism, that is, the idea of 'adapting as far as possible the external life of the Church to supposed modern cultural ideals'. Belloc, when he reached Rome, very much hoped for an audience with the Holy Father. 'Leo XIII had sent for me,' he recalled later, 'but the ass who got the message delivered it too late. . . Thus I missed the greatest of Popes since the Reformation.'[1]

Leo XIII's successor, Pius X, was to continue the task of standing firm against the forces of doubt and scepticism. He was an entrenched opponent of modern biblical scholarship, and is best known, perhaps, for his suppression of the modernists. His encyclicals *Pascendi* and *Lamentabili* complemented the theological firmness of Leo XIII's *Providentissimus*, asserting the incompatibility of Catholicism and a free pursuit of scientific enquiry. Between them, in their various utterances, Leo XIII and Pius X condemned the notion that Moses had not written the five books of the Pentateuch (including the description of his own death); the idea that the pains of hell were not physical; the theory of evolution; the use of the electric light; and (like all their predecessors) the ideas of the French Revolution. The sceptic, and even the modern Catholic, might very well be puzzled by the

[1] Mells, April 11, 1934.

enthusiastic swing towards his religion which took place in Belloc's life at this date. In general political terms, in matters of social justice, as we have already seen, the encyclical *Rerum Novarum* was deeply sympathetic to Belloc. Pius X's condemnation of Belloc's beloved French Revolution, on the other hand, must have been less welcome, when it came. Belloc was renewing his commitment to the Catholic faith at a time when the papacy, and with it the hierarchy of the European church, was becoming more hardened in its anti-intellectualism, more doggedly reactionary, than at any date, perhaps, since the Counter-Reformation. Father Tyrrell, for instance, the English Jesuit condemned and suspended by Pius X, wrote books which now seem positively traditionalist in their emphasis. At the time of his death he was regarded as so dangerous a heretic that he was refused a Catholic burial.

Fashions change; in religion, faster than in many other areas. The popularity in the early 1980s of Pope John Paul II, in many ways a traditionalist in theology, perhaps shows that the majority of Roman Catholics were disturbed by the liberal developments in their church since the Second Vatican Council. Nevertheless, there would be few outside the ranks of Archbishop Lefèbvre's break-away church who would subscribe to all the encyclicals of Pius X.

The change of atmosphere has made Belloc's religious position unsympathetic to the majority of his present-day coreligionists.

> Heretics all, whoever you be,
> In Tarbes or Nîmes, or over the sea,
> You never shall have good words from me.
> *Caritas non conturbat me.*[1]

The belligerence, and the humour, of this are at odds with the rather solemn air of benevolence which comes from the well-meaning utterances of most Roman Catholic pulpits today. (Pulpits, indeed, are themselves hardly ever used.) Even in Belloc's lifetime, his passionately held, and yet so often humorously expressed, theological conservatism was a source of embarrassment to intellectual Catholics. Dining one night with the Jesuits of Campion Hall in Oxford, he was asked by a sceptical fellow-guest how he could possibly believe that the Bread and Wine at the Mass were transformed into the actual Body and Blood of Our Lord. Belloc replied that he would believe that they were changed into an elephant if the

[1] *The Path to Rome*, p. 147.

Church told him so.[1] It was the Jesuits, not the sceptic, who were scandalised by this very characteristic reply.

Belloc's career as an apologist became most active fifteen or twenty years after he had written *The Path to Rome*. But it is in that book that he expands most lyrically on the basis and origin of his Catholic convictions.

> Now in the morning Mass you do all that the race needs to do and has done for all these ages where religion was concerned; there you have the sacred and separate enclosure, the Altar, the Priest in his Vestments, the set ritual, the ancient and hierarchic tongue, and all that your nature cries out for in the matter of worship.[2]

The *fons et origo* of his devotion to Catholicism was that it was the ancient faith of Europe. The villagers of Undervelier, singing the Latin psalms and hymnody, were at one with their ancestors. And the church which enshrined their belief was also, in some measure, a continuation of something even older than Christianity itself. In its very language, it perpetuated the unifying force of the legions and magistrates of the Roman Empire; and, in many of its temples and shrines, it worshipped, with different words and gestures, on the very stones where the old gods had been invoked centuries before Virgil.

Belloc was not a naturally pious man. But he felt that he had to choose between the uncertainties of modern secularism, and the Faith that had sustained Europe for nineteen hundred years.

> I have never said that the Church was necessarily European. The Church will last for ever, and on this earth, until the end of the world; and our remote descendants may find its chief membership to have passed to Africans or Asiatics in some civilisation yet unborn. What I have said is that the European thing is essentially a Catholic thing, and that European values would disappear with the disappearance of Catholicism.[3]

This was the conviction which *The Path to Rome* celebrates. He was not at that date – nor was he ever to be – particularly concerned about the individual whims and utterances of Popes. Still less, though he always revered holiness, was his religion pursued in order to have a personal relationship with the Deity.

Indeed, so little did he sympathise with the idea of 'personal religion', that there is a wonder he had any at all. He has often been

[1] Speaight, p. 376.
[2] *The Path to Rome*, p. 53.
[3] Letter to the *Catholic Herald* 1936, quoted Speaight, p. 387.

compared with Charles Maurras, the editor of the right-wing periodical *L'Action Française*, many of whose ideas are remarkably similar to Belloc's. They shared a devotion to the common Latin past of Europe; a delight in classicism and the Roman Empire; a horror of international capitalism, particularly where it appeared to conceal the Jewish interest; a conviction that Catholicism was the best bastion against the forces of modern materalism and socialism. But they differed very markedly, even in their earliest days, not only in so far as Belloc pooh-poohed nationalism (particularly Prussian nationalism) but also in the matter of whether Catholicism was true. Maurras dreamed of a monarchist Catholic France. But he did not actually believe in God. Belloc always found it hard to submit to the intellectual discipleship which was demanded of the faithful. But he did submit. The tears at vespers in *The Path to Rome* are characteristic, though (for him) rare. He believed in his religion, and he practised it. He attended mass whenever he could (though he seldom received the Holy Sacrament) in the morning, and he regularly muttered his prayers at night. Without such observances, and such beliefs, his defence of Europe and of the faith, as ideals, would have been – as he would be the first to have said – a sham.

With them, they were mighty and ancient banners under which to fight. When he returned from Rome to London in the summer of 1901, he was refreshed for battle. His life was clearer now, and the direction in which his ambitions lay. He had rediscovered, in the most powerful way, where he came from and where he was going; where Europe, and England, came from, and where they ought to be going. Capitalism, Materialism, Scepticism, Prussianism, Imperialism, Nationalism lay in the path. Belloc was to use all his powers as an artist, a journalist and a politician to wage war on them.

Have you ever noticed that all the Catholic Church does is thought beautiful and lovable until she comes out into the open, and then suddenly she is found by her enemies (which are the seven capital sins and the four sins calling to heaven for vengeance) to be hateful and grinding? So it is; and it is the fine irony of her present renovation and those who are the most angered by her appearance on this modern field all armed, just as she was, with works and art and songs sometimes superlative, often vulgar. Note you, she is still careless of art or songs, as she always has been. She lays her foundations in something other, which something other our moderns hate. Yet out of that something other came the art and song of the Middle Ages. And what art and songs have you? She is Europe and all our past. She is returning. *Andiamo*.

SIX

KING'S LAND
1901–1906

The Path to Rome, which 'made' Belloc's literary reputation, presented a full-square caricature of its author to the world: an opinionated supertramp, happy so long as there is Mass at the beginning of the day, wine and Catholic good cheer at the end of it. The caricature does not, in Belloc's case, distort the truth. This is very much what he was like.

But the unshaven, hard-drinking rambler through Catholic Europe was only part of the truth; and Belloc had no sooner finished *The Path to Rome* than he began to doodle – on a proof copy of the book[1] – 'a description of my own county of Sussex'.[2] He described the book as 'fantastic, just as "The Path to Rome" was, though I believe and hope it has the sentiment of Sussex running through it. It promises to be a little sadder than "The Path to Rome" but I cannot be certain whether it will be or not until it is written'.[3]

The book that he was planning was *The Four Men*. Ten years were to elapse before it was published, and in the meantime he published some thirty-five books, including an admirable and highly personal account of *Sussex*. In its finished form, though obviously written by the same pen as *The Path to Rome*, *The Four Men* is different, more poignantly elegiac, more hauntingly religious. The 'I' of the Roman pilgrimage has been joined for the ramble through Sussex by three others – by a sailor, full of the lonely wisdom of the sea; by a cynical old countryman called Grizzlebeard; and by a poet, his heart steady in the love of one woman, his ears sharpened by old songs. And these characters are, really, all Belloc himself.

In describing Belloc during the Edwardian era, between the ages of thirty and forty, one pines for some such device, which will enable one to do justice to the many rich strands of his life. He was, after *The Path to Rome*, an acknowledged, and important, presence on the

[1] Copy kept in BC
[2] Princeton, Charles Scribner's and Sons. October 27, 1902.
[3] Ibid.

literary scene, as a poet, essayist, biographer, historian and novelist. Poles apart from Belloc in everything they believed, Shaw and Wells became his friends. He detested literary coteries – his interests always lay outside them. Nevertheless, when in 1901, he became a naturalised British subject (in the same month that *The Path to Rome* appeared) he described his profession as 'man of letters'.[1] Joseph Conrad was to present Belloc with a copy of *Nostromo*, and figures as diverse as Edmund Gosse and Max Beerbohm crossed his path in London. On hearing that Belloc had been seen at a cricket match, Max remarked, 'I suppose he would have said that the only good wicket-keeper in the history of the game was a Frenchman and a Roman Catholic.' Belloc and Beerbohm liked each other and in Beerbohm's magnificent series of parodies and caricatures, *A Christmas Garland*, the brilliantly captured spoof Bellocian prose appears alongside skits of Henry James, Thomas Hardy, Rudyard Kipling, H.G. Wells and George Bernard Shaw.

Yet, while having to chronicle Belloc's literary activity, one faces the difficulty that this was only a part of his life during this decade. 1901–1910 were the years in which he wrote his finest books: his three funniest novels, his best travel-literature and one of his finest biographies belong to this date. They all deserve attention. But, for some readers, all his prose would pale beside the serious verse he wrote in this decade. And, then again, it would be a strange biography of Belloc which did not celebrate the publication in 1907 of his *Cautionary Tales*. Certainly, nowadays, for every one reader of *The Path to Rome*, there are probably ten thousand who are intimately acquainted and delighted by the Chief Defect of Henry King, by the Dreadful Lies of Matilda, by the miserable fates of Godolphin Horne and Rebecca Offendort and by the happy rewards bestowed by providence on Charles Augustus Fortescue.

Had he chosen to devote himself wholly to letters during that decade, his reputation would, perhaps, be more solid today. For there can be no question at all that Belloc was one of the finest prose-writers of the century; one of the most distinctive minor poets and *the* most accomplished practitioner of 'light' or 'comic' verse. He is out of fashion, out of print, in most cases out of mind, not because of the quality of his *literary* output, but, very largely, because of the nature of his political and religious beliefs. He regarded politics as far too important a matter to be taken wholly seriously. He was rewarded by not being taken seriously himself. Although we can now see that

[1] The passport is kept at BC.

many of his political judgements were right, that was not to prevent him being a complete political failure. Being in the right is not infrequently the unforgivable sin in politics. He began as a republican. He ended as an authoritarian monarchist. At no stage did he have any noticeable sympathy with parliamentary institutions. This angered people. He regarded 'the party system' as humbug, and said so. He saw increasingly little difference between the Front Benches of the Conservative and the Liberal Parties; and he said so. As for the House of Lords, he was a keen abolitionist, not slow to point out the elevation to peerages of those who had made generous contributions to party funds. And yet, although his political function in Asquith's parliament was largely that of an irritant, Belloc nursed a quite genuine political ambition. In spite of himself, he wanted office, and he liked the idea of power. Although he behaved from the first in a way which was calculated to annoy all the professional politicians, he was aggrieved that he did not have a more successful political career; just as, at Oxford, he had gone out of his way to irritate the dons and then been astonished that they did not elect him to a Fellowship. His mother, and Sarah Mew, perhaps, had much to answer for, in those leisurely summers of the 1870s in Sussex and La Celle St Cloud, when they had taught the strutting, posturing little boy that he was most charming when most aggressive.

* * *

These were the years of his blossoming friendship with G.K. Chesterton, and the continuing company of Maurice Baring, Edmond Warre (known as 'The Bear', now studying architecture in London), with aristocratic families such as the Herberts and the Stanleys. He was separated from many of his close friends in the early years of Edward VII's reign. Basil Blackwood wrote inconsolably gloomy letters from the Government Offices in Bloemfontein; the Phillimores, established now in Glasgow with a young family, seemed almost as far away.

Life at Cheyne Walk was the reverse of dull. Belloc's political resolve had clearly hardened so that, by 1902, he was starting to make political contacts with a view to getting a seat in the House of Commons. On February 22, 1902, Elodie noted in her appointments diary, 'Mr Lloyd George asked to dine here.' And then, in bolder ink, she has added, 'He promises to come. I have asked Lady Kershaw and her son to meet him.'[1] It would seem that Lloyd George, very much a

[1] BC February 22 1902.

rising star in the Liberal Party at that date, attended several of Elodie's dinner parties during the course of that season. In turn, they were invited everywhere. Belloc, in most moods intensely clubbable, would accept all invitations at this period, and Elodie, likewise, would come along, unless exhaustion or pregnancy prevented her.

It is not true, as has sometimes been alleged, that Belloc went off on his own to house parties or grand social occasions, leaving his wife behind. Elodie was, in fact, very popular, and often she was entertained in comfort and grandeur while Belloc was obliged to go off making money by journalism or lecture-tours. Elodie's American voice and manner had been completely discarded by now, and the misconceptions which this caused did on occasion, give rise to awkwardness. In the summer he made the journey to Rome, for instance, Belloc arranged for the children to be looked after so that Elodie could have a few days rest and holiday with Lady Carnarvon, mother of their friend Aubrey Herbert. Elodie wrote to her husband from The Manor House, Teversal, Mansfield, that she was having a pleasant time exploring the 'castles and dukeries' of that thickly aristocratic region of England.

> I had a horrid experience at Newstead. For some reason they got things mixed & they thought I was a noble! They all kept calling me 'my lady' & such kow-towing – it was painful. But I said nothing & grinned to myself as I drove away. The house keeper asked me most humbly if I had been kind enough to put myself in the visitor's book. I had been so kind. So I grinned at the shock which she must have got when she found the name of Citizen Belloc! It was creepy, dear, for a Democrat.[1]

Elodie surely gravely exaggerated the shock value of not being possessed of a title. The housekeeper had been muddled by her arrival at Newstead (Byron's seat) in the company of a countess, but Lady Carnarvon must have had dozens of friends who were called plain 'Mrs'.

However much the republican Bellocs poured scorn on the titles of the English aristocracy, they were both capable of seeing the delights which could be provided and enjoyed by a landed class. She wrote again from Teversal:

> The wood was like part of heaven. And how the birds sang & a tribe of cuckoos called and checked the world. You are quite right, dear heart, as soon as God will let us we must have a patch of earth

[1] BC summer 1901.

somewhere near a wood. The world is now like heaven. How can I thank you for this delightful rest? God bless you.[1]

Belloc and Elodie had absolutely no desire to ape the manners or customs of the landed aristocracy. She (as the letter just quoted indicates) never lost the sense of her origins and was frightened by the idea of people getting her wrong. For his part Belloc had too great a pride in his true family history to be a snob. He liked 'high life'. As life went on, the majority of his friends belonged to the upper class. But the same could have been said of both his French and his English grandfathers. When, for a variety of reasons, they conceived the ambition to live in Sussex, the Bellocs were not aspiring to be a sort of fake landed gentry. If anything, the move to Sussex was a step down in the social scale, exchanging as they did the smart elegance of their little house in Chelsea for the rigorous squalor of rural life.

Elodie disliked the cramped existence of a town house. She pined for 'a patch of earth somewhere near a wood'. Belloc, for his part, could not possibly afford to run 104, Cheyne Walk. The prospect of an enlarged family (their son Hilary was born in 1902, Peter in 1904) created the necessity of a larger house; and, on his uncertain income, there was not much chance of buying a capacious London establishment. Poverty, and the demands of a young family, drew them increasingly to country life. While Belloc was away from home, rambling, lecturing, and speechifying, Elodie more and more found herself living with his mother in Slindon; and, in the summer months, this enabled them to sub-let the Cheyne Walk house, and provide a little useful extra income.

As the Sussex habit grew on them, they decided that they could not continue casually to batten on Bessie, particularly since there was so little room in Slindon House. By great good fortune, in the summer of 1903, a neighbour of Bessie's, Mr Wedgwood, was looking for a tenant for Bleak House, Slindon. 'Grandmama is in so amiable a frame of mind that I believe that if we were taking an unfurnished place now she might be moved to give us *some of her superfluous traps*,' Elodie reported. 'I shall let you know at once the result of the Wedgwood negotiations.'[2]

Bessie and Elodie looked round Bleak House that afternoon, and were delighted by it. Belloc wired his approval, as well he might, for Wedgwood let them have it for two guineas a week from June until

[1] Ibid.
[2] BC June 6, 1903.

October.[1] It was their first extended period of life together as Sussex householders. They were successful months. The cheapness of Sussex, its obvious suitability for children, and the proximity of grandmama who, whether or not in an amiable frame of mind, provided Elodie with companionship during Belloc's long absences were only a part of what drew them to that area of England. Since the age of ten, Sussex had been to Belloc a still place in a constantly shifting existence; an oasis of stability for that most restless of beings.

> The great hills of the South Country
>   They stand along the sea;
> And it's there walking in the high woods
>   That I could wish to be,
> And the men that were boys when I was a boy
>   Walking along with me.

With one part of himself, Belloc thought he could only be at home in France, far from the 'stench of Protestantism', swilling wine and tasting good food and singing old Republican songs. But the other fantasy, in which he believed intensely, and kept constantly in play, was of himself as a Sussex man, deeply English and rustic in prejudice, who had had a lot of jolly mates during his boyhood in that county of ale and farms and sailing ships. In fact, his boyhood was rather solitary when he was at home, and companionship, when it came from other little boys, was to be found with his boarding-school chums at the Oratory. Friendship meant so much to him in grown-up life precisely because there were not all that many 'men that were boys when I was a boy'. Sussex, far from having been his only childhood home, was but one of the many places to and from which Bessie had flitted, squandering time and money. But it had been there, as he tells us in his essay 'The Mowing of a Field', as a solitary child, pushing his way through the glade of beeches beyond Slindon and glimpsing the sea, that he had first felt at home. That was why the poetic fantasy had a deep and important place in Belloc's heart.

> If I ever become a rich man
>   Or if ever I grow to be old,
> I will build a house with deep thatch
>   To shelter me from the cold,
> And there shall the Sussex songs be sung
>   And the story of Sussex told.

[1] BC June 8, 1903.

They did not move finally from London until the summer of 1906. When they did so, it was not to the neighbourhood of Slindon and Arundel but to the hamlet of Shipley (near Horsham) in the Weald. It was in March that they found and bought it: 'a lovely old long brick house', as Elodie described it.[1] They managed to scrape together £900 for the freehold[2]. For that, they got the house, five acres of land, and a mill. It was called King's Land.

Belloc described it as

> exactly suitable to oneself, though a kind that no one else would like…It went very cheap because not every modern man would care to live in a house which was planned as it is, and also because most townsmen coming to it and finding no water supply and not appreciating that a full water system, well, pump cistern and closets and all could be put in for £100 were put off.[3]

This was (that uncharacteristic figure of speech for Belloc) an understatement. Although they managed to put in a primitive water supply, the place had nothing deserving the name of a bathroom for years. This did not trouble the Bellocs. As one of their grandchildren remarked much later in the century, when it was suggested to him in hospital that he might wash, 'In our family, we don't take baths'. Electricity was not installed there until well into the mid-century. Nor was there gas. It was lit by oil lamps and candles throughout Elodie's lifetime.

Yet the setting was, and is, irresistible. Even though it was markedly nearer London than Slindon, King's Land was deeply remote; and it preserves its remoteness even today, in spite of the cacophonous proximity of Gatwick Airport.

You turn off the main road into thickly rolling, gently wooded country; it is the sort of highway Chesterton celebrated when he fancied that 'the rolling English drunkard made the rolling English road'. And, after getting lost, as you inevitably will if you try to find it, you come to an inn at Shipley which feels as if it is in the middle of nowhere; but a benign and not a hostile nowhere. At the inn, they have not heard of King's Land, nor of Belloc. But, if you ask for the mill, they set you on your road, and setting off even further into the depths of nowhere, you see, after less than a mile, the shape of the old windmill against the sky. It is still in use.

Next to it is the long rambling brick house, and beyond that house

[1] Speaight. p. 214.
[2] BC March 1906.
[3] Speaight. p. 215.

there is a green, surrounded by old trees, and the squat boxy tower of the twelfth-century parish church.

Parts of King's Land are very old, said to date from the fourteenth century. Eleven gables make a chaotic zig-zag along the roof. It is the chaos, more than its antiquity, which strikes you at first. Indeed, quite a lot of it is Victorian, and the newest extension had been built in 1890, only sixteen years before the Bellocs moved in.

When they arrived, it was the village shop. You walk straight in to the drawing-room, which is still lined by all the old shop fittings: tiny drawers for spices and sugars, shelves for the packets and tins. Now, thanks to Belloc's constant tinkering with the place, doors lead off in all directions into an anarchy of rooms and corridors.

This dank and inconvenient house, always dark because of its tiny windows, was to be Belloc's home for the rest of his life; Elodie and he were both to live out their lives here; his children, and four of his grandchildren, were to grow up there. It was to be the focus and the background of all his most intense emotional experiences for nearly half a century. Of course, if he had been a rich man, he would have bought a nicer house; but, as things turned out, he is unimaginable without King's Land. It was as much a part of him as Abbotsford was of Sir Walter Scott. The pseudo-grandeur of Kipling's Bateman's (that other great Edwardian celebrant of Sussex life) would, somehow, never have done for Belloc. There is nothing stately about King's Land, and nothing finished. Men of fervent imaginative energy (one thinks of Dickens and Milton) have often lived out their lives in poky, overcrowded rooms. Their houses did not contain them, like elaborately polished show-cases. Rather, it as though they were, in part, burrowing and bursting out of them; and in part, like the bees, fashioning their most magnificent creations in a confined space. King's Land, in its place and setting, offered Belloc the remoteness from modern life and the complete silence and stillness which his soul required when he dashed back there sweating from the London train. On the other hand, it bears all the marks of his restlessness. It is a house which leaves its lines of retreat open. Apart from his study, all the rooms on the ground floor have doors which lead directly outside. Most of them also have doors leading into other rooms, like the stage-set of a farce. By entering the dining-room, you are not committed to staying there. You can press on into the hall, and up the great staircase, which Belloc installed, ludicrously out of proportion with the rest of the house (a gift from Lord Astor). Or you can dive into the kitchens and endless sculleries. Or you can return, almost certainly knocking your head on every low-slung lintel, through the drawing-room, and either back into the garden through the old shop front, or on into another back passage, which Belloc added, leading to Elodie's damp little work-room and the garden beyond.

Belloc hated to be tied down. If he knew he was stuck in one place, he was miserable. He was always on the move. And yet, with another part of himself, he longed for sameness and security. King's Land, with a curiously inelegant poetry, satisfied both needs. Had he pursued simply the life of a man of letters, who farmed five acres and made the occasional sortie to the continent of Europe, it would have been the most entirely perfect setting for his genius. In fact, the course of his life in the five years after he moved to King's Land made living there seem astonishingly and exhaustingly inappropriate.

* * *

The quest for his Sussex home did not, of course, take up the whole of Belloc's time in the first five years of this century. As always, there was a great deal of travel, by land and sea. In the summer of 1901, he and Arthur Stanley had bought the *Nona*. 'She was a nine-ton cutter, built somewhere about 1870 at Bembridge in the Isle of Wight, a sturdy little boat made for leisurely fun, and not for racing. She was rather more than thirty feet over all, broad in the beam, with a draught of five or six feet'.[1] Neither Belloc nor Lord Stanley had as much chance as they would have wished to sail in the *Nona* at this time, but she was to be an important part of his existence in the future.

He travelled in the Pyrenees, he travelled, following the collapse of his health during the winter of 1905, in North Africa, and wrote of what he found there in that magnificent book *Esto Perpetua*. He travelled, repeatedly, and compulsively, in France. In the spring of 1904, he and Elodie even managed to snatch a rare holiday together without the children. They set off on bicycles on Tuesday, March 22. 'We got to Beauvais at 11 o'clock. The Mayor and his son were having a Requiem Mass in the cathedral,' Elodie recorded in her brief holiday-diary.[2] Normandy was racked by gales, and for the first few days they appear to have done nothing, except be rained upon and absolved from their sins; Elodie went to confession three times in the course of the week. Had she been brought up to believe that the normal intimacies of married love were matters which had to be confessed? Or was it simply good to be in Catholic Europe, with an

[1] J.B. Morton: *Hilaire Belloc, A Memoir* (1955) p. 46.
[2] BC March 22, 1904.

occupied confessional in every village church past which they pushed their sodden bicycles?

To avoid the rain, they pressed on south, abandoned the cycles and got on the train. Elodie wrote back to G.K. Chesterton,

> My friend, let me tell you and Frances that for the first time in eight years, I have been below the parallel of 45° North. And there, by God's grace, I found his Sun and hills and sheep and vineyards and happy blessed people who have high horizons – away up in the air and purple at that – and who work in the fields and who sleep at night and who go to Mass and say their Rosaries in trains and behind their market stalls. May God give back to England some such strong hold upon her own heroic soil.[1]

The Chestertons, in a very different way, felt that God was giving such a strong hold to their native country; or, that he would do so, if allowed the chance, through such means as guild socialism in politics and ritualism within the worship of the Established Church. Conrad Noel, the priest who married Gilbert and Frances Chesterton, was unquestionably one of the greatest influences on their lives. It was he who ultimately achieved notoriety, when he had left London for the living of Thaxted in Essex, by hoisting a red flag above his church tower there. Inside, worship at Thaxted was not imitative of contemporary Roman Catholic worship. It sought rather, inspired largely by Percy Dearmer's *Parson's Handbook*, to recreate the atmosphere of medieval English Catholic liturgy. Noel taught his congregations to sing simple vigorous Gregorian chant. He cleared his churches of pews. The worshippers stood, rather than kneeling or sitting, to watch the sacred ministers, clad in the vestments of Old Sarum, sing the language of the Book of Common Prayer, accompanied by the music of the Middle Ages.

This variety of Anglican worship, of which Frances Chesterton was a particular devotee, baffled Protestants and Romanists alike. G.K. Chesterton, in his autobiography, tells how Percy Dearmer, Conrad Noel's mentor, would walk about his parish in Primrose Hill clad in sacerdotal garb of his own idiosyncratic design.

> And he was humorously grieved when its strictly traditional and national character was misunderstood by little boys in the street. Somebody would call out, 'No Popery' or 'To hell with the Pope', or some other sentiment of larger and more liberal religion. And

[1] Quoted Speaight. p. 193.

Percy Dearmer would sternly stop them and say, 'Are you aware that this is the precise costume in which Latimer went to the stake?'[1]

It was the slightly absurd pedantry of all this which led some people to label Dearmer's unquestionably beautiful liturgical achievements as 'The British Museum Religion'. None of it meant anything to Belloc. Yet it was the Englishness of Anglicanism, the very fact that it was local, national, parochial, which appealed to Chesterton's very different nature. When he developed a wider view of Christendom, it was under Belloc's influence. And it never achieved more amusing expression than when, in 1914, F.E. Smith declared that the Bill to Disestablish the Church in Wales had 'shocked the conscience of every Christian community in Europe'.

> Are they clinging to their crosses,
> F.E. Smith,
> Where the Breton boat-fleet tosses,
> Are they, Smith?
> Do they fasting, trembling, bleeding,
> Wait the news from this our city?
> Groaning, 'That's the Second Reading'
> Hissing, 'There is still Committee!'
> If the voice of Cecil falters,
> If McKenna's point has pith,
> Do they tremble for their altars?
> Do they, Smith?
>
> Russian peasants round their pope,
> Huddled, Smith,
> Hear about it all, I hope,
> Don't they, Smith?
> In the mountain hamlets clothing
> Peaks beyond Caucasian pales,
> Where Establishment means nothing
> And they never heard of Wales,
> Do they read it all in Hansard
> With a crib to read it with –
> 'Welsh Tithes – Dr Clifford Answered',
> Really, Smith?

Even so, it was years before Chesterton came to feel that the Church of England did not actually have a claim to belong to the greater

[1] G.K. Chesterton: *Autobiography* p. 164

church of Christendom, and changed his allegiance to that of his hero and friend.

Belloc and he saw a lot of each other in the opening years of the century. 'It was a masculine period of hard thinking and hard drinking, a recrudescence of the Old Grub Street', as Chesterton's sister-in-law remembered.[1] The bars of Fleet Street were their usual place for meeting, El Vino a favourite haunt at this date.

> Under the shelter of a vast cask of sherry, on the corner of an old mahogany table, G.K. would reel off hundreds of words and talk in a glowing flow of epigram and paradox. It became a custom to look in round about six in the hope of finding him. Those who arrived early sat at G.K.'s table, the others pushed in where they could. It was a mixed and most amusing crowd, with continual fresh arrivals. Belloc might rush in like a nor'easter, and expound the universe, insisting that some particular manifestation, political, social or psychological, could only happen at three places in the world, all of them widely and wildly apart – say a village in the Pyrenees, a walled City in Central China, or a fishing hamlet in Sussex. Maurice Baring, the most modest and distinguished of special correspondents, famous for his Russian studies, would drift along with that brilliant essayist the Abbé Dimnet, who had a unique knowledge of vintage claret, while Arthur Machen, his scholarly face alight, would discourse on demonology.[2]

Both Chesterton brothers, and their wives, liked coteries. Belloc did not, particularly if they were literary coteries. He had an idiosyncratic, and wide, range of literary interests, but he was not, like Chesterton, a literary critic, nor even a consistently voracious reader. In addition to a constant stream of journalism, sometimes republished as books of essays; and volumes of very uneven verse, Chesterton had started to make a name for himself as an interpreter of English literature. His *Robert Browning* (1903) and *Charles Dickens* (1906) are models of criticism, stimulating, entirely personal accounts which make you want to re-read the authors he elucidates. There is no pretence at accuracy. He was entirely unruffled, having declared that every postcard Dickens wrote was a work of art, when a reviewer pointed out that Dickens died on June 9, 1870 and that the first postcard appeared on October 1 of that year.[3]

But in addition to the man of letters, the poet and the comedian,

---

[1] *The Chestertons* p. 44.
[2] Ibid. 45.
[3] Christopher Hollis: *The Mind of Chesterton* (1970) p. 54.

there was a side of Chesterton which longed to be led, and to have his opinions formed. He shared with George Bernard Shaw a passion for opinions, which is not the same as saying that he was an intellectual who lived in the world of ideas. Of course, there was a grain of seriousness in both men when they chose to attack 'the science ridden, culture ridden, afternoon-tea ridden cliffs of old England'.[1] But in their endless, perfectly good-humoured controversies, their public debates, their essays refuting each other's notions about science, politics and religion, Shaw and Chesterton seem essentially frivolous characters, more like men knocking a shuttlecock over a net rather than discussing issues which affect life.

If Chesterton's controversial writings became more hard-hitting in the course of Edward VII's reign, one does not have to look further than Belloc to discover the reason.

In the *Daily Mail* articles which he gathered up into the book entitled *Heretics*, Chesterton poked fun at Ibsen (Shaw's great discovery) and at Kipling. He hit out to left and right, assailing both the vulgarity of commercial imperialism and the aridity of scientific agnosticism; the blind selfishness of modern conservatism and the implausibility of Fabian Socialism.

'I am delighted with what I have read in the *Daily Mail*. Hit them again. Hurt them. Continue to binge and accept my blessing,' Belloc wrote. 'Give them hell.'

When *Heretics* appeared, he said, 'It is the only book of yours I have read right through.'

Undoubtedly, the distinction between ideas which are 'serious' and ones which are not, could provoke a whole flood of Chestertonian rhetoric, proving that seriousness of mind was an uproariously comic malady; laughter, on the contrary, the most gravely important characteristic of all the best philosophers and sages. This, indeed, is the notion which runs through his absurd little fantasy *The Napoleon of Notting Hill,* dedicated to Belloc and published in 1904. It is hard to resist the feeling, having read that book, that what attracted Chesterton to Belloc's intellectual position was not its soundness, but its outlandishness. With his zest for paradox, Chesterton saw in Belloc a man with whom almost everyone disagreed and concluded that he must have bee in the right. It became an axiom to him that the truth is always the opposite of what it appears. In time, he came to believe this in sober truth. But, initially at least, the thrill of it consisted in a kind of mental gymnastics. The Napoleon of Notting Hill, Wayne, the

[1] Samuel Butler, quoted Maisie Ward: *Gilbert Keith Chesterton* p. 194.

heroic shopkeeper who beat back the armies of Bayswater and North Kensington by the simple ruse of switching off all the street lamps, makes this declaration to the King:

> 'Crucifixion is comic. It is exquisitely diverting. It was an absurd and obscene kind of impaling reserved for people who were made to be laughed at – for slaves and provincials – for dentists and small tradesmen…This laughter with which men tyrannize is not the great power you think. Peter was crucified, and crucified head downwards. What could be funnier than the idea of a respectable old Apostle upside down? What could be more in the style of your modern humour? But what was the good of it? Upside down or right side up, Peter was Peter to mankind. Upside down he still hangs over Europe, and millions move and breathe only in the life of his church.'[1]

Here one sees in the most grotesque and tasteless form the absorption of a Bellocian idea – that of the Primacy of St Peter and the fact that the Catholic Church is the one place where the human spirit has 'home and hearth' – transformed into a piece of Chestertonian nonsense. *The Napoleon of Notting Hill* has ideas – plenty of them. But it has ideas in the way that a warehouse or a lumber-room has furniture – stacked up, piled upside down, crammed together in any order. Belloc's mind was much more like a drawing-room furnished with immovables (only the French noun will do) of the French Second Empire, perhaps, heavy, recognisable, well arranged and fixed.

The contrast between the two friends can be most amply demonstrated by comparing the novels which they both wrote in that year of 1904. *The Napoleon of Notting Hill*, crammed with wonderful jokes and absurd paradoxes, is a fantasy of absurd nonsense. It purports to happen in 1984. England is governed by monarchs, who are appointed entirely arbitrarily. When a humorously-minded clerk called Auberon Quin becomes King he decides to give each of the London districts its independence. It is an extension of an idea running through many of Chesterton's writings, the glory of things, places and people being *themselves*. The King says, as he looks towards 'old inviolate Notting Hill, "Look up nightly to that peak, my child, where it lifts itself among the stars so ancient, so lonely, so unutterably Notting".'

The districts of London only discover their essential identity when they have abandoned the humbug of a general patriotism, and learnt,

---

[1] *The Napoleon of Notting Hill* (1904) (p. 62, Penguin Edition).

through battle and bloodshed, to feel intense and romantic patriotism for their own little patch of earth. Chesterton, in reality the most benign and harmless of men, loved to fantasise about battle, murder and sudden death, as his many swashbuckling poems and his tales of murder show. He liked playing with swords and pistols. At the end of *The Napoleon of Notting Hill*, the humorous monarch, King Auberon, and the bloodthirsty shopkeeper, Adam Wayne, stand amid the smouldering ruins of battle-torn London. Yet, they conclude,

> When dark and dreary days come, you and I are necessary, the pure fanatic, the pure satirist. We have between us remedied a great wrong. We have lifted the modern cities into that poetry which every one who knows mankind knows to be immeasurably more common than the commonplace.[1]

The first time one reads this, it seems rather magnificent. The second time one reads it, one is hard pushed to say what it is intended to mean.

The world of Belloc's fiction is much more penetrable. It is not the London of an imagined 1984. It is the Edwardian London in which Belloc himself moved, and had ambitions to exert power, viewed with relentless irony and satire.

Emmanuel Burden (1904) is Belloc's first novel. He was not a novelist in the tradition of Trollope, George Eliot or Henry James (all friends of his mother). He was astonishingly incurious about the mystery of human character. And he would certainly not have been equal to the kind of fiction which makes psychological realism its business and aim. *Burden*, like all his novels dealing with the contemporary scene, is really a prose extension of the side of his genius which produced the humorous rhymes. His novels should not be judged in comparison with Hardy or Henry James or George Meredith; rather, with Firbank, Max Beerbohm or Saki.

As such, they stand up remarkably well, and deserve to be better known. *Emmanuel Burden* is the farcical parable we should expect from one whose view of the British Empire descended from his mother's, who 'hated the name and hated the thing'. The book's relentless irony is wearisome if read at a stretch; but, in short doses, it is exceedingly effective. And, for all its irony and exaggeration, there can be no doubt that he is describing a quite recognisable, real world. Here, the English aristocrats of ancient lineage turn out to be the very recent descendants of Irish publicans; and the great Imperial expansion

[1] Ibid. p. 158.

is exposed as nothing more than a commercial swindle organised by cosmopolitan financiers. A typical aside is to be found early in the novel describing the village of Mallersham: 'of course Mallersham was originally Malden Land and the sign of the inn is a touching example of the deep roots which our English families strike into the soil. For though the Gayles, who sold the estate to the Howleys last year, had originally purchased it in 1857 from the Marlows, who were heirs by marriage to the Hindes, yet the Hindes themselves had bought it from the Kempes of Hoverton, whose early efforts in finance bring us directly through the Rinaldos to Geoffrey Malden, the famous soldier husband of Maria Van Huren, the witty Dutch companion of William of Orange.'[1]

The story concerns the fortunes of Emmanuel Burden, merchant, 'of Thames St in the City of London, exporter in Hardware'. He is an old-fashioned Gladstonian Liberal, who has been an honest trader all his life. Financial speculation, gambling with stocks and shares, dabbling with the whims and chances of international finance, have always been abhorrent to him, as they have been to his doughty City friend, Mr Abbott.

Mr Burden and Mr Abbott represent all that is best in the honest English commercial tradition. They are, one could say, the spiritual heirs of men like Belloc's grandfather Joseph Parkes, of families like the Wedgwoods and the Priestleys. But Mr Burden has a son appropriately named Cosmo. And Cosmo goes to the University, and gets into debt, and has to extricate himself from a possible breach of promise case by borrowing money. It is his Levantine friend Mr Harbury who lends him the money, and it is through Mr Harbury that he comes into touch with Mr I.Z. Barnett, the great international financier.

Mr Barnett is a recognisable type; perhaps cruder than his Rothschild or Oppenheimer Edwardian originals, infinitely less so than his modern equivalents, like 'Lord' Kagan or Sir James Goldsmith. Mr Barnett is a Jew of German origin, now domiciled in London, with a finger in every pie. He is a rising man, a respected member of all the smartest clubs, and with power over bankers, aristocrats, and Parliamentarians, as well as over the Press. He is a near monopolist. And he uses his influence over Cosmo Burden to bring respectable old Mr Burden into a gamble with an African swamp called the M'Korio Delta Scheme.

A syndicate is formed. Against his better judgment, Emmanuel Burden is roped into it, even though his friend Mr Abbott holds out,

---

[1] *Emmanuel Burden* (1904) p. 24.

and denounces the whole scheme from first to last. The M'Korio Delta (where it is thought there might be gold) is an obvious South Sea Bubble, designed to enrich Mr Barnett and his syndicate. No sooner are the shares placed on the open market than the prices fluctuate wildly, no one profiteering more by these changes and chances than Mr Barnett himself.

Too late, Mr Burden sees the light. He has allowed himself to be carried along on the wave of humbug which described the M'Korio Delta as the Brightest Jewel in the British Imperial Crown. Too late, he returns to his old Liberal view of the Empire as (in Mr Abbott's phrase) 'the giant Blunderbore'. The support of figures like Canon Cone (a thinly disguised Hensley Henson) for the scheme is diminished morally by the disclosure of how many shares this cleric has in the venture. Poor Burden's friendship with the honest Abbott is broken irrevocably before he sees the truth, and can denounce his fellow members of the syndicate as 'swindlers and thieves and scum'. He dies apoplectically in his house in Upper Norwood, and his son inherits his considerable fortune.

The economic and political message of *Emmanuel Burden* is crudely inescapable: British involvement in Africa stems from purely commercial motivation. Ardent Imperialists, carried away by the fervour of religious evangelism or of political rhetoric (Kipling, in the course of the book, writes a poem about the M'Korio Delta called 'It 'im in 'is mouf') might believe that something else was at stake in Africa. In fact, it was simply being exploited to make a few rich men even richer. Such was the 'British Empire'.

The rich men in question were, some of them, British; some of them were not. Their ideals and standards of behaviour were abhorrent to the majority of old-fashioned English merchant-men, whose interests were in trade and in shipping, not in gambling with stocks and speculating in strange parts of the world where it is hinted that there might be gold.

The central figure in all this, therefore, is the Jewish financier, Mr I. Z. Barnett, who, as we learn in a preface to the work, is subsequently elevated to the peerage with the title of Lord Lambeth. By the time Belloc's series of political novels comes to its conclusion, with *Pongo and the Bull*, we see this villainous figure – 'the Peabody Yid', as he is known in society – as the Duke of Battersea. He is one of Belloc's most amusing creations. The methods by which he takes over the clubs, the Press, the City and the politicians, while appearing to do no more than smile and shrug and lisp with a foreign accent, are all richly comic; and the prose never flags. This paragraph, towards the end of the tale, gives some of the book's flavour and shows how it is written in a manner which would not have disgraced P.G. Wodehouse or Evelyn Waugh:

> The session was lagging to its end. Within a week or two the grouse would be whirring and the chance would come for the transference of the M'Korio from the Government of the Foreign Office to that of the Colonial; the moment approached when a few men, undisturbed by the necessities or accidents of the debate, could go right forward and do their best for England. But if time was propitious, time also urged them. Soon the great editors would have left their offices, the heads of the great businesses would be abroad or in the provinces. I have already alluded to the grouse; but a very few weeks and the shadow of the partridge would appear between Mr Barnett and the best laid of his plans. Already multitudes of the middle class were asleep upon beaches of sand. Anxiety, a mood that cannot long disturb such minds, had begun to cast a wing over Mr Barnett's clear and creative intelligence.[1]

Belloc's publisher in this instance was A.M.S. Methuen, who justly commented that 'I don't think it will fetch the public because the note of irony is too subtle, restrained and continuous. But it is a most admirable book and exceedingly clever'.[2]

The narrator's tone, throughout the novel, is one of aggrieved astonishment that anyone could question the excellence of Mr I.Z. Barnett's motives. Unlike Belloc's historical works, the novel has footnotes. In the discussion of how Mr Barnett bought up large sections of the British Press, for instance, the narrator concedes that the editor of the *Gazette* 'was connected with Mr Barnett in the old business of the Haymarket Bank; but if that is taken as evidence of corruption, or even of undue influence, who would be safe from such accusation? A footnote adds: 'As an example of the lengths to which folly can go, I may quote the accusation made against Mr Barnett that he influenced three of the great dailies upon a critical date by *threatening to cut off their supply of paper!!!*'

These ironies were not lost, of course, on Lord Basil Blackwood, still incarcerated as a colonial civil servant in the Government Offices in Bloemfontein.

My dear Belloc
   I am very slowly and with great delight reading 'Mr Burden'. I

[1] *Emmanuel Burden* p. 243.
[2] BC July 21, 1904.

think it is your masterpiece. I am sorry of course that you should *always* harp on the same string and that your general scheme should be such a commonplace one. That is, eternal mockery and denunciation of the rich. I also think that it is a pity to impute baseness and personal interest to every one who follows ideals with regard to the destiny of England as a wide-world-power. I know that's your hobby & you share it in common with the demagogues of Trafalgar Square, Hyde and Regents parks but on this common place base you have erected a most original structure & I have rarely been so diverted before as I am now reading this biography. I can't congratulate you too warmly.

It's a book one will always be able to take up & to read a page or two because on every page there is a chunk of wit. I think the pictures too are excellent & the titles printed under them are of quite superfine wit, I suppose they are yours...

...I hope that it is a financial success. Do tell me. I must say I have been most genuinely amused by it.

Enough for the present, if only you could be persuaded to change your strings, if only you were able to curb your petty jealousy of those who are richer & more prosperous than yourself!!! I am as poor as you but I am not perpetually writhing under the knowledge that others – a limited few – are rich and well.

Yrs BTB[1]

Perhaps Blackwood felt a pang to notice the brilliance of the comic illustrations. They were not (like the drawings for *The Path to Rome*) by Belloc himself, but by Chesterton. The letter, though, shows how warmly it was possible (and should remain possible) to feel about Belloc and about his work, while not swallowing whole his prejudices, obsessions and opinions. Belloc did not expect his friends to be sycophants or disciples. 'HB hated to be treated as "cher maître".'[2] It is perfectly possible to enjoy his fiction while not believing that the British Empire was rotten to the core, or entirely in the hands of international Jewish financiers.

There was, of course, a strong element of truth in Blackwood's humorous twitting of Belloc with *envy* of the rich. His mother's youth was truly opulent. Belloc himself had grown up thinking of himself as a rich man; and the fact that the family fortune was lost, half because of Bessie's conversion to Romanism, and half because

---

[1] BC November 10, 1904.
[2] JSN to the author.

of her unwise adviser's speculations on the Stock Exchange, gave him a particular and abiding horror of the capitalist world.

For all that, what gives Belloc's fiction its cutting edge, is that there is a measure of truth in his caricatures. His friends, perhaps, wearied of his harping on the same string, in 1904. He was still tirelessly harping on it forty years later. It was his conviction that the British Empire, particularly in its African manifestations, was founded on purely commercial considerations, and that talk of Imperial glory or the White Man's Burden was sickening and hypocritical. It was equally his conviction, that the old trading instincts of the English were being eroded by speculators and financiers, who were more interested in dabbling with stocks than buying and selling *things*.

This development of capitalism was what led to the sickening inequalities in society. The divisions between rich and poor could not be healed, he believed, by State socialism. The poor could only regain dignity and independence if they were given the chance of *owning* their land and their houses.

In terms of the actual political events which sharpened these preoccupations during the first few years of the century, one may mention two major concerns. The first was the use of imported Chinese labour in the goldmines of the Rand. The mine-owners pleaded that, without the recruitment of cheap labour from China, it would have been impossible to make the mines profitable. The peasant Boers were deeply suspicious of the Chinese imports, many of whom had been brought from prison, or from the dregs of society in Hong Kong; they were not only depriving the Boers of work; they were a threat to property and person. The British Labour Movement was naturally opposed to the recruitment of cheap foreign labour. Liberal opinion in general was scandalised. It seemed, for the Pro-Boers, to be the final proof, that the Boer War had been fought solely to remove the Boer obstructions to the profiteering of families like the Beits and the Oppenheimers. The importation of the serfs, according to Lloyd George 'brought back slavery to the British Empire'.[1]

In this, Belloc stood full square behind the Radical wing of the Liberal Party. In the area of property versus capitalism, however, Belloc supported at least one measure of Balfour's Conservative administration. This was the Irish Land Act of 1903. As far back as 1886, Gladstone had tried to introduce a measure in Parliament which would allow the Irish peasants assistance with the purchase of their own land. It was rejected at the time. And it was left to George

[1] John P. McCarthy: *Hilaire Belloc, Edwardian Radical* (Indianapolis 1978) p. 102.

Wyndham, the handsome young Chief Secretary for Ireland, to bring this measure to pass. Wyndham, who had served as Balfour's private secretary, belonged to 'The Souls'. He was to become one of Belloc's closest friends. The passing of his Land Act showed, for Belloc, that 'the Irish people have deliberately chosen to become peasant proprietors…when they could have become permanent tenants under far easier terms'. This proved to him that in 'a universal Catholic society', there would develop 'from the very sancity in which it held property, a society in which the mass of citizens would own property'.[1]

This view of things derived directly from Belloc's conversations as a young man with Cardinal Manning, and with his reading of the Papal Encyclical *Rerum Novarum*. It was to develop into the political creed known as Distributism; the view that wealth could be shared by the distribution of property, a movement which would be inimical to Capitalism and to Socialism alike.

These were the 'strings' on which he harped ceaselessly in all his political utterances. There was a further obsession, but it was not to develop fully until he had entered Parliament; and that was that the distinction between the Front Benches of the Conservative and the Liberal Parties was purely notional, that they all belonged to the same families, the same 'set', shared fundamentally similar attitudes to life, and that 'the Party System' itself was a sham.

As Arthur Balfour's Conservative administration tottered to its close, Belloc saw this less clearly. He had begun to conceive the desire to enter Parliament at the next General Election. Although his political opinions did not exactly square with any major grouping at that date, it was no surprise that, with their enmity to Chinese Labour in South Africa, their desire to relieve the lot of the poor, their suspicion of Capitalism and Empire, that he should ally himself to the Radical wing of the Liberal Party.

[1] Ibid. p. 271.

CHAPTER SEVEN

PARLIAMENT
1906 – 1910

'Are you still standing for Parliament?' Basil Blackwood asked Belloc at the beginning of October 1905.

> The election is still sufficiently remote to render it unnecessary to survey the constituencies but in a month or two I suppose we will see the photographs of the rival candidates . . . I suppose you and your crew will drive us crown colony officials into the desert. On public grounds I regret the fate you have in store for South Africa – for private reasons I eagerly look forward to it as it may bring me back to civilization.

This letter was dated from Bloemfontein, with the plaintive note under the Government letter-heading, 'on this day pheasant shooting begins in Christian lands'.[1]

Belloc had in fact been on the look-out for a constituency for some time, and had been selected by the Liberals to fight the 'marginal' seat of South Salford, on the borders of Manchester. It was a working-class constituency then held by the Conservatives with a majority of 1,227.[2] The voters were a mixture of Irish Catholic immigrants and an indigenous population with a strong adherence to the various other nonconformist sects, particularly to the Methodists, and the Congregationalists. The strong Temperance Movement in Salford was strong, which hardly made it the ideal constituency for the poet who had pined for the company of 'Catholic men that live upon wine.' On the other hand, the sitting candidate, J. Greville Groves, belonged to the wealthy firm of Groves and Whitnall, which owned (contrary to Belloc's Distributist principles) no less than a hundred public-houses in the district.

Arthur Balfour resigned in December 1905. Sir Henry Campbell-Bannerman, leader of the Opposition, became Prime Minister, formed a Liberal Government, and dissolved Parliament. Belloc plunged at once into his election campaign.

[1] BC October 1, 1905
[2] Speaight.p. 204.

If the whole of political life were conducted on the hustings, Belloc would probably have been the most successful politician of his generation. At thirty-five, he was more rugged, and in many ways simpler, even than the President of the Union who had held Oxford spellbound ten years before. The rowdy atmosphere of election meetings, the shouting and the heckling, the bellowed exchange of over-simplified views, was entirely to his taste.

> A Frenchman there was named Hilaire
> And Réné – the names make you stare;
> He wanted to be
> A Salford M.P.
> But they wanted no foreigners there.

he read, to his delight, scrawled on a wall. He probably wrote it himself. It certainly gave him the opportunity to quote it in his next speech; to say that he had as much French blood in his veins as Lord Lansdowne or Lord Edward Fitzmaurice; and that he had served in the French army for the same reasons as Lord Kitchener – to see what it was like.[1]

His religion was undoubtedly not in his favour. The first meeting of his campaign was held in the schools of St John's Roman Catholic Cathedral in Salford. The clergy, and his campaign manager, Sir Edward Wood, were alike in warning Belloc not to make allusion to his religious allegiance for fear of alienating Protestant voters. He rose to his feet in a packed hall and began by saying: 'Gentlemen, I am a Catholic. As far as possible, I go to Mass every day. This' (taking a rosary out of his pocket) 'is a rosary. As far as possible, I kneel down and tell these beads every day. If you reject me on account of my religion, I shall thank God that He has spared me the indignity of being your representative!' After a shocked silence, there was a thunder-clap of applause.[2]

It was a bold technique, analogous to placing a statue of Our Lady on his desk during the All Souls' examination. The dons had accepted his challenge by voting him out. But the electors of South Salford were more impressed. Undoubtedly, one of the things in his favour was his indignation at the deeply unpopular importation of Chinese labour into the Transvaal. Those who could see South Africa at first hand, like Basil Blackwood, were naturally sceptical about the Liberal line, which stood for a white, rather than a yellow, Labour force, dominated rather by English than by Dutch administration. No one

[1] Speaight. p. 205.
[2] Ibid. p. 204.

appeared to recognise, on the Liberal side, the rather obvious fact that a proportion of the inhabitants of South Africa were neither Chinese, Dutch, nor British. The intense feelings engendered at the time about that province of the Empire in the electorate at home never foresaw for a moment that plans for the future of South Africa ought to take account of the position of the Blacks. It was tacitly assumed by both sides that their position of subjection was entirely natural and proper. Perhaps not surprisingly, it was left to a high Tory Imperialist, John Buchan, to see the potency, as well as the romance, of the idea of a black Africa. *Prester John* is a sort of black *Redgauntlet*. The good Scotch hero accuses the last of the great Kaffir kings of wanting 'to wipe out the civilisation of a thousand years and turn us all into savages'. But when he hears Laputa's own speech to the blacks, urging them to throw off white oppression ('a bastard civilization which has sapped your manhood'), Davie is impressed. 'By rights, I suppose, my blood should have been boiling at this treason. I am ashamed to confess that it did nothing of the sort. My mind was mesmerized by this amazing man.'[1] The Liberals like Belloc who first read Buchan's adventure story must have viewed it as the sheerest fantasy. From the perspective of seventy years, it is the British public and the politicians who seem like fantasists; and the great romancer who seems to have had a curious glimpse of what was to come.

None of that would have troubled the Salford constituents, most of whom, if they were literate, would not have had the means to buy books or subscribe to libraries. Belloc wooed them hard, returning exhausted whenever he could to stay with Lord Stanley of Alderley, who made his house Belloc's campaign headquarters.

Polling day was on January 13, 1906. He and Elodie went in triumph to the Manchester Reform Club, a splendid Gothic edifice, where some were singing hymns and some were opening bottles of champagne. They cried for a speech, and Belloc asked them to be completely silent. 'For this is all that is left of my voice. If you desire to hear that voice in Parliament for purposes on which we are agreed, you must spare it. You know how hard the fight has been in South Salford. It is especially hard because I chose to be, and shall continue to be a thorough-going Radical. As I had the hardest fight, so it will probably appear I have the smallest majority . . .'

This turned out to be true. He was elected by 852 votes. The Manchester North-West constituency was won more easily from the Conservative Joynson Hicks by Winston Churchill, who was there at

[1] *Prester John* (Nelson repr. 1949) p. 155.

the Reform Club to share in the jubilation. The North-East constituency – a sign of the times – was won by J.R. Clynes for the Labour Party.

When all the votes were counted, throughout the country, it was realised that there had been a great Liberal 'landslide'. In the new House of Commons, there were 377 Liberals, 157 Conservatives, 53 Labour and 83 Irish Nationalists. Never before, in the history of British politics, had one party held such a substantial majority over the rest.

Belloc and Elodie returned to London by train. Chesterton and Dorothy Hamilton were there to receive them. 'This is a great day for the British Empire,' Belloc remarked, 'but a bad one for the little Bellocs.'[1]

*   *   *

This was unquestionably true. Belloc was never a man to spend much of the week at home, but with his new parliamentary commitments there was even less time for his family. The first thing he did after the election was to get a tiny flat in Victoria Street, midway between the House of Commons and the trains to Sussex from Victoria Station. For it was in March of that year that they bought King's Land, and in the summer that the caravan trundled over from Slindon with all their things.

A near neighbour in Sussex was Wilfrid Scawen Blunt, the eccentric, lecherous poet whose enthusiasms included the Arab world and Irish Nationalism. He was married to Byron's grand-daughter, Lady Anne Noel, an accomplished painter who, in the early days of their marriage, had depicted her husband in full Arab costume on a neighing charger. 'After her Eastern experience she thought it wrong to be without a hat or turban, even in her bedroom. Thus in bed she would wear a small Irish fishing hat and mackintosh, instead of a nightdress, to go with it, lying against her pillows, "dressed", in the words of her son-in-law Neville Lytton, "as though for a southwest gale in the channel".'[2]

The year before the Bellocs arrived at King's Land, Lady Anne had left her husband, worn out by domestic disputes, and by his repeated infidelities. Belloc and Elodie, however, enjoyed the company of Blunt himself. Sometimes, if Belloc was at home, he would take his wife over to Newbuildings, Blunt's magnificent Charles II mansion at

---

[1] Speaight p. 207.
[2] Max Egremont: *The Cousins* (1977) p. 67.

Southwater. Blunt at this date was an agnostic with strong Moslem sympathies, but he had been brought up as a Roman Catholic and educated at Stonyhurst. In this, as in most other particulars, he differed wildly from his cousin George Wyndham, another constant visitor to Newbuildings.

Wyndham was believed by many to be the handsomest man of his age. He had enjoyed a glitteringly successful career as a Guards officer, and he was distinguished both as a horseman and as a man of letters. In 1887, he had married Lady Sibell Lumley, the young widow of Earl Grosvenor (heir to the first Duke of Westminister), and daughter of the Earl of Scarbrough. Over eighty men were said to be painfully in love with her, (if one counted curates) and even before her husband's demise, Lord Curzon had repeatedly pressed his besotted suit on her. She refused them all, even the curates, who might have tempted her more than some, for she was of a religious (high Anglican) disposition; and married George Wyndham.

Apart from the ties of blood, one would not have thought that Blunt and Wyndham had much in common. Wyndham was a High Tory, the protégé of Arthur Balfour. It was widely assumed that he would one day be Prime Minister. He was an ardent Imperialist; Blunt deeply opposed to the Empire. Wyndham believed in a European presence in Egypt; Blunt was an enthusiastic Egyptian nationalist. In spite of all political and temperamental differences, however, the two men retained a profound affection for each other. And, over the matter of Ireland, they were surprisingly close. For it was Wyndham, as we have seen, who implemented the Irish Land Act of 1903, which, within five years, had enabled 228,930 tenants to take possession of their holdings. John Redmond, the Nationalist M.P., called Wyndham's Act 'the most substantial victory gained for centuries by the Irish race for the reconquest of the soil of Ireland by the people'.[1]

All this did not do much to endear Wyndham to his Tory supporters and, when his party was defeated at the election of 1906, he himself abandoned hope of holding high political office. 'My sympathies,' he wrote, 'are more and more with the real Tories; less and less with Americanism and Teutonism or rather with their awkward adaptations to our life in these islands . . . My brief sojourn abroad has made me feel that the "gentry", whether of territorial birth or literary distinction, throughout Europe represents something that is valid more truly than the domestic politics of "nation-states" and the world politics of would-be Empires.'[2]

[1] *The Cousins*, p. 154.
[2] Ibid. p. 256.

This was Wyndham's position when Belloc first met him in the House of Commons at the beginning of 1906. Both in London, and at Blunt's table, they quickly became firm friends. Wyndham was eight years older than Belloc; he was forty-three. The two shared many views and attitudes in spite of the fact that they sat on opposite sides of the House of Commons, and there can be no doubt that Wyndham's friendship determined the shape and course of Belloc's career in the House. 'Both he and Belloc are admirable talkers,' Blunt recorded in his diary towards the end of the year, 'Belloc's best story was of an Italian brigand who had regularly confessed his sins every Saturday from his youth up in his own village, but who was refused absolution at last at the age of eighty, as profaning the sacrament of penance, by going on with his confessions about women. "E cosa impossible", said the priest.'[1]

G.K. Chesterton remembered that 'the one Front Bench man who seemed in the days of my youth still eternally young was, for me, in those days, on the opposite Front Bench. The wonderful thing about George Wyndham was that he had come through political life without losing his political opinions, or indeed any of his opinions. Precisely what gave him such a genius for friendship was that life had left in him so much of himself; so much of his youth; so much even of his childhood. He might never have been a Cabinet Minister; he might have been any common literary or artistic fellow with a soul to save and some dim secretive ideas about saying it. He was not always trying, like Charles Augustus Fortescue, "to take a judgment broad and wide".'[2]

Charles Augustus Fortescue was one of the magnificent *galère* who composed Belloc's *Cautionary Tales for Children*, which he started to doodle in the opening months of his parliamentary career. They are infinitely funnier and sharper than the previous volumes of comic verse; technically faultless, there is not a syllable out of place, not an epithet which could be improved. Grown-ups, once they have read them, go on loving them; and to read them only a few times is to have them quickly by heart. Much more striking, is that they still appeal to children. Young boys and girls who know nothing of the geography of London, nor of the ways of the world, can repeat with endless and manifest delight that:

> The House itself began to fall!
> It tottered, shuddering to and fro,

[1] Wilfred Scawen Blunt: *My Diaries* (1932) p. 570.
[2] *Autobiography* p. 122.

> Then crashed into the street below –
> Which happened to be Savile Row.

Children who have no idea how their country is allegedly governed
beg to hear again the rebuke of 'the Duke – his aged grand-sire' to the
tearful Lord Lundy:

> 'Sir! You have disappointed us!
> We had intended you to be
> The next Prime Minister but three:
> The stocks were sold; the Press was squared:
> The Middle Class was quite prepared.
> But as it is . . . My language fails!
> Go out and govern New South Wales!'

Much of one's pleasure in the volume derives from Basil Blackwood's illustrations. He was still in South Africa when Belloc began
to write them, and wrote back, 'I'm glad to hear that you have not
abandoned the intention of sending verses in order that we may
embark on a new venture. I believe my pencil has acquired merit in the
long period during which it has lain fallow.'[1] The letter is
accompanied by a drawing – evidently the Wealthy Banker, whose
daughter Rebecca slammed doors for fun and perished miserably –
sitting on a Chinese serf and squashing him flat.

'How do you like Parliament?' Blackwood asked in another letter,
as if an aside,

> The Natal 'crisis' provoked an uproar for information. I regret that
> you should be handicapped by blissful ignorance as to the senti-
> ments, conditions, realities of the country. For you, the world was
> always haunted by capitalistic bogies, but you are stark staring mad
> about South Africa and share the popular delusion that no one
> whatever his antecedents or character can maintain any freedom in
> S.A.[2]

Belloc's maiden speech in Parliament had been on the subject of
Chinese labour in South Africa. 'The *Morning Post*, naturally trying to
hurt the Government, said that I alone of the Liberals had shown
courage. *The Times* said in a leader that what I had said was "dangerous rant".' Thus he boasted to Maurice Baring[3], adding the confession, 'I have made my maiden speech. After it I was sick. This is true
and not an exaggeration.'

[1] BC April 6, 1906.
[2] BC April 4, 1906.
[3] Quoted Speaight pp. 210–11

The House could not fail to have noticed Belloc, and he quickly became a familiar figure there; though never one who was taken wholly seriously. At the time of his election, the parish priest of St James's, Spanish Place, wrote that 'it is a matter of great rejoicing to me that one who has proclaimed his Catholicism as loudly and plainly as you have done in your "Path to Rome" should be returned to Parliament . . . I am certain that your presence in Parliament will be a very great gain to the cause of Catholic education. I am already prophesying that if the Liberals remain in office for 5 years, and are then again returned to power, you will hold Cabinet rank in the second administration.'[1] The prophecy was fairly wide of the mark. But Belloc did not disappoint his Catholic supporters in fighting for the preservation of the Catholic schools. He reminded the House that what was at issue was the Catholic Faith. 'The House may tyrannically insist on their having less, but English Catholics cannot be content with less for their Catholic children than Catholic schools with Catholic teachers teaching the Catholic religion and impressing the children all the time.'[2] Those members who were prepared to accept this unambiguous statement of things were probably nonetheless a trifle astonished to be told that 'since Diocletian nothing can compare with the persecution of the Catholic people of this country by the wealthy and official classes': a striking utterance if one remembers the 'dungeon, fire and sword' endured by recusants in the sixteenth and seventeenth centuries.

Though happy to stand up for his co-religionists in this way, Belloc was anxious to make the point to the House that he was not simply sitting for South Salford as what he sometimes contemptuously called 'a professional papist'. He supported the reform of the House of Lords (Campbell-Bannerman's measure of 1907), being unable to resist the observation that not all the English peers were of 'strictly English blood';[3] he made loud speeches about military policy; he moved, 'That this House regrets the secrecy under which political funds are accumulated and administered and regards such secrecy as a peril to its privileges and character'. The notion that financiers influenced public events by giving or withholding party funds runs through all his political fiction. In real life, it was an awkward matter to prove, and it did not make him popular to raise it.

*   *   *

---

[1] BC January 15, 1906.
[2] Quoted Speaight. p. 211.
[3] Speaight. p. 221.

Meanwhile, in time that was not taken up with his constituency, his House of Commons life and his incurable addiction to European travel, Belloc had a home. He had managed to pick up the Literary Editorship of the *Morning Post* and this undemanding job helped to pay for some of the improvements to King's Land. The building work, even of the most essential kind, had been far more expensive than he reckoned at first, and there were perpetual worries about money. Where others would have spent time and energy improving the domestic offices, Elodie devoted herself to creating a chapel. It was on the first floor, just along the corridor from her bedroom (the Bellocs slept separately), little more than a narrow boxroom in proportions. The photograph of Thérèse Martin was pinned up on one wall. A rudimentary altar was erected and furnished, vestments purchased.

They still needed permission to use the chapel for the purposes of Sunday mass or for the hearing of confessions; permission, that is, from the local Roman Catholic bishop. This was a point of ecclesiastical discipline which Elodie had overlooked. She was adamant, however, that they should have their own way:

> My Beloved Heart:
>
> I went to West Grinstead today to have our dead prayed for on All Souls' Day. And while I was there I found that Father Measures was troubled as to whether he could have outsiders at confession here. I carefully avoided telling him that we had done so – because it would have been an appalling business if we had got Father Godfrey into trouble. I am greatly troubled about this last business. So will you, like the sensible and good angel that you are, go to the Bishop tomorrow and find out quite clearly what are our privileges and what are forbidden . . . Do try, my beloved, because if I can't go to Confession here the whole point of our having Mass is nearly lost . . . Drag, my beloved, if you can, permission for *us* of the household to go to Confession from the Bishop.
>
> Above all things don't tell the Bishop unless you must that we have been . . .
>
> The flock revels. I hunt the post . . .[1]

The flock revelled up to a point. When their cousins Mary and Susan Lowndes (daughters of Marie Belloc-Lowndes) came to stay, they were always struck by how very fierce Elodie was, how many rules there were that could be broken. The rare appearances of Papa were

[1] BC October 31, 1907.

built up and looked forward to, but when he came, as often as not in a fury, the children did not enjoy it much and went to hide in the mill or play in the fields. More fun was had when they could go and play with neighbours, such as the children of Sir Walter Burrell at Knepp Castle[1], leaving Elodie to her congenial domestic tasks, such as placing a crucifix over every low door-lintel, so that unbelievers, visiting the house, would be forced to bow to Our Lord.[2]

Not all visitors, unbelieving or otherwise, were impressed. Arthur Benson, son of a former Archbishop of Canterbury, and author of 'Land of Hope and Glory', was taken over by Percy Lubbock to see King's Land. He was horrified. The house was 'unutterably frowsy, mean, with a vulgar accumulation of hideous objects, old and new'; and Belloc himself emerged from the shadows 'in slippers, very dishevelled, beery, smoky, unpleasant, with a shiny tail coat'. The whole atmosphere was that of a 'gypsy encampment'.[3]

Yet, for those who saw it with less prim or malicious eyes, King's Land had poetry, and even a kind of holiness. The accumulation of clutter struck Arthur Benson as hideous, but it had not been chosen for its beauty. Much of the furniture came from the old Belloc household in La Celle St Cloud. The objects and icons – a bust of Demosthenes, a portrait of Danton, a bas-relief of Joseph Priestley and Josiah Wedgwood – adorned the walls because of their associations more than for their appearance's sake. It certainly was not 'tasteful'; and Belloc's fondness for the dark wall-hangings and panelling, much of which he installed with his own hands, deprived the rooms of light. It was above all a house with a chapel, and Elodie's efforts to maintain that, in spite of the opposition of bishops, paid off. The great feasts of the Church became, therefore, great domestic events. During Holy Week, they would pin cards with the Fourteen Stations of the Cross round the drawing-room. At Christmas, the three masses would be offered, if a priest could be found to stay the night. The day previous, on Christmas Eve, village children would be entertained in the hall by the songs of the miller; they would be shown the crib, and given presents from around the tree. After the masses on the next day, eating and drinking – particularly, drinking – would go on until late in the afternoon or evening.[4]

The tradition of the King's Land Christmas developed gradually, but it was inescapably memorable for all those who experienced it.

[1] The Dowager Countess of Iddesleigh to the author.
[2] Dom Philip Jebb OSB to the author.
[3] David Newsome: *On the Edge of Paradise* (1980), p. 285.
[4] Morton p. 28.

Friends, however 'unutterably frowsy' the house, came back to it, when they could easily have arranged to see the Bellocs in less uncomfortable surroundings. The place had, and has, a magic.

The pattern of life there at the very beginning of 1908 is captured in one of Elodie's diaries. On Wednesday, January 1, they drank a bottle of port with Nurse Allen, and the domestics, Ernestine and Marie Staule, in the kitchen. Next day, 'Hun went back to town', but returned 'with Gilbert and Frances Chesterton'. On Friday, January 3, 'Maurice Baring arrived about 1 o'clock in a taximotre [sic] from London. We all had great fun over our lunch & in the afternoon we all taximotred up to Hammer's Ponds to see the sources of the Arun. It was unspeakably lovely. It still freezes. Maurice Baring stayed all night. After some debate we sent the taximotre back to town. We all said the Litany of Loretto in the Chapel. Maurice Baring loves King's Land'.[1]

One of the reasons Baring and others liked coming to King's Land was that it was so far in spirit from the smart social scene in London: the world which the schoolmistressy Arthur Benson (who had taught and befriended Baring at Eton) anathematised for its horrid orgies, 'tasteless extravagance hobnobbing with Asquith, Cromer and Haldane, and concluding their revels with eggs being fried in Max Beerbohm's hat'.[2]

Belloc, through his friendship with Baring and Raymond Asquith, also belonged to this world, while nursing very ambivalent feelings about it. He would have been as amused as everyone else by some of the absurd pranks and jokes which they played, such as on the occasion when Margot Asquith (stepmother of Raymond and second wife of H.H.) took Baring to the Albert Hall to watch the great Torrey-Alexander mission. They soon began to get bored and to chatter to each other. Torrey, on the platform, detected them and stopped a hymn in mid-course. 'There are two ladies and a gentleman who are talking together in a box,' he thundered. 'Now they must come down to the front and sing the next verse alone.' 'Maurice Baring fell to the ground and lay there – but Margot Asquith and the other came cheerfully forward and, in the silence, accompanied by a vast organ sang the next verse in tones like the squeak of mice or rats to the Great Hall.'[3]

Jowett had called her 'the best-educated ill-educated woman that I have ever met'. Margot Asquith (neé Tennant) was satirised in

[1] BC January 3, 1908.
[2] *On The Edge of Paradise* p. 275.
[3] Ibid. p. 128.

Belloc's novels as Mary Smith, the intriguing gossipy political hostess, related to most of the aristocratic families in England, forever shoving her relations and her rich Jewish friends into positions of prominence and twisting the arm of her cousin Dolly, 'the young and popular Prime Minister': a fairly unmistakeable portrait of Asquith himself. 'Mary Smith was related to all of them and they were all related to each other, and in their relationship there was friendship also, and they governed England . . . '[1] Certainly, there was not much exaggeration in this. 'The Souls' were nearly all related or intermarried – and a very high proportion of men in public life during the Edwardian era were connected by blood or marriage to Charterises, Grenfells, Tennants, Horners, Lytteltons or Mannerses.

They whooped from house to house, literate, rich, clever; self-contained, but unself-conscious. Most of their private language ('dewdrops' for a compliment, 'dentist' for 'tête-à-tête', 'ridge' for 'depression', 'ibsen' for 'ordinary') derived from Baring family slang. In the households of Lady Desborough, Lady Elcho, Lady Horner or Margot Asquith, they could safely use this language, because everyone present could be expected to understand it; just as, if they poured out their private life to one of the circle, they could be sure that their secret was safe and would not spread beyond the sixty or eighty people who made up that intimate band.

Baring and Belloc had a life-time of composing spontaneous Ballades on every subject under the sun. None of these poems captures the atmosphere of Edwardian high life so perfectly as Belloc's 'Ballade of Hell and Mrs Roebeck', and its sense of social satiety contributes to our picture of what made the 'gypsy encampment' at King's Land so attractive;

> I'm going out to dine at Gray's
> With Bertie Morden, Charles and Kit,
> And Manderly who never pays,
> And Jane who wins in spite of it,
> And Algernon who won't admit
> The truth about his curious hair
> And teeth that very nearly fit: –
> And Mrs Roebeck will be there.
>
> And then tomorrow someone says
> That someone else has made a hit
> In one of Mister Twister's plays,

[1] *A Change in the Cabinet* (1909) p. 19

And off we go to yawn at it;
And when it's petered out we quit
For number 20 Taunton Square,
And smoke, and drink, and dance a bit; –
And Mrs Roebeck will be there.

And so through each declining phase
Of emptied effort, jaded wit,
And day by day of London days
Obscurely, more obscurely lit;
Until the uncertain shadows flit
Announcing to the shuddering air
A Darkening, and the end of it: –
And Mrs Roebeck will be there.

Envoi
Prince, on their iron thrones they sit,
Impassible to our despair,
The dreadful Guardians of the Pit: –
And Mrs Roebeck will be there.

As a satirist, Belloc's lonely sense of absurdity made him feel like a stranger and a sojourner in the houses of the rich; and, as a Radical, their wealth, their power, their clique-ishness revolted him. And yet, they were his friends: Raymond Asquith, Maurice Baring, George Wyndham meant as much to him as his cronies in Fleet Street, probably more. Basil Blackwood thought Belloc's radicalism sprang from 'your petty jealousy of those who are richer and more prosperous than yourself'. In the next three years, this radicalism was to be tested and tempered. Politically, they were the years of Mrs Roebeck Triumphant. For, on April 22, Sir Henry Campbell-Bannerman died, and Herbert Asquith became Prime Minister. Asquith, though not a close friend, was the father, or the friend, of many of Belloc's closest companions. Yet his Liberalism was distinctly unRadical. Asquith represented the 'Right' of his Party. Lloyd George, his Chancellor of the Exchequer, embodied many of the Radical ideals which Belloc cherished most warmly. Belloc, however, by the end of Asquith's first parliament, felt a complete revulsion against Lloyd George's policies. The implicit cynicism of his attitude to Parliamentary government, present in his utterances since the Boer War, became outspoken and vitriolic. It is by no means easy to say how or why this came about; but it owed much more than Belloc ever wanted to admit to a conflict, not so much of loyalties, as of attractions. He minded about the poor. His radical convictions were sincerely held. But his friendship with George Wyndham, and all that it involved, tugged at his heart with an even deeper claim to be heard.

*   *   *

It will seem paradoxical to speak of Belloc at this date as muddled or uncertain. He appears in print as a man of pugnacious certitudes. Indeed, surveying him from the perspective which the length of his life provides, these certitudes seem almost tediously simple and few. As we read the books he wrote immediately before the First World War, and follow his career as a political thinker until his death, the wonder is that he modified his views so little. Europe and the Faith are one; the further away you got from either, the less civilised you became. Capitalism and Socialism are two names for the same hideous phenomenon: they are both at war with individualism; they can only be crushed by owning property and practising the Catholic faith. Such is the essence of Belloc's political creed. It affected what he had to say about almost every world issue between 1910 and 1940. It inspired his reading of the world map: Poland and Ireland being the great tests and examples of what Europe could become, if set free from the threats of Prussianism, and the Anglo-Judaic Plutocracy.

Yet, it is very easy to have 'views', and to go on expressing them outside the context of a Parliamentary career. A Member of Parliament is obliged to decide what he thinks, not in general, but in specific terms. Given his general view of life, which way is he going to vote for this or that stage of a particular Bill? Frequently, Parliamentary votes are not matters of principle. They simply require detailed knowledge of the particular legislation under debate. Thus, the edges of ideology become blurred, and strange alliances are formed.

But the great and dramatic issue before Asquith's parliament was not blurred, and, initially at least, Belloc was perfectly clear in his mind where he stood over it. This was Lloyd George's Budget on April 29, 1909. Paradoxically, although it was, as Belloc himself said, 'in every sense, in every detail, and in all its extent . . . a radical budget', it was made necessary partly because of the demands of right-wing Members of Parliament for more Dreadnoughts for the Royal Navy. 'We want eight, and we won't wait,' George Wyndham had chanted,[1] and it became a rallying-call for all those who wanted an increase in Defence spending.

Yet the necessity of paying for the Dreadnoughts was not what

[1] *The Cousins.* p. 270.

made Lloyd George's Budget controversial. It put twopence in the pound on to income tax, added a supertax on very high incomes, and increased death duties by one third. It increased the duty on tobacco, and (more controversially) on whisky. But the major sticking-point was a new land tax which taxed capital gains on the unearned increment of land value, and placed a duty of a halfpenny in the pound on the capital of undeveloped lands.

It all seems mild enough by the standards of a modern 'mixed economy'. At the time, it provoked a violent reaction from the landed classes, an influential proportion of whom sat in the House of Lords. For, the underlying purpose of the Budget was not to buy Dreadnoughts, but to provide the money for the first steps along the road to the Welfare State: a non-contributory pension scheme (five shillings a week to men over seventy, if their income was less than ten shillings a week); sickness and maternity benefits.

Asquith, never given to overstatement, was inclined to underplay the controversial nature of his Government's intentions. But this was hardly the tone set by Lloyd George in the peroration of his Budget Speech:

> This is a war Budget. It is for raising money to wage implacable warfare against poverty and squalidness. I cannot help hoping and believing that before this generation has passed away, we shall have advanced a great step towards that good time, when poverty, and the wretchedness and human degradation which always follows in its camp, will be as remote to the people of this country as the wolves which once infested its forests.

The war was being conducted against the landed and plutocratic classes and they were not slow to realise it. Lord Rosebery, who, so few years before, had been a Liberal Prime Minister, was the chief speaker at a meeting held in the City of London at the Cannon Street Hotel. The chairman of the meeting was Rosebery's brother-in-law, Lord Rothschild. It was, he protested, 'not a Budget, but a revolution: a social and political revolution of the first magnitude'.[1]

It looked inevitable that the House of Lords would reject the Budget and it was not long before Lloyd George was taunting them with his gleeful question: 'whether five hundred men, ordinary men, chosen accidentally from among the unemployed, should over-ride the judgement – the deliberate judgement – of millions of people

[1] For this, and preceding matter, John Grigg: *Lloyd George, the People's Champion* (1978) p. 198.

who are engaged in the industry which makes the wealth of the country'.[1]

The constitutional crisis which this confrontation provoked led to the General Election of January 1910. Opinions differ about the extent to which Lloyd George deliberately forced the issue. Asquith, one can have no doubt, hoped that the Budget (perhaps suitably amended) could be passed in the Lords without an election, and without a constitutional crisis.[2] But, for the purposes of this story, what is noticeable is the ambivalence of Belloc in the affair.

The only point of the Budget with which he disagreed was its imposition of a tax on whisky. He was torn, even over this question, between holding on to his teetotalling support in Salford while not losing the Irish vote. In *The Path to Rome* he had written that a Catholic was able to distinguish between Bacchus and the Devil; 'To wit: that he should never drink what has been made and sold since the Reformation . . . not whisky, nor brandy, nor sparkling wines.' This being so, it was odd that he had to complain that 'the Budget overtaxes Ireland by a new heavy tax on whisky, which is the National Drink, and it has the same effect in Ireland as though you were to put 50 centimes a bottle on Vin Ordinaire in France or a penny a glass on the working man's beer in England'. Yet, while that was doubtless meant to please his Irish constituents, what of the Wesleyans and the Temperance League? 'The Whisky Tax is an excellent thing,' he averred for their benefit, 'so far as England is concerned, because whisky is not the national drink in England; I am certain in our climate or at any rate with our inherited bodies it does us harm.' Is the English climate really so different from the Irish? What if you had inherited an Irish, or Scotch body and were living on English soil? Belloc's stand on the issue made no kind of sense, except in so far as he was obviously anxious for his political future.

Belloc believed, when the hurly-burly of his Parliamentary career was over, that he was always forthright in telling the truth. This matter of the whisky tax is very small, but it is significant. If the Budget were rejected by the Lords, there would certainly be an election. Belloc had a majority of only 852. He had to be prepared.

Much more striking, in view of what he was to say after he left Parliament, about Lloyd George's social reforms, is the general fact that he supported them so warmly at the time. With the one exception of the whisky tax, he thought it would 'be difficult to

[1] Ibid. 225.
[2] Roy Jenkins: *Asquith* (1964) pp. 194–211.

imagine a better Budget': that its proposals were 'perfectly excellent'.[1]

The excellence consisted in its firm embodiment of the two fundamental principles of Belloc's radicalism during the election campaign: a concern for the poor and a suspicion of the House of Lords. Lloyd George's Budget set the Poor and the Lords in opposition. This should have been precisely what Belloc liked. But, when the actual implications of the policy dawned on him, he did not seem to like it. Belloc was always better at attack than at constructive proposal. He always found it easier to say what was wrong with a policy than to suggest a constructive alternative. Belloc had been huffing and puffing with Revolutionary fervour since his late teens, proclaiming his republicanism, his enmity to privilege, his hatred of the rich, his longing for a radical government in England. At the first hint that such a thing might actually take place, he realised what the destruction of privilege would actually entail.

It was easy enough for him to cheer and halloo at the idea of 'bleeding' 'eurasian' peers like Lord Rothschild. It was a much more difficult matter to be entirely opposed to the lifestyle of a peer such as Lord Derby who, before he succeeded to his father's title, had been Conservative M.P. for Westhoughton in the previous parliament and Postmaster General from 1903 to 1905.

'I think him so thoroughly honest a man that I will do anything for him,' Belloc wrote to Baring at the end of the year.

> He talked more sensibly about the Budget than any man I have yet heard. And he is the only man living who has given me complete and immediate and full-hearted free run of his library. Everybody else of the many rich people I know, who have libraries, put some sort of irritating restriction, moral or material, upon the use of it, and they are indeed to be excused. But Lord Derby gave me the Library exactly as though it were my own and that detail argues all the best qualities that are to be found in a rich man; indeed, he almost set me to think that great wealth can in some cases fail to corrupt. I should be glad to think so.[2]

There is no reason why Belloc should have been mixing in purely radical company while the Budget crisis lasted. But his hours in Lord Derby's library tell their own story. He was bored, for much of the time, by politics. Even if his financial position did not demand it, he would have wanted to write more books and this year he saw three through the press (another satirical novel called *A Change in the*

[1] Speaight. p. 234.
[2] *Letters* p. 21.

Cabinet, his substantial biography of *Marie Antoinette*, and a collection of newspaper essays entitled *On Everything*).

However 'excellent' Lloyd George's Budget, Belloc had come to regard him with personal abhorrence. He was dishonest (how dishonest even Belloc, at this date, did not guess); he was unchaste and, worse, he was not a gentleman.

> He excelled even the ruck of politicians in his desire for what he thought was fame, as well as his extravagant greed for money. The two things do not usually go together but in his case it was difficult to say which was the stronger. He fully achieved both . . . [Lloyd George] began as a small Nonconformist Radical member of Parliament, a solicitor by trade and at first with no particular bad marks against him that I ever heard of. He dined with me once or twice in my house at Chelsea during the Boer War when he was advertising himself – with a certain courage, but with still more cunning – by appealing to the strong Nonconformist feeling there was against the war. He was a fluent speaker of what is called the 'tin chapel' order, and appealed strongly to the audiences which in an earlier generation had also been appealed to by Spurgeon, Moody and Sankey and people of that kind. There was a great deal in him of the Welsh revivalists, but he had none of their high sincerity. He may possibly like other men of the sort who enter public life have had some sort of convictions when he began, but he had certainly lost them by the year 1900 and was purely on the make.[1]

Belloc wrote these words nearly thirty years after his career as an M.P. came to an end. To many people, it will seem grossly unfair to miss the extraordinary paradox in Lloyd George's nature, in which unrepentant personal corruption and a perfectly genuine passion for social justice existed mysteriously side by side. But, by the time he wrote this secret account of Lloyd George, the whole matter had been sufficiently distorted to be clear in Belloc's mind: the vulgar little Welshman's rise to eminence was purely the result of a plot by bankers and financiers.

He elbowed his way up through the ruck of professional politicians and became Chancellor of the Exchequer at the moment when the policy of the Boer War had for the first time introduced acute financial pressure. Income tax had as a result of the Boer War risen

[1] BC 1937.

to over five per cent and was becoming appreciable, but the main squeeze was on Death Duties.[1]

At the time, Belloc had been in favour of the increase in death duties, for the same reason that Lloyd George gave for it: that it provided money to help the poor, to provide pensions for the old and assistance for young mothers and the sick. Looking back on it afterwards, Belloc thought it had all been a fiddle and a plot: the Peabody Yid was somewhere at the back of it.

> Lloyd George was put up by the Banks as spokesman for the necessity of beginning the confiscation of capital through taxation. In his name there was introduced by the Treasury a new and much more drastic scale of death duties which have of course gone on increasing from that day to this [1937]. He was turned on to talk the ordinary demagogy about making the rich pay, there was some resistance in the House of Lords which it was pretended to meet by threatening to make a large number of new Peers – but that of course was all the usual political clap trap, there was no real intention of making new peers nor any intention on the part of the House of Lords to resist seriously, for the money had to be found or else the whole banking monopoly sacrificed.[2]

Seen from the perspective of nearly half a lifetime, in which Belloc himself had had endless battles with tax authorities, it is striking how differently the 1909 Budget, which seemed at the time 'perfectly excellent', appeared to him. He does not suggest what evidence there was for the 'plot' which he believed to have happened. He appears to have forgotten Rothschild, saying that it was not a Budget, but a revolution; faded from memory, too, is the rejection of the Budget by the House of Lords. The possibility of creating a large number of peers to force the matter through the second House certainly seemed real enough to Asquith at the time. When the Prime Minister put the matter to King Edward VII, the monarch was horrified and said it was tantamount to 'the destruction of the House of Lords'.[3] Since that was what Belloc had said he wanted, he had not at the time accused the Chancellor of the Exchequer of being in cahoots with these mysterious bankers.

Yet, even in 1909, there were strong indications that Belloc's radicalism was on the wane. The changes which were taking place in

---

[1] Ibid.
[2] Ibid.
[3] Roy Jenkins: *Asquith* p. 203.

the social structure of England depressed him, for he loved old things, and civilised things. Having had the run of the houses of Blunt, Wyndham and Lord Derby, he must have felt the same regret as Yeats, 'among a rich man's flowering lawns', that the old order was passing away.

> Mere dreams, mere dreams! Yet Homer had not sung
> Had he not found it certain beyond dreams
> That out of life's own self-delight had sprung
> The abounding glittering jet, though now it seems
> As if some marvellous empty sea-shell flung
> Out of the obscure dark of the rich streams,
> And not a fountain, were the symbol which
> Shadows the inherited glory of the rich.

In one of his most perfect essays, 'The Old Things', Belloc puts it in a way more positively than Yeats.

> Those who travel about England for their pleasure, or, for that matter, about any part of Western Europe, rightly associate with such travel the pleasure of history; for history adds to a man, giving him, as it were, a great memory of things – like a human memory, but stretched over a longer space than one human life. It makes him, I do not say wise and great, but certainly in communion with wisdom and greatness.[1]

When a man writes as much as Belloc, he writes on many levels, sometimes only engaging a part of himself in the texture of his prose. But, in this essay, we have the very core of Belloc, the quintessence of what made him such an interesting political phenomenon, and such a distinctive writer. The 'old things' which he sees and meditates upon lead, on one level, to the kind of fantasy which created Kipling's *Puck of Pook's Hill*:

> Up this same line went the Clans marching when they were called Northward to the host; and up this went slow, creaking wagons with the lead of the Mendips or the tin of Cornwall or the gold of Wales.[2]

But there is something more fundamental revealed by 'The Old Things' than a purely nostalgic ability to imagine the past. It is akin to the fact that Belloc was closer, in spirit and sympathies, to the paganism of the ancient world than to any of the reformed traditions

[1] *First and Last* (1911) p. 155.
[2] Ibid. p. 159.

of Christianity. In 'The Old Things', he remembers a man, a thatcher, who said to him, 'We must have straw from the Lowlands; this upland straw is no good for thatching.' 'Immediately when I heard him say this there was added to me ten thousand years.'[1]

It is central to the whole Bellocian way of looking at the world that being aged by ten thousand years is a good thing. Politically, we tend to divide the human race: between those who do not wish to change things for fear that they will become worse (and these we label conservative); and those who believe that things are so bad that they must be changed; or, alternatively, believe that it is in the nature of things to change and that we must direct these inevitable changes into a desirable direction. (These we label progressives.) Belloc, whose politics owed much to the William Morris socialism of *News from Nowhere*, and much to the radicalism of Cardinal Manning, is equally at variance with 'conservatism' and 'progressivism' thus defined. The ancient dignity of the human race (a myth strengthened in his mind by repeated perusal of Rousseau) can only be recovered; not gained by a new system, but rather by a reversion to an old. These ideas were to be articulated most clearly when Belloc had left Parliament and was working in close collaboration with G.K. Chesterton and his brother Cecil. But they were there, firmly enough, in 1909. The unpublished memoirs which he wrote in 1937 distort what actually happened in 1909, in terms of his own political development. Can one doubt that Belloc imagined, if the 'Radicals' looked for a leader after 1906, they should have found it in the grandson of Joseph Parkes? Jealousy played a very big part in his attitude to Lloyd George.

> His rise at that moment was a first striking example of the degrad-
> ation coming upon politics in this country, a degradation almost
> certainly due to the mixture of cowardice and greed in the gentry,
> who should have defended public life from corruption.[2]

The aristocracy, who had hitherto held the reins of government in this country since the collapse of the monarchy (and, by aristocracy, he did not simply mean the House of Lords, but the cultivated upper class to which Balfour and Campbell-Bannerman had belonged, and which Asquith had joined by marriage), were allowing power to pass into the hands of upstarts and vulgarians. Belloc in general had a low view of Asquith's premiership; a view hardened, after Raymond's death, by their subsequent quarrels over religion. 'Notably he was responsible for having fallen into the hands of a gang of Jews from

[1] Ibid. p. 160.
[2] BC 'Memoirs' 1937

none of whom he had taken any favour, and yet to whom he gave all the advantages which his office permitted him to bestow.'[1] Yet he found gentlemanly qualities in Asquith.

> He was the last in a long series of English Prime Ministers begin-
> ning with Sir Robert Walpole, all of whom had been men acquain-
> ted with the classics and having the ordinary manners at table and in
> a drawing-room of the cultivated classes. With him the prestige of
> position perished.[2]

Belloc is careful not to say that Asquith belonged to the cultivated classes; merely that he had acquired their manners. It would have spoilt his argument to observe that the Nonconformist Yorkshire family of Asquith's grandfather was, if anything, as low in the social scale as that of the Nonconformist Lloyd George. No one could have accused Herbert Asquith of vulgarity.

And it was the vulgarity of his fellow-M.P.s which increasingly irked Belloc. That is why he spent more and more time in the company of George Wyndham. The more they saw of each other, the more the two men saw eye to eye. Wyndham came to share Belloc's view that Parliament was a sham, a waste of time, riddled with corruption. Belloc, while never quite admitting as much, came to see that he had been wrong about the House of Lords. And, of course, their views on Ireland were remarkably close. Belloc never wavered in his defence of the Irish position in the House. He made many speeches on their behalf. For instance, a month before the Budget, on March 3, 1909, there was a very heated debate about the arrest of the editor and manager of the Clonmel Nationalist newspaper, W.J. Murphy, who had been dragged from his house with great violence by the police before dawn. John Edward Redmond, the nationalist M.P., rose to protest against this deliberately provocative act of cruelty. He was followed by Belloc, whose speech was a splendidly turned combination of fury and satire:

> My only object in rising is that it shall not be said in a matter of this
> kind that no protest arose from the Liberal benches. There was a
> time, not a time, of course, which I can remember, for I am a young
> man, when it was impossible for a definite Irish grievance to be
> raised without there being a body of support from the party, if it is
> still a party, to which I am supposed to belong. I am quite certain if I
> did not rise, no one would rise on this side in the matter. And yet

[1] Ibid.
[2] BC 'Memoirs' 1937.

the weight of Liberal opinion in this, as in countless other cases, minor and major, is wholly with the Irish people . . .

He then launched into a wholly characteristic fantasy:

Consider some man – it is an outrageous consideration which will shock all your most tender susceptibilities – some wealthy man, the owner of one of our great newspapers, one of the Levi family or the Harmsworth family – breaking the law. Consider him being dragged out of his bed in Berkeley Square – as it is being dragged out of bed to be wakened at six o'clock in the morning in the snowstorm of last evening.

An Hon. Member: 'I should like to see them.'

Belloc: I should like to see them too. The whole spirit in which your law is administered here is different from the spirit in which it is administered in Ireland.

There is no doubting here where Belloc's loyalties lay. But, like John Redmond himself, Belloc was an enthusiast for Wyndham's Land Act of 1903, and an opponent, at this date, of the out and out Sinn Feiners. If a peaceful solution to the Irish question could be found, if the English could dispense the economic justice to the Irish which they owed them, Belloc, like Redmond, was in favour of it.

It was the only issue over which Belloc ever had a serious quarrel with his wife. It happened in July 1909. Belloc had not been home for periods longer than a week in the course of the whole year; and, when he returned to Sussex, testy and exhausted, he evidently exploded with rage at the way in which she expressed her excessively simple pro-Irish sentiments. She, an American of wholly Irish stock, felt she could not be expected to be loyal to an England that had, in her view, treated her ancestors so brutally. In normal circumstances, Belloc would certainly have sympathised with her point of view. But his friendship with Wyndham was then at its height, and when he went back to London, the quarrel was clearly not patched up.

'My love and Chosen One,' she wrote after him,

Why are you so troubled? I cannot change my nature any more than I can change my eyes and hair. If I said too much about England last night I am very sorry. But if there is the possibility of 'treason' anywhere, it always means that there are two lines of advance. And surely, my beloved, you will bear me witness that I have never been treacherous nor asked treachery of you. Ireland can go her way, and so can England; and since I was the age of Peter [then 5 years old] I have found my consolation in leaving alone those affairs that are not intimately my own. What I *feel* does not matter a penny weight. I love those whom I love, and they are usually those who have loved me. The rest – from them I only ask peace.[1]

Elodie, devoted as she was to making a home at King's Land, must have felt intensely isolated there in the course of 1909 while Parliament was in session. 'This house is an experiment,' Belloc told Wyndham,

> I have pinned everything on to it: I desire to found the little place and to make a security since I was forbidden to inherit one. But it has come so late in my life that it is like a big gamble instead of a quiet creation. The cheques that come in and should build – or now that the building is at last over, be invested – go to that big hole of the past. The whole game depends on how far these large prices I am getting will hold and how long I can go on doing three jobs at once.[2]

The three 'jobs' – being a very prolific author and lecturer; being a Member of Parliament; and being a Sussex householder – were scarcely compatible with one another, and placed severe strains on Belloc's iron strength. In general, the Edwardian period was a leisurely one in which to pursue a political career. By modern standards, the demands made of Members of Parliament – in terms of attending the House, and of visiting their constituencies – were minimal. But Belloc arranged his life at this period in a way which compelled the maximum expenditure of energy and effort.

An article in *Punch* declared,

> Inquiries at the House of Commons elicited the fact that Mr Belloc is the most hard-worked of our younger Parliamentarians. The week-end brings him no respite from his labours, as he invariably spends it in the great heart of Salford among his constituents, where he conducts classes in military history, conversational French, medieval theology and thorough Bass.[3]

He was genuinely concerned to better the lot of the poor. But he was also very anxious not to lose the support of his constituents. And it was hardly practicable, if he was obliged to spend the week in

[1] Bc July 15, 1909
[2] BC August 19, 1909.
[3] Speaight. p. 236.

London, and Friday to Monday in the north, to devote much time to his 'experiment', in Sussex.

'My darling heart, I am so sorry you cannot come home,[1] wrote Elodie to the Reform Club towards the end of April. The reason for his absence in that particular week is given in a letter to Wyndham:

> I have just seen Maurice Baring off to Constantinople with tears in my eyes for I am very fond of him. We had breakfast together, during which I caused a German to act with vivacity: the first time this feat has been accomplished since the charge up the hill at Wattignies on the 16th of October 1793, at about ten minutes to twelve o'clock mid-day, and even then the retirement was carried out with greater precision and *lenteur*.[2]

Baring had, that very week, at last become a Roman Catholic. 'It is an immense thing,' Belloc wrote to Charlotte Balfour. 'They are coming in like a gathering army from all manner of directions, all manner of men each bringing some new force: that of Maurice is his amazing accuracy of mind which proceeds from his great virtue of truth. I am profoundly grateful!'[3]

It is interesting that he should have written so fully of this to Charlotte Balfour, and not mentioned it to Elodie. However little, at this stage in their lives, his wife shared his political interests; however alien she might have felt from his northern constituency, she would surely have responded warmly to this momentous news. Baring was, after all, a friend of hers as well as of her husband.

This was not really the case with George Wyndham. Belloc's devotion to Wyndham was a source of friction with Elodie. The dedicated week-ends which, according to *Punch*, were spent, 'in the grimy heart of Salford', were passed, very largely, in Saighton Grange, Wyndham's beautiful house near Chester. Elodie never went there, although, when Wyndham largely abandoned Saighton in favour of Clouds, his Wiltshire residence, he often urged her to come to stay. Belloc wrote to his friend,

> Your conversation is a thing I actively seek and perpetually wish to enjoy. In early manhood, talk is pleasant for itself and pretty fluid, but when one begins to hear the rumble of the river, & when one begins to notice youth as a thing separate from oneself, then one comes up against the gate of the Quaratine, talk becomes different.

[1] BC April 22, 1909.
[2] BC April 1909.
[3] Quoted Speaight. p. 245.

It divides itself into half that is convention and half that is a sort of food and necessity. One gets at last into communion with other men. You cannot but reject my 'elbowing'. I talk like that from two vices. One, that, when I talk, my machinery gets set to a pace & warms, & one that the more my thought develops under the friction with another mind, the more the externals leave me: it is like the Dervishes who when they are dancing cannot feel knives. All that is the devil for conversation, but nevertheless I must meet minds – high minds – or starve: and I reassert the huge pleasure I have had in so many hours' talk with you. [1]

No one ever called Elodie 'a high mind'. Belloc did not have to spend such long periods away from her; the sad truth is, that he chose to. He was devoted to his wife; he convinced himself that he was still 'in love' with her. Their letters to each other continued to be peppered with endearments of a kind which make Mr and Mrs Mantalini, in *Nicholas Nickleby*, seem positively prosaic in their forms of expression. But, for someone who needed 'friction with another mind', King's Land was not the place. And yet, if he was to continue paying the builders and the servants, there could be no letting up in the strenuous literary activity.

In Holy Week 1909, Belloc descended on his family and, 'in honour of my crucified Saviour', abstained from wine. 'It is hell! Drink muck, think muck! I can't think. I'm thinking like a Cambridge man or an editor of a rag. Oh! Oh! It is abominable, it is a destroyer of guts.'[2]

In this foul mood, he dictated a satirical novel to his new secretary, Miss Ruby Goldsmith, a Jewess who had come to work for him six months before and taken rooms in the village. The finished work was *A Change in the Cabinet*, a somewhat creaking satire, in which a Cabinet Minister called Sir Charles Repton goes mad, gives utterance to all Belloc's own political beliefs, but is cured by quack medicine and elevated to a peerage to make way for a protégé of 'Mary Smith'. Many of the familiar characters are here; the Peabody Yid still exercises his smiling influence over the nation's destiny, and the 'young and popular Prime Minister', as obvious a portrait of Asquith as ever, drifts in and out of the drawing-rooms of pretty young women without very much control over either his parliamentary colleagues or his political 'backers'. As soon as the novel was done, and the Stations of the Cross removed for another year from the drawing-room shelves, and Easter had bibulously arrived, and he had

[1] BC October 11, 1909.
[2] BC Good Friday 1909.

made his communion and then drunk a bottle of Burgundy with his breakfast, Belloc rushed off by the first possible train to London.

★ ★ ★

Wyndham and Belloc used to swap sonnets. Wyndham was a devotee of that poetic form, and one of the many people who has edited the sonnets of Shakespeare. It is to this year of 1909 that the series of Belloc's sonnets belongs which begin, 'The world's a stage'.

> The world's a stage, – and I'm the Superman,
> And no one seems responsible for salary.
> I roar my part as loudly as I can
> And all I mouth, I mouth it to the gallery . . .

The sonnets reflect the violent contrasts in Belloc's life and temperament during this period. On the one hand, there is his passionate involvement in the world of politics, speeches in the House, journeys to Salford, public lectures, loud pronouncements on all the issues of the day. On the other hand, there is the sense that the whole political world was a farce, an artificial charade which he gazed at with the detachment of a stranger.

Equally, in the social world, the poems reflect the contrast between the roaring and jesting and drinking which went on when Belloc was in the company of his friends; and the impulse which made him buy a house on the remotest edge of the Sussex downs, or take to sea in the *Nona*.

> The scenery is very much the best
> Of what the wretched drama has to show.

And yet, while he was in Sussex, the world of Mrs Roebeck always beckoned, 'the day by day of London days'. Anyone who knew the story of Belloc's life, and who found these sonnets, updated, would assume that they belonged to the period of his lonely widowerhood.

J.B. Morton, writing of a much later phase of his life, recorded,

When he was not in the midst of laughter and talk, the expression of his face was not merely pensive but melancholy, and his eyes, which could blaze with anger or light up with gaiety, were the eyes of a man who had suffered . . . On an occasion . . . when my wife was abroad, and I unable to join her, I was surprised to find myself bored (a new experience for me) and at a loose end and disinclined to make any effort. I told Belloc this, and he said: 'I know all about it. It is astonishing how lonely a married man is without his wife, how pointless everything seems. I used to feel exactly as you do now.'[1]

Morton evidently believed, like all Belloc's younger contemporaries, that the habits of melancholy and introspection developed largely after Elodie's death, the enforced solitude, and the solitary nights at the Reform Club. The truth is odder. Life forces upon men burdens which are appropriate to their temperament. Tennyson mooned about in pubs, worried whether there was life beyond the grave, and suffered from a nebulous sense of lost joy long before the death of Arthur Hallam could give these painful sensations of melancholy a focus. In a somewhat similar way, Belloc's sonnets had already created the role which life was going to force him to play. The best of them is (in spite of a regrettable eighth line) very good indeed; in the A.E. Housman league. And it actually seems to contain this intimation that Fate is going to take him at his word, even though he is as yet in ignorance of the programme. The sense here of life's pointlessness is as bleak, certainly, as anything in Housman; and no one reading this poem without a knowledge of its author would guess that it was penned by a devout Catholic. The doughty stoicism of the sestet is grand, exquisitely underplayed. This is what he wrote to Wyndham, differing slightly from published versions:

> The world's a stage: the trifling entrance fee
> To see the show is paid the Registrar.
> The Orchestra is very loud and free,
> And plays no music in particular.
> The programme isn't published that I know:
> The Cast is large. There isn't any plot.
> The acting as a rule is far below
> The very worst of transatlantic rot.
> The only part about it that I like
> Is what they call in English the Foyay
> There I can sit alone awhile & strike
> A match and set my cigarette alight
> And then, when I am weary of the play –
> On with my coat and out into the night.[2]

His letters to Wyndham reveal a longing to write 'serious' poetry. (The sonnets are not considered to be 'serious'.) But the necessity of earning money for King's Land meant that he was unable to choose

[1] Morton. p. 129.
[2] BC Easter Tuesday 1909.

what he wanted to write. In this busy year of 1909, as well as *A Change in the Cabinet*, he published a book on *The Pyrenees* and gathered up a series of newspaper essays with the title *On Everything*. But the major literary labour of the year was the finishing of *Marie Antoinette*.

He had been writing it, on and off, for five years, snatching every available moment for research in the British Museum. When it at last appeared, in the autumn, it was dedicated to George Wyndham. It was, on the whole, well-received, and justified the faith its publishers had placed in it. *The Times Literary Supplement* enjoyed its liveliness and unashamed bias. 'The author is an artist and an historian, with strong prejudice and a definite point of view,' wrote the reviewer. 'He has something of Carlyle's eye for the graphic and the pathetic – and a tendency to fall into Carlyle's exclamatory style when recreating scenes best known to us through Carlyle's descriptions'.[1]

The reviewer was right to comment on the scenic quality of the biography, for it is memorable as a series of magnificent *vignettes*, particularly in its latter stages, when the King has been arrested and executed. 'For yet another hour the silence endured unbroken: ten o'clock struck, amid that silence, and the quarter . . . The Queen heard through the shuttered window the curious and dreadful sound of a crowd that roars far off and she knew that the thing had been done . . .'

Marie Antoinette's childhood in Austria, her bewildered and juvenile reception in the corrupt world of the decayed Bourbon court, her love for Axel de Fersen, are all very competently handled. For all this, it is a biography written under constraint, in fits and starts. He can rise to the great scenes. Indeed, it could be argued that the last three or four chapters, the closing in of the mob, the victory of the revolutionaries, the capture of the Royal Family, the battle of Wattignies and the death of the Queen on the guillotine, are, considered purely stylistically, among the best things Belloc ever wrote. The reconstruction of historical tableaux is something at which he excelled. Has anyone ever equalled his description of June 20, 1789?

That very middle class sight, a great mob of umbrellas wandering in the streets, was full of will: wandering from one place to another, they landed at last in a tennis court which was free, just where a narrow side-street of the southern town makes an elbow. Into that shelter they poured: and over against them, watching all they did from above, from his home across the lane, was Barentin, Keeper of the Seals. He saw the umbrellas folded at the door, the hundreds

[1] October 28, 1909.

pressing in, damply; he saw through the lights of the Court their damp foot-prints on the concrete of the hall – the table brought: Bailly, the president, standing upon it above the throng and reading out the oath that they *'would not disperse till they had given the nation a constitution'* – then he saw the press of men signing that declaration one by one.[1]

The faults of the book, on the other hand, are obvious; and, probably of a kind, were *Marie Antoinette* reprinted today, which would make it impossible for a modern audience to enjoy it. There is the blustering, throat-clearing loudness of the man on a lecture-tour. ('I have repeatedly insisted in this book upon the inability of Marie Antoinette to perceive the French mind.')[2] Then again, for all the scenic effect and the purple prose (of the dying Louis XV: 'Gusts of strong faith swept over him in these failing years, as strong winds, filled with a memory of autumn, will sweep the dead reeds of December'[3]), there is a major flaw in the narrative. He is really far more interested in the French Revolution than he is in Marie Antoinette. At the same time, he is so deeply versed in the story of the Revolution itself that he takes much of the essential background as 'read'. The final effect is of a series of well-worked scenes against a narrative chaos in which opinions are constantly given when what we were seeking was information. Those who tolerated these aesthetic blemishes in the book might yet draw the line at the absurdity and irrelevance of its repeated anti-Jewish gibes and asides. It was perhaps necessary to describe Beaumarchais as a man 'whom the older and higher world remembered as the associate and perhaps the partner of the Jewish clique in London that had published the first dirty lie against Marie Antoinette's chastity when she was yet a child of eighteen'. But there was really no justification for playing Belloc's boring old gramophone record of obsession with the Dreyfus Case. Equally, one wonders whether there might not have been better ways of defending Marie Antoinette's extravagance than this: 'It was never really excessive in amount: the sums we mention when we speak of it are trifling when we compare them with the financial debauchery of our own age. Why, that whole annual increase in her allowance which Turgot had been blamed for making would not have paid for one night's riot in the house of our London Jews.'[4]

[1] *Marie Antoinette* (1909) p. 205.
[2] Ibid. p. 297.
[3] Ibid. p. 67.
[4] Ibid. pp. 89–90.

Whatever the propriety of the sentiments, it was to his own age that he was soon forced to return, to the age of vulgar debauchery and London Jews. For the constitutional crisis forced him once more on to the hustings.

EIGHT

DISILLUSIONMENT
1910–1913

When the House of Lords rejected Lloyd George's Budget proposals, a constitutional crisis was forced upon the Liberal Cabinet. Asquith decided to go to the country.[1] A resolution was passed in the Commons: 'That the action of the House of Lords in refusing to pass into law the financial provision made by the House for the service of the year is a breach of the constitution and a usurpation of the rights of the Commons.' Parliament was then prorogued, on January 8, 1910. The election which followed was to be a quick one. Polling day was on January 15.

Belloc was not in good shape for the election campaign. He had made a lightning lecture-tour of Scotland in the month before Christmas; developed severe laryngitis, which was worsened by dictating every day to secretaries during the Christmas holidays.

Moreover, any Liberal M.P. might have shared his doubts about the party 'if it still is a party to which I am supposed to belong'. It was only Asquith's skill as a diplomatist which held together the disparate elements of the Liberal Party at this date. Like the Labour Party in the parliaments of the 1970's the party of the government was really an alliance, or coalition of quite various political creeds, and over all major issues of the day, except perhaps Free Trade, it was divided: over Ireland, over the question of Imperial and military expansion; over social reform and female suffrage; and over fiscal policy.

When a group of Salford Liberals wrote to the Press giving their reasons for not supporting Belloc's candidature for re-election, he offered to fight the seat as an independent; but, in the event, he was adopted. Privately, to Maurice Baring, he regarded the issue of the election rather jadedly:

> Either at the last moment, men will say 'I don't care how good the Budget is, I simply cannot tolerate this filthy beastly Government with its licensing bills and its educational balderdash and its

[1] Roy Jenkins: *Asquith* p. 202

humbug about the privilege of the Commons'; or else they will say, 'I can't bear the idea of the rich deciding not to tax themselves, and beastly as the Government is, I shall vote for the Budget'.[1]

Publicly, he was, naturally, more defensive of Asquith's administration. The doctor ordered him not to use his voice for three days before the campaign began. Elodie and his eldest son Louis came north with him to appear on the platform; and Baring came along to lend moral support. Then, on January 8, the doctor could restrain him no longer, and the speechifying began. He loved the almost festive air of rudeness which characterised election meetings; the baying, the interruptions, the cries of 'Hear hear!' or 'Nonsense' were meat and drink to him. Although his voice was still croaky, he was possessed of an hilarious and demonic energy on the platform, at thirty-nine already an archaic sight in his long dark overcoat and well-curled bowler hat, gesticulating with an umbrella as he spoke.

'England is at a turning-point,' he shouted. 'Society is trembling with the desire to produce a new and better England. But it cannot be done without raising great sums of money and without putting burdens on the rich. If it is going to be done at all, it is going to be done in the next few weeks. An old man said to me the other day, "This is the first election I remember in which something is going to happen." That is true. You are either going to push the great weight of social reform and democracy over the edge and send it down on the other side, or you are going to allow it to slip back on yourselves and crush you.'

His record as their M.P. was puzzlingly independent, as far as the electors of South Salford were concerned. His teetotalling constituents remembered against him his opposition to the Licensing clauses in the Budget. Even moderate Protestants, perhaps especially moderate Protestants, would have been dismayed by his belligerent insistence that public money should be spent on the maintenance of sectarian schools teaching what the majority of Christian opinion in England regarded as error. And there were strong rumours that Belloc was about to join the ever-increasing ranks of the Labour Party; rumours which had been fanned by his voting with the tiny Labour minority on the Trade Disputes Bill. On the other hand, thorough-going radicals would probably have been dismayed by his extremely conservative attitude to the question of women's suffrage: 'I am opposed to women voting as men vote. I call it immoral, because I think the bringing of one's women, one's mothers and

[1] *Letters* p. 23.

sisters and wives into the political arena, disturbs the relations between the sexes.'[1]

His own mother, together with her friend Barbara Bodichon, had been wanting to get into the political arena since the 1860's, and it had not noticeably marred her relations with Belloc. But in this, as in most public issues, he simply followed the current Roman Catholic party line. His idiosyncratic turns of phrase, and his eccentric appearance, doubtless gave to Belloc's political character the air of wild independence. In fact, if one examines all his most distinctive standpoints – support for Irish nationalism; limited support for the Trade Unions; fear of the Jews in public life; unbending desire for sectarian schools for Jews and Roman Catholics; hostility to female emancipation; a desire for peasant ownership and 'distributed wealth' – one sees that these are the natural views of a man who regarded Cardinal Manning as his mentor.

There were just enough tolerant Protestants and ardent Roman Catholics in Salford to return him to Westminster for a second time; he won the seat by a mere 314 votes. The campaign left him quite exhausted; but, rather than go home, he set off at once for France and tramped about, sometimes on foot, sometimes in trains, in Louviers, Chartres and Paris ('where I hobnobbed with soldiers and renewed my youth'[2]) Gisors, Beauvais, and Amiens ('where I talked learnedly to Commercial Magnates and laid hands on my friends and blessed them and walked all over the roof of the Cathedral with a jolly old man who stank'[3]).

Repose was impossible for him. When he had drained himself of energy in one direction, he could only 'renew his youth' by expending it in some other way, equally exhausting. As the train rattled through the cathedral towns of Normandy, he began to doodle *More Peers*.

> During a late election Lord
> Roehampton strained a vocal chord
> From shouting, very loud and high,
> To lots and lots of people why
> The Budget in his own opin-
> -Ion should not be allowed to win.

Unlike Lord Roehampton, Belloc recovered from his laryngitis and took his seat on the Government backbenches when Parliament reassembled in February. He did so with very mixed emotions. The

[1] Speaight p. 280.
[2] BC February 5, 1910.
[3] Ibid.

election triumphs of 1906 had not been repeated. Asquith did not have an independent victory, since he now depended on the support of the Labour members and Irish Nationalists. The Liberals had 273 seats, the Unionists 273; the Labour Party had 40 seats, the Irish Nationalists 70 and the Independent Nationalists 12.

Belloc's reaction was contemptuous: 'I could have laughed on the floor if I had not been so ill! It is indeed a treat, as the story says. The Party System is "up against it". I am glad Winterton represents me in Parliament and that Sussex is itself again but that is the nearest thing I can get to party feeling.'[1] Winterton, of course, was a Tory.

Belloc's disillusionment with the party system was to increase in the course of the year. The question of the House of Lords remained crucial and delicate. Belloc was all in favour of their power being removed from them absolutely, 'by popular movement! . . . A revolutionary change followed by an act of will need not hurt a nation, but the clinching and making final of a slip or lowering of efficiency does hurt a nation – greatly'.[2]

For Asquith, the matter appeared much less simple. He could not get the Budget proposals through the Commons, let alone through the Lords, without the approval of the Irish members; and they would only lend him support against the Lords on condition that he upset his own nonconformist supporters and removed the duty on whisky which was still a part of Lloyd George's proposals. Asquith would not have been where he was had he been devoid of political cunning; but it was not he who had determined to reduce his absolute majority in the Commons. It was the electorate. The Unionists were not the only ones who would oppose his attempts to reform the House of Lords. Many of his own Cabinet were unhappy about the idea of creating five hundred peers to bring about a *coup d'état*. Sir Edward Grey, the Foreign Secretary, threatened to leave the Government if this proposal went any further; so did John Morley, Gladstone's biographer. Moreover, the King was exceedingly displeased by the notion of the kind of 'revolution' which Belloc and the other Radicals longed for so eagerly. It was indeed a major constitutional crisis, perhaps the most important of the century. Asquith, with no independent majority, only owed his power under obedience to the King, and he would have been behaving with grave constitutional impropriety had he forced through the virtual abolition of the House of Lords without consulting the other parties.

After the most delicate negotiations with all parties, lasting two

[1] BC February 5, 1910.
[2] *Letters* p. 45.

months (amendment of the Budget to suit the Irish, audiences with the King, pacification first of the radicals, then of the 'right wing' Liberals, discussion with the Unionists about their preparedness to reform the Lords in the event of a Liberal government's resignation), the Budget was finally passed through the House of Commons on April 27 and, the next day, through the Lords. The revolution, which so many M.P.s dreaded, and for which Belloc had pined, had been averted. 'Thursday night', wrote the Government Chief Whip, the Master of Elibank, 'saw a grand Parliamentary Triumph for the Prime Minister. All his lost prestige has been recovered.'[1]

For Belloc, it was all sickening. Unlike most of the radicals and Labour members, who looked forward to the abolition of the House of Lords, Belloc did not have in mind a socialist revolution. He wanted a revolution which would get rid of the plutocrats, limit the money-power; the hidden force, as he saw it, which held a sinister control over the Government. He wanted the plutocrats to be replaced, not by plebeians, but by the landed gentry. They were the ones who owned the land (always the test in the Bellocian view); and he blamed them for not standing for parliament in greater numbers. 'The Squires won't come, all the experts will,' he moaned.[2]

Asquith's diplomatic triumph in the spring of 1910 was therefore seen by Belloc as a piece of double-dealing and corruption. On the most important issue facing the Commons, it appeared that the two main parties, the Liberals and the Unionists, were, in the last analysis, prepared to collaborate. Belloc ignored the reduced Government majority, the fact that only radical Liberals (a small proportion of the parliamentary party) wanted a serious conflict with the Lords, the fact that the King was technically the head of state and deeply opposed to the measure. For him, the issue just showed that the whole idea that the Opposition was really opposed to the Government was a sham. 'Balfour and Asquith have come to an understanding which the country in general may not be told but which is now fairly generally known. By this understanding all real attack on the House of Lords will be prevented.'[3]

It is this tacit alliance between the two major parties which forms the core of the comedy in his novel *Pongo and the Bull*. Dolly is still the young and popular Prime Minister, as he had been in *Mr Clutterbuck's Election* and *A Change in the Cabinet*, and he is very recognizable once more as Asquith, of whom Belloc wrote in his 'Memoirs', 'What gave

[1] Jenkins p. 210.
[2] *Letters* p. 45.
[3] Ibid., p. 25.

him the position he did ultimately attain was his second marriage to Margot Tennant . . . She counted as being in the heart of the smart people, not from descent of course, for of that she had none, but from the wealth of her family (though greatly exaggerated) and still more from her associations, coupled with her own demeanour. [Asquith] therefore found himself suddenly swept into a new world, wherein he was rather bewildered. Its inhabitants jeered at him behind his back, as his obviously middle-class manner struck them as ridiculous. On the other hand, as his wife's husband, he was certain to go far'.

In the novels, Asquith (Dolly) is not married to Margot (Mary Smith); she is the widow of an American millionaire and he himself is married to a connection of the Peabody Yid, who, having started life at the beginning of the series as Mr I.Z. Barnett, has now risen to eminence, through the ranks of the peerage, to achieving a dukedom, that of Battersea. ('Battersea House, as all the world knows, occupies the bottom of St James's Street where the gateway to St James's Palace used to stand until it was pulled down under the Broadening of the Streets Bill.')[1]

It is a silly enough tale, full of all the familiar ingredients of Belloc's political fiction – two-dimensional thumb-nail sketches of Edwardian politicians, drawn with a scathing irony. It is set, futuristically, in 1915. One of the biggest jokes is that the railways have been nationalised. Ireland, to Dolly's and Pongo the Leader of the Opposition's intense relief, gained its independence years before. The current crisis is India, which is presenting all the problems Ireland had presented in the bad old days of 1910–11. There have been uprisings, food shortages, and a desire for Home Rule. If the British Government is to maintain its view of itself as altruistic and compassionate, it must find some money for famine relief. The core of the plot, therefore, is a Budget: how to raise cash? Do they borrow from the aged Duke of Battersea? Or will they be able to get a much easier loan (with less conditions attached) from the eccentric American millionaire G. Quinlan Smith, who spends awkwardly long times abroad, hunting for relics of Disraeli on the continent of Europe?

Pongo is not Arthur Balfour. He is a Celt, and although he is not Welsh, but Cornish, it does not take much imagination to notice, in Pongo's stinking dishonesty and ludicrous self-seeking, a resemblance to Belloc's view of Lloyd George; 'He was in height but five feet four inches, and few men who have made a great impression upon their contemporaries could boast so little personal beauty . . .

[1] *Pongo and the Bull* pp. 63-64.

There must have been, as journalists perpetually maintained, some magnetic charm about the man to compensate for physical defects that would otherwise have marred his career.'

The jokes in *Pongo and the Bull* would be impenetrable today to anyone who had not taken the trouble to remind themselves of the political events of 1909–10. But they reflect, as do Belloc's letters of the period, an absolute disillusionment with the Parliamentary system. As early as March, he had written to his Liberal agent in South Salford and told him that he no longer felt any loyalty to the Liberal Government or to the Party System. He realised that another election was quite likely to happen soon, 'and I can't believe the Grocers and pawnbrokers who control the caucus in Salford will stand a candidate pledged to ridicule & criticise the Party System & if they won't have me independent they shan't have me at all: if they *will* have me they will be idiots, for I shall be defeated & they will have paid for nothing'.

His predictions were right. The constitutional crisis concerning the Lords continued throughout 1910, complicated in May by the death of Edward VII and the accession of George V, who handled the whole matter with great delicacy and acumen. George V very much resented the secrecy with which the negotiations were undertaken, and was personally anxious to preserve the ancient privileges of the House of Peers. But the King agreed, once Asquith had been forced into the position where he had to go to the country for a second election within the year, that, in the event of a Liberal majority being returned, the five hundred necessary peers would be created.

The election, actually, solved nothing. It was the 'most apathetic in living memory', according to Sir Sidney Low. Only a million votes were cast in the entire country. Many seats changed hands. There was one fewer Unionist than in the previous Parliament; three fewer Liberals; the Labour Party and the Irish Nationalists each gained two seats. Those who had bothered to vote had refused to treat the election as a mere referendum over the Lords issue, and in many constituencies the main topic debated was Tariff Reform.[1] Thus it was, in spite of the enthusiasm of some remaining Liberal Cabinet Ministers like Winston Churchill for the reform of the House of Lords, that the situation went on much as it had done before.

> Lord Calvin thought the Bishops should not sit
> As Peers of Parliament. And argued it.
> In spite of which, for years, and years, and years,
> They went on sitting with their fellow-peers.

[1] *Edwardian England 1901–1914*, ed. Simon Nowell Smith (1964) p. 82.

Mutatis mutandis, Roy Jenkins, in his biography of Asquith, presents the year 1910 as a political muddle, a cataclysmic storm which threatened to burst over the Prime Minister's head, which resolved itself into a series of unpleasant little squalls. Other commentators and historians, too, make it clear that opinion on both sides of the Commons was divided over the issue; and it is unlikely that the majority of Liberal M.P.s wanted to change the constitution, or even radically to modify the powers of the second chamber. To this day, abolitionists, such as Belloc professed himself to be, are thin on the ground. Late into the century plans from the Left to create enough peers to vote in their own abolition are regarded as disadvantageous electorally.[1]

But, although most observers regarded the history of Asquith's Parliament as a subtle and difficult one, the whole matter was as clear as day to Belloc. He surveyed scornfully 'the usual flood of third-rate rhetoric' from Asquith over this 'sham battle with the House of Lords'.[2]

When the election came round – 'this tom-fool election' – Belloc did not stand again. Before dissolution, he declared in Parliament that 'I shall be quite unable to meet any constituents unless local opinion is so indicated and local machinery is so controlled that I may come forward in complete independence of the system which I now fully understand and which I now clearly believe to be both unreal and dangerous to the country. I do not see how anyone can stand in an English constituency today and say; "If you return me I will vote in favour of this or that set of men, self-appointed, who are going to bring forward some programme I know not what." '[3]

Just before he made this speech, Belloc had been over to Ireland, 'What an eye-opener to revisit Ireland after ten years & to be in the midst of those realities after the ridiculous stench of Westminster!'[4]

Can he really have been as *naïf* as he seems? Can he really have been surprised that all political issues get blurred and muddled in parliamentary debate, and that they change as a result of electoral accident?

[1] See *The Times*, June 12, 1982. 'Labour's plan for the abolition of the House of Lords, which is likely to be endorsed by the party executive next week on the basis of a home policy committee decision taken on Thursday, produced no nervous reactions from the Government ministers yesterday. They believe that Mr Wedgwood Benn's plan for the creation of 1,000 peerages among Labour supporters for the sole purpose of getting rid of the Second Chamber will prove to be a vote loser at the next General Election.'
[2] BC 'Memoirs' 1937.
[3] Speaight p. 295.
[4] BC November 14, 1910.

The constitutional crisis was, in a way, an irrelevance, as the indifference of the electorate showed. They *were* interested in Lloyd George's Budget; but there is no evidence that the electorate wanted the House of Lords destroyed because of it. Would it really have been the act of a responsible government to force through the issue in a hung parliament against the wishes of the King, the Lords, most of the Commons and the electorate? Apparently Belloc thought it would.

It is hard to know, precisely, what he was complaining about, as he grumbled out his last few weeks as M.P. for Salford. He knew all about the party system of the Asquith world, and he knew quite well that members of both Front Benches were intermarried; that they attended the same dinner parties, went to the same schools and flirted with the same selection of Tennant, Horner, Elcho, Asquith and Grenfell womenfolk. These were not reasons for conscientious objection to pursuing a parliamentary career in 1906; they were, apparently, in 1910. Asquith had been compromised; bought, no doubt, by the rich Jews in his wife's circle, just as Lloyd George's very radical Budget had (for some reason) been devised by 'bankers'.

'Perhaps they did not bribe me heavily enough, but I am relieved to be quit of the dirtiest company it has ever been my misfortune to keep,' he said, when he had finally left the House. This is all the sheerest fantasising. No one pretends that politicians are the most honest or congenial of men. Whatever Belloc's motives for entering politics; he certainly had no excuse for any such supposition. He moved in the same drawing-rooms for ten years before mixing with them in the smoking-room of the House. He had assiduously cultivated the company of Lloyd George since 1902. But, when he actually came to do the job, he did not enjoy being an M.P. It was very tiring, and it was very boring. A good parliamentarian has strong principles which he need never abandon. At the same time, he must be flexible enough to see that events move rapidly and frequently to shed new light on issues which, the previous week, had looked quite different. Accidents happen. Change sometimes occurs by chance rather than by design. Very few matters for debate, in what is fundamentally a legislative assembly, are all 'black and white'. This was something which Belloc never recognised in the House of Commons. *All human conflict is ultimately theological*, Manning had told him, words which ate into his soul. He evidently took them to mean that every politician who did not conduct himself in the way he hoped was in a state of mortal sin.

Men do not go to the trouble of becoming M.P.s unless they want political power. The priest at St James's, Spanish Place who predicted that Belloc would have Cabinet office echoed ambitions over which he had no control. Did he not dine with the Front Bench? Did they not know his qualities? Belloc was not the only example of a man who made a clown of himself, and yet expected to be taken deeply seriously. The novels he wrote and the speeches he made in his latter years as an M.P. reflect the awkward love-hate feelings which he nursed for the English establishment. He wanted to be inside. But, once in, he wanted to tell them that they were doing it all wrong; everything was better in Catholic Europe: in Ireland, Poland, or France. It had happened at Oxford, and given him an obsession with the 'Whig' view of history then promulgated. In the same year as he left Parliament he was also attacking such institutions as the *Edinburgh Review* which 'has a shit (si j'ose m'exprimer ainsi) writing on it whom I strongly suspect to be *George Macaulay Trevelyan . . .* '

Almost as bad was the British Academy. 'The New English Academy! The 40 immortals – have you read the list? Wow, wow! Christ help us what a list . . . '

His disgust with Parliament, therefore, needs to be seen beside his disgust with almost all institutions except the Church of Rome. In almost all cases, there was an initial fascination followed by a most violent feeling of revulsion. He was bored with Parliament. He was hanging on to a tiny majority, and he was almost certain to lose his seat at the next general election. But he gives as his reason for leaving: 'Perhaps they did not bribe me heavily enough . . . ' Who were 'they'? The Rothschilds? The Isaacses? The Master of Elibank? What were they bribing him to do, or not to do? Certainly not to take office. The really intolerable thing about his fellow M.P.s was that they were not, for the most part, interested in being lectured on military history, nor being treated to very predictable Roman Catholic arguments on all the other social issues of the day. This hurt. Furthermore, when confronted with the confused processes of parliamentary debate, with committee stages and second readings, Belloc's ideas were thrown into confusion. M.P.s for most of their debating lives are not interested in wide general principles but in what the Honourable Member for South Salford thinks about Section C, Paragraph 28 of some particular suggestions. As we shall see, his claim that Lloyd George's Budget was 'excellent' was quickly forgotten. It is hard not to feel that his desire to abolish the House of Lords was not the merest posturing, the position likeliest to attract most attention to himself. There is a ludicrous romanticism about his fury with the 'squires' for not 'coming down' instead of the 'jumped-up' working class and lower-middle class types who now seemed to be in the ascendancy.

So much for his position vis-à-vis the Party. As far as his job was concerned – the hours when the House was in session, the days he had to spend in his vile constituency, the tedious travel which it involved: Belloc was understandably bored by the whole thing. Four years was enough of it. He wanted, and needed (if he was to make enough money for his family and household), to go on writing. In April, he had exclaimed, 'The sight of work makes me sick! It lies about my table.'

> A Book of Essays. Dull to Extinction (in proof)
> An uncompleted Novel. ,, ,, ,, (In M.S.S)
> An Essay on Economics. Good but I won't [finish it].
> 3 Rhyme Stories for Basil Blackwood to illustrate. The sight of them is like the tooth-ache.
> The 4th chapter of the Child's History of Sussex, poor little bugger!
> ½ my article on the Song of Roland for the Quarterly. All of which God forfend.[1]

This was by no means an uncharacteristic work-load. Of course, it was, by most sane standards, 'too much'. But Belloc was now addicted to working in this way. There are many easier ways of making money than by churning out book after book. Belloc did not wish to take them. In the course of only a few months, this pile of paper and rubbish on his table at King's Land would turn into *On Anything*, and *Pongo and the Bull*. The economic essay would gell a little in his mind before it became *The Servile State*. But, by a supreme irony of literary history, it was the nonsense verse, awaiting its illustration by 'BTB', which was to carry Belloc's name down to posterity. As in his parliamentary speeches, he strove to create *More Peers*. Those whom the Government had already ennobled had less kind words from Belloc. The Barony of Swaythling had been created by Campbell-Bannerman in 1907, and Belloc celebrated the demise of the first Baron Swaythling with a memorial verse which he had printed and circulated among his friends:

> Lord Swaythling whom we loved and knew
> On earth as Mr Montagu,
> Will probably be known in hell
> As Mr Moses Samuel:

[1] BC April 2, 1910.

> For though they do not sound the same,
> The latter is his real name.[1]

The next few years were to prove many of Belloc's apparently outrageous hunches right, and to reveal that parliamentary life had, indeed, sunk into the pits of corruption. In 1910, he did not know half of it; he merely sensed its 'ridiculous stench'. He left, not because it was corrupt, but because it prevented him from doing work which interested him more.

In the smoking-room of the Commons. Lloyd George approached his erstwhile supporter towards the end of 1910, and said that he was sorry that Belloc's political career appeared to be over. 'So I replied to him: "One day, you will be finished and forgotten. But I, like my Saviour, will rise again on the Third Day": which shocked that little Welsh Nonconformist.'

*   *   *

It is hard to avoid the feeling that Belloc emerged from his parliamentary career a harder man, a bitterer man, and, which is more difficult to forgive, a less funny man. Much of the bitterness undoubtedly stemmed from his poverty. He had inherited his mother's inability to deal with money. He had also inherited his mother, who needed perpetual financial support. He had a wife and five growing children. The essential and very basic improvements to King's Land had been more expensive than he had predicted. He had, as he never tired of reiterating, no private fortune. He was compelled to earn his keep.

Earning a living is, doubtless, a very irksome necessity. But Belloc sometimes spoke as if it were a burden he alone had been called upon to bear. And he did not make it easy for himself when employment did come his way. In the autumn of 1910, at the very moment when he should have been consolidating his journalistic career, in preparation for his abandonment of politics, he broke his link with the *Morning Post*. He had been a Literary Editor of the paper for five years. No one pretends that the relations between Literary Editors and their superiors have always been easy. From above, there is often a resentment that too much space in the paper is being snatched for 'literary' material; or that authors are being used to review books whose views do not coincide with that of the paper as a whole. Literary editors, moreover, are notoriously lazy men, apt to regard their job as a sinecure. From below, on the other hand, there are natural feelings of

[1] Polite version.

resentment at 'editorial interference'. The books pages are not taken sufficiently seriously, and not enough space is devoted to them.

At the *Morning Post*, the editor, Sir Fabian Ware, was a strong personality, and there were frequent eruptions, a note surviving from March 23, 1909 gives the flavour of his relationship with his Literary Editor:

> Dear Belloc,
> I owe you an apology for the way I shouted at you this afternoon; but *please* don't, on your rare and unexpected visits to the office (about which I shall say more on another occasion), stand in my door and wag a finger at me when I am engaged on a private and difficult business. Yours F.W.[1]

The clash between the two men was inevitable. One of the difficulties which always arose when Belloc took employment was that he could not tolerate having a superior; nor was it temperamentally possible for him (for all his prodigious energy, and power of hard work) to keep hours. He only ever took 'jobs' as a way of making money. What is nowadays called 'job satisfaction' is not something which he ever found in employment. He found satisfaction on his own farm; in his own boat and (very occasionally) writing his own books. But he could not be dictated to.

Of course, once he had broken with the *Morning Post*, the quarrel with Ware was elevated into a matter of principle. Since Belloc's visits to his office had become increasingly rare, and since he did nothing about the Literary Page of which he was nominally in charge, Ware not unnaturally asked him to abandon his position as Literary Editor and, instead, to become a weekly columnist in the paper. This row blew up in June 1910. By September, Belloc, failing to recognise who was calling the tune, issued Ware with an ultimatum. If he did not have a written undertaking by September 2 that Ware intended to keep him on his old salary, he would be compelled to sever his connexion with the paper. Unsurprisingly, Ware did not reply; he saw no reason why the *Morning Post* should continue to pay a man who was not doing his job. From Belloc's position, it had come to feel, quite sincerely, like a matter of burning principle. Ware was getting rid of him, he felt, because he had written articles 'disrespectful to the wealthy'.[2]

Belloc was cutting off his nose to spite his face. Had he been

[1] Quoted Speaight p. 258.
[2] Speaight p. 257.

temperamentally capable of working regular hours as another man's subordinate, he would have been able to see more of King's Land and more of Elodie. He did not realise it, but time was running out on his marriage.

1911 and 1912, rather than providing him with respite, were among the busiest years of his life. Abandoned by the *Morning Post*, he wrote over thirty articles in the year April 1911–April 1912: for the *Glasgow Herald*, for *The Academy*, for the *National Defence Magazine*, for *The Bellman*, for *The New York World*, for anyone who would publish him.

Nor did his freedom from obligations at Salford mean that he had any more time to spend in Sussex. An essential source of income for him, since he scorned conventional employment, was the money he managed to collect by lecturing. During this same period, 1911–12, he got thirty guineas from Folkestone Girl's School for three talks. But he was evidently prepared to sink his price to as low as five guineas for the Richmond Athenaeum. That winter was dominated by weekly, sometimes twice-weekly, treks to address the Hull Catholic Federation on the Battle of Crécy; the Hale Literary Society on French poetry; the Bristol and District Fabian Society on the Party System; and on unspecified subjects at Crouch End, Harrogate, Leeds, Merthyr Tydfil and Worthing, all of which he visited in the space of seven weeks.[1]

This would have been an exhausting programme had he merely thought to combine it with family life. But, of course, this lecturing and writing of articles was merely a money-spinning sideline to the main business of his life at this date. For, in these years 1911 and 1912, he wrote seventeen books; he founded, organised and ran a periodical of his own, which was to play a uniquely important role in the political life of the nation; he had increased, rather than diminished, the extent of his foreign travels.

Even if you modify this statement and say that, of the seventeen books, some are extremely short and at least two are almost word for word the same;[2] and even if you take the view that Cecil Chesterton really did all the work on *The Eye Witness*, these years provide strong evidence of Belloc's almost preternatural energies. For out of the teeming hurry and steam of these years – the drunken nights and bleary-eyed mornings, late for mass and late for trains; the lost tickets and the lost temper; the tedious hack-work, and the pot-boiling – out of all this cauldron came bubbling some of Belloc's finest works: two

[1] The previous two paragraphs derive from work-sheets, income tax returns and appointment diaries at BC.
[2] *The Servile State* and *Socialism and the Servile State*.

brilliant books of political analysis (*The Servile State* and *The Party System*), one of his best works of historical topography (*The River of London*) a quite excellent series of little battle books (*Blenheim, Waterloo, Crécy, Malplaquet, Turcoing*); two works, one imaginative and one analytical, on his pet subject of late eighteenth-century France (*The Girondin* and *The French Revolution*), a splendid volume of *More Peers* and, in the middle of it all, the book which is perhaps his masterpiece, *The Four Men*.

*   *   *

By the time Belloc collaborated with Cecil Chesterton to produce *The Party System* (1911), he had already given repeated vent to feelings of outrage that the Front Benches of both Government and Opposition belonged to the same 'set', and, very often, to the same families.

We are not surprised at Romeo loving Juliet, though he is a Montague and she is a Capulet. But if we found in addition that Lady Capulet was by birth a Montague, that Lady Montague was the first cousin of old Capulet, that Mercutio was at once the nephew of a Capulet and the brother-in-law of a Montague, that Count Paris was related on his father's side to one house and on his mother's side to the other, that Tybalt was Romeo's uncle's stepson and that the Friar who married Romeo and Juliet was Juliet's uncle and Romeo's first cousin once removed, we should probably conclude that the feud between the two houses was being kept up mainly for the dramatic entertainment of the people of Verona.[1]

Lest any modern reader be tempted to think that this analogy is far-fetched, one does well to remember the letter Belloc wrote to Maurice Baring shortly before his Parliamentary career came to an end:

On Thursday is the big division which will wind up the session, I suppose; the division which will give the resolution of the Commons defying their brothers-in-law, stepfathers and aunts' lovers in the Lords. Thus Geoffrey Howard will defy Lord Carlisle while the more dutiful Morpeth will acquiesce in his father's power. Kerry will similarly support the privilege of Lansdowne but Fitzmaurice (oddly enough) will be of an adverse opinion. Alfred Lyttelton will think the power of the peers reasonable; not his sister's husband, Masterman, who will however be supported by his wife's first cousin Gladstone; while the Prime Minister will not find his brother-in-law, Mr Tennant, fail him, nor need he

[2] *The Party System* (1911) p. 76.

doubt Mr. McKenna, since he had married the daughter of the Tennants' chief friend. Oddly enough, however, while Pamela Tennant's husband will support the Government, her brother Mr. George Wyndham, will not find it possible to agree with them. His stepson, the Duke of Westminster, has privileges not to be despised, and it is curious that the young gentleman's wife's step-nephew, Mr Winston Churchill, should be found in the Liberal ranks. However it is some compensation to this member that his aunt is the mother-in-law of the Tariff Reform League in the person of Lord Ridley, called by the vulgar Fat Mat.[1]

The Party System was Belloc's first sustained essay in the journalism of political analysis. To the modern eye it will seem innocent in its anger. It is decades in England since anyone imagined that back-bench M.P.s had any power. They are simply 'lobby-fodder' who, obedient to their whips, must walk through the 'aye' or the 'no' doors in defence to the wishes and policies of the 'front bench', the Cabinet or the Shadow Cabinet. In recent years, a surprising amount of fuss was caused by the publication of the *Diaries* of Richard Crossman. They caused a stir because they showed that all major political decisions in this country are made, not in the House of Commons, but in the Cabinet, by a tiny clique surrounding the Prime Minister. This style of government was labelled by Crossman 'presidential', as though things had ever been otherwise. All that the diaries did was to show, once again, that Great Britain, which calls itself a 'democracy', is, and always has been, an oligarchy.

Fifty-five years before this fact came to excite Richard Crossman, it became clear to Belloc as he sat on the Government back benches in the House of Commons. Astonishingly to us, it was not publicly known at that date. There was a widespread belief that the Government or the Opposition listened intently to each opinion expressed in the Chamber before making up its mind on all the issues of the day. And it was further imagined (at least by Belloc, apparently, when he was new to the game) that all the M.P.s on one side of the House were passionately opposed to everything believed by those on the other side. In fact, as Belloc came to see, decisions made in Parliament were made by small groups, close to the Party leaders. And it became his further belief (as we have seen, over the constitutional crisis of 1910) that the Leaders of Government and Opposition were actually in cahoots. It does not seem to strike him that it would be very dangerous to this country if this were not the case: if one party, say,

[1] Quoted Christopher Hollis: *The Mind of Chesterton* p. 114.

were capable of changing the constitution radically by abolishing the second chamber against the wishes of the majority of the electorate, and the wishes of Parliament. In what he took to be the great days of Parliamentary democracy, Pitt and Fox minded so much about the issues which divided them that they did not speak to each other outside the Chamber. Asquith and Balfour hobnobbed like gentlemen, or, as Cecil Chesterton and Belloc would have it, like hypocrites.

All this is precisely and vigorously argued in *The Party System*. The analysis is devastatingly built up; and its idealistic position is made clear from the moment that it is asserted that 'it is surely ridiculous to say that a man represents Bethnal Green if he is in the habit of saying "Aye" when the people of Bethnal Green would say "no".'[1]

The authors move on from this position to an analysis of the Party System as a whole; *en passant*, side-swipes are delivered against corruption in high places, and, in particular, against the sale of peerages. The political ills of the day are attributed with heady simplicity to the bi-party system. For it is a system which itself depends on 'the secret funds, the unmentionable truth'. As for the source of these funds, 'everyone acquainted in the smallest degree with the inside of politics knows that there is a market for peerages in Downing Street, as he knows that there is a market for cabbages in Covent Garden'.[2]

The Party System retains its historical importance today, not because, in lashing out against abuse, it happened to hit a few well-deserved targets, but because of the effect it had on the public attitude to journalism. Its claims were only implicit, and had not been worked out fully by Belloc, or by Cecil Chesterton, at the time of publication. Perhaps they were never fully worked out by either man. But, however unspecific their analysis, they were making an implicit claim that political power should pass out of the hands of party backers, out of the hands of suppliers of funds, out of the hands of politicians themselves and into that of journalists. If politicians could not be trusted, where could we look for the truth? If their representatives said 'aye' against their wishes, where could the people of Bethnal Green say 'no'?

Historically, the answer has been an enormous increase in the power and importance of the Press. The cliché that 'we ought to be told' did not originate solely with Belloc. Ours is the century of the

[1] *The Party System* p. 17.
[2] Ibid. p. 104.

great Press barons in the USA and in Great Britain: in Italy, Mussolini, the first great dictator of modern times, was not merely in awe of the Press, he was in some ways its creation. Perhaps *The Party System*, and what followed it in Belloc's career, had little to do with that. But it has much to do with another strand of journalistic history. President Nixon fell, not because of Watergate, but because Watergate was discovered by journalists. Minor versions of the same calamity go on all over the West, month by month. Politicians live in fear of being found out. The serious downfall of at least one senior British politician was started as a piece of apparently fantastical tittle-tattle in *Private Eye* (a highly Bellocian periodical). When *The Party System* was published, there was no *Private Eye* which could bring to light the scandals and secrets which that book hints at so darkly. There was no newspaper which would take that risk. (The crowing of W. T. Stead over poor Sir Charles Dilke in the 1880s had happened *after* Dilke's "exposure" in the divorce courts.)

The immediate consequence of the publication of *The Party System* was that Charles Granville and a few others put up the money for the foundation of a new paper to expose the cant and the hypocrisy of the British political system. It was called *The Eye Witness*. Belloc was made editor with Cecil Chesterton as his second-in-command.

Belloc lacked 'staying power' in literary or journalistic enterprises. His interest in the books and periodicals on which he was engaged could never be sustained for longer than, at most, six months. But, before *The Eye Witness* had become 'the wretched thing' to him, and when he was still enthusiastic about it, Belloc was an inspired editor. He attracted as contributors many of the most interesting writers of the day. George Bernard Shaw, H.G. Wells, H.A.L. Fisher, Maurice Baring, Sir Arthur Quiller-Couch and Wilfrid Blunt all wrote for its early numbers. It was an age, unlike our own, in which weekly journals were read, and bought, extremely widely. After Belloc's first six months as editor, *The Eye Witness* had a circulation larger than any other weekly except *The Spectator*. Even so, without sufficient advertising, it was hard work keeping the enterprise financially solvent. It was reckoned that, in order to pay its way, *The Eye Witness* needed to sell 100,000 copies each week.[1] Nowadays, this figure seems extraordinarily large. The habit of reading 'weeklies' has generally died; their place has been swallowed up, partly by the Sunday newspapers, and partly by

[2] Speaight p. 308.

television. Papers like *The Spectator* and *The New Statesman* would think they were doing extremely well if they had a circulation half that of the original *Eye Witness*.

The Eye Witness was, as has been said, a new thing in English journalism. It was, in effect, trying to establish an alternative source of power to that of Westminster, to substitute government by a clique of well-born or wealthy families with government by a posse of journalists. At the time, they did not realise the import of what they were doing. They saw themselves merely as irritants, deliberately worrying the public, and threatening the politicians, with hints of corruption in public life. G.K. Chesterton, Cecil's elder brother, had no doubts, in his *Autobiography*, of the historical importance of it all:

> I can remember old Tories like my grandfather would actually pause in the full sweep of their denunciations of Mr Gladstone, to wave away the faintest suggestion that there could be any fiends rending the souls of our statesmen less erected, as Milton says, than the fiends of ambition or jealousy: 'Heaven forbid that I should suggest that any English Prime Minister'. . . . No; Frenchmen might have discovered the negotiable value of coins of the realm; Italians and Austrians might think it well worth while to double their income; the statesmen of Bulgaria or Bolivia might have some notion of the meaning of money; but English politicians passed their lives in an absent-minded trance, like that of Mr Skimpole; kept their eyes fixed on the fixed stars, never enquired whether politics had made them richer or poorer; and received their salaries with a start of surprise. Well, for good or evil, all that is dead. And what killed it was primarily the journalistic explosion called *The Eye Witness*.

Although GKC revered the memory of his brother, he was honest enough to recognise that the relentless exposure of skulduggery in high places was, in fact, a mixed blessing. The object of the paper had been, very largely, to make the public aware of the evils of public corruption. The danger is that, once they know, the public will begin to take corruption for granted. Too much exposure of the human frailty of politicians merely has the effect of making the public cynical.

> I know that my Victorian uncles did not know how England is really governed. But I have a strong suspicion that if my Victorian uncles had known, they would have been horrified, and not amused; and they would have put a stop to it somehow. Nobody is trying to put a stop to it now.

Thus, in a typically GKC paradox, one sees that an enterprise designed to combat corruption actually had the opposite effect. And this is a phenomenon which one sees in succeeding generations. The American public is more, and not less, hardened to the idea of political corruption since Watergate. The English public is more corrupted in its political innocence by *Private Eye* than by the private misdemeanours of peers or Cabinet Ministers.

But there was a further disadvantage in *The Eye Witness*'s crusade, and that was in the character of Cecil Chesterton himself. Because of his early demise, his friends liked to speak of him in the hushed tones which are reserved for discussion of the Sanctified. In GKC's *Autobiography* Cecil emerges as a benign good-hearted creature, whose argumentative nature was never known to quarrel. A similarly rosy view of Cecil emerges in the memoirs of his widow, *The Chestertons*. Others formed a different impression. Sir Thomas Beecham remembered

> that the first sight of him was a distinct shock. I had pictured to myself a dashing and romantic knight of the pen, a champion of dangerous but righteous causes, and here was one of the most ill-favoured and unprepossessing individuals I had ever looked on. His method of speech – or rather delivery of it – it was hardly better, for he stammered, stuttered and spluttered and seemed to swallow his tongue as well as his words when he became carried away by enthusiasm or indignation.[1]

From the first, the shrill tone of editorials in *The Eye Witness* reflected Cecil's approach to public questions; and, as Belloc gradually lost interest in the paper, Cecil's influence over it increased, until he eventually became editor, with unhappy results.

But perhaps the most important thing about Cecil, from the point of view of Belloc's life-story, is the warmth of feeling which soon developed between him and the Bellocs. He fast became 'Uncle Cecil'. Evidently, he was one of those characters, so frequently, and justly, unattractive to grown-ups, who are 'good with children'. The Bellocs all liked his jokes, antics and high, squeaky stammer. Moreover, unlike so many of the Belloc's friends, he appeared to have all the time in the world for Elodie. In March 1912, Elodie had still not so much as seen the inside of George Wyndham's houses.[2] But she had frequent and warm conversations with Cecil Chesterton.

It was his friendship with these two very different men – Wyndham

1 Frances Donaldson: *The Marconi Trial* (1962) p. 69.
2 BC March 16, 1912.

and Cecil Chesterton – which shaped the development of Belloc's political opinions in 1911–13. And one sees this fact most nakedly displayed in Belloc's *volte-face* about Lloyd George. Although he had cultivated Lloyd George's company when he hoped to profit by it, there is no evidence that Belloc ever liked 'that little Welsh Nonconformist' personally. On the other hand, apart from this desire to levy a duty on whisky and to bring in Licensing laws, Lloyd George had represented, in the Parliament of 1906–10, all the things which Belloc, as an advanced radical, had cherished. Lloyd George was 'the people's champion'; and was welcomed as such by the member for South Salford. His Budget of 1909 had been 'excellent'. By 1911, however, when Belloc was out of Parliament, Lloyd George's Insurance Bill was greeted in *The Eye Witness* with explosions of horror and derision.

The British nowadays take National Insurance so much for granted that it is hard to appreciate how much animation it aroused when it was first introduced. All who have enjoyed sickness benefit, maternity benefit, child benefit, unemployment benefit or an old age pension take it for granted that the only way to pay for these advantages is to put aside a proportion of our weekly income and stick the stamps on the card.

Belloc, one might have thought, would have welcomed the measure. He had been passionately keen on eliminating poverty. Lloyd George's Act was the first stage of a social programme which provided tangible, practical ways of bringing the worst extremity of poverty in Great Britain to an end. That, whatever the inadequacies of Lloyd George's private life, is why the poor of England and Wales loved Lloyd George and still love him. His sexual conduct, his untrustworthiness with money and his humble social origins all rankled with Belloc. None of them can be denied. But it seems petty to concentrate on them to the exclusion of remembering that at the beginning of the twentieth century the poor were dying of starvation on the streets of London; by the middle of the century, they were not; and this was very largely due to the enterprise of David Lloyd George. Belloc, who assailed Lloyd George so persistently from 1911 onwards, achieved nothing of an analagous beneficence.

Belloc, rather oddly for a man who had been so rigid in his radical republicanism for twenty years, dicovered an emotional kinship with men who were neither radical nor republicans. On the one hand, he had befriended George Wyndham. This meant that his opposition to the Lords underwent a subtle transformation. His objection to the power of the House of Lords was that it was a body composed of parvenus and plutocrats, with no prizes for guessing the ethnic origins of some of the more recently elevated 'peers'. He pined, instead, for 'the squires' to come down and purge the House of Commons.

In Cecil Chesterton, Belloc found his hostility to the Jews mirrored, distorted and magnified to an almost grotesque degree. Cecil was spittingly, uncontrollably anti-semitic. Never having had the responsibility of being a practical politician, Cecil's views never needed to come down to the ground. Having dabbled with various forms of socialism and found them unsatisfactory, he discovered, in his conversations with Belloc, that it was possible to be a radical without socialism. The great political principle at stake for a disciple (as Belloc still was) of the French Revolution was that of Liberty. Having decided that he detested Lloyd George, that he was jealous of his success and horrified by his lifestyle, Belloc realised that he could not maintain a political position which had anything in common with the 'jumped up' Chancellor of the Exchequer. He further discovered, after writing several articles on the subject in *The Eye Witness*, and after discussing it with Cecil, that the new Insurance Bill was actually a threat to Liberty as Danton would have understood it. What would one expect from an idea which had originated with Bismarck? 'Licking stamps for Lloyd George' was, among all its other absurdities, kowtowing to 'Prussianism'.

It can not be denied that a confusion of motive led to Belloc's disillusionment with English politics. His friendships have been mentioned, always passionately important to him. Nor can one ever forget, when reading his economic and political analyses, two of the most fundamental catastrophes in his own personal mythology: the destruction of his French family home by the Prussian soldiery of 1870; and the destruction of his English family fortune by 'speculators' on the Stock Market a few years later.

But that is not to deny that the book which grew out of all these broodings, reflections and experiences, *The Servile State*, is a sharply brilliant analysis of what was past, and passing and to come in the capitalist powers of the West.

One might think, given his objection that the Insurance Act was a 'tax on the poor', and his contempt for the collectivist views of Sidney and Beatrice Webb ('"running" the poor is their hobby'[1]) that *The Servile State* is a futuristic vision of the horrors of socialism. But this is not so.

The Servile State is the capitalist one. Belloc believed that modern

[1] McCarthy p. 284.

industrial society had produced a new kind of slavery; whereby a small majority of rich men persuaded the majority of their fellow-citizens to work for wages. The wage-slaves were never going to earn enough or own enough to make them independent of their employers or owners.

Belloc saw very clearly, as did his friend Shaw, that the obvious alternative to this sort of exploitation was a socialist or collectivist state: the sort of state which the Insurance Act of 1911 appeared to herald, and to which Shaw, H.G. Wells and the Webbs eagerly looked forward.

The rhetorical brilliance of *The Servile State* is its demonstration that these two apparent opposites, Capitalism and Socialism, are in fact different words for the same thing. He predicted that the collectivists would work harder and harder to take industry into public ownership and to increase taxation to a level of confiscation to pay for their enterprises. How right he was. But the twist of his argument is contained in the insight that 'all so-called socialist experiments in municipalisation and nationalisation were merely increasing the dependence of the community upon the capitalistic class'.

When we consider that Belloc's Utopian contemporaries really believed that a collectivist state could flourish *without* Capitalism, his economic grasp seems quietly admirable. In fact, as we can see from the history of modern Russia which, after its revolution in 1917, tried to abolish money itself, collectivist states depend more, and not less, than capitalist ones on the power of bankers and brokers to bail them out and pay their bills.

There was in Belloc's view, only one solution; and it was a solution contained in the political encyclicals of Pope Leo XIII. The only solution to the dilemma of Western society, poised between bankruptcy and slavery, was to spread the restoration of private property. Very simply, this was that every man should own three acres and a cow. It was an anti-industrial, anti-capitalist, anti-modern view. And all Belloc's love of Sussex, and King's Land; his admiration for George Wyndham's Irish Land Act; his devotion to Catholic Europe went into the apparently dry analyses of *The Servile State*. The fundamental position of *The Servile State* is this; that an Irish peasant who earns almost no money but owns his own land, burns his own peat, grows his own potatoes and milks his own cow is a freer creature than a clerk or factory hand who might earn ten times more money, but is compelled to work for someone else, and to live in a rented or leased house, and to be dependent on shopkeepers for his sustenance.

If one concedes that the Distributist ideal was desirable – that it would be a good thing if more people owned more property – was there ever a chance that such a dream could be put into practice? Belloc's secretary and friend of forty years, J.S. Nickerson, wrote, 'It is impossible to avoid the question: To what extent did Belloc and Chesterton believe in the practical application of Distributist principles? And it is hard to avoid the conclusion that neither of them really tried to answer it.'[1] This is true. But it has to be conceded that there was never a political system in Great Britain which would have allowed the Distributist ideals to be tried. Belloc's view was that widespread private ownership was *more* practical than collective ownership; and, of that, the modern world has hundreds of examples to prove him right. Writing thirty-five years before any British Government attempted to do such things, he claimed that taking the waterworks or the railways into public ownership would fail to make them any more efficient. It would leave the position of men and women in society at large in precisely the same position. Distributism, on the other hand, would fundamentally change the position of millions of men, women and children. It would make them free.

In *The Servile State*, he did suggest immediate economic measures to benefit small savers:

> If I desire to benefit small savings at the expense of large, I must reverse the whole economy under which interest is paid upon deposits today. It is far easier to save £100 out of revenue of £1000 than to save £10 out of revenue of £100. It is infinitely easier to save £10 out of a revenue of £100 than £5 out of a revenue of £50. To build up small property through thrift when once the Mass have fallen into the proletarian trough is impossible unless you deliberately subsidise small savings, offering them a reward which, in competition, they could never obtain; and to do this, the whole vast arrangement of credit must be worked backwards.[2]

This remains, it is true, rather vague. What would there be to prevent the Duke of Battersea dividing his huge fortune into an infinite number of tiny fortunes in order to benefit from the advantageous rates of interest meant for those of modest savings? And what of the stock market, which would hardly be free to pursue its business if it was only possible to trade in a limited number or stocks and shares? Perhaps, however, there might have been found answers to these questions if any government ever felt the slightest desire to put

[1] *The Chesterton Review*, Vol. VII No. 4 pp. 340–1.
[2] *The Servile State* p. 110.

Belloc's ideas into practice. None has. His analysis of society as an increasingly cumbrous collectivist state, shackled to a dependence on the vicissitudes of the capitalist world, the big businesses, the fluctuations of the world market: this has been a prophecy all too manifestly fulfilled in the history of the modern world.

* * *

During the first six months of 1912, Belloc was still nominally editor of *The Eye Witness* though there can have been few weeks in that period when he spent more than a couple of hours at his editorial desk. From January to March, he undertook an exhausting series of lectures, which ensured that he was never in the same place for more that twenty-four hours at a time. Penrith one night, Crewe the next; then on to Huddersfield. The comparatively easy journey from Huddersfield to Sheffield was hampered by the fact that he had to go, to fulfil a lecture engagement, by way of Merthyr Tydfil in South Wales. He came south again to King's Land for Holy Week and, for once, he was too busy to devote the sacred days to writing political fiction. Throughout that exhausting spring, he had been at work on his series of British Battle books. By March 16 he had finished Tourcoing and Waterloo and he felt confident enough to sign a contract with a publisher to write a history of France. By April 7 he had finished 'Crécy and half Poitiers!'[1]

That little task done, he set off for a short tour of France, Belgium and Germany. On his first stop he visited his mother, who was spending the summer, as was her custom, at La Celle St Cloud. Bessie was displeased by the anti-Jewish tone of some of the articles which she had read in *The Eye Witness* and he felt constrained to justify himself. 'I do not argue the Jewish question much in the Eye-Witness or out of it. It seems to me like arguing about a house that is on fire. Here you have two bodies which, under certain conditions re-act disastrously one upon the other. We know from history what these conditions are. We know that if the Jewish race is recognised and given privileges of its own, things work more or less well, and we know that all attempts to shirk the problem lead to the most horrible results of violence. There was a desperate attempt to shirk the problem for three generations and it has come back and hit us.'[2]

Whether one regards it as 'shirking the problem' or not, Bessie's generation undoubtedly had a different attitude to the Jews from that of her son. A.L. Rowse has written, 'When Disraeli was being made

[3] BC, to George Wyndham April 7, 1912.
[2] BC.

leader of the Conservative Party it was not objected against him that he was a Jew, but that he was not a landed gentleman. A sensible old Duke therefore proposed that he be made one, and Hughenden was bought for Disraeli to qualify him.'[1] While that does not mean that there was no anti-Jewish feeling in Victorian England (one thinks of the villainous Jews in Trollope and Dickens), there was undoubtedly a positively pro-Jewish feeling in George Eliot's circle, to which Bessie, as a young woman, had belonged. There is an absolute contrast between the spirit which created *Daniel Deronda* and T.S. Eliot's fear that

> The red-eyed scavengers are creeping
> From Kentish Town and Golder's Green.

Between the two Eliots, there had grown up a whole literary generation who were unashamedly hostile to the Jews. Buchan, Kipling and Rupert Brooke all loathed and feared them. Belloc, by contrast, who had employed a Jewess as a secretary since 1908, claimed, to the end of his life, to have good personal relations with his Jewish friends. 'As for me, I get on famously with them,' he wrote during the Second World War. 'English people used to boast all day long that England had no Jewish problem because they were so just, so kind, so God knows what: but the real reason was the strong Anglo-Judaic alliance all over the world.'[2]

Belloc detested humbug far more than he disliked the Jews. He protested:

> There is not in the whole mass of my written books and articles, there is not in any one of my lectures (many of which have been delivered to Jewish bodies by special request because of the interest I have taken) there is not, I say, in any one of the great mass of writings and statements extending now over twenty years, a single line in which a Jew has been attacked as a Jew or in which the vast majority of their race, suffering and poor, has received, I will not say an insult from my pen or my tongue, but anything which could be construed even as dislike.'[3]

The blustering syntax here will suggest to some readers that Belloc was protesting too much. The question of whether he was or wasn't must be postponed until we reach 1922, when Belloc published what he called his 'admirable yid book': *The Jews*. It was undoubtedly a

[1] A.L. Rowse: *Portraits and Views* p. 80.
[2] JSN October 6, 1941.
[3] BC September 6, 1924.

question which interested him to the point of obsession, and the reasons for this have already been tentatively suggested. But it was not the only thing on his mind as he cascaded through the summer months of 1912.

* * *

Belloc had promised to send his mother a copy of *The Servile State* in a letter dated April 21, 1912.[1] In fact, at this date, the thing had not been written. It had existed merely as notes on a page, a concept in his head. The book was not finished until August. In the course of writing it, he also decided to resign the editorship of *The Eye Witness*. Cecil Chesterton took the job over, and Belloc sold his few shares in the thing back to the proprietor, Charles Granville. 'So that's good riddance' was Belloc's view.[2] On August 12, he handed in the manuscript of *The Servile State* to the publishers (T.N. Foulis) and he hung about in London for a day awaiting payment. The Reform Club was shut, so he was obliged to smoke, write letters and read the newspapers at the Devonshire Club. He slept at the G.K. Chestertons' house in Battersea, and while making travel arrangements for himself, he interviewed a French maid for Elodie (a Mlle Corbin: 'she seemed to me excellent . . . I do hope, my sweet, she will suit you . . . '[3]), packed her off to Sussex by train from Victoria, and, the next day, was staggering into the same railway station himself laden with luggage. He had been commissioned, for £40, to write a series of articles for 'the stinking *Pall Mall Gazette*' about the Napoleonic battlefields. The series had already begun to appear, so it was with some speed that Belloc set out, exactly one hundred years after the great French emperor, for Moscow.

His travelling companion was Evan Charteris. They crossed a very rough Channel hoping to reach Boulogne, but the boat was compelled to put in at Calais. ('I was unhurt and enjoyed it,' he wrote back to Elodie. 'Oddly enough: for usually a bad sea makes me sick.')[4] The next twenty-four hours were devoted to a sequence of tedious calamities. They got to Brussels that night, slept in a station hotel, and the next day hired a car to take them to the battlefield of Laffeldt. The car got stuck in the mud and had to be tugged out by horses. Then, on the road to Maastricht, the doomed automobile caught fire; and they had to complete their journey by tram, which meant that they missed their

[1] BC April 21, 1912.
[2] BC August 14, 1912.
[3] BC August 13, 1912.
[4] BC August 27, 1912.

express train to Cologne. Nevertheless, by lunchtime on August 28, Belloc was calmly writing to Elodie from Frankfurt: 'Things are already *quite* out of the old order of Europe and half barbarous. The Oder flows by, a huge shallow stream, and the country is a dead flat with vast pine forests. The Pines low and ugly. I shall be on the Russian frontier in four hours.'[1]

Joined by his old school friend Charles Somers Cocks in Berlin, they were in Warsaw by one o'clock the next morning. 'The moment one is over the Russian border into *Russian* Poland (out of *Prussian* Poland) everything changes. To begin with, everybody treats everybody else as an equal and they all lounge about.' This considered view, based on about twenty minutes' experience of Warsaw, derived of course from the knowledge that the Poles, unlike the Prussians, were thoroughly Catholic. The only non-Catholics about the place were the Jews, and it is not surprising that they, too, should have engaged his attention.

'After crossing the frontier all the Jews appear in caps and *Gaberdines* . . . not unlike a cassock. The Jews are treated in a most friend¹ · manner by everybody, but openly talked of as a foreign race. Most of them are hideously poor.' In spite of the discomforts of Warsaw – no proper cafés, only one 'ordinary hotel', and the discomforts of sleeping in what sound like modern 'duvets' ('the beds have *no bedclothes*, only one big hot covering, a sort of cross between an eiderdown and a pillow-case') – he found much to like about the Polish capital. 'It is intensely Catholic.' At Mass the next morning, he saw 'Just the same inside of a church & pictures & every thing which you may see wherever the Church is, as in Dublin or Valparaiso'.

He was not there long, however, for at midnight he caught the express to Moscow where, although there were only two Roman Catholic churches, he managed to hear mass at eleven o'clock the next morning. 'It is astonishing how *half-baked* everything in Moscow is. You cannot get a plan of the City even in hotels and no one has a clear idea of the time at which anything is to happen.' Still, there were compensations. 'All Russian men and women laugh and smile the whole time like contented animals . . . ' and 'the Hotels and Inns are astonishingly cheap'. Another advantage was that there was 'not a single Jew . . . to be seen except occasional travellers in the great hotels. The Russians have wisely determined to keep them beyond a sort of fence'.

From the authoritative tone in which he writes to Elodie on

[1] BC August 28, 1912.

Moscow, its population, its architecture, its familiar customs, sights and sounds, you might suppose that he spent a few weeks there at least. It was a 'curious little old walled city' within which was an enclosure called 'the Kremlin. It has a few ugly churches in it and an uglier palace & it is in no way remarkable'. In fact, having found that it was impossible to buy a map of Moscow (why did not he bring one with him?), he merely went to the Roman mass (which he could have heard anywhere in the Western world: no sampling of Orthodox rites for him); he had a meal afterwards; he wrote a long letter while he drank his coffee and in the afternoon he moved on. He was in Moscow for less than *six hours*.

From the train, he glimpsed the battlefield of Borodino. 'There is a gilt and beribboned tent for the Czar & specially made triumphal way for him five miles long from the train to the Battlefield, with flags and all manner & all, & a special life-size station has been built for little Tiddlywinks the Czar who is but one degree less crapulous than his cousin George the Henpecked,[1] or rather huge great urchin-china-pecked.'

At the station, which they obviously had time to inspect, he managed to fraternise briefly with 'a colonel of the line & talked to him at great length' – probably about ten minutes – 'about Borodino and about Napoleon, for whom the soldiers here had a high veneration'. That is a very characteristic piece of Belloc generalisation. He himself revered Napoleon to the point of idolatry and scorned the British Royal Family and their Russian cousins the 'Tiddlywinkses'. He therefore understood (with no dishonesty) that the Russians, celebrating their great victory over the French dictator, were all burning with the same pro-Napoleonic zeal as himself.

Whether his impressions were accurate, he had no time to check. Nor would it have occurred to him to do so. Somers Cocks met him at the frontier and they hastened westward by train as fast as they could. At Salzburg, though there was time to disembark, he would not even get out of his railway carriage. He said that one could tell at a glance that it was like Earl's Court. The scenery, moreover, was 'practically Switzerland' and therefore 'detestable'. Alas, the train was compelled to pass through Switzerland, through all the Zwinglian mountain passes, with their capitalist snow and their Calvinist evergreens, but, to his enormous relief, they were soon back in France. 'I must say Switzerland is the nearest thing to moral hell the rich have yet erected. It amazes me that any one who can avoid it should go there. I rushed

---

[1] George V, 'henpecked' by his wife, Queen Mary.

through with great speed and am now here. (Bourg). What a heaven is the Republic after that outer Barbarism from Moscow to the Rhine.'[1]

Belloc judged everything to the advantage of Gaul. On September 7, he wrote to Elodie, 'I spent today walking slow up the Burgundian vineyard – of which there is a thousand feet in height looking eastward . . . I should be in Tours tomorrow . . . I shall get Mass at Bourges just one week after the one-horse but touching Mass at Moscow.'[2]

That makes things very clear. At Tours he was 'enormously moved' at the tomb of St Martin. Although he had loved the sense at Warsaw that the Church is everywhere the same, he could never shake off his instinctive sense that the Church was most truly herself in his father's homeland. By Monday, September 9, he had reached Paris, where it was bitterly cold, and the next day he saw his mother at La Celle St Cloud. Within the space of ten days, he had travelled thousands of miles, worn himself out, and merely confirmed his prejudices about Prussia and Eastern Europe by watching them scud past the window of a railway carriage. This was one of the silliest and most extreme examples of Belloc's compulsive restlessness. Except in his journeyings through France, which he knew very well anyway, he rarely noticed anything *en route*. He did not learn from travel. Indeed, his capacity to be touched by new experience was quickly evaporating. He arrived in places with his impressions of them ready-formed. His desire to be on the move perpetually was but a symptom of his demonic, almost crazed energy.

*   *   *

Seeing his mother had worried him. She was 'much older. She sometimes mixes things a little, but her whole pleasure now is to live in the past there [at La Celle St Cloud] and the village is still conversation enough for her'.

In spite of the alleged limitations of her interests, Bessie was soon receiving exultant letters from her son in London about a public scandal which was about to burst upon the world.

'Lloyd George has been dealing on the Stock Exchange heavily to his advantage with private political information, a thing which I think was never done before by an English Cabinet Minister. The facts are now so generally known that he may not survive their exposure. When I was in London yesterday everyone was talking about it.' This, of course, was what came to be known as 'the Marconi scandal'.

It is as well to consider the story of it after Belloc's dash to Moscow,

[1] BC to Elodie September 6, 1912.
[2] BC September 7, 1912.

the journey in which he only saw what he wanted to see, in which Salzburg looked like Earl's Court, for then all due allowance can be made for his interpretation of the scandal. But to make allowance for his bias is not to suggest that he was wrong. A man of Belloc's temper only sees what he wants to see, whether he is looking out of the window of his railway-carriage or reading the newspaper. But the Marconi scandal seems, even without reference to Belloc, to be a tamely hilarious repetition of one of his own political satires. The deviousness of the Liberal Cabinet Ministers involved is as gross as anything in *A Change in the Cabinet*. Men get rich quick with the absurd arbitrariness of Mr Clutterbuck's change in fortunes. And (no cause for surprise) at the back of it all there are a family called Isaacs and a politician called Samuel. The whole story reads like a Belloc 'fantasy'.

The bare facts of the case are these. The Imperial Conference of 1911 had approved the plan of a chain of state-owned wireless stations to be erected throughout the Empire. The Postmaster General, Mr Herbert Samuel, was asked to find a company to undertake the work; and, after a certain amount of purely notional 'looking around', lighted upon the Marconi Wireless Telegraph Company of which his friend Mr Godfrey Isaacs happened to be the managing director. There was, perhaps, nothing outrageous about this choice. Marconi were a very reputable firm. But here the slippery slope begins: here business transactions begin to slither into shady dealings.

Godfrey Isaacs, the managing director of the English Marconi company, had a brother called Sir Rufus Isaacs, who was Attorney General in Asquith's Government. He did not join the Cabinet until three months after the contract with Marconi had been made: a point he always made in his defence. But it is inconceivable, as a close friend of Samuel, that he did not know of what was going on. His brother knew of the contract and would undoubtedly have informed him.

The contract, not surprisingly, enormously increased the value of the Marconi shares. In August 1911, they stood at £2.8s.9d; in December, they were £3.6s.3d.; and by March 1912, when the contract had been agreed (but *not* made public), they had shot up to £6.15s. By April they were at £9. Their value had therefore multiplied fourfold in eight months.[1]

The facts were not lost on Cecil Chesterton who published gleeful weekly accounts of the matter in *The Eye Witness* while Belloc continued to work on British Battles of an earlier era. By the time

[1] Frances Donaldson: *The Marconi Scandal* p. 19.

Belloc was in Moscow, the *Eye Witness* allegations had become quite explicit. It was claimed that Rufus Isaacs had gambled with Marconi shares, being on the one hand privy to the secrets of the Cabinet (through his friend Herbert Samuel) and on the other to that of the Marconi company (being brother of its managing director). Christopher Sandeman wrote in *The Eye Witness* that either these accusations were true or they were false. 'If false, they cannot be ignored in silence by the men against whom they are directed. If true, it is inconceivable that two Hebrews unable to refute such accusations should continue to occupy positions hitherto supposed to be filled by honourable English gentlemen.'[1]

Rumours flew hither and thither. Some said that Sir Rufus had made £160,000 out of the deal; others put it at a million. It now came to be realised that the two Hebrews were not alone in the fiddle. Lloyd George himself, the Chancellor of the Exchequer, had been buying and selling Marconi shares before news of the Government contract was made public. So had the Chief Whip of the Liberal Party, the Master of Elibank.

In the debate in the Commons on October 11, 1912, all Government Ministers concerned denied the allegations made in *The Eye Witness*. They had the fullest support of Asquith. He advised them,

> I have read carefully the scurrilous rubbish, and I am clearly of the opinion that you should take no notice of it . . . I suspect *The Eye Witness* has a very meagre circulation. I notice only one page of advertisements and that occupied by books of Belloc's publishers. Prosecution would secure it notoriety, which might yield subscribers.[2]

In the parliamentary inquiry which followed, in January 1913, it was revealed that Cecil Chesterton's allegations (and the generally believed rumours) were not strictly accurate. But none of the men concerned ever denied that the Attorney General had bought £10,000 worth of shares, though he did not buy them directly from his brother Godfrey Isaacs, and they were not shares in the *English* Marconi company. What happened was that his brother Harry bought 100,000 shares of the *American* branch of the company. Rufus then bought 10,000 of these shares at £2 and immediately sold 1,000 of them to the Chancellor of the Exchequer and 1,000 to the Chief Whip. No money changed hands during these rapid transactions, because these 'sales' took place *before* the shares came on the public market. On April 19, when they

[1] Donaldson p. 25.
[2] Ibid p. 57.

Hilaire Belloc aged twenty.
A photograph he gave to Elodie in 1890

Hilaire Belloc as an undergraduate with
Lord Basil Blackwood

Elodie Belloc

Louis Belloc, Hilaire Belloc's father

Bessie Parkes Belloc, Hilaire Belloc's mother, at about the time of her wedding

G. K. Chesterton as he appeared at the time of his first meeting with Hilaire Belloc

George Wyndham

Maurice Baring

Father Vincent McNabb O.P.

Cecil Chesterton

Hilaire Belloc in middle age

Gilbert and Frances Chesterton

Drawing in pencil and chalk of Hilaire Belloc by Daphne Pollen (1932). Belloc said of it: 'You have made me look like Blake, seeing a vision.'

H. G. Wells playing 'soldiers' in a scientific manner, by S. Begg

G. G. Coulton in old age

An after-dinner speech

'Mr Belloc's visit to the Vatican'
by Max Beerbohm

Hilaire Belloc on board the Nona

*Conrad Russell, Hilaire Belloc, Lucy Pollen
(later to marry Belloc's grandson Philip Jebb)
and Katharine Asquith*

*Hilaire Belloc in his study at King's Land,
February 1948*

did become publicly available Rufus Isaacs sold 7,000 of his shares at £3 6s. 6d., thus making a clear profit in a single day of £3,000. Not the million pounds that had been spoken of, but a fairly profitable way of passing from dawn to dusk. He still had 1,000 shares left.

It was when Rufus Isaacs had made his safe £3,000 that the 'speculation' had begun. He, the Postmaster General (Samuel) and the Chief Whip bought 3,000 more shares at £2,532 on May 22. Since they were not due to deliver the shares previously sold by them at £3 6s. 6d. till June 20, this new purchase had something of the look of a 'bear' transaction.[1] In April and May, moreover, the Master of Elibank, who had charge of the Liberal Party funds, bought 3,000 shares on behalf of the Party.

All this was eventually admitted by the three Cabinet Ministers in the public enquiry. No more was admitted. The modern historian of the affair, Frances Donaldson, believes that Belloc comes out of it all very badly. She believes that he gravely and unjustly injured the reputation of Rufus Isaacs and Herbert Samuel with his persistent implication that there had been corruption at the very start of the affair, with the placing of the contract. 'This charge was never believed except by the people of extraordinary prejudice who would not be convinced of the facts.'

It is hard to see why Lady Donaldson's heart bleeds for these obvious crooks. The Master of Elibank, Isaacs, Lloyd George and Samuel manifestly tried to make themselves rich by the Marconi contract. Why else had they bought shares? The fact that they did not make themselves as rich as they hoped, or as their enemies believed, does not materially alter the fact that Ministers of the Crown were using their knowledge of decisions made in Cabinet for their private enrichment. The honourable thing to do, if they had no scheme afoot when the contract was first mooted, would have been to refrain from buying any Marconi shares. The whole thing stinks. The fact that Cecil Chesterton was poisonously and notoriously anti-semitic does not affect the issue at all. As Belloc himself said, when he spoke to the Committee of Inquiry, and was accused of having a prejudice against the Jews, there was no one less Jewish than David Lloyd George.[2]

There can be no doubt that there would not have been a public inquiry into the scandal had it not been for the journalism of Cecil Chesterton and Hilaire Belloc. When they came, the denials of these accusations (largely, as we now know, penned by Asquith himself

[1] Maisie Ward: *Gilbert Keith Chesterton* p. 286.
[2] Donaldson p. 65.

and read out by his disreputable colleagues)[1] were shockingly specious, appallingly circumspect. Perhaps, when the contract was drawn up, there had been, in the formal sense, no plot. But it looks poor that the best of their defence was that they had bought shares in the American, not the English, branch of the company; and that they were unable to deny that Harry Isaacs had bought these shares (and sold a portion of them to the Attorney General) days before they came on the public market in London. Even if the collusion which all this implies, and which *The Eye Witness* gleefully announced, did not take place, there is enough here, for a few ministerial resignations to have been in order.

No such thing happened. Lloyd George went on to become Prime Minister. Sir Rufus Isaacs, less than two months after the public inquiry had revealed his part in the affair, became Lord Chief Justice and took the title of Lord Reading. Kipling's poem on that occasion expressed what many felt:

> Well done, well done Gehazi,
> Stretch forth thy ready hand,
> Thou barely scaped from Judgment,
> Take oath to judge the Land.
> Unswayed by gift of money
> Or privy bribe more base,
> Or knowledge which is profit
> In any market place.

Lady Donaldson is 'terrified' by this 'poem of hate'. Similarly, she finds Belloc's part in the affair 'disgraceful'. And she takes the view that 'all might have been well if Belloc had kept out of politics. In the literary circles where he properly belonged his eccentricities were understood and could not have been seriously damaging'.[2]

Belloc, of course, did not belong, properly speaking, to 'literary circles'; and, even if he had done, it is hard to see why this should have prevented him from speaking out on a matter of public importance. The phrase 'all might have been well' would seem to mean here that the scandal would never have come to light. In the Marconi affair, he saw a very muddled and unclear case of jiggery-pokery and he smelt a rat. There can be no doubt at all that there was a rat to smell. To be precise, there were five rats. The anti-semitic tone of *The Eye Witness*

[1] Denis Judd: *Lord Reading*.
[2] Donaldson p. 65.

is, beyond question, distasteful. Belloc was not writing for it during the height of the scandal. The only aspect of Belloc's part in the Marconi affair which we may deplore is not that he persecuted Cabinet Ministers without a cause; but that he left their persecution in the hands of Cecil Chesterton. When he should have been on the trail of Herbert Samuel, Godfrey and Rufus Isaacs, Lloyd George and the Master of Elibank, he was gadding about the Continent and writing military history. When talking of the matter, Belloc always recognised that Cecil Chesterton was unbalanced on the matter of the Jews; and that he spoilt the position of *The Eye Witness* by failing to check his facts, or to investigate the villainous five with sufficient rigour. It was this which enabled Godfrey Isaacs, in 1913, to pursue a successful libel action against Cecil.

So far, in spite of a great deal of character assassination in the English Press, none of the accused Ministers had prosecuted anyone. Asquith had held them back, evidently knowing, if the half of the story came out, at that moment of critical division in the Liberal ranks, that it would be the end of the Party. This indeed turned out to be the case. On February 12, 1913, L.J. Maxse, editor of the *National Review*, was examined by the Committee of Inquiry. He expressed surprise that the Ministers had not denied that 'they had any transactions whatsoever . . . in any financial centre in any shares in any Marconi company throughout the negotiations with the Government'. This, of course, was something which none of them *could* deny, which is why they failed to appear before the Committee. But their chance of a successful prosecution for libel came two days later when a Paris newspaper *Le Matin* wrote a distorted account of Maxse's words. They said (and the dates are crucial) that Samuel, Godfrey and Rufus Isaacs had bought shares in the *English* Marconi Company *before* negotiations with the Government had started; and that they had sold them, at four times the price, when the public learnt that the contract was going through. This of course was not what Maxse had said. Nor was it what the Cabinet Ministers had done. (One is forced to the conclusion that, though dishonest, they were not clever enough for this.) Almost identical allegations had appeared in *The Eye Witness* (which folded in November 1912 and was almost immediately resuscitated under the title of *The New Witness*) but no one dared to submit the facts of the case to an English court. Herbert Samuel and Rufus Isaacs, however, *did* decide to prosecute *Le Matin*, with Sir Edward Carson and F.E. Smith as their counsel.

It provoked from G.K. Chesterton the 'song of Cosmopolitan courage':

> I am so swift to seize affronts
> My spirit is so high,
> Whoever has insulted me
> Some foreigner must die.
>
> I brought a libel action,
> For *The Times* had called me 'thief'
> Against a paper in Bordeaux,
> A paper called *Le Juif*.
>
> *The Nation* called me 'cannibal'
> I could not let it pass –
> I got a retractation
> From a journal in Alsace . . .

The case was settled out of court, with *Le Matin* withdrawing every item of their story. Cecil Chesterton's turn came next. On January 9, 1913, he published an article in *The New Witness* attacking the City record of Godfrey Isaacs. Entitled 'Ghastly Record', the article exposed some twenty commercial failures with which Isaacs had been concerned. He asked whether this person was fit to be given one of the largest Government contracts ever placed.

> The files at Somerset House of the Isaacs companies . . . cry out for vengeance on the man who created them . . . who filled them with his own creatures, who worked them solely for his own ends, and who sought to get rid of some of them when they had served his purpose by casting the expenses of their burial on to the public purse.

He further claimed that, had the Attorney General not been his brother, Godfrey Isaacs would have been prosecuted. 'This is not the first time in the Marconi Affair we find these two gentlemen swindling.'

> What happened to Lord Henry Chase?
> He got into a libel case . . .

Cecil's account of Godfrey Isaacs's business career was largely accurate. But, lest the not very subtle insults in the article had been missed by his victim, a sandwich man was hired to parade up and down outside Isaacs's office bearing the legend GHASTLY FAILURES. Cecil Chesterton would not disclaim responsibility for this; it would seem to have been arranged by his wife.

The placard angered Isaacs. Finally, on February 27, Cecil Chesterton got what he wanted. 'I am pleased to hear,' he wrote to Isaacs's solicitor, 'that your client Mr Isaacs proposes to bring an action against me.' Once more, as in the *Le Matin* case, Sir Edward Carson and F.E. Smith were employed as counsel. The charge was criminal libel, and Cecil Chesterton insisted on facing the charge alone. He refused to disclose the names of the writers of any of the unsigned articles in his periodical.

He behaved with a sort of conceited gallantry and, of course, he was found guilty of criminal libel, while claiming a moral victory when he was fined only £100. Looking back on it all now, the Marconi affair seems 'a ghastly failure' on both sides, for both Isaacs and the *Witness*. Chesterton accused the wrong man of the wrong things at the wrong time. He phrased his accusations in hysterical anti-Jewish language; he did not bother to check his facts; he spoilt, forever, an investigation which needed making and which could, with more subtlety, have toppled his enemies. After it had become apparent that the Isaacs brothers did not negotiate the sale of the shares on the dates he claimed, he persisted in putting it about that Godfrey Isaacs had wickedly tried to corrupt Ministers of the Crown. This was nonsense. The scandal consisted, largely, in the things which Belloc had, by his early investigations, forced Rufus Isaacs and Lloyd George to admit publicly; that they had, while Ministers of the Crown, profited directly from the policies of the Government. This was in itself scandalous. They did not need to speculate about things they did not do on dates which it was later proved were impossible.

Had they been prepared to fight on surer ground, Belloc and the Chestertons would have exposed the extent of Rufus Isaacs's involvement in the affair, as well as that of Lloyd George and the Master of Elibank. Godfrey Isaacs was, in a way, an irrelevance. As it was, the real villains got away scot free. Cecil Chesterton claimed in *The New Witness* that had he not struck in the dark, the nation would still be in the dark.[1] This was a euphemism for saying that, had he not told lies, none of the truth would have emerged. The precise opposite is true. If Cecil had not muddied the water, it might have been possible to catch one of the villains out. In the event, the investment itself was bungled, and the Cabinet Ministers concerned did not make very much money. Modern historians of the affair have tried to write it off as a storm in a teacup. G.K. Chesterton in his *Autobiography* (published in 1936), said, 'It is the fashion to divide recent history into Pre-War and Post-War conditions. I believe it is almost as essential to divide them

[1] Quoted Maisie Ward p. 302.

into Pre-Marconi and Post-Marconi days. It was during the agitations upon that affair that the ordinary English citizen lost his invincible ignorance; or, in ordinary language, his innocence.' Again, almost the precise opposite is true. The Cabinet Ministers concerned were involved in dirty tricks; but, as far as can be known, the tricks were far less dirty than public cynicism and rumour and newspaper reports suggested. The Isaacs brothers were not the monsters of Cecil Chesterton's imaginings; corrupt Jews, bribing the greedy Presbyterian Chief Whip and the Welsh Nonconformist Chancellor of the Exchequer. They merely saw the way to making some money in the course of their Cabinet work. They hoped to make a lot of money, but did not do so. It was profoundly dishonourable; but that is all there is to be said. The degree to which Belloc's friends had the whole matter out of proportion is indicated by G.K. Chesterton's final judgment: 'I think it probable that centuries will pass before it is seen clearly and in its right perspective; and then it will be seen as one of the turning points in the whole history of England and of the world.'

Chesterton wrote histrionically about the affair because his brother Cecil was killed not long afterwards in the Great War. The libel trial, too, took on a somewhat sanctified glow because, on the day it began, Cecil became a Roman Catholic. He had been toying with the idea for some time. Elodie finally talked him round; and the ceremony happened conveniently near the Old Bailey at the 'actor's church' – Corpus Christi, Maiden Lane. Years later, Godfrey Isaacs took the same step, shortly before his death. 'It is the only reconciliation,' Chesterton wrote; 'and it can reconcile anybody. *Requiescant in pace.*'[1]

The public scene did not occupy the whole of Belloc's attention in those times. His five acres in Sussex provided solace from the hurly-burly of politics and scandal. Every now and again, he would even have time to work in the fields with Laker, who farmed the land and acted as a family factotum. His children, too, were growing up and occupying his sporadic attention. But, as often as not, even in Sussex, his attention was devoted, not to his family, but to his friends.

His daughter Eleanor, remembering the visits of Charles Somers Cocks, wrote, 'Once I met H.B. and Mr Cocks walking and talking along White Hall, the top lane of the parish. I was meandering slowly on a bicycle and they were so entirely engrossed in conversation that they never so much as saw me. It was the only genuine case of its kind I have encountered, though I have heard of such concentration.'[2]

[1] *Autobiography* p. 208.
[2] Eleanor and Reginald Jebb: *Testimony to Hilaire Belloc* (1956) p. 127.

George Wyndham was, perhaps, the friend who meant most to Belloc at this time. Wyndham finally invited Elodie over to Clouds, and the effect of the visit was characteristic. 'I enjoyed much in the Bellocs' visit, but he does tire me. He rejoices in disputation for the sake of disputing, whereas I care for discussion only in so far as it extends the area of possible understanding. And he shouts.'[1]

Wyndham, by 1913, was worn out. His public career was effectively over. Drink had begun to play a larger part in life than was altogether healthy. But although the two men differed over many things and still shouted at each other, the area of agreement had become greater. They both mourned a rural, hierarchical England which was vanishing forever. They both shared a sense that Westminister had become corrupted and that politics was a game not fit for gentlemen to play. 'I am now persuaded that you were right over the falsity of Parliament and the venality of the Press,' Wyndham wrote to Belloc.[2] But the chief thing that they had in common was a devotion to poetry. Wyndham was one of the most attentive and constructive readers of Belloc's verse. Sometimes, he offered helpful criticism. More often, he was humble in his admiration. His favourite among them was 'The Prophet Lost in the Hills at Evening', which he considered 'the best I have read by any man now living' . . . and, 'By God 'tis good. I don't suppose you know how good it is'.[3] And probably he didn't. For, even at his most sombre and skilful, there is always an innocence about Belloc's verse, an innocence which, once again, was Wyndham's delight.

Any man who can sing

> To see the yellow mustard grow
> Beyond the town, above, below;
> Beyond the purple houses, oh!
> To see the yellow mustard grow –

is happy and *safe*. He doesn't know why he is happy and safe. But he knows that he is secure. He breaks out of the prison of Time into Eternity. Like God, in the first chapter of Genesis, he sees that it is good.[4]

---

[1] *The Cousins*. p. 281.
[2] *The Letters of George Wyndham* p. 724.
[3] Ibid. p. 680.
[4] Ibid. p. 680.

Wyndham spoke more truly than he knew. The days of his friendship with Belloc, and of his own life, were numbered. So were the days when it could be said of Belloc that he was happy or that he was safe.

NINE

THE DEATH OF ELODIE
1914

The Four Men is one of Belloc's most beautiful books, a hymn to stability by one of the most restless beings who ever crashed about the surface of the earth; a prose elegy by a man who was homesick for a home he was never really prepared to enjoy.

> Ah! but if a man is part of and is rooted in one steadfast piece of earth, which has nourished him and given him his being, and if he can on his side lend it glory and do it service (thought I) it will be a friend to him for ever, and he has outflanked Death in a way.[1]

In the year in which these sage reflections were published, Belloc was never still for a single week. It was in 1912, the year of his visit to Moscow. Even at a generous calculation, adding up all the odd days and nights he snatched at home in the middle of his busy-ness, he cannot have spent five weeks out of fifty-two at King's Land. He loved his house; and, even more, he loved what it stood for: a hearth for his friends, a haven for his family, a shrine for his household gods. But, in practical terms, at this date, he was too busy, and too restless, to be able to live out this dream. In *The Four Men*, as in his song of 'The South Country', Sussex stands for something solid, permanent and salutary:

> I will gather and carefully make my friends
> Of the men of the Sussex Weald,
> They watch the stars from silent folds,
> They stiffly plough the field.
> By them and the God of the South Country
> My poor soul shall be healed.

But, of course, nothing can 'outflank Death'. And, in 1913, he began to walk into the valley of the shadow.

The first blow, as it were a dress rehearsal for the great tribulation,

[1] *The Four Men* p. 309

fell in June 1913. In the spring he had declared to Wyndham, 'Life is not long and the humanities are rare'.[1] The two friends had resolved to see more of each other. Much of May was spent together; and, in the last week-end, Wyndham came to stay at King's Land. The two men discussed the immortality of the soul. Belloc said that he accepted the doctrine of the after life merely because his church told him to do so. Wyndham believed in it with passionate certitude, unprompted by an ecclesiastical discipline, though sharing his wife's Anglican faith. They planned to meet again soon. Wyndham decided to dash over to France. Belloc was to join him if it were possible, and then Wyndham was to stay at King's Land again on June 13. As it turned out, that was the day of his funeral.[2]

Much of what the two men enjoyed together and held in common is displayed in a magnificent letter written four days before he died. Belloc had, in the event, followed Wyndham over to France, where they had an expedition together to St Germain and the Bougival woods. But he did not have time to delay Wyndham the next day. Accordingly, Wyndham ambled about Paris on his own, looked into bookshops and then dined at Ledoyen.

Now I would not for the world – a phrase, but let it pass – have missed revisiting with you the woods that were a part of your boyhood, and therefore - *à ma guise* – an index to Man's Immortality. But – again – I would not for the world – let us pass the phrase once more – have missed the dinner I ate and the wine I drank at *Ledoyen*: Potage St Germain. A Barbue – the whole of him with a sauce that was Mâitre d'Hôtel sublimated with mushrooms. A cold quail, stuffed with truffles and garnished with aspic and parsley, and supported by a salad.

Hot Asperges vertes, as big as the white ones, with sauce mousseline. A cold salade Russe – without ham – but with a perfect mayonnaise. And then the best strawberries I can remember. For wine a Richebourg of 1890 which stood as other wines – and stands – in the relation of Homer and Shakespeare to other poets. It was a miracle of Earth's entrails searched by the sun and responding with all the ethereal perfumes of a hot day in Summer tempered by the whispering and cool shadows of a breeze. No Jew was there. No American. No Englishman but myself. The French were dining under a sapphire sky, by an old willow tree, a fountain and a nymph in bronze. I had struck an oasis of civilis-

[1] BC March 11, 1913.
[2] *The Cousins* p. 284.

ation. There were few women and that was fit. For how few
women understand![1]

It is perhaps not surprising, after penning this masterpiece, that
Wyndham began to feel severe pains in his chest. By Sunday, June 8,
he had a congested lung and, by nightfall, he died of a passage of a clot
of blood through the heart.[2]

Belloc saw the news on a newspaper placard as he was ambling
down the Strand the next day with Maurice Baring. It was the most
stunning blow that he had yet endured.

> I cannot get the Dead Man out of my thoughts . . . Today in
> rattling through the prayers for the living in my head, at Mass, his
> name halted me suddenly and abominably: I remembered, or rather
> stumbled, and left it unspoken: it has to come later now in the much
> longer list of names one runs through in a chain night after night
> and at Mass, too; for whom we ask three things, Refreshment,
> Light and Peace. We agreed and were continuing to agree more
> nearly in everything; he was the only man older than myself whom
> I sought, and I sought him eagerly always. I loved him with all my
> heart, and so surely as I have no horizon beyond that plain horizon
> of this world, so surely will some years of mine to come be full
> *desiderio tam cari capitis*.[3]

Stunned with grief, Belloc set off for the Pyrenees. But this time, he
was not making a journey away from his family, but towards them.
Elodie, after an exhausting winter, worn out by family colds and flu,
had been ordered to have a complete rest, and she took rooms in
Lourdes at the Hôtel de la Chapelle for herself and her two daughters.
Elizabeth was now aged twelve, and Eleanor celebrated her fourteenth birthday there. The boys (Louis was now nearly sixteen,
Hilary eleven and Peter nine) remained in Sussex, being tended in part
by Edith, the faithful cook, and partly by Ruby Goldsmith, who was
as much a family friend as she was Belloc's secretary.

Belloc joined Elodie and the girls briefly at Lourdes and was pleased
to see his wife's strength returned. It had been a year, all in all, of
strain. Elodie feasted on the change of scene and had been half sorry
when the post was forwarded on and she had to open a bag, 'simply
stuffed with letters about Marconi and Cecil'.[4] Prayers were offered
for Cecil, nonetheless, at the Grotto of Our Lady.

[1] *The Letters of George Wyndham* p. 372.
[2] *The Cousins* p. 284.
[3] Speaight. p. 331.
[4] BC June 1913.

Lourdes always had a special place in Elodie's heart. It was appropriate that she should have spent her last summer there. The largeness and simplicity of its claims were, and are, entirely consonant with her faith. Here was a place where the Blessed Virgin had been seen, and spoken to, during the reign of Queen Victoria. The supernatural, always immediate and wholly real to Elodie, was here taken for granted. When, after a few days of it, Belloc felt compelled to hurry back to England, he was pursued by wonderfully happy letters from his wife and daughters. Eleanor wrote,

> Dearest Papa,
> The weather is still lovely and dry.
> There are two pilgrimages at Lourdes now, a Toulouse one, and a Spanish one: the dear Spaniards are still here in all their dignity and pride. I like them very much indeed with their gay colours and black hair. They have had three miracles, two of which we were witnesses.
> Elizabeth and I are allowed to play in the garden, and its great fun there with the dogs and the little children, who continue to hit each other as much as ever . . .
> When you see Uncle Cecil, will you give him my love and tell him that I do not forget him in my prayers. And when you reach beloved King's Land please give my love to the boys, and Miss Goldsmith, and ask the boys to write to us and tell us about *all* the animals. We are going to benediction in an hours time.
> with best love to all from
> your loving daughter Eleanor.[1]

At the end of July they too returned home. Harvest came, and Belloc spent more time in Sussex. Elodie was better, but her near-collapse at the beginning of the summer was a reminder of what a heavy burden had been placed on her when they first went to live at King's Land. It was unheated and unlit and wildly impractical to run. And it was Elodie, not Belloc, who had been responsible for it. She personally supervised the trimming of thirty-five lamps every day. It was her care to organise not only the domestic management of the house – the cooking and the shopping – but also the maintenance. As well as giving instructions to the cook, she had to remind Laker to mend the gutters or repair the roof. For women more robust, or of a more practical cast, this might have been easier than it was for Elodie.

In September 1913, Belloc organised the building of the Troll's Hut

---

[1] BC June 1913. Spelling and punctuation as printed.

at the end of the garden. Its name implied that it was meant for children, but Belloc soon inhabited it himself, using it as a study, with an immense Ordnance Survey Map on one wall, of the whole of England, measuring fourteen by twenty-two feet (a gift of Auberon Lucas) and Maurice Baring's printing press in the corner. Here he would sit, as the summer passed into the autumn and as the children went back to school.

The girls were being sent away for the first time, to the Dominican convent at Stone in Staffordshire. It was a school with a high reputation, founded by Newman's friend Mother Margaret Mary Hallahan. The Madonna there was believed to be responsible for reducing Newman's costs in the Achilli libel trial.

H.B. met us at Victoria with a large box of chocolates and a waiting taxi. He seemed remarkably cheerful and full of plans and talk. London always exhilarated him. He took us across the Park to Euston and saw us on to the train for Stone, reminding us about changing at Stafford and streaking off to the bookstall to buy a lot of papers for himself and some for us. The dark gloom and bustle of Euston left me stunned, and when H.B. suddenly said, 'Oh my poor lambs, you are going so far away from us', I did not know whether to smile or weep.[1]

It was a pitiable parting, on both sides. As September wore on, the days grew shorter, darker, colder. Not long after the girls returned to school, Belloc and Elodie were driving together to Slindon to visit his mother. Coming over Halnacker Hill they saw the mill in ruins. It was a sight which saddened and shocked them both; and he went home and wrote down the words which he later set to music, and which he would sing in a high, almost elvish tenor. It was as though, in the sight of the ruined mill, he had a greater desolation in view, as when a cold shiver passes down our spine and we do not know why. It was the last autumn of Elodie's life and the last autumn of pre-war England.

> Ha'nacker Hill is in Desolation:
> Ruin a-top and a field unploughed.
> And Spirits that call on a fallen nation
> Spirits that loved her calling aloud:
> Spirits abroad in a windy cloud.
>
> Spirits that call and no one answers;
> Ha'nacker's down and England's done.

[1] *Testimony to Hilaire Belloc.* p. 167.

> Wind and Thistle for pipe and dancers
> And never a ploughman under the Sun.
> Never a ploughman. Never a one.

There is nothing sufficiently explicit here to make Belloc's lament prophetic; it is a mere intimation of worse to come. So far, he had seen the decline and ruin of England as the result of corrupt political and economic systems. Death, bereavement, and war lay in the future.

It is a sad song: 'Sally is gone that was so kindly.' But more is lost than Sally, or the old mill. The God of the South Country no longer seems able to heal the poet's troubled heart. He has lost faith in England. The future, somehow, was not there.

On October 10, his mother wrote to him from La Celle St Cloud, 'from the house where you were born. . . . I am very anxious to keep up this house, which is the only thing your father left you, and if there were any catastrophe in England the house over here might be some refuge. . . . '

Whatever the catastrophe they felt or foresaw, the mother or the son, Bessie's conviction, less than a year before the outbreak of the First World War, is poignant: 'I have never believed that France would suffer twice.'[1]

In November, as the weather grew colder, Elodie's health began, once more, to decline. And when the children returned for their Christmas holidays, she suddenly became much worse. Presumably, Elodie was suffering from cancer. We shall never know. On December 23 she became unable to swallow her food. Christmas itself, normally marked with neo-medieval high cheer at King's Land, passed in terrified silence. On January 2 of the new year, Belloc wrote to his mother:

> It is mainly heart, but the heart is influenced in a secondary degree by insomnia and digestive trouble and if we can get the digestion and the sleep right the heart will pick up again. Everything depends on that. She is getting on very well with both nurses, one of whom is an old friend of our family's, having come to look after the children in the past; and the doctor comes at regular intervals twice a week from London. It will, I fear be a few weeks before we can be certain one way or the other, but I will keep you always informed. All the neighbours have been very anxious to call and enquire and she sees her children for a few moments every day, which is a great consolation to her.[2]

[1] BC October 10, 1913.
[2] BC January 2, 1914.

Six days later, however, he was much less anxious. 'Elodie is appreciably better and the doctor was relieved by the change at his last visit. I will tell you regularly how things go. She is getting regular sleep now and retaining nourishment fairly well. My great object is, of course to move her to some warmer place, but the doctor tells me it will still be a good time before I can do that.'[1]

Bessie felt that the children should be moved away; she foresaw now what was to happen. But Belloc was anxious that the young should remain at King's Land for the duration of the school holidays. They would be going away soon enough and, besides, as he pathetically believed. 'Elodie is very distinctly better.'[2] For all this certitude, there is almost, in his letters of that week, an unhappy sense that he would not be brave enough to face Elodie's illness on his own. The presence of the children provided a welcome distraction. The sprightly appearance of a normal Christmas holiday was kept up. Miss Goldsmith took the children to the pantomime in Brighton; and, on January 13, the Feast of St Hilary, there was a solemn inauguration of the Troll's Hut. Belloc himself painted the motto around the door: 'St Hilary my kith and kin: bless this hut and all therein.'

But time was running out. The children went back to school. Gilbert and Frances Chesterton came to see Elodie on January 20, but the next day Belloc was far from cheerful. He complained,

> Elodie gets no worse and no better. Certain of the symptoms have improved, but others are more distressing and I am bound here very anxiously . . . Elodie is stronger *functionally*, i.e. in digestion and nutrition but weaker *nervously*; she eats almost normally but she can see no one, she can read but little and she sleeps more and more ill. I cry and pray God to take her to the *Sun*. The doctor won't let her move – not even out of bed – and it will be long, long.[3]

But it was not, in the event, long. By the end of the month Elodie was much weaker. Elizabeth and Eleanor were summoned back from their convent school in Staffordshire. The unimaginably dreadful thing was about to happen. The illness had entered its last phase. Elodie had started to wander in her thoughts and to become delirious. The English accent which she had so painstakingly acquired in 1896 began to fall away and her incoherent mumblings became, once more, unmistakably Californian.

She had only lived forty-two years in the world. She had been the

[1] BC January 8, 1914.
[2] BC January 10, 1914.
[3] BC January 21, 1914.

wife of Belloc for seventeen of those years. On February 1, 1914, she became unconscious. All through the next day, they waited. Just before midnight on February 2, she died. Belloc, who had been watching by her bed with devoted terror for five weeks, at once became hysterical. He threw himself on to the corpse and held it, in a paroxysm of sobbing. The nurses and the older children had to tear him from the scene and lead him to his own bedroom.

The next day, her body was carried down to the hall at King's Land where it lay surrounded by candles. Neighbours and friends came to pray beside it. Belloc wandered upstairs again and along the narrow corridor to her room. He glanced round once more at her dressing table, at her clothes, at her bed with its scarlet coverlet. It had always been a dark room, its small windows preventing it from getting much sunlight. He came out of the room and turned the key in its lock. From that moment, Elodie's bedroom was sealed up forever. So, too, was her little parlour downstairs. No one entered them again in Belloc's lifetime. Nor would he ever pass that bedroom door without pausing to kiss it or trace upon it the sign of the cross. And this he did for the next forty years.

★   ★   ★

'My father told me that after a great loss and abiding grief there is always duty and toil left to pull us together and to enable us to start life again.' So Eleanor Belloc recalled.[1] She added, 'He did his very best for us as far as he could, but without Mamma it must have been an intolerable burden at times.'

Having attended their mother's funeral at West Grinstead, Eleanor and Elizabeth returned to their convent school at Stone until Easter. They were aged fourteen and thirteen respectively. Louis, at sixteen, was away at school too, at Downside, where his mother had hoped he would become a monk. Hilary, aged eleven, and Peter, aged nine, were still at home.

Belloc was not equipped, in practical or emotional terms, to meet the 'duty and toil' of parenthood. As his loyal daughter said, 'he did his very best'. It was not that he failed to care. But the inadequacy of his 'very best' had disastrous consequences in the lives of all his children. And, in the initial moments of his grief, he could not help or support them. He was shattered and terrified. Father Vincent McNabb, that holy eccentric whom Belloc revered so deeply, did what he could to console. The pair of them were seen often together in

[1] *Testimony to Hilaire Belloc* p. 169.

those days, both in the gardens of King's Land, and in London. 'Of the great dogmas I feel few,' Belloc confided to Maria Lansdale, his old American friend, who had written him a letter of condolence, 'but of the Creator and common disposer I have had little blindness in my life. How she wished you over here again! She did in the last years of that exile of hers get what she loved in the Sussex home. I keep on all night and all day wishing to God that this place achieved after such trials had been ours together till a common and quiet end. But it is ordered.'[1]

A few days after penning these thoughts, Belloc set off for abroad, leaving his two little boys in the hands of his secretary, Miss Gold-smith, who, together with Laker and Edith the cook, had to keep house, and to clear up after the chaos of the previous sad months.

'It is very strange,' Miss Goldsmith wrote to him, 'but I now seem to have come to understand for the first time how and why she so dearly loved King's Land, and I think it would be a desecration to leave it (or any part of it) shut up and unused, and I so hope you will never do that. But I now realize more than ever, how overwhelmingly difficult it will be for you to live there again. Perhaps at Easter when the children are home we can fix up the Trolls Hut – move the books and maps in – and do some work there? Do you think it will be at all possible?'

Belloc never *did* abandon the idea that he, notionally at least, lived in King's Land, but for the present, his mind was in a tortured turmoil. 'It is an anarchy of the soul.'[2]

Seized by the pain of this anarchy, he made at once for Rome, a bastion against anarchy for more than two thousand years. He enjoyed a 'splendid' audience with St Pius X, who blessed medals for the Belloc children. From there, he pressed on southwards to Naples, took a boat to Sicily, walked about for a few days, took a boat to Tunisia, disliked it; sailed to Marseilles; spent a further few days in Provence before weaving his way back through France.

From Lyons, he wrote despondently to John Phillimore:

I write you this brief line because I know no one else intimately on earth who is fully possessed of the Faith. I desire you to take such means as should be taken, whether by prayers or by Masses, or any other means for my preservation in this very difficult task. I am in peril of my intelligence and perhaps of my conduct and therefore of my soul, which deserves little through the enormity of what has

[1] Princeton February 20, 1919.
[2] Princeton February 20, 1914.

happened . . . It is not as though I had any vision, comprehension or sense of the Divine order. All that was done for me as by another part of me: therefore I find myself without powers, like a man shot in the stomach and through the spine. I was content to keep the door and fight the crowd outside the church and now my office is valueless to me. I wish to God it were the body that was in peril. For I must make a third journey, as I took those two others in my boyhood and early manhood, but those were to California and in the unknown world: for the third journey, in which I must also do all to succeed, there is no plan and no knowledge in me. The body will I fear be strong and will keep me too long from that start upon that journey.[1]

Belloc, in those days, came closer to despair than at any other period in his life. Some weeks later, he was still confessing to an 'increasing doubt whether I can live my life'.[2]

The importance of personal 'commitment' in religion is so highly valued nowadays that there are many modern Catholics who would hardly recognise Belloc as a religious man at all. He could not 'feel' the truth of the great dogmas. He had no 'vision', no 'comprehension of the Divine order'. He hung on, rather, in blind, dry intellectual faith. There was nothing in his experience to confirm the Church's teaching that the Soul was immortal, or that Elodie had merely preceded him upon that 'third journey' towards the Light. He clung to this in the very blackest depression, in the very darkest fear. Hitherto he had 'fought the crowd outside the church'. He was to do so again, when he emerged from this great trial of faith. He was to do so with renewed hardness and strength. The modern Catholic is taught to be as different from Belloc as possible. An eirenical attitude is preached not merely towards heretical Christians, but to those of other faiths, or no faiths at all. In the year in which this page was written (1982) the Catholic Bishops of England and Wales decreed that the Rastafarians – a Jamaican sect who believe in the divinity of the late Ethiopian emperor, Haile Selassie – had a 'valid' contribution to make to religious debate. Catholic parishes were urged to lend their church halls to the Rastafarians, where their smoking of marijuana was likened by the Bishops to the sacramental life.

Small wonder that, in such a world, Belloc's dedication to fighting the crowd outside the church is viewed with tacit disapproval by the hierarchy of England. Similarly, the piety encouraged by the new

[1] March 17, 1914 quoted. Speaight p. 344.
[2] Ibid.

liturgy – an affair of strong emotional fellowship, both with Christ and one's fellow-worshippers – seems to have little in common with the arid darkness of Belloc's time of trial. But, if one cannot allow that Belloc showed Faith, in the fullest Christian sense, during the spring of 1914, one has failed to understand the meaning of the word.

He returned, after his lonely sojourn in France, to find his children all at home for the Easter holidays. Auberon Lucas lent him a motor-car and a chauffeur, insisting that he spend time with the poor orphans. Miss Goldsmith accompanied them on the journey they took to Wales: 'Mr Belloc put up a good "front" of joviality and sang lustily as we travelled along; when we returned to London, we stopped first at Lord Lucas's town house and then went on . . . to his country home in Hampshire.'

As if the strain and expense of looking after his own children at this date were not enough, Belloc began to be assailed, during the summer of 1914, with the financial worries of his mother and his sister. His sister Marie, who had already established herself as an author, found herself to be overdrawn at the bank by £350. This was in spite of the fact that she had published, in the previous year, her brilliantly successful novel of suspense, *The Lodger* (a story in which two impoverished people in Marylebone unwittingly let rooms to Jack the Ripper). Belloc, who was never above 'touching' rich friends himself when he needed money, was also recklessly generous. He agreed to guarantee his sister's overdraft, on condition that her husband, *The Times* journalist Frederic Lowndes, paid his salary into her account, until the debt was redeemed. It was an agreement which was to rankle and rumble over the next five years. Belloc himself, meanwhile, whose income depended entirely on his fluent pen, was unable to settle to work. In the very months when he was airily guaranteeing his sister's overdraft, he was himself getting badly into debt. It is doubtful whether he even noticed.

Grief still hung heavily upon him throughout the brilliant summer of 1914. Unsurprisingly, in May, he turned to the *Nona*, that sturdy nine-ton cutter that he had bought, first in conjunction with Lord Stanley, and of which he was now the sole owner, that nobleman, having, like Lord Lundy, 'gone out to govern one of the Australian Colonies.'[1] She was Belloc's contemporary, 'built somewhere about 1870 at Bembridge in the Isle of Wight, a sturdy little boat made for leisurely fun and not for racing. She was rather more than thirty feet over all, broad in the beam, with a draught of five or six feet'.[2]

[1] BC May 27, 1914.
[2] Morton p. 46.

Having paid Lord Stanley £50 for the boat – money which he did not possess – Belloc set out to pick up the boat in Anglesey, arriving at Holyhead on May 22.

The sea has taken me to itself whenever I sought it and has given me relief from men. It has rendered remote the cares and the wastes of the land; for of all creatures that move and breathe upon the earth we of mankind are fullest of sorrow. But the sea shall comfort us, and perpetually show us new things and assure us. It is the common sacrament of this world . . .[1]

'I hope to have her round Littlehampton this summer,' he wrote enthusiastically to his mother, the first sparkle of happiness in his letters since the death of Elodie.[2]

In the book which he made of this journey – one of the volumes which displays Belloc at his discursive best – the impression is given that the Cruise was continuous; that he and Kershaw sailed from Holyhead to Sussex, putting into shore now and then, but 'continuing in the same', like Sir Francis Drake, 'until it be thoroughly finished'. In fact, the seven or eight weeks which they spent on the enterprise were interrupted, as one would expect, by frequent sorties elsewhere. While the *Nona* was anchored in harbour, Belloc would abandon his sailing companion and go to stay with friends, or to spend a few nights at the Reform. It was on June 29 that he went to Mass at Salisbury.

During the Mass, the priest, after his announcements, asked the congregation to pray for the soul of the Archduke Heir-Apparent of Austria, who had been murdered at a place called Sarajevo. I had never heard the name and I had but a vague idea who this archduke was, of his relationship to the Emperor, and of his heirship to the throne of Hapsburg-Lorraine. I came to the 'Nona' where she lay, and sailed out with her into the sea for some days. I had no conception that anything could be brewing.[3]

There is something highly endearing about this confession of ignorance of European affairs, particularly in a man, who within weeks, was to be selling himself to Fleet Street editors, as a great expert on the War. At sea, and in solitude, we glimpse a more impressive Belloc than the blustering self-appointed know-all that he presented to the public in some of his speeches and writings. The

[1] *Cruise of the Nona*, last page.
[2] May 27, 1914.
[3] *Cruise of the Nona* p. 145.

magic of his surprise encounter with the Fleet, sailing out of Plymouth on that summer day, is one of the best things in his prose. Belloc is always best, whether in poetry, or in his essays, or in his historical writings, when he is *observing*. Many of his declarations on the subject of politics, or of economics, or of theology, however true they may be, sound like the utterance of a wind-bag. Such passages should not blind us to the best of Belloc's prose. When he *notices* things – the look of sunlight on water, the great ships, appearing out of the mist – we realise that there are few more observant, or more artfully evocative, writers in our language.

We had just rounded the Start at dawn. My companion went below to sleep. I watched, over the quarter, the Start Light flashing pale and white in the broadening day, and at last extinguished. Then the sun rose, as I have said. Immediately after its rising a sort of light haze filled the air to eastward. It was denser than it seemed to be, for it did not obscure the low disc of the sun, nor redden it, but as you will read in a moment, it performed a mystery. The little ship slipped on, up past the Skerries Bank, and I could see far off the headland which bounds Dart Bay. There was no sail in sight. I was alone upon the sea; and the breeze neither freshening nor lowering, but giving a hearty line of course (along which we slipped, perhaps, five knots or six) made the water speak merrily upon the bows and along the run of our low sides. In this loneliness. and content, as I sailed northward, I chanced to look after an hour's steering or so, eastward again towards the open sea – and then it was that there passed me the vision I shall remember for ever, or for so long as the longest life may last.

Like ghosts, like things themselves made of mist, there passed between me and the newly risen sun, a procession of great forms, in all line, hastening eastward. It was the Fleet recalled.

The slight haze along that distant water had thickened, perhaps imperceptibly; or perhaps the great speed of the men-of-war buried them too quickly in the distance. But, from whatever cause, this marvel was of short duration. It was seen for a moment, and in a moment it was gone.

Then I knew that war would come, and my mind was changed.[1]

[1] *The Cruise of the Nona* p. 150.

PART TWO

Mr Belloc

TEN

THE GREAT WAR
1914–1918

A patriotic hostess, shortly after the outbreak of the Great War, was foolish enough to ask G.K. Chesterton, 'Why are you not out at the Front?' to receive the inevitable reply: 'Madam, if you go round to the side, you will find that I am.' Another reason for his absence from the trenches was that he fell ill in the autumn of 1914, with a mysterious combination of bronchitis, malfunctioning kidneys and coronary disorders. His bed at Beaconsfield broke under the vast bulk, and he was presumably propped up on mattresses on the floor when he sank into a coma at Christmas, from which he did not emerge until the following Easter, of 1915.[1] He tells us:

> When I first recovered consciousness, in the final turn of my long sickness, I am told that I asked for *Land and Water*, in which Mr. Belloc had already begun his well-known series of war-articles, the last of which I had read, or been able to understand, being the new hope from the Marne. When I woke again to the real things, the long battles before Ypres were over and the long trench war had begun. The nurse, knowing that I had long been incapable of really reading anything, gave me a copy of the paper at random, as one gives a doll to a sick child. But I suddenly asserted in a loud and clear voice that this was an old number dealing with the first attempt before Nancy; and that I wanted all the numbers of the paper that had appeared since the battle of the Marne. My mind, such as it is, had suddenly became perfectly clear . . .[2]

For all the very bellicose, or rather Bellocose, nature of Chesterton's hatred of the Prussians, there is an appropriateness about that fey and childish figure sinking into an obese and comatose sleep for three months when hostilities really began to destroy Europe.

Belloc's position was very different; and, as he tells us in *The Cruise of the Nona*, his 'mind was changed' by the coming of war. He was, in

[1] Alzina Stone Dale: *The Outline of Sanity, A Life of G.K. Chesterton* (1982) p. 202.
[2] *Autobiography* p. 250.

any case, by the summer of 1914, a completely changed person. The first phase of his life, stretching from his birth to the death of his wife, began with a violent thunderstorm and the breaking of nations.

It is appropriate – for Belloc was thoroughly a European, and rooted through all that he loved and believed in European soil – that the second phase of his life, from Elodie's death until his own, should also have begun with great European turmoil. Before one traces his life during the Great War, there is a case for standing back and for meeting Belloc, at the age of forty-four, as it were for the first time. Up to now, this biography has remarked his extraordinary constancy. The old Belloc is very recognizable in the young; the controversialist of later years can be clearly seen in the undergraduate; we even glimpse him in the tiny figure of 'Master Hilary', stomping about the lawns of La Celle St Cloud and banging a drum. But there can be no doubt that, after the death of Elodie, a great change had come upon him. Put simply, he was now a man whose heart had been broken.

How did this figure strike those who had never met him before? Two examples may be chosen: one of a man who never met him again, and another of a woman who was to become a dear friend. They both belong to the early months of 1915.

On February 25, 1915, Belloc paid one of his frequent visits to the Continent. (His passport is stamped over twenty times for the year 1915–16).[1] He was met at Bologne by Evan Charteris and Maurice Baring, who were both on active service, Baring in the Royal Flying Corps. Together they inspected Ypres, and then made their way back to Cassel to dine with Sir John French, who was a friend of Bessie Belloc's.[2]

> On the way back from Ypres, Belloc sang a good many songs; some of them were about bishops. When we got home, and the car was waiting to take us to the Commander-in-Chief's house, while we were washing, someone asked the driver who he was waiting for. The driver said: 'Two officers and a *clergyman*.' The clergyman was Belloc, I should mention he was wearing a broad wide-awake hat.[3]

Baring told the story, of course, because of its ludicrous inappropriateness. Anyone less clerical in manner than Belloc would have been hard to find. But the mistake, so grotesque to Baring who had known the younger Belloc, was quite understandable. Belloc was swathed

[4] BC.
[2] BC August 20, 1914.
[3] Maurice Baring: *Flying Corps Headquarters (1914–1918)* (1930) pp. 82–83.

from head to foot in black. This widower's uniform was to remain his daily wear until he died: a black suit of thickest fustian, a black tie, a black overcoat or cloak, black shoes and large black hat, all made for him, strangely enough by Lanvin, the Parisian couturier. A chauffeur who did not mistake him for an undertaker would very naturally think him a priest. From now on, in all outward forms, he was to maintain his mourning. The King's Land writing paper and envelopes would, henceforth, be edged with black. Some of his friends, and even his own mother, began, as the months and the years passed, to urge him to do otherwise. It would not have been in his nature to do so. The death of Elodie halted life. After it he was less unwilling than incapable of change. In the matter of the outward observances of mourning, he was simply following family custom. His Irish grandmother at La Celle St Cloud, and his English mother, had both been widows for as long as he could remember them; and they both chose to be widows in what has been regarded as a very 'French' way. That is to say, they were widows in the mould of that very unGallic figure, Queen Victoria. Bessie never abandoned her blacks, her dabbing of her eyes at the mention of her late husband. She had brought up her son to regard this as normal behaviour. There was no cause for wonder, when he came to be widowed, if he followed family custom.

On the road from Ypres to Cassel, then, we glimpse 'two officers and a clergyman'. Back in the salons and drawing-rooms of London, where Belloc was so frequently and enthusiastically received, we glimpse the same figure. His passport of the time describes him for us: 'Age: 45. Profession: Man of Letters. Height: 5 feet 8 inches. Forehead: Medium. Eyes: Grey. Nose: Short. Mouth: Medium. Chin: Strong. Colour of hair: Brown. Complexion: Fair. Face: Oval.' Lady Diana Manners (later Cooper) described Belloc as 'perhaps with Winston Churchill the man nearest to genius I have known, one of the most complex, contradictory and brilliant characters ever to rumble, flash and explode across this astonishing world of ours . . . He was the "Captain Good" in life as well as the minstrel, the story-teller, the soothsayer, the foundation and the flush of the feast'.[1]

And yet, her first impression, as a young woman was that Belloc was an old, old man.[2] When they met, he was in fact about forty-five and she perhaps twenty-three or twenty-four.

Both impressions – Diana Manners seeing an old man stomping into the drawing-room of her mother, the Duchess of Rutland; the chauffeur imagining that he had a clergyman in the back of his car –

[1] Diana Cooper: *The Rainbow Comes and Goes* p. 239.
[2] Conversation with the author.

tell us more than the blurred memories of those friends – G.K. Chesterton, Maurice Baring, Raymond Asquith, Basil Blackwood – who knew Belloc before and after the change had come upon him. They laughed at the idea that he looked like a clergyman; and they, who had drunk with him, wasted midnight hours with him, and witnessed his prodigious physical energy, would not think of him as an old man. But he had come to be possessed with a melancholy detachment, a divine discontent with the world, which is perhaps more commonly found in the aged and the clergy.

> I stood in the desert, and I watched the snows
> On Aures, in their splendour from the west.
> Sahara darkened: and I thought of those
> That hold in isolation and are blest.
>
> They that in dereliction grow perfected:
> They that are silent: they that stand apart:
> They that shall judge the world as God's elected:
> They that have had the sword athwart the heart.

*   *   *

It was natural, as soon as war broke out, that Belloc should have pronounced on the subject in the British press. Since undergraduate days, he had reckoned himself an expert on European military history. and foreign policy. 'Mr. Belloc, Balliol,' noted *The Isis* in 1893, 'spoke eloquently and clearly as he generally does, though we think he might sometimes leave poor Germany alone.' That was not the mood of the Fleet Street editors twenty years later. By then, Belloc's anti-German feelings had refined and hardened. He had also built up an unrivalled knowledge, through his ceaseless ramblings, of the terrain which was to become the battlefield between the German armies and the Allies. He had, moreover, served in the French army, and was uniquely well-positioned to tell the British public what to expect in the opening months of the war: from their allies, from their enemies, and from their battle-grounds. He had contributed an article on this subject to the *Sunday Chronicle* before the war was many weeks old.[1]

Many of the group – slightly younger than he – whom he had befriended in Oxford during the early days of married life were joining up: Auberon Herbert, Lord Lucas; Raymond Asquith; Maurice Baring; Evan Charteris. Immediate contemporaries like Lord Basil Blackwood managed to get commissions. Belloc did not.

[1] Speaight p. 347.

Shortly after the outbreak of the war, in August 1914, he went to see General Macdonough at the War Office to volunteer, Macdonough was not sure what to do with him, or where to send him,

'Not a sign of a staff for me to go to yet,' Belloc wrote to Lady Juliet Duff, 'not even a divisional one. It is an abominable shame, and when I chuck it in disgust and try through the French, it may be too late – they will wonder why I didn't ask before.'[1]

That was on September 12, 1914. But three days before he had been visited at King's Land by a Sussex neighbour called Jim Allison. Allison was advertisement manager on *The Times*, and by birth an Australian. He was the chief shareholder and guiding light in a new periodical, to be called *Land and Water*. It was to appear weekly, and it was to deal exclusively with the war. Belloc signed a contract, agreeing to a weekly article. This showed very great common sense. Even as he traipsed from the War Office to the drawing-rooms of London hostesses, he must have known in his heart that he would not be acceptable as a soldier in the British army. He would have struck any recruiting officer, as he struck Diana Manners and the chauffeur, as a creature apart; someone who was too old for active service. The appearance would have been deceptive. Belloc at this date could have outstripped any young subaltern on a day's march. But his appearance was of a broken and unhappy man, prematurely aged and extremely dirty. Belloc would have been impossible to use in any military capacity. He would have wanted to boss his commanding officers, to lecture his generals on strategy. It was much better that he should do so in print, and from the sidelines.

So, within only a fortnight of war breaking out, Belloc had regular weekly employment. The circulation of *Land and Water* was vast – well over 100,000. It was the most lucrative work he had ever enjoyed, and it brought him his widest public. After a few issues, not having heard from Belloc for a few weeks, Basil Blackwood wrote, 'I am sorry to find that I had attributed your silence quite falsely to the insolence of wealth. I had hoped that much riches had made you rude. However you are paying debts, that at all events is a good moral exercise & the process tends to keep ones nose above water.' Blackwood clearly took Belloc's new career as a military expert with a certain measure of satire. This letter is decorated with two delightful BTB drawings: one of 'H.B. lecturing on Armageddon or the final battle of the war' (note the plan drawn in the Bellocian manner). In the other, two aged London clubmen hover in a smoking room; the more

[1] Speaight p. 347.

aged and venerable is saying, 'Belloc says etc. etc', and the caption is, 'This is what goes on all day at the Naval and Military'. 'I believe you will end life as a lecturer at Sandhurst, I hear you quoted on all sides as a military authority,' Blackwood averred. By October, Lord Basil was experiencing the horrors of the Front.

As you say, one's safety or otherwise in this war is simply a matter of Fate. The Germans have specialised in shells and it is a few days that we have not been under shell fire. Some have played upon us with effect but of course the vast majority go wide. However who can scheme to escape shells? Many guns have a range of eight miles, shells fall so impartially they can't be dodged, one must simply await with resignation what fate has in store. The most horrible scene I have witnessed was one that followed the explosion of two shells of the largest calibre on our billets killing 24 & wounding 20. I was on the spot & helped to remove the shattered debris. I shall never never forget the hateful sight or the long drawn out melancholy business of digging graves & giving the 18 bodies of the others christian burial – nor shall I forget the idiotic address of the military chaplain who was brought up from the neighbouring hospital for the purpose.[1]

It must have been hard to read this communication from his old friend, illustrator and travelling-companion and not to feel woefully inadequate at home. As if the ugly horrors of war needed emphasis, Blackwood asked Belloc to send him:

1/ a small bottle of morphia tabloids which are of great use when a man is wounded w. no doctor available and in great pain (which alas is frequent). A chemist would probably know the best dose to dull pain.
2/ a small bottle of permanganate tabloids to put in water to wash a wound, otherwise it is better not to wash it.
3/ A tourniquet. The colonel has one it is simply a band such as you might file papers with, with a lump attached which is put over the artery to secure great pressure at that point.

The items were posted. To reassure Belloc that he should not pine for an active part in the war, Lord Basil wrote:

I can understand your extreme anxiety to take a direct part in this war but for your consolation let me say that as far as I can see there is no sort of hurry as there will be an abundance of opportunity in due

[1] BC October 15, 1914.

course for all those who have been unsuccessful hitherto, to come, and secondly that you are probably of far greater use in England writing lecturing and illuminating. I must tell you that your articles in Land and Water are enormously appreciated here by soldiers & it occurred to me at once to suggest to you that it might be worth your while to get the job of writing the official history. I expect it would be a gold mine & one of the works (such as the poem on the bishops) which will live for ever.[1]

It has to be said that Belloc's histories of the First War have *not* lived for ever. At the same time, the enthusiasm of the common soldier for *Land and Water* was, to say the least, volatile. A volume was soon in circulation entitled *What I Know about the War* by Blare Hilloc. When opened, it was discovered to be a notebook with blank pages.[2]

If one turns the pages of Belloc's reflections on the Great War now, however, one is struck less by his inevitable mistakes than by his attitude. In each year of the war, he underestimated the potential size of the German armies, and overestimated their casualties. Lord Northcliffe's *Daily Mail* exposed some of these errors in September 1915, and the placard advertising that day's issue read 'Belloc's Fables'. Of course, people were angered by his mistakes. But mistakes, we can now see, were hardly avoidable. Belloc was in close touch with friends and soldiers at the Front; he visited France frequently; he had a deep knowledge of the terrain, and an above average understanding of the strategy, of the war. But he wrote for the most part from a desk in London. He was not a 'war correspondent'. From the point of view of accuracy, one is impressed by how few mistakes he made in the course of his *Land and Water* work, not by how many.

But much more is one struck by his attitude. The War of 1914–18 has come to seem to later generations a ghastly struggle between two highly similar Imperial powers – Germany and England – with the victims the flower of Europe's manhood, and the pride of many of her loveliest buildings and towns. Belloc saw it in much larger, historic terms. Looking back on it all in later life, he believed that there had been a 'moral revolution and breakdown' in Europe, beginning in the 1890s. 'Only the war accentuated it and prevented a reaction.'[3] He did not therefore believe simply that the cause of the Allies was untainted. He had no illusions about defending a 'way of life' which had produced the Marconi scandal and the Dreyfus affair. He was the last

[1] BC October 15, 1914.
[2] Speaight p. 349.
[3] Mells, April 20, 1933.

man to be tempted to think that the Allies had produced the best of all possible worlds, or that the 'democratic' system, with Lloyd George at the top of it, was worth defending with a single drop of human blood.

The struggle in Europe between 1914 and 1918 was, as far as Belloc was concerned, something other. It was a clash between Catholic civilisation and pagan barbarism and it was to be welcomed only in so far as England, quite by accident, found herself fighting on the side of Catholic civilisation. It was forty-four years since German armies had last goose-stepped their way through France. They had vandalised the house where Belloc was born, they had destroyed the furniture, desecrated the family portraits, defiled all that his mother and grand-mother had held sacred. It was deeply ingrained in him, therefore, this identification of Prussia with pagan barbarism; by contrast, he identified all that was good and lovely with his mother's religion, and the nation of his father. So, at the end of the first year of the war, he could see the German armies as the enemies of all the things he had loved since his youth, of all that he had celebrated in *The Path to Rome*.

> Comprehend the mood of the French, contrast and oppose it to that of the Germans, and you will have viewed almost in its entirety the spiritual theatre of this gigantic struggle. No don's talk of "Slav" or "Teuton", of "progressive" or "backward" nations, mirrors in any way the realities of the great business. This war was in some almost final fashion, and upon a scale quite unprecedented, the returning once again of those conflicting spirits which had been seen over the multitudes in the dust of the Rhône Valley when Marius came up from Italy and met the chaos in the North. They had met again in the damp forests of the Ardennes and the vague lands beyond the Rhine, when the Roman auxiliaries of the decline pushed out into the Germanies to set back the frontiers of barbarism. It was the clash between strong continuity, multiple energies, a lucid pos-session of the real world, a creative proportion in all things – all that we call the ancient civilization of Europe – and the unstable, quickly growing, quickly dissolving outer mass which continually learns its lesson from the civilised man, and yet can never perfectly learn that lesson; which sees itself in visions and has dreams of itself; which now servilely accepts the profound religion of its superior; now, the brain fatigued by mysteries, shakes off that burden which it cannot comprehend.[1]

[1] *A General Sketch of the European War: The First Phase* pp. 370–372.

Belloc's francophilia had long been a source of amusement to his friends. But the First World War made Belloc's vision of Europe no matter for jest. France, which he had loved since childhood, embodied enough of 'the Old Things' to save the world. Prussian militarism embodied enough of the new and ugly things to destroy it. So, as the war continued, one recognises why Belloc's immediate commentaries on strategy and battles were only partially important. Out of the smoke of battle and the bitterness of personal loss, his mind would clear for the next round of conflicts. Prussian militarism was, in the event and, until the rise of Hitler, defeated: at what cost! It did not prevent Belloc noting, long before the end of the war, the enthusiasm among the British for those things about the Germans which were most odious and most dangerous. Nor was he so pre-occupied with anti-Prussianism as not to notice, after the October Revolution of 1917, that Civilisation, Europe and the Faith, would have other enemies to face when the Germans were subdued:

> In one of his articles in *Land and Water*, he must have rather puzzled many of his readers, I fear, by an elaborate historical reconstruction of the outlook on the future, in the mind of a Greek official in Byzantium, at the beginning of the sixth century, calculating and combining all the forces of the Roman Empire and the Catholic Church. He noted how such a man might think he had accounted for all the possibilities, the danger of a religious split between East and West, the danger of the barbarian raids on Gaul or Britain, the situation in Africa and Spain, and so on; and then say he had in his hand all the materials of change. 'At that moment, far away in a little village of Arabia, Mahomet was eighteen years old.'[1]

* * *

Belloc did not, in the event, get the offer of a commission in the British army. But Basil Blackwood's fantasy about HB lecturing the troops did come true, and Belloc was in quite constant demand on the rostrum. Throughout the First War, as he said, 'I travel *without stopping*.'[2] One week would find him lecturing the fleet at Rosyth[3]; another would find him explaining the progress of the war to troops at the Front, or to civilian audiences at home.

But the closest he came to official 'war work' was his mission to the Vatican in 1916. It was felt in Foreign Office circles that the Vatican

[1] G.K Chesterton: *Autobiography* p. 255.
[2] Cockerell Papers. BM ms 52704.
[3] BC January 19, 1917.

was hostile to the Allies, and, as Robert Speaight has observed, this was hardly surprising. 'Neither the Masonic governments of France and Italy, nor the Liberal government presided over by Mr Lloyd George, gave much ground for hoping that the rights of Catholic populations would be respected in the post-war settlement, should the Allied Powers prove victorious.'[1]

A visit made to the Italian front in June 1916, when Belloc inspected field guns and lunched with General Caputo, gave the Foreign Office the opportunity to arrange a papal audience. And the great Catholic apologist was received by the Supreme Pontiff on June 3; indeed, though he did not know it at that time, he met two Supreme Pontiffs, for the man who ushered him into Pope Benedict XV's apartments, Mgr Pacelli, was himself one day to become Pius XII, last of orthodox popes.

Belloc was not given to a sentimental attachment to individual popes. The very fact that he revered the office of the Papacy led him to take a dim view, very often, of St Peter's successors as individuals. He did not have very high expectations of Benedict XV. 'I had thought to see one of those rather subtle and very *bornés* Italian officials – *bureaucrates*.'[2]

He was pleasantly surprised and 'had a long, long talk with him'. 'He spoke of individual conversion as opposed to political Catholicism in a way which – with my temperament all for the Collective Church – profoundly impressed me.'[3]

Poland was also discussed. As when he had dined with the Fellows of All Souls', Belloc evidently felt constrained to put the Holy Father wise. 'I spoke to him at great length *on Poland*; that is the key after the war.' For thirty-five years, until his wits began to fade, this was Belloc's repeated view of the European scene: that Poland is the *test*. By that, he meant that Poland, like Ireland, was a Catholic nation, and the future of what he called 'political Catholicism' could be gauged by how far the civilisations of Europe allowed Poland to survive: against Prussian militarism, later against the atheistic dictatorships of Hitler and Stalin. We can now see very clearly that Belloc was truly prophetic here. As I write these words, for the first time in history, there is a Polish pope whose entire European policy proclaims the Bellocian point of view. The extent to which the 'free' nations of Europe support Poland reflects the extent to which they care about the

[1] Speaight p. 358
[2] Speaight p. 359, letter to Charlotte Balfour.
[3] Ibid.

survival, or revival, of Christendom. Benedict XV was less sure. For one thing, Belloc's lecture on the Polish question presupposed that the Allies would win the war. 'But do you think they will, Mr Belloc?'[1]

It is perhaps not surprising that the Holy Father, who took such an openly weary view of international politics, struck Belloc as 'sad and weak. One thing moved him, which was the sending of Jews to the Holy Land. He kept on saying to me, "C'est une honte! C'est une honte". I told him that it would bring its own reward. My daughters rebuked me afterwards for putting the Pope wise . . . '[2] In the matter of the Polish future, Benedict XV seems, perhaps, incomprehensibly secular. With regard to the idea of a 'Jewish homeland', his attitude perhaps seems to a modern and post-Hitlerian readership almost grotesquely religious. It was such sentiments as these which sent men on Crusades in the twelfth century. The Roman Catholic Church had not revoked, still less had it apologised for, its medieval decrees, forbidding the faithful to mix with the race who condemned Our Lord to death. Pope Eugenius IV in 1442 had decreed and ordered 'that from now on and for all time, Christians shall not eat or drink with Jews nor admit them to feasts, nor cohabit with them, nor bathe with them'.[3]

Repugnant as this may be to a modern sensibility, it was an attitude which persisted into our century. It was piously harsh; as are the similar prohibitions placed by Holy Scripture on the Jews themselves, against mixing with the Gentiles. A Pope who did not take this line, however, in 1916, would have been regarded as extraordinary. The holiest place in Christendom – the Sepulchre of Christ, the mount where He died, the stable where He was born – could not, without blasphemy, be handed over to the race who, according to the Gospel tradition, took upon their own heads the blood of His death. There have been other Popes, and other events in Jewish history since 1916. Pius XI, in answer to the anti-Jewish lunacy of the Nazis, proclaimed that all Catholics were spiritual semites. Pius XII, condemned by Belloc and others for not speaking out against the slaughter of Jews by Hitler, did much to shelter them as refugees. It was a tribute to his devotion to these Jews, his preparedness to offer them fake baptismal certificates in Gentile names to save them from the hands of the bullying tyrants, that Rome's Chief Rabbi, at the end of the Second World War, was converted to the Catholic religion. Since then we

---

[1] Speaight p. 359.
[2] Mells April 11, 1934.
[3] Quoted Corrin op. cit. p. 86.

have had Pope John XXIII's rejection of his church's anti-semitic decrees, and the Second Vatican Council's collective expression of contrition for the centuries in which Catholics were encouraged to avoid, or to persecute, the Jews. Finally, more eloquent than any words, we have the pictures of a Polish pope, kneeling silently at Auschwitz.

All these things have passed in the sixty-five years since Benedict XV spontaneously exclaimed, 'C'est une honte! C'est une honte!' at the idea of European Jews settling in Palestine. When one considers the ineradicably disastrous consequences of the Balfour declaration, it is hard not to feel that the Pope's unselfconsciously 'medieval' reaction to the matter was not as prophetic as Belloc's vision of the future of Poland.

*   *   *

By an irony he would have disliked, we can see that Belloc's chief 'war work' was not in the analysis of campaigns, nor in the interviewing of popes, but in keeping amused and informed the kind of women who had asked G.K. Chesterton why he was not 'out at the Front'. Belloc longed to be at home in the world of the generals and the politicians. He was in fact much happier in the world of Mrs. Roebeck. The war involved him in a ceaseless round of travelling, lecturing, writing and journalism. But the centre of his life at this date was not King's Land, associated so painfully with the greatest catastrophe of his existence, so much as the drawing-rooms of London. He wearied of

> each declining phase
> Of emptied effort, jaded wit,
> And day by day of London days.

At the same time, he was wanted by the 'bright young things' of the hour; and he was addicted to their company. Much as he had enjoyed baiting and tormenting the generation of their parents – H.H. Asquith, Lady Desborough, Lady Horner ('Hag Horner', as he called her)[1] and the rest – he was devoted to the next generation: Raymond and Katharine Asquith, Julian Grenfell, Diana Manners, Harold Baker ('Bluetooth') and all those clever, well-born young people who kept up the feverish pace of social life in London during the First World War. We glimpse the world Belloc inhabited at this date in the

[1] BC May 12, 1917.

incomparable diaries of Lady Cynthia Asquith[1], in which the practical jokes, the private language, the flirtations and the whoopee intensified as the news from the trenches got bleaker, every month bringing the information that a brother or a cousin or an intimate friend of that brilliant coterie would cast their 'dewdrops' no more. Small wonder that they drank and hooted and took cocaine and did all in their power to blot out the torture of consciousness.

> Mary [Herbert] . . . had witnessed wonderful Coterie episode. After dinner Diana [Manners] ejaculated, 'I *must* be unconscious tonight!' And away went a taxi to fetch chloroform from the chemist. 'Jolly old chlorers.' Aubrey [Herbert, Hon.] firmly removed Mary before the orgy began.[2]

One captures the same atmosphere of frenetic hilarity, a nerve-racking blend of heroism and frivolity, in the letters Maurice Baring wrote from the Front to Lady Juliet Duff. Read today, they reflect much of the charm and humour and linguistic refinement of Baring, that excellent and too-little-read figure. His novels deserve to be revived, but his letters, delightful as they are, are hardly approachable by the modern reader. The nicknames, the 'in' jokes and the flights of private fancy are impenetrable to anyone outside the coterie.

Baring makes it perfectly clear in his letters to Lady Juliet ('Dear Animated Bust') that he finds it impossible to take her quite seriously. All who knew her remember that she was 'a good sort', 'terrific fun'; but she was gangling (all of six foot three in height), clumsy, empty-headed and very, very silly. 'I do think her the ugliest beauty,' was Cynthia Asquith's verdict in 1916, at about the time when Belloc fell in love with her.[3]

> How did the party go in Portman Square?
> I cannot tell you; Juliet was not there.
> And how did Lady Gaster's party go?
> Juliet was next me and I do not know.

The infatuation led to an endless stream of letters, poems, epigrams and other compliments from Belloc's pen, from the middle of the First War, when he was perhaps forty-five and she thirty-five, to the

---

[1] Lady Cynthia Asquith: *Diaries 1915–1918.* (1968) She was the daughter of the 11th Earl of Wemyss and married Herbert, second son of H.H. Asquith, the Prime Minister.
[2] Ibid p. 112.
[3] Ibid p. 223.

time when he could no longer hold that pen in his hand. Her husband, Sir Robert Duff the second baronet, had been killed in action in 1914, leaving her with one young son, Michael. Although she was evidently attractive to men, there was always an element of jesting, as far as her name was concerned, which must, for Lady Juliet herself, have been irksome. When Eddie Marsh proposed marriage to her, for instance, everyone refused to believe the story. In his late fifties, Maurice Baring came up to Duff Cooper in Whites, breathlessly excited, and said, 'Duff, Duff, there's something I must tell you.' 'Can't it wait till after lunch, dear Maurice?' 'No! I've done it, I've finally done it.' 'Done what?' 'Been to bed with a woman.' It was believed by all Baring's friends that this unique experience (never repeated) had been with Juliet Duff; not because there was any likelihood of it being true, but because she was the woman whose name was introduced into the conversation if you wanted to tell a story in which the opposite sex was made ridiculous. As the years progressed, her reputation for clumsiness, affectation and absurdity became almost mythic. She lived in a world of beautifully-furnished houses (her taste was impeccable), surrounded by the friends and associates of her son Sir Michael Duff, in whose education Belloc had tried to take a hand.

It is inevitable that the prurient will ask themselves whether he was granted the privilege once allegedly vouchsafed to Maurice Baring, of sharing the bed of Juliet Duff. There is no documentary evidence to support any view of the matter. On the one hand, we have to consider the miserable atmosphere of war-time London, its hurried social whirl carried out against a certainty that at any moment there will be 'a darkening and an end to it'; we have the suggestion, and more than the suggestion, that Juliet Duff was not averse to the affectionate companionship of men; we have the fact that Belloc was in love with her. On the other hand, we have the fact that Lady Juliet, when referring to 'poor darling Hilary', would try to make it clear that she had not allowed him the privileges of a lover. Although, from 1916 onwards, his engagement books show that he dined with her almost every night that he was in London, there is no reason to suppose that he was able to express his adoration in physical terms. It was a thing of frantic telephone calls; telegrams, billets doux, and tête-à-tête dinners snatched in the middle of evenings in which dozens of other figures flooded in.

Belloc was Juliet Duff's peculiar indulgence. He was the one man in the world who took her totally seriously, and she would not have wasted this flattering truth by seducing him. Her relationship with him was really characterised by Sir Andrew Aguecheek's 'I was adored once'. He was a man who did not seem to notice that she could barely walk into a room without upsetting a vase of flowers, wrenching the door from its hinges or demolishing lampshades.

> Two visions permanent: his native place
> Found after days at sea, and Juliet's face.

But in that, as in all his quests for permanence, Belloc was misled. Towards the end of the war she made a lightning and foolish marriage to a man called Major Trevor, whom 'nobody knew'. Belloc was furious:

> I have written enough
> For Juliet Duff.
> I'll write nothing whatever
> For Juliet Trevor.

Although the 'marriage' only lasted a matter of months, it destroyed forever the prospect of her becoming Mrs Belloc, for it would have been unthinkable that Belloc, as a public defender of the Catholic faith, could have married a divorced woman. This meant that, long after the war, and her separation from Major Trevor, Juliet Duff could still claim Belloc as her lap-dog.

> Goodbye my Juliet; May you always be
> Polite to all the world but kind to me.

On the whole, she answered his plea, and as she developed the somewhat idiosyncratic lifestyle which revolved around her son's friends her trundling old black coated devotee never ceased to be 'poor darling Hilary'.

*   *   *

Of course, another, and more pious, way of describing the course of Belloc's relations with Lady Juliet Duff would be to emphasise the fact that he was still inconsolable for the death of Elodie. And there cannot be any doubt that, after his wife's death, he was a changed man. His grief was of a peculiarly guilt-ridden kind. In her life-time, he had neglected Elodie while he gadded about on his travels. Moreover, he always felt that the cold, rambling damp house where he had taken her to live had helped to kill her.

His feelings of attachment to Juliet Duff increased, rather than diminished, the guilty piety of his devotion to Elodie. Whenever he saw his children, it was to encourage them in the canonisation of their mother, a process into which his daughters entered with particular relish. 'We missed her beyond measure,' Eleanor wrote some forty-two years after her mother's demise, 'and made up our minds to go on missing her, and we would never accept the guidance or help offered in her place by other kindly people. She had been the queen of our hearts and home, and much will be forgiven us because we loved much.'[1]

The Belloc girls were at St Dominic's Priory in Stone for the duration of the war: and, towards the end of their time there, the headmistress, Sister Rose Ismelda, was rash enough to suggest that Elizabeth was prepared for some examinations. Belloc was astonished:

> I am still thoroughly opposed to any examination system, especially of the Oxford and Cambridge type. I do not see what sort of use they can be except to those who are going in for the teaching profession. The three things which Elizabeth could study with profit and which will make her happier later on are Latin, French and Drawing. Drawing she has a natural taste for and I should give her what opportunities I can further when she has left school, but if she can have a good grounding in French and Latin in her last year it will be invaluable.[2]

For the first time in his life, Belloc had money to spend on his family. *Land and Water*, although he claimed that 'the non-Belloc part gets stupider and stupider every week'[3], had brought him in such a considerable income that he had been able to save. As a shareholder as well as a contributor, Belloc found himself, half by accident, in the possession of a capital sum. He decided to invest it, and to play the games of the rich, of which he professed to disapprove. If they could speculate with stocks and shares, why should not he? In the middle of 1917, he proudly announced to Maurice Baring that he had invested *all* his savings in Russian bonds. Baring, who knew Russia well, not unnaturally expressed astonishment, and urged Belloc to withdraw at least a part of his capital from this very 'high risk' investment. He even hinted that he thought there might, conceivably, be a revolution in Russia. Belloc's features twinkled with a knowing Irish grin. 'Ah, but Maurice. It will be a *Jewish* revolution . . . ' A word to the wise; the presence of Jews in the bolshevik Leninist camp would ensure that

[1] *Testimony to Hilaire Belloc* p. 169.
[2] BC February 10, 1917.
[3] BC March 17, 1916.

international capital was safe. Needless to say, by the end of 1917, the Bellocs were paupers once more. It would have been unnatural, eery, had it been otherwise.

* * *

As for almost everyone else in Europe, the war was for Belloc a ceaseless tale of death and loss. Because Baring, Belloc and his friends went on believing that the 'Prussianism' was an evil which would destroy Catholic Europe, they went on believing that the appalling carnage of the trenches was not merely necessary, but almost glorious. In a spine-chilling poem published in *The Spectator* in September 1916, Maurice Baring could write of a dear coreligionist, Dermot Browne:

> Thus with clear eyes and laughing lips he went,
> Rejoicing in the soldier's sacrament,
> And ready to salute and to obey,
> Should the High Captain beckon he was there,
> Shriven and houselled, happy when the blare
> Of trumpets called him on St Michael's day.

Not all of the soldiers were so lucky; most of Belloc's friends who died were Protestants. That very week, Raymond Asquith was killed, and Baring wrote home;

> Raymond's death is a crushing blow, isn't it? I am proud for him - for how far nobler a fate that is than if he had been a successful barrister or even Curator of Big Ben or even a "Politician" – & the splendour of his death is doubled by his not being a regular soldier and his having had so much to give. But for us it adds to the gloom and takes away more of the sunlight.[1]

Six weeks later Bron Lucas was killed on November 3, 1916. Belloc wrote to Juliet Duff that 'he was the noblest and the best and therefore they took him from this vile world, and our lives are changed'.

The catalogue was to continue. Basil Blackwood was killed on July 3, 1917, leaving in Cynthia Asquith's eloquent understatement, 'a bewildering blank'.[2] The same year was to claim Edward Horner; and, in that year also, Belloc's great friend Cecil Chesterton left the *New Witness* in the charge of his new young wife, Ada Jones, and joined up, to be discharged after only a few months with a septic hand.

The chief worry of the year was that the eldest Belloc child, Louis,

[1] Jebb September 21, 1916.
[2] Cynthia Asquith. p. 339.

having started his army career as a sapper on the Somme, was mildly gassed in August 1917. He had always been more melancholy, less exuberant than his two brothers, Hilary and Peter, who were still at school. Elodie had intended Louis to be a monk and written off to his headmaster at Downside about the matter on more than one occasion. Now he languished in hospital, covered in blisters. But he recovered, and as soon as he was fit for active service he got out of the army and joined the Royal Flying Corps, of which Maurice Baring had been so surprisingly accomplished a member ever since the beginning of hostilities.

By the following summer, 1918, it was becoming clear to most observers that, with American help, the war would soon be over in Europe. A bucolic Belloc wrote to Maurice Baring from King's Land on July 5, 1918:

> I have got all my hay in. Thirty tons. The jays are eating my beans. Now that I have my hay in I am praying for rain and great quantities of it. Four bullocks have come and also Louis on leave from the North. He now does all things in the air in a terrifying manner, including looping the loop, and the day before yesterday went careering all over the North of England in what they call a Cooks Tour, a go-as-you please by oneself for many hours in the air.

For Belloc, who was not persuaded to step into an aeoplane until he was well over seventy, his son's aerobatic activities must have seemed particularly brave and bizarre. At the end of August 1918, the boy returned to the Flying Corps and his Squadron set out to bomb the German transport columns.

He was reported as 'missing' a few days later. Baring, being on the spot, did all he could to find information. 'The suspense is cracking . . . I am so sorry, for you, Dear Hillary [sic] and I wish I could do anything.' Belloc persisted in hoping that Louis might only have been taken prisoner.

Only two months later, there was the Armistice, and while Belloc was still making inquiries, to find out if Louis had been taken prisoner by the Germans, came the astonishing news that Cecil Chesterton, suffering from nephritis in a hospital near Boulogne, had died of the illness at the beginning of December. He was buried on December 6, and on December 14 his friends assembled at the little church of Corpus Christi, Maiden Lane, where Cecil Chesterton had been received into the Catholic Church, and where he had been married. He has, on the whole, received harsh judgements from posterity[1], and he has been seen as vitriolic, malicious and vindictive. But, for Desmond MacCarthy, he was 'the most pugnacious journalist since Cobbett,' and we may regret, not that he hounded the politicians of his day too cruelly; merely that he failed to be sure of his facts. 'He never in his life checked an action or a word from a consideration of personal caution,' wrote Belloc, paying tribute to the courage of his friend. But he could equally and simply have just written, 'He never in his life checked a word.'

Vincent McNabb preached at Cecil Chesterton's requiem, and Belloc believed it to be the finest piece of oratory he had ever heard.[2] As he knelt in that friendly little church, crammed with statues, and prayed for the soul of his friend, he was, of course, thinking about his missing son. The fiction that he might one day come back, that he had been taken prisoner, that he was in hiding, was forcibly discarded by Christmas-time.

'The first step is undertaken lightly, pleasantly, and with your soul in the sky; it is the five hundredth that counts,' Belloc had written in *The Path to Rome*.[3] As Belloc approached his fiftieth year, he was to be tested as he had never been tested before. Louis had gone the way of Elodie. The boy's bedroom, like Elodie's was now kept locked at King's Land, also never to be opened in Belloc's lifetime. The locked rooms tell their own morbid story, corresponding in an obvious way to the imprisoned tortures of Belloc's own soul. The exhibitionistic paraphernalia of mourning announced to the world that there were whole emotional areas which were out of bounds. So he went on using mourning paper, and wearing black clothes, for the rest of his life, outwardly bluff and sarcastic and funny as before, but with a face almost perpetually darkened with the shadow of death. 'These things have the evil effect of clouding the mind,' he wrote. 'They destroy its vision. Dogma alone remains: that is its supreme value. But vision is lost for the moment. He is undoubtedly safe and his mother has him. But the mind in this world has no relief.'[4]

As in his grieving for Elodie, the sorrow he felt for Louis was strongly intermingled with remorse, for he had neglected his children and, in later years, failed to 'get on' with his son. He still had left a fourteen-year-old boy, Peter; a rumbustious sixteen-year-old,

---

[1] An exception is *Cecil Chesterton* by Brocard Sewell (1975). It goes without saying that his widow's book, *The Chestertons*, gives a favourable view and speaks of Gilbert as 'the lesser brother'.

[2] Speaight p. 370.

[3] *Path to Rome* p. 18.

[4] Princeton 5 November 1918.

Hilary, and his two daughters who were on the verge of womanhood. But he could only give them a part of his affection, a part of his time. As he settled to post-war life, Belloc doggedly and unavoidably felt unable to leave the dead alone. Since 1914, he had lost his wife, his son, and the cream of all his younger friends, as well as older mentors such as George Wyndham. Like Yeats, and with rather more justice, Belloc felt his friends to be 'all the Olympians, a thing never known again'. His emotional range narrowed now. He went on, of course, meeting hundreds of people: journalists, politicians, co-religionists, disciples, and the friends of his children. But his closest intimates, closer to him in a way than his own family, were the fellow-survivors of the Great War, the widows and the brothers and sisters of all the Olympians.

Yeats, contemplating the desolation of post-war England and Ireland in 'Nineteen nineteen', and surveying the ghastly violence of the Irish scene, could only exclaim that

> Man is in love and loves what vanishes,
> What more is there to say?

Belloc, who was never stuck for words, tried to provide answers precisely to this question in the second half of his writing life.

ELEVEN

THE BOSSES AND THE CHIC
1919–1922

In May 1919, Belloc took Katharine Asquith and her daughter Perdita out for a drive in his car. ('They never last more than four years.')[1] He was an exuberant, rather than a careful driver, and in the roar of his conversation, he took his eyes off the road in order to speak to his passengers. They collided with a motor-cycle. No one was hurt; but, although a nasty experience, it helped to break the ice between Belloc and Raymond Asquith's widow.

'I never told you and I thought all the time I would like to,' she wrote to him, 'though perhaps it seems rather impertinent – how perfect I thought you were about the accident. I was quite glad it happened because of that, though you will say it is an expensive and dangerous way of getting to know your friends – and I was terribly sorry that you should have lost the motor-car through taking us out.'[2]

From this moment, Belloc showered the Asquiths with presents of claret, chocolates, crystallised fruits, outings to Gilbert and Sullivan, visits to the sea and offers of foreign holidays. On June 27, 1919 they both attended the wedding of Duff Cooper to Lady Diana Manners, after which Belloc proposed that they should take a holiday together. Since the Asquith children (Helen eleven, Perdita nine and Julian three) were hardly of an age to enjoy mixing with the Belloc children (Eleanor twenty-one, Elizabeth eighteen, Hilary sixteen and Peter fourteen) the idea of a joint family expedition to the Continent was abandoned. Mrs Asquith took a bungalow at Mullion in Cornwall and set off there on her own. But she was soon writing to 'Mr Belloc' (as he yet was to her): 'Couldn't you get your boat out of dock & swoop round the Lizard to our bay? I shall be rather lonely with nothing to think about but the sunsets and the crabs'[3].

In the event, he was only able to pay them a flying visit on that occasion, though it was not the last time that he would join them on

[1] BC April 5, 1918.
[2] BC May 4, 1919.
[3] BC May 1919.

Cornish holidays and take them out in his boat. In the previous few months, he had been half crushed with depression. So had Mrs Asquith. When the children were in bed, they talked, far into the night.

When he had gone, she wrote,

> The Times when we've talked have been a relief to me and made me feel less desperate – partly because you are so sure of certain things & though I don't suppose I shall ever feel sure myself I have to live as if I were and I can't help feeling glad when someone who is so much above me in understanding is quite certain & partly because I think you are the only person that I know who has been unhappy in the way that I am. My mother is the only other person who has experienced it all but even she understands more by sympathy and making comparisons than from having had the same personal experiences. It just so happens that no other people I know mean the same things as I do when they talk about either marrying or dying.

When they spoke of 'marrying' and 'dying', they spoke, of course, of something that was in the past. There was no question of their marrying each other, as some members of their families supposed. As late as 1922, Belloc was still under the impression that her name was Kathleen[1]. Even if they had loved each other passionately, it would have taken much to break down the walls of his grief for Elodie, and of Katharine Asquith's own statuesque diffidence. Their relationship deepened in a consideration of religious inquiry.

It was Belloc's irrecoverable losses, wedded to an unshakeable faith in the strength of dogma, which were to fashion his remaining years as a writer. Like his own 'Prophet lost in the hills at evening', Belloc could 'feel the footsteps of the dead' shuffling softly close; he could feel darkness gathering, change threatening, and despair mocking the wasted years which lay behind. But like the Prophet, he could say that he had kept the Faith.

Two things, abundantly and immediately, filled his mind at the close of the First War, and they both concerned the Faith. One was the private horror of death, forced by the war on to the individual consciences of every man, woman and child. There could be no one, in 1919, who had not lost, at the very least, an acquaintance or a friend in the previous five years. In many families, of course, there were many more than one loss. Katharine Asquith lost her husband, Raymond, and her brother, Edward Horner. Belloc himself lost his

[2] BC June 19, 1922.

first-born son. Many of the most brilliant of their young friends, or relations, had been removed, savagely, from their lives. And, in the shade of this terrible experience, Belloc found that 'dogma alone remains'. He could not *feel*; he could only cling to what he knew.

And, if this was true in the area of private grief, it was equally true when considering the state of Europe at the end of that war. 'Europe must go back,' he lamented. 'Northern France will maintain the tradition, as usual, but a general decline is inevitable.'[1]

To both these things, the blank personal horror in the face of death, and the great political horror of Europe broken and divided by the most terrible war in history, there was, for Belloc, only one antidote, one gleam of light for travellers on an otherwise benighted path. 'One thing in this world is different from all other. It has a personality and a force. It is recognised, and (when recognised) most violently loved or hated. It is the Catholic Church. Within that household the human spirit has roof and hearth. Outside it, is the Night.

> In hac urbe lux sollenis,
> Ver aeternum, pax perennis
> Et eterna gaudia.'[2]

Nearly all his energies as a writer and a controversialist from this point on were devoted in one way or another to a propagation of this certitude. It would be wrong to suppose that Belloc was solely responsible for the great wave of conversions to Catholicism which took place in England during the decades after the First World War. But his role was a unique one. The household of the Faith had always been home to him. There is a characteristic story of him standing in the French fashion at Mass in Westminster Cathedral and being told by a whispering sacristan, 'Excuse me, sir, we kneel here.' 'Go to hell', said Belloc. 'I'm sorry, sir', said the sacristan, 'I didn't know you were a Catholic.'

Belloc's devotion to his Faith had none of the sentimental enthusiasms of a convert. He took it as a natural, sane part of life. He did not have to be on his best behaviour either in church, or when talking about the Faith. This was, and is, a common characteristic of Catholic men and women. But it is also noticeable that, contrary to what is often supposed, 'cradle Catholics' have not been conspicuous in their attempts to proselytse. Frank Sheed, the Catholic publisher, chronicled a great list of prominent writers in the between-war years: 'the philosophers Christopher Dawson and E.I. Watkin, the poets

[1] Cockerell papers.
[2] *Essays of a Catholic* p. 305.

Alfred Noyes and Roy Campbell (though he did not take the actual plunge until the thirties), the biographer D.B. Wyndham Lewis, the satirist J.B. Morton, the writer-of- all-trades G.K. Chesterton, the artist writers Eric Gill and David Jones, novelists Compton Mackenzie, Philip Gibbs, Maurice Baring, Arnold Lunn, Sheila Kaye-Smith, Bruce Marshall, Graham Greene and Evelyn Waugh . . . Notice one strangeness. Almost all the Catholics who entered the nation's reading-lists were either converts or (in Europe) reverts, people who had been born inside the Church but had for a time lost touch. The one born Catholic was Hilaire Belloc.'[1]

The reasons for this are rooted in the history of the English Roman Catholic community during the nineteenth century. After the re-establishment of a Catholic hierarchy, Catholic dioceses and parishes under Cardinal Wiseman, it might have been thought that the days were over in which the recusant community need feel self-protective or self-contemplative. Manning's leadership banished forever the concept of the Catholic Church in England as a mere 'Italian mission'. His ultramontane view of Church polity insisted on the Church in England and Wales recognising itself as part of the Universal Church of Christ. His evangelism among the urban poor earned him the respect and affection of many outside his communion. And yet, by the beginning of the twentieth century, the Roman Church in England was still composed, very largely, of three distinct groups: There were the Old Catholic families, few in number, who for the most part resented their church being taken over by a lot of ex-Anglican clergymen; there were the Irish immigrants in cities like Birmingham and Liverpool; and there were converts.

As the Roman Catholic community was constituted at that date, it was only likely that converts would take much interest in the non-Catholic world in the first generation. Thereafter, their children were educated at Catholic schools, and, in Manning's day, they were forbidden to attend the Universities. Within a generation, they had joined the self-enclosed clique to which educated Catholics naturally belonged. The huge majority of middle and upper class Englishmen remained untouched by their existence.

Belloc was fully aware of this, and he made the point in a letter to his old friend Professor Phillimore in 1920:

> My book *Europe and the Faith* is now passing through the press and will be out very soon. It is quite abominably ill written. I did not know that I could write so badly even if I tried. For the first time in

[1] Frank Sheed, *The Church and I*, p.33, corrected by Dom Philip Jebb, OSB.

my life I feel I am making a sacrifice, and like Danton, may my style be *flétri* but may the book do good! Every bit of work done for the Faith is of enormous importance at this moment, and though there is not the least chance yet of England's conversion – many disasters must come upon her first – still the immediate future is going to be chaos of opinion, and in that chaos the order, the civility of the Faith will make a deep impression *if it is presented*, but it has to be presented. The difficulty just now is that English Catholics do not present it at all. They fiddle about with unimportant things of detail or fill the air with the hymns of praise of Protestants for being allowed to live. It is essential for us to impress it upon our contemporaries that the Catholic is intellectually the superior of everyone except the sceptic in all that region cognate to and attached to that which may be called 'Intellectual appreciation' – pure intelligence.

Four powers govern man, avarice, lust, fear and snobbishness. One can use the latter. One cannot use the first three. Blackmail is alien to Catholic temper and would cut little ice. Pay we cannot, because we are not rich enough and because those of us who are will not use their money rightly. Threaten we cannot, because we are nobody, all the temporal power is on the other side. But we *can* spread the mood that we are the bosses and the *chic* and that a man who does not accept the Faith writes himself down as suburban. Upon these amiable lines do I proceed.[1]

It would be foolish to take this wholly seriously. On the other hand, it can hardly be denied that Belloc was wholly successful in this modest aim. He knew that the English were a race of snobs, and that if he could not convert them to Catholicism, he could put about the idea that his religion was smart. When Manning became a priest of the Roman obedience, he felt that he had abandoned any claims to be a gentleman. Within two generations of his death, the English-speaking world was wallowing in *Brideshead Revisited*. And this was quite largely because Belloc had put about the idea that 'a man who does not accept the Faith writes himself down as suburban'.

While he was M.P. for South Salford, he had, for instance, stayed as the guest of the Bishop of Manchester, Edmund Knox. He had 'suffered terribly from the sour claret; when asked how he slept, he replied that he hadn't, and had had to sit up all night reading'.[2] Within the decade that followed, Bishop Knox's son Ronald had rebelled

[1] Speaight. p. 391.
[2] Penelope Fitzgerald: *The Knox Brothers* (1977) p. 167.

against the Protestantism of his father and become one of the most brilliant stars in the Anglo-Catholic firmament: an effortless debater at the Oxford Union, a fluent classicist, the beloved contemporary of that prodigious Etonian generation who were butchered in the trenches, a fashionable preacher much in demand. The Roman Catholic church never produced men of such calibre, and when Ronald Knox finally toppled over into that Church Belloc was among the first to appear at the Brompton Oratory, where he was staying, 'and exuberantly congratulate him on his conversion'.[1] '*Être Catholique, c'est tout*,' he wrote to Knox. 'To remake Europe is our intense and urgent call. Of the higher things I know nothing. I was not called to them. But I know *that*: and I know that very few men can so act anywhere: in England but a dozen, and that you are one of them.'

Knox was his guest at King's Land for the Christmas of 1921. Although his elegant and witty accomplishments as a homilist did not go unused in the church of his adoption, he never in fact found a central place in it. Apart from a spell as Catholic Chaplain at Oxford (and the chaplaincy in those days admitted only young men, most of them from a tiny handful of private boarding-schools) he was to have no official appointment in the church. His days were spent in country houses, rapidly solving *The Times* crossword and composing, on a battered typewriter, an idiosyncratic translation of the Latin Vulgate which was soon to be swept away by a flood of more scholarly versions after the Second Vatican Council.

Within a limited circle, however, Knox was an influential figure; and his influence was precisely of the kind Belloc would have approved. On the one hand he employed his comic and satirical gifts for laughing his readership into agreement. On the other, his writings have an air of casual superiority, which makes one feel that membership of the Church is vaguely analagous to an *entrée* into the best social circles.[2]

If a snob is a social climber whose ambition is to intrude himself into the lives of his social superiors, then Belloc was not a snob. It simply happened that most of his friends belonged to a high social class. Most of the men in this class were not of Belloc's faith. Basil Blackwood had

[1] Evelyn Waugh: *Ronald Knox* (1959) p. 197.
[2] For example 'If you are at all shy, you can imagine how appalling it would be if your mama told you quite suddenly one morning that you were going to be presented at Court. If she went on to say that unfortunately there would be no time to get any special clothes, and you would have to go just as you were, that would put the lid on your misery, wouldn't it? And that is how a priest feels or ought to feel when he goes to the altar. He is presenting himself at the Court of Heaven.' *The Mass in Slow Motion* p. 7.

declared himself immune from 'the hellish charms of your sect'.[1] He died, like Lord Lucas and Raymond Asquith, invincibly ignorant of Catholic consolation. 'The absence from the Faith of such souls in England turns us all into exiles,' Belloc had written to Maurice Baring.[2]

It was partly a consciousness of the *manner* in which he grieved for his heroic friends which led their widows to embrace Belloc's faith. Raymond Asquith's widow, for instance, found, for a long period, that she was unable to believe in life after death, still less in the resurrection of the dead. But, the more she grieved and fretted, the more intolerable, and unreasonable, her unbelief appeared to her. This was very largely a development of her sense that no one else in her circle, apart from Belloc, meant 'the same things as I do when they talk about marrying or dying'.

She was slow in her conversion. Even after hours of discussion with Belloc, and mountains of correspondence, she had still only reached the point where she could write, 'I shall always be grateful even if I remain where I am now.'[3]

When she did come to embrace the Faith, she encountered the hostile opposition both of Asquiths and of Horners. It was not quite as horrific to her father-in-law as the conversion of Venetia Stanley to Judaism ('Mr Asquith has told Venetia that, if she persists, he will never speak to her again'[4]) but it was seen as a betrayal of the values to which she had been brought up.

Belloc, recalling H.H. Asquith, wrote,

In quite the last years of his life he developed a violent antipathy to the Church. He had always held the rather provincial attitude of the English cultivated atheist towards the main doctrines of Catholicism, as they had been filtered through to him through the drab and worn cloth of English Protestantism. How he came to know anything about the Church I know not, it was perhaps the obviously approached conversion of his daughter-in-law which first made him take an interest in something which he had not sufficient travel or cultivation to understand. He had presumably thought of the Catholic Church as a sort of picturesque survival. But now on the approach of death he became fanatical in the matter. He refused to take any share in the putting up of a memorial of his son in the Cathedral of Amiens; he was exasperated by the idea that his

[1] BC October 25, 1914.
[2] Speaight. 370.
[3] BC January 1, 1921.
[4] Lady Cynthia Asquith: Diaries p. 50.

> grandson and heir to his empty title would during childhood at least be brought up as a Catholic by his mother . . .[1]

There was certainly every reason to suppose that Mr Asquith had a marked antipathy to the Catholic Faith. But Belloc did nothing to lessen this antipathy, and his allusion to the matter of Raymond Asquith's memorial in Amiens displays the most breath-taking insensitivity.

He arranged with the authorities at Cambrai Cathedral to erect a tablet to the memory of his son Louis and, at the same time, it struck him that it would be pleasing to put up a similar memorial to Katharine Asquith's late brother, Edward Horner. As visitors to the church at Mells will know, the Horners had already made arrangements for their own memorial in their own church, and produced what is perhaps (with the effigy of the infant Lord Haddon carved by the Duchess of Rutland in the Chapel at Haddon Hall) one of the most poignantly beautiful church monuments of the modern period. It did not occur to Belloc that, if anyone might decide about tablets erected to the memory of Edward Horner, it should have been his mother. She had already fallen out with Belloc, first over a trivial domestic issue when, invited to stay at Mells, he had arrived with two or three of his children, unannounced, in tow. When she had expressed surprise at the size of the party, he had bawled her out and told her that her ancestors had stolen Mells from the Abbots of Glastonbury. There then followed the much more serious coolness arising from the conversion of Katharine Asquith. Thereafter, because she did not wish her daughter to adopt a religion which she regarded as false; and because she did not consider it Belloc's business to put up tablets in foreign cathedrals, with epitaphs composed by Professor Phillimore, to the memory of her son, Lady Horner was dismissed by Belloc as a 'hag'.[2]

Exactly the same intrusive insensitivity involved the Asquiths, when Belloc thought it appropriate that he should supervise the erection of a monument in Amiens to Raymond Asquith. There is no reason to suppose that, had he lived, Raymond Asquith would ever have embraced the Catholic religion, nor even had sympathy with it. There seemed no particular appropriateness, apart from his widow's change of ecclesiastical allegiance, why he should have a memorial in a Catholic cathedral. And once again, as in the case of Edward Horner, it was felt that his father and step-mother should have a say in whether

[1] 'Memoirs' BC 1937.
[2] BC July 1, 1929.

this memorial was to be put up. H.H. Asquith's feeling that Belloc was being intolerably intrusive was dismissed as 'fanatical'.

There can be no doubt that Belloc in his blundering way was trying to be kind, in this matter of monuments and tablet. But, as his letter to Phillimore shows, there was more to it than that. *Threaten we cannot, because we are nobody . . . But we* can *spread the mood that we are the bosses and the* chic *and that a man who does not accept the Faith writes himself down as suburban.* Edward Horner and Raymond Asquith were, of course, friends of Belloc. And his faith taught him to believe that they did not die, but journeyed on towards the Truth through the fires of purgatory. Belloc undoubtedly believed, therefore, that though they disputed the Faith in life, in death they would know better. There was therefore something perfectly acceptable to him about erecting shrines for them in Catholic cathedrals; just as there was nothing inappropriate about the Requiem which Belloc organised every year for the soul of the Protestant Bron Herbert.

On the other hand, it is noticeable that, by claiming 'all the Olympians' who died in the trenches as so many honorary R.C.s after their death, Belloc was promoting the idea that 'we are the bosses and the *chic*'. The Catholic upper class, in Victorian England, had either been disappointingly reticent, from the point of view of ultramontane propagandists, or dangerously wishy-washy. One thinks of Lord Acton, an opponent of almost all the resolutions of the First Vatican Council and an unbeliever in Papal Infallibility. Raymond Asquith, Edward Horner and Lord Lucas had not been Catholics. But they had been the *jeunesse dorée* in a world which, almost before it vanished, was preternaturally brilliant and beautiful. Looks, wealth, and cleverness seemed to have been poured out for them by a benign providence until they marched away to the mud of Flanders and northern France. Raymond Asquith, certainly, was for that generation in England what Robert Gregory was for his friends in the aristocratic Anglo-Irish world: 'Our Sidney and our perfect man.' The English were not accustomed to associate Roman Catholicism with the aristocratic qualities, not least because in England since the Reformation freedom of the intellect has been so much prized and valued. Belloc's quarrel with H.H. Asquith showed how deeply he had come to believe, not in the Faith, for he had always believed in that, but in his own ingenious notion that the Faith in England went naturally hand in hand with the social and intellectual superiority of such as Raymond Asquith. Why did his father object, so 'fanatically', to the idea of the plaque in Amiens cathedral being erected at the instigation of a stranger? The answer is simple. Raymond Asquith, now an honorary Catholic, had moved in the highest circles of intellectual and social brilliance. But his father, in origin, *au fond*, did not belong to those worlds. He had only entered them by his second marriage. Raymond's 'high intelligence and sense of duty' were inherited from his mother. Mr Asquith himself, who was 'jeered at behind his back' for his 'ridiculous middle-class manner', [1] only objected to Catholicism because he 'had not sufficient travel or cultivation to understand' it. In short, 'a man who does not accept the Faith writes himself down as suburban'.

When one sees the extent to which Katharine Asquith's wholly private journey towards faith could be used in Belloc's propaganda war, one understands a little of why he was not a welcome guest at Mells; and why . . . Asquith, having been amused by Belloc in the days when they both sat together in the House of Commons, the one as Prime Minister, the other as a colourful back-bencher, came, in later years, to abominate him.

A conversion with more public consequence was that of G.K. Chesterton. This change surprised Belloc more than any of the others. Chesterton had showed no sign of wishing to follow his brother Cecil into the Church of Rome in 1913. Since young manhood, he had shared, with his wife Frances, a seemingly happy faith in the Church of England. He was, as *Orthodoxy* and the Father Brown stories show, sympathetic towards the Roman Catholic Church. But it was precisely this which had made Belloc think he would never join it. He had imagined him always, like George Wyndham, as a romantic fellow-traveller. 'Faith,' as he wrote to Maurice Baring when discussing Chesterton's change, 'is an act of will and as it seemed to me the whole of his mind was occupied in expressing his liking for and attraction towards a certain mood, not at all towards the acceptation of a certain Institution as defined and representing full reality in this world. There is all the difference in the world between enjoying military ideas and even joining the volunteers, and becoming a private soldier in a common regiment.'[2]

As it happened, Belloc had been much preoccupied with his own affairs – finishing books, foreign travel, and the doings of his children – in the immediate months before Chesterton was received into the Church. Chesterton, who felt that he owed so much of his faith,

---

[1] All these phrases come from Belloc's 'Memoirs' BC. H.H. Asquith came from a family of Northern manufacturers. His first wife, Helen, was a doctor's daughter from Manchester. It is from her Belloc averred, that Raymond's qualities descended. Belloc never met her.

[2] *Letters* p. 124.

under God, to Belloc, was anxious to discuss the matter with him. He wrote, explaining that he had decided to embrace the Roman obedience and that a date was set in Beaconsfield for the ceremony to occur. He wanted to talk the matter over with Belloc, and to explain why he had decided to take the step at that juncture.

This, incidentally, is something which he never satisfactorily did. There seems no discernible difference, in his writings or general outlook, between the Anglican and the Catholic Chesterton. In both, the relentlessly whimsical prose breathes the same attractive air of the *anima naturaliter Christiana*. He claimed to Father Ignatius Rice O.S.B. that he had joined the Church 'to restore his innocence'. But all who knew Chesterton agreed that a more manifestly innocent man never lived. The decision, however, by the summer of 1922 was made. It seems to have been one of those unaccountably impulsive steps, such as matrimony, which suddenly seem unavoidable to a man, even though, to all outward appearances, there is no reason why things should not continue as before. In his letters to Maurice Baring and Ronald Knox, it seems really more like a divorce than a marriage. He appears to have felt, during the Anglo-Catholic Congress of 1922, that mysterious sinking of the ground from beneath his feet which has been the end of so many careers in the Church of England. 'Human kind', as another, unrepentant, Anglo-Catholic poet put it, 'can not bear very much reality.' 'A young Anglo-Catholic curate has just told me that the crowd [in the Albert Hall] cheered all references to the Pope, and laughed at every mention of the Archbishop of Canterbury.'[1] Inevitably, this came to hurt Chesterton's sense of honour. If his bosom returned an echo to the cheers for the Pope (which it did), he could not honourably remain in the ranks (with the cheering curates) of the Archbishop of Canterbury. Some chivalry of this kind seems to have helped him through the last painful stages of what Newman called an Anglican death-bed. Ronald Knox, who had trod the same path five years before, corresponded with him regularly. Father O'Connor, the 'original' of Father Brown, came down from his Yorkshire parish; Maurice Baring and Laura Lovat rallied about with help and advice. The only voice which was silent was Belloc's.

The day was fixed for the ceremony itself, in a corrugated iron hut on the edge of the Railway Hotel at Beaconsfield, the town at that stage having no recusant place of worship. Father Ignatius Rice came over from the nearby Douai Abbey. Ronald Knox arrived from Oxford, and they all sat awaiting the appearance of Mr Belloc. The

[1] Maisie Ward p. 389.

moments ticked by, turning first into half an hour and then an hour. Frances Chesterton, still loyal to her Anglicanism and broken-hearted by her husband's defection, was in floods of tears, and Father Rice had to take her into the bar of the hotel for a drink to calm her nerves, while Father O'Connor heard Chesterton's confession in the tin tabernacle. At length, they abandoned any hope of Belloc's appearing, and they proceeded with the ceremony in an agony of awkwardness. Father O'Connor remembered too late that he had neglected to bring his Ritual, the order of service by which a person is received into the Church. Chesterton thought that he had one, and fished about in his elephantine pockets and produced 'a threepenny shocker' before the prayer book, mingled with string, chalk, sweet papers and tobacco, made its unexpected appearance. The perfunctory rite was performed to the accompaniment of Frances Chesterton's lachrymose sniffing, and Ronald Knox felt afterwards that the occasion had been 'spoilt' by Belloc's negligent failure to appear.[1]

A month later, Maurice Baring wrote to Belloc to ask if it was true that Chesterton had at last been reconciled to the Holy See. He received the reply, dated from the Reform Club on August 25. 'Yes, Gilbert was received in the end of July. I think the date was Sunday, the 23rd, but on that I am not absolutely sure. It is a very astonishing occurrence, but these things are always astonishing.'[2]

To Chesterton himself, Belloc wrote a letter which was deeply revealing of the contrast between the two men, and of Belloc's own attitude to the Faith.

The thing I have to say is this (I could not have said it before your step: I can say so now. Before it would have been like a selected pleading.) The Catholic Church is the exponent of *Reality*. It is true. Its doctrines in matters large and small are statements of what is. This it is which the ultimate act of the intelligence accepts. This it is which the will deliberately confirms. And that is why Faith through an act of the Will is Moral. If the Ordnance Survey Map tells us that it is 11 miles to a place then, my mood of lassitude as I walk through the rain at night making it *feel* like 30, I use the Will and say, 'No. My intelligence has been convinced and I compel myself to use it against my mood. It is 11 and though I feel in the depths of my being to have gone 20 miles and more, I *know* it is not yet 11 I have gone'.

I am by all my nature of mind sceptical . . . And as to the doubt of

[1] Ronald Knox to Auberon Herbert, reported to the author.
[2] *Letters* p. 124.

the soul I discover it to be false: a mood: not a conclusion. My conclusion – and that of all men who have ever once *seen* it – is the Faith: Corporate, Organised, a personality, teaching. A thing, not a theory. It.

To you, who have the blessing of profound religious emotion, this statement may seem too dessicate. It is indeed not enthusiastic. It lacks meat.

It is my misfortune. In youth I had it: even till lately. Grief has drawn the juices from it. I am alone and unfed, the more do I affirm the Sanctity, Unity, the Infallibility of the Catholic Church. By my very isolation do I affirm it, as a man in a desert knows that water is right for man: or as a wounded dog, not able to walk, yet knows the way home.[1]

Catholicism was the only alternative in Belloc's mind to Atheism. Either Christ had been the Incarnate God and founded a Church, or He had not. The whole thing hinged on this: and, with it, the burning personal question of whether the dead will rise to greet one another on the day of resurrection. There was therefore only the Thing, It, and chaos: nothing in between. 'Outside is the night.' Belloc was once asked to Oxford to debate with Lord Halifax about the differences between the Church of Rome and the Church of England. He accepted, but said that to speak of the Church of Rome and the Church of England was like comparing the Carlton Club with the Club of Hercules. You were using the same word in two completely different senses. Any Anglican who came to use the word 'Church' in the Catholic way would, eventually, come to accept 'the Faith. It.'

Belloc, who had never belonged to the Church of England, and had no interest in it, was not concerned to convert individual Anglicans, even though he might take a cynical delight in the submission to Rome of the more socially desirable adherents of the established religion. 'Personal religion', indeed, was something from which he diffidently shied away. When, after her conversion, Katharine Asquith recommended him to read an essay on St John of the Cross, he replied that he found 'the whole thing *repulsive*. I don't say – I am not so foolish as to say – that it is false. But I do say that I was never made for understanding this "union with God" business: St Theresa and the rest. I don't know what it is all about and the description of "isolation and detachment", "the necessary night of the soul", disgusts me like Wagner's music or boiled mutton'.[2]

[1] Maisie Ward. p. 404.
[2] Speaight. p. 381.

Malcolm Muggeridge, meeting the aged Belloc, was struck by the fact that although he had written about religion all his life, there seemed to be very little in him.[1] And it is clear that by 'religion', Muggeridge was speaking of 'this union with God business'. Belloc's faith was a much more absolute thing than that, dependent, as his letter to Chesterton shows, less on feeling than on Will. When he had his audience with Benedict XV, the Pope 'spoke of individual conversion as opposed to political Catholicism in a way which – with my temperament all for the Collective Church – profoundly impressed me'. It is important to remember this. Although the emotional side of the Faith was something which made very little appeal to him, he was relentless in the maintenance of his own personal religion. If possible, his day would always begin with Mass. He would end it by muttering formal evening prayers such as the *Salve Regina*. Two things, in all the reminiscences of his friends, are said to have moved him deeply. One was personal holiness, of the kind manifested by his friend Father Vincent McNabb. Another was Benediction of the Blessed Sacrament. In this service, largely discontinued today, the consecrated host is placed on a throne above the altar for the adoration of the faithful. It is not Mass. No communion follows it. It is a very brief affair (Belloc maintained that it was impossible to concentrate for longer than twenty minutes in church and suspected any priest who took longer than twenty minutes over his Mass of heresy). It is an act of pure faith in the presence of Christ in the Sacrament of the Altar. Before the priest lifts the sacrament in its show-case or monstrance over the heads of the worshipping faithful, they sing two Latin hymns, of which the first, *O salutaris hostia*, contains the very essence of Belloc's creed. The visible and material sacrament – a tangible token of that Thing, that It which is called the Faith – has opened the gate of Heaven.

> O salutaris hostia,
> Quae caeli pandis ostium . . .

It is frequently recorded that Belloc could not hear the closing lines of the hymn without being moved to tears:

> Qui vitam sine termino
> Nobis donet in patria.

If, to a modern Catholic, Belloc's faith seems rigorously materialistic and, in his own words, *desiccate*, one can only say that it *was* his

---

[1] Malcolm Muggeridge: *Like it Was* (1981) p. 420.

religion. Belloc would probably have found the new vernacular mass, and the religion which gave birth to it, irritatingly inchoate, time-wasting. The Mass, for him, was a daily chance to be present at the material and true miracle of Christ's incarnation. When the priest had finished his business at the altar, that was it: time to shuffle off for bread and eggs and coffee. As often as he knelt there, wherever he was, at that scarcely audible and universally identical rite, Belloc renewed his intellectual appreciation of the fact that he belonged to the one institution on earth founded, guided and daily visited by Almighty God. To this piece of historical and theological fact, it is unlikely that he would have wished to add the many features of the modern rite which beside its supernatural effect, *ex opere operato*, would seem an irrelevance. In Northern France, in which Belloc placed such hopes of the future, it is almost impossible today to hear mass without the inclusion of lengthy extempore 'bidding prayers' relating to the contents of the morning newspaper. There are daily homilies. There are periods set aside for members of the congregation to shake each other by the hand. Hymn-singing is a frequent part of the rite even on weekdays. And there are invariably lengthy readings of what Belloc would have regarded as 'Yiddish folklore'. By some merciful providence, these reforms did not come upon his beloved liturgy in Belloc's lifetime. 'I am by all my nature of mind sceptical.' One rather doubts whether his faith would have survived the Second Vatican Council. But, since it was not put to this scarcely superable test ('The Vatican Council has knocked the guts out of me,' Evelyn Waugh wrote; Belloc would surely have said the same),[1] it is important to recognise the underlying and quotidian existence of Belloc's personal religion before discussing his attitude to what he called 'political Catholicism'.

*   *   *

By 1919, nearly a decade had passed since Belloc had even attempted to reconcile his own independent radicalism within the confines of one wing or another of the British Liberal Party. He had decided, by the time of 1911, that the Party System was a sham, and the violent upheavals and destructions brought about by the Great War had served to clarify his vision of Europe and its future.

In *Europe and the Faith*, published in 1920, he sets out in three hundred pages of declamatory and pugnacious sentences to elaborate his view that 'Europe is the Church and the Church is Europe'.[2]

[1] *The Letters of Evelyn Waugh*, ed. Mark Amory p. 638.
[2] *Europe and the Faith* p. 32.

What we call civilisation was the Roman civilisation. All that is good in our European civilisation – roads, justice, poetic metre, architecture, reading and writing – comes from the fact of the Roman Empire; and there is an absolute division between areas colonised by the Romans and those which were not. It is this which explains the 'barbarism' of Prussia, which has been responsible for most of the historical disasters from the Reformation until the Great War. 'Prussia was an hiatus. In that small neglected area, neither half cultivated from the Byzantine East nor fully from the Roman West, rose a strong garden of weeds. And weeds sow themselves. Prussia, that is, this patch of weeds, could not extend until the West weakened through schism . . .'[1]

Now, with civilisation, the Roman Empire also spread the Catholic Faith, the creed adopted 'by the intellect of antiquity and especially the Roman intellect . . . in its maturity'. The next thing to happen was the Dark Ages. 'Europe survived.' And the reason that books, law and civilisation survived was that they were all kept going by the Catholics, the inheritors of the Romans. For a Catholic, 'the Europeans are of his flesh. He can cônverse with the first century or the fifteenth; shrines are not odd to him nor oracles; and if he is the supplanter, he is also the heir of the Gods'.[2]

The appeal of all this might be felt strongly by someone who had no faith at all. 'The Oriental pagan, the contemporary atheist, some supposed student in some remote future, reading history in some place from which the Catholic Faith shall have utterly departed, and to which the habits and traditions of our civilisation will therefore be wholly alien, would each, in proportion to his science, grasp as clearly as it is grasped today by the Catholic student who is of European birth, the truth that Europe and the Catholic Church were and are one thing.'[3] But, unlike Charles Maurras and his followers in the *Action Française*, Belloc asserted the crucial importance of believing in the truth of Catholic doctrine. Maurras was in love with the kind of Europe Belloc described, a unified culture drawing its strength from Imperial antiquity which would purify and supplant the monied interests of both 'democrats' and parliamentarians on the one hand and of international financiers on the other. The difference between Belloc and Maurras was that for Belloc the whole thing depended on the Incarnation of Christ. It was no good simply embracing 'Europe and the Faith' as an ideal. The Faith had survived, against barbarian-

[1] Ibid. p. 12.
[2] Ibid. p. 28.
[3] Ibid. p. 32.

ism and bankers and heretics, not because it was attractive but because it was true. Nor does it relate in any way to an individual's *personal* feelings about Christ, the Bible, or anything else.

Belloc imagines a man at a dinner party in late antiquity who has read the Gospels with pleasure. He ends by saying, 'For my part I have come to make it a sort of rule to act as this Man Christ would have had me act. He seems to have led the most perfect life I ever read of and the practical maxims which are attached to His Name seem to me a sufficient guide to life.' Such a person, Belloc points out, would never have been persecuted as a Christian. Christians would not have recognised him as one of their number. He was not of the Faith. 'For the Christian religion (then as now) was a thing, not a theory. It was expressed in what I have called an organism, and that organism was the Catholic Church.'[1]

Such was his vision of Europe, broken at the time of the Reformation, when the Money Interest and Prussian Barbarism and Nationalism all conspired to threaten the ancient unity. Since that time, there has been a conflict in Europe between the old thing and the new. In so far as it was a Roman colony, prized as Mary's Dowry until the reign of Henry VIII, and the birthplace of so much good Catholic architecture, law, philosophy and literature, England was not beyond the pale. But its ancient freedoms had been taken from it by the Reformation, even though the process by which that freedom evaporated was a slow one. The rich oligarchy who snatched the monastic lands and dominated the House of Commons inevitably wanted to fight against the Crown, the last protector of the Common Man against the Money Power of rich families such as the Cromwells. With the defeat of the Monarchy in the English Civil War, England became an aristocratic oligarchy, ruled by a few families of wealth and influence.

That is to paraphrase, but it is roughly how Belloc saw the history of England unfolding. It was partly his reading of Cobbett which led him to this conclusion, and partly his ambivalent feelings about the English upper class. He had upset Lady Horner in all kinds of ways; when she displayed her distaste for his company, he could stand in the hall at Mells, and confront her with his view that her ancestors were thieves who had stolen the house and lands of the Abbot of Glastonbury.

We would not expect the great republican biographer of Danton to have became a monarchist until we turn the pages of *The House of*

[1] Ibid. p. 73.

Commons and Monarchy to see what he means by that term. He had always supported the French Revolution, and with it the Terror, because it was in his view a restoration of the *status quo*. In the same way, he believed, England and the other so-called democracies of the West were in need now of a monarchist revolution. Why?

England, since the days of Oliver Cromwell, had been governed, in effect, by an oligarchy. And the only form of oligarchy which ever works is an aristocracy. 'Men never tolerate an Oligarchy imposed without Aristocratic excuse of value. Why should Tom, Dick or Harry, in no way distinguished from you and me, and millions of the rest of us, have these extraordinary powers?'[1] Modern politicians are no longer tolerable because they are no longer gentlemen. 'The series of Prime Ministers which began with Walpole and ended with Asquith (all men of much the same classical culture, and all men dependent upon much the same system of a clique) had in common the fact that they were members of an oligarchy in a state which had very strongly at the beginning of the process, and still slightly adherent to it at the very end, the Aristocratic quality . . . They were honoured.'[2]

The same could not be said, of course, for Lloyd George and his henchmen, figures like the triumphant Rufus Isaacs.

Belloc's view is that the House of Commons is no longer taken seriously by the working man. He has at last seen through its 'filth', 'the personal corruption in which it is soaked'. 'The House of Commons having gone morally to pieces, the Trade Unions are rapidly taking its place.'[3] But there are two faults he sees in the Trade Unions. One is that they are limited in their objectives, but speak in *general* terms of their desire for nationalization or the rights and privileges of trade organization. Belloc proposed the purging, and virtual abolition, of the House of Commons, to be replaced by a number of committees, Trade Unions among them, in which specific group interests were put forward. At the moment, the self-interest of powerful groups in society is kept hidden. Only an absolutist, and only an individual, can root out corruption on this scale, and can remain personally answerable to the people.

'Who prevents an Englishman to-day from getting a glass of beer when he wants it? Fifty years ago the answer would have been clear – "The Governing Class" (only no governing class would have been so tyrannical). Who today? You cannot answer. It is anonymous. A lot

[1] *The House of Commons and Monarchy* (1920) p. 69.
[2] Ibid. p. 186.
[3] Ibid. p. 161.

of (unknown) rich men got richer through it. That is all you can say; and that sort of thing cannot last. Well, under *monarchy* the answer would be clear. "Who stopped your beer?" "King John".'

Belloc longed, then, for a great, inspiring personal hero who would purge society of its corruptions and inspire the masses to return to the strong, the Roman, ideal. Such a figure was to emerge, and the author of *The House of Commons and Monarchy* was to meet him and regard him with a besotted admiration which was undiminished until his death. His name was Benito Mussolini. No such inspiring figure was ever to rise up at home. The absolute monarch of Belloc's dreams was not to be found in the ruling royal house (Jewish on Prince Albert's side, Prussian through and through on Queen Victoria's) of George the Hen-pecked. He looked airily at the conclusion of his survey, towards a transformation of society '(and that would be the best way, because the most continuous) through the return to power of what is now the Hereditary House'. But this was a surprising view, considering his earlier hostility to the House of Lords (when himself in the Commons) and his repeated conviction that, through the corruption of Lloyd George, the Second Chamber was being filled with 'a lot of (unknown) rich men'.

The fear that society is being quietly taken over and governed by international financiers and faceless bankers finds its parallel in much of the anti-semitic writing of the period, notably the French contributors to Charles Maurras's paper *L'Action Française*. 'Every financial operation, especially if it be of doubtful morality, must certainly have a Jew behind it; wherever a number of partners, Jewish and non-Jewish, are engaged in some bad work (as, for instance, in our innumerable Parliamentary scandals), a Jew must always for this sort of person be the prime mover and the evil genius of the whole. As is the case with every other mania, this mania rapidly obscures the general vision of its victim. His prejudices soon lose proportion altogether. He comes to see the Jew in everything and everywhere, and to accept confidently propositions which he would himself see to be contradictory, could he give a moment's thought to the matter . . . The Anti-Semite is a man so absorbed in his subject that he at last loses interest in any matter, unless he can give it some association with his delusion, for delusion it is.'[1]

I quote so much from Belloc's own definition of the anti-semite to show how much he wished to be distinguished from the vulgar anti-semitic excesses of continental journalism with which he was

[1] *The Jews* (1922) p. 150.

probably more familiar than most people in England. It is in the general context of his belief in Europe, as the household of Faith and of Roman civilisation, that one sees most clearly both what his attitudes to the Jews were and why he entertained them.

They are set out in *The Jews* – 'my admirable Yid book' – and before turning its pages one naturally recalls his (to us) tasteless rhyme on the same subject, describing the great Rothschild residence, next to Apsley House, which was demolished at the end of the Second World War.

> At the end of Piccadilly is a place
> Of habitation for the Jewish race.
> Awaiting their regained Jerusalem.
> These little huts, they say, suffice for them.
> Here Rothschild lives, chief of the tribe abhorr'd
> Who tried to put to death Our Blessed Lord.
> But, on the third day, as the Gospel shows,
> Cheating their machinations, He arose:
> In Whose commemoration, now and then,
> We persecute these curly-headed men.[1]

Either you find this funny or you don't. Belloc's friends divided between those who laughed at his Jewish preoccupations, and those, like Duff Cooper, who shouted him down and found, for instance, his use of the term *Yid* intolerable.[2] The funny thing about the rhyme, if you find it funny, is that Belloc almost believed it. 'Kindly remind Mr Belloc, as quietly as you can, that his neighbour is of the Jewish faith,' muttered a hostess to her butler, when Belloc sat at her table yelling his head off about the bloody yids. When the message reached him, he replied in a loud voice, 'How very interesting. You can tell Lady – that I am a Catholic.'

He knew perfectly well that his baser nature was dominated by a strong streak of the crude anti-semitism which he dissects so mercilessly in *The Jews*. He wrote that book partly to lay the latent anti-semitism in his own bosom; partly to clear his head; partly to set out, as dispassionately as possible, an analysis of a major and crucially dangerous phenomenon, to which liberal opinion in England was wilfully blinding itself. That phenomenon he defines in the opening paragraph of his book by saying that 'the wholly different culture, tradition, race and religion of Europe make Europe a permanent antagonist to Israel, and that the recent and rapid intensification of

[1] Oral tradition.
[2] Lady Diana Cooper to the author.

that antagonism gives to the discovery of a solution immediate and highly practical importance'.[1]

One can argue till Kingdom come about whether the first part of the thesis is valid or fantastical – the fundamental antagonism between Europe and Israel. What was indisputable throughout Europe in 1922 was a strong feeling of such antagonism. English liberals wanted to sit at home; to say that there was no essential difference between the Jew and the nation of his adoption; that, if one ignored the problem, it would go away. This was not what was happening in Vienna and Warsaw and Berlin and Paris in those years immediately after the Great War. In his chapter on the anti-semite, Belloc makes it quite clear that the prejudice against the Jews was for the most part irrational. But that does not alter the existence of a Jewish problem in Europe at that date, a problem exacerbated, according to Belloc, by three factors: first, 'the Jewish reliance upon secrecy'. This concealment, in Belloc's view, went very deep, and was designed in part to disguise the international range of Jewish interests and connections. 'Why,' I can understand some distinguished Jewish publicist in England saying, 'should I be compromised by people knowing that such-and-such a Bolshevist in Moscow or in New York is my cousin or nephew?' From such habits of concealment, Belloc believed, sprang the anti-semitic fantasies of Jewish plots to take over the world. A second factor which exacerbates the Jewish problem is their belief, religiously ingrained, in their superiority to the rest of the human race. 'The Jew cannot be absorbed,' Disraeli is quoted as saying, 'it is not possible for a superior race to be absorbed by an inferior'. Third, and worse than either of these factors, is the disingenuousness of Gentiles. 'The Jews who mix with the wealthiest classes to-day, especially in London, have no true idea of their real position in the eyes of their guests and the fault is with their guests.'

Much of the 'admirable Yid book' makes disturbing reading precisely because there remains something true in this latter idea. We are all aware – Jews, Gentiles, semites and anti-semites – of the existence of Jews. We all know that the Jews regard themselves as a separate group within society. And yet there remains something unacceptable about Gentiles sharing the view Jews take of themselves. Jews are allowed to distinguish themselves; but it is embarrassing if the Gentiles do so. For this reason, Belloc's 'admirable Yid book' will go unread today. Its pages are too upsetting. And yet they contain two very chilling prophecies. The antagonism between Israel and Europe

[1] *The Jews* p.3.

would lead, he predicted, to greater and more hideous persecution of European Jewry than had ever been known. He wrote in 1922 when, perhaps, the majority of his English readers would have thought it faintly embarrassing to talk of a 'Jewish problem'. Sixty years later, one's reaction cannot be the same.

There is a second, and more paradoxical, prophecy in the book. It is, that the existence of a Zionist movement would exacerbate anti-Jewish feeling in Europe. If the Jews claimed Palestine as their national home, then the anti-semite persecutors in Europe would, for the first time in history, be able to say, 'Go back to your own country.' This would in fact worsen the lot of the poor Jews left behind.

It goes without saying that Belloc burned with anger and pity in making these prophecies. They began to be fulfilled in his lifetime, and he was loud and outspoken of his condemnation of the butchers and persecutors, and furious with those, such as the Pope, who kept silence when the Nazi outrages began. Of all his books, *The Jews*, read nowadays, delivers the greatest reproach to his critics and detractors. Perhaps the persecution of the European Jews could not have been avoided. Belloc's was one of the few voices which dared to speak about it, and which dared to offer a solution. But that solution – the recognition of Jews as Jews, whatever their nationality – shocked the consciences of those who wished to pretend that 'the Jewish problem' did not exist. When Hitler rose to power and insisted on all the grotesquely cruel paraphernalia of Jewish houses being daubed with yellow stars, Belloc was accused of having proposed a similar scheme in his book. Only a reading of the book would determine whether it was fair to bracket Belloc with the Nazis.

Over the Zionist question, it has perhaps taken longer for the power of Belloc's prophecies to be seen. His attitude to it would seem to anyone outside the household of the Faith to be almost comically, medievally superstitious. It was, quite simply, that no good would come of handing over the Holy Places to the Jews. He regarded it as 'this most perilous of all the results of Zionism'.[1] In his book, he confines himself to some routine attacks on Sir Herbert Samuel: 'I also refrain from making comment here – I have made it strongly enough elsewhere – upon the strange selection made by the Jews for their first ruler of the Arabs and Christians in Palestine. I will do more than to say that a desire to shield the less worthy specimens of one's race is natural and even praiseworthy. One may even take a certain glory in that one is able to protect them from outsiders. But to give them too

[1] Ibid. p. 244.

great a prominence is a mistake, and it is indeed deplorable that of the whole world of Jews – from crowds of Jews eminent in administration, and political science, known for their upright dealing and blameless careers – Mr Balfour's Jewish advisers (whoever they were) should have pitched on the author of the Marconi contract and the spokesman of the famous declaration in the House of Commons that no politician had touched Marconi shares'.

In private, however, he was not so reticent. His reaction to the Balfour Declaration was precisely what Richard Coeur de Lion's or Frederick Barbarossa's might have been. It was an anti-Catholic blasphemy which would bring ill-luck on England and on the world. His vigorous repetition of this idea brought him many enemies. Perhaps it led him into bizarre exaggerations. But one never reads a newspaper account of that little strip of land which Belloc called *The Battleground* without being reminded of his audience with Benedict XV, and the Pope's murmured words, *'C'est une honte, c'est une honte'*.

TWELVE

PEARLS AND CAVIAR
1922–1924

Belloc reckoned himself an expert in the field of economics, and, particularly in his comic writings, he loved to anatomise the extraordinary workings of capitalism. So, Mr Clutterbuck, having purchased a warehouseful of rotten eggs (a million in all) makes his fortune in the City by selling them to the Government at the beginning of the South African war.

The Mercy of Allah was probably Belloc's most sustained, and amusing, money-fantasy. It tells how Mahmoud, a merchant of Baghdad, made, and lost, and made again many fortunes. When wealth pours into his lap, it is usually as a result of some extraordinary sharp practice on his part. But he attributes all his good fortune to The Mercy of Allah. And, by the end of the book, one realises that this is, indeed, an important element in his success. No amount of unscrupulous skill succeeds in the financial world without the element of luck. To emphasise this fact, Mahmoud abandons, towards the end of his adventures, his speculations in gold, camels, dates, and other 'commodities' and becomes a banker. By dishing out large quantities of paper money, Mahmoud is able to lay his hands on his customers' gold as a security. One of his little nephews, to whom he is telling the story of his fortunes, exclaims, 'But the wealth wasn't *there* uncle!' And thereby he touched on the essential mystery of wealth. In the end, in a capitalist economy, it is impossible to say where wealth 'comes from' or whether it is real. It is not wholly a measurement of a man's possessions, as we had supposed at the beginning of *The Mercy of Allah*. It is a matter of confidence. And anti-capitalists of Belloc's mould would unquestionably have regarded it as a 'confidence trick'.

His contribution to the public debates about the Western economy – State versus private ownership, on or off a gold standard – were always firmly based on the conviction that state socialism and international capitalism, tied to banking and borrowed wealth, were alike unhealthy. The only real wealth, in his view, was tangible: land, livestock, things.

Belloc's writings about money are among his best. But, although he felt himself to have a peculiar understanding of the workings of high finance, he was incapable of managing his own affairs efficiently. To both his sons, Hilary and Peter, he wrote, on more than one occasion, insisting on the value of saving 'a nest egg'. To Hilary, when he tried his hand as a businessman in New York, Belloc wrote:

> I enclose you a cheque for £35, the object of which I will explain. With it, start your banking account of which I spoke and pay it in at once, while I still have the money. Then treat £25 of it as a nest egg, the extra £10 is your allowance for the month of August, of which you can draw and spend as much as you like. The £25 I want you to regard as absolutely sacred, and I do want you, my dear boy, to try and add to it, however little it may be. See to it that at the end of each month it grows a little, even if it be only by a pound or two. It is of the greatest possible importance in life to begin like that.[1]

This excellent counsel was not something which Belloc was ever able to follow himself, as is revealed by the disarming advice that his son Hilary should pay the cheque for £35 into the bank fast, before it bounced.

Brought up by his mother Bessie to imagine that there was a huge family fortune which would one day be at his disposal, Belloc had never wholly shaken off the notion. He was incapable of being prudent or ungenerous with his money. Foreign travel was a necessity to him; and that cost money, even though he eschewed expensive hotels and the absurd paraphernalia of the rich. His friends received an endless flood of lavish offerings. He liked to have joke poems, such as his tribute to the late Lord Swaythling, privately printed. Often, when giving a book to Katharine Asquith or Juliet Duff, he would spend double the price of the volume on having it expensively rebound. When he took his friends, young or old, out to restaurants, the champagne flowed and the most expensive dishes were borne to the table. Once, when someone asked him why he wrote so much, he said, 'Because my children are howling for pearls and caviar.' Their tastes, in fact, were probably never as expensive as his own.

In addition to his children, Belloc also felt obliged to give financial help to his mother and his sister. Bessie was as 'hopeless with money' as any of them. Once past her eightieth year, there was not much chance of her suddenly acquiring high economic acumen. By the beginning of the First World War, her little trickle of savings had

[1] BC July 17, 1924

H.B.—16

evaporated. But, happily, this coincided with the period of Belloc's greatest prosperity, when he was earning regular and high income for his contributions to *Land and Water*. He paid her £40 a quarter, something he could do easily during the war years. But, in 1920, when his own income diminished and he needed money to help launch his children into the world, it was less easy to find the money for his mother's allowance.

Less reasonable, and therefore harder for him to tolerate, was the extent to which his sister, Marie Belloc-Lowndes, relied on his financial support. At least one of her books, *The Lodger*, had been a best-seller, and she was married to Frederic Lowndes, the *Times* journalist. She lived in some *chic* in the old Parkes house of 9, Barton Street, as one of what she called The Merry Wives of Westminster. At the beginning of the war, Belloc had not only guaranteed his sister's overdraft at the National and Provincial Bank for £350[1], but he had also lent Lowndes the money to buy the lease of the house. By the end of the war, the £1,250 which Belloc had lent to the Lowndeses was something which he desperately needed himself. 'I have lent you altogether £1,250 on which the promised interest has not yet been paid by you for some years,' he complained to Marie, 'nor any proposal about it made by you, nor even a word written about it . . . I simply cannot afford to be out of such considerable sums of money.'[2] In a desperate effort to get some cash out of his sister, he proposed cancelling half the debt if she or her husband could pay him regular interest on the remainder. The matter was never, in fact, settled.

Quite certainly, there was wrong on both sides in this quarrel. Belloc had not made it sufficiently clear when he lavishly doled out £1,250 to the then-impoverished Lowndes's what terms he attached to the loan; how much of it, indeed, was a loan and how much a gift. It was only when things got tight that he started to specify how much he needed the money back. It poisoned their relationship for the rest of their days. Belloc's friends, and his children, were often struck by how little he appeared to like his sister. He made no particular effort to see her, and spoke slightingly of thrilling popular crime novels. He also mocked her calling herself Mrs Belloc-Lowndes, 'as though the great estates of the Lowndes' had been allied to those of the Bellocs'. But the 'coolness' between them never had the quality of a feud. Neither Belloc's children, nor the children of Mrs Belloc-Lowndes, had any inkling that there had been a financial awkwardness. Mrs Belloc-Lowndes, for her part, who was endowed with more warmth

[1] BC September 17, 1914
[2] BC August 4, 1919

of heart and sweetness of nature than her brother, never failed to speak warmly of him. She never reciprocated either his coldness or his satire; she was genuinely proud of him. Towards the end of Bessie's life, she did her best to assist Belloc with the allowance. She paid a quarter of it. She also tried to arrange for the sale of La Celle St Cloud. Belloc was depressed, after the war, to visit it and find that his cousins lived 'in Palaces crowning the heights, while my poor little dusty ancestral house which bred the whole boiling lot of them lies down below like a slum with a pocket-handkerchief of a garden all in ruins'.[1] By the time he and Marie got round to selling it, having lost the deeds,[2] the place had mouldered to the point where it was worth almost no money at all.

And meanwhile the children howled for pearls and caviar. Long before, in their infancy, Arthur Benson had squeamishly likened King's Land to a gipsy encampment. And there must be many Romany children who had a more stable and orderly upbringing than Belloc's children. Belloc was warmly affectionate towards them all, but it was not easy to have him as a father. For much of the time, during their adolescence, when they might have wanted to see him at King's Land for the school holidays, he was dashing hither and thither, between London and the Continent. His was not an equable temperament. There were explosions. And those who knew and loved the Belloc children as they grew up into the world must often have felt that the union between the parents had produced a mixture almost too strong for conventional tastes. The fey, semi-psychic qualities of Elodie were certainly passed on to her daughters Elizabeth and Eleanor. So were her hot temper and her practical ineptitudes. To this were added, in all the children, a strong dose of Belloc's own violent energy and a strain of his dismissive, satirical attitude towards the world. But they made many friends, who would be invited back to King's Land. This could be an intimidating experience.

It was as an undergraduate at the Society of Oxford Home-Students (now St Anne's College) that Jane Soames (universally known as Bonnie) first encountered the Belloc phenomenon. Hilary Belloc was her undergraduate contemporary, at his father's old college of Balliol. In 1922, she also came to know Elizabeth and Eleanor who, although they were not undergraduates, had both spent periods of time living in Oxford with the nuns of Cherwell Edge.

When the occasion arose for Bonnie Soames to visit King's Land for the first time, she was smitten with the thickest of head-colds which

[1] Speaight p. 438
[2] BC April 26, 1920

somehow added to her feelings of nerves and awkwardness as she was led in to the rambling, dark old house. Herself the daughter of an eccentric Wiltshire clergyman, she was no stranger either to rambling houses or to formidable older gentlemen. But she was, understandably, in awe. She did not set eyes on Belloc until dinner, when he shuffled into the dining-room, and, having been introduced, bellowed down the thick refectory table – as he did to all guests – 'My child, I want to know your plans!' Streaming with misery and catarrh into her handkerchief, she made flustered apologies for being there at all and said that she really did not intend to stay long; if it were convenient, she would be able to leave in the morning. 'No, no, no, NO!' came the response. 'My child, you may stay as long as you like; you may stay a month, you may stay three months. But I want to know your *plans*.'

This was a completely routine procedure. It is described by J. B. Morton in his memoir of Belloc in exactly the same way.

> 'Mr Martin', he said, 'I must know your plans.' I, who had made no plans, probably looked surprised, for he went on, 'You can stay as long as you like, or go as soon as you like, but I must know your plans'. This military precision was so foreign to my own nature that, with anyone less formidable, I should have laughed, and made a jest of it. But he produced a time-table, and I chose a day and a train at random. He was satisfied. The 'staff-work' as he always called it, was finished, and we settled down for the night.'[1]

Bonnie Soames, however, climbed the miserable stairs to bed early, feeling that she had not been a 'success', while the voices of the men, who sat drinking and smoking, roared up from below. She had undressed, and climbed in between the sheets with a shuddering sneeze, when the door of her bedroom opened. To her amazement Belloc stood there. In one hand he brandished a heavy stone hot water-bottle wrapped in a piece of flannel. In the other, there was a beaker of whisky. This roaring, formidable monster was worried about her cold. From that moment, her heart melted to him, and they became the firmest of friends. When, a few days later, he emerged, cursing and bellowing from his study to complain that he could find no typist for a piece of work on which he was engaged, Bonnie Soames offered to do it and unwittingly fell into the role which was to occupy her, sporadically but constantly, for the next seventeen years, as Belloc's factotum, secretary, research assistant, and, in her

[1] J.B. Morton p. 25

inimitably combative way, devotee. But this did not prevent her pursuing her own life, which, at that date, was that of an Oxford undergraduate.

For Bonnie Soames, the hold and influence of Belloc was just beginning. For his children, young adults on the threshold of existence, it was less easy to come to terms with his overpowering strength of character. Eleanor, the elder daughter, perhaps felt the force of it more strongly than any of them. As she grew to womanhood, she fell into the pattern of many elder daughters (now the eldest child living, too) of being her father's consort. She caught many of his attitudes, accents and affectations, and at the same time, with a part of herself, she wanted to escape. With equal strength, she felt her sister Elizabeth to be a rival for her father's affections. A little before her twenty-first birthday, Eleanor got engaged to a young man called Eric Cumming, and then, with almost equal precipitation, she broke the engagement. Some months later, she decided to go back to the convent where she had been at school, St Dominic's Priory at Stone, and try her vocation, as her mother had done before her, as a religious.[1] The experiment lasted about as long as Elodie's had. She quickly abandoned the veil, 'wherein,' her father wrote, 'she was very wise, for though the religious life is extremely happy if it suits one, to try and stay in it when it does not suit one is great folly. No life can be happier or unhappier, according to temperament'.[2]

In fact, the whole episode of Eleanor's sojourn in the convent had annoyed and angered her father. Elodie had dreamed of making Louis a monk of Downside. And, when he was fifteen years old, Peter Belloc had told his father that he felt a religious calling, possibly for the Benedictine life. Belloc's retort had been absolute. 'Put that idea out of your head. You're not meant for that. No Belloc can do that sort of thing.'[3]

In the fullness of time, two of Eleanor's children were to do that sort of thing quite happily. But she herself was certainly not 'meant for that'. After a few unendurable weeks of keeping her silence and custody of the eye, the vow of obedience which she was preparing to take had begun to seem less attractive than at first. She accordingly went to the Sister Almoner (as an old girl of the school she knew all the nuns well) and said that she needed five pounds for a charitable

[1] It is the proud boast of the Headmaster of Downside that both his mother and his grandmother were nuns.
[2] Letter to Hoffman Nickerson BC April 1, 1921
[3] Speaight p. 381

purpose which she was not at liberty to disclose to the Mistress of Novices. The money was to give relief to a young person in great distress. The crisp white note was somehow handed over and Eleanor Belloc, still clad in the simple habit and veil of the postulant, walked straight to the railway station and took the first train to Euston. She arrived in a friend's house breathlessly excited and she was taken to a ball that very night.[1] Her father was furious with her. He had regarded her testing of her vocation as a tomfool exercise. But the way in which she left the convent was insulting to the good Dominican nuns who had been so kind to the Bellocs since the death of Elodie. And, moreover, it was precisely the kind of tale which brought the Faith into disrepute.

Shortly afterwards, Eleanor renewed her acquaintance with Reginald (Rex) Jebb, a friend of her former fiancé Eric Cumming. Jebb, who had returned from the trenches with an M.C., had set up as a prep-school master not far away from King's Land.

> My engagement to Eleanor in 1922 came as something of a shock to Belloc. A Protestant and a schoolmaster – that was a combination of attributes he would certainly not have chosen for his future son-in-law. His summing up of the situation was characteristic: 'But, my darling child, that is almost as bad as marrying a parson'. Nor was the somewhat Victorian interview I had with him in the drawing-room at King's Land to discuss the matter altogether encouraging. We talked at some length about my financial position and the difficulties that might arise when a Catholic marries a non-Catholic. He seemed somewhat relieved when I told him that I owned a small house in Horsham and that I was far from feeling any aversion to the Catholic Faith, but his gloom did not entirely lift, and his parting words, 'Well, I suppose we must go on with it', were hardly enthusiastic.[2]

Eleanor had just reached the stage of 'replacing her mother: maturing, of spiritual wisdom, full of life and altogether my household'.[3] Her marriage was therefore a grave disruption of her father's domestic life. Just when he had begun to feel that he could hand over the household management to Eleanor she had gone off and married Mr Jebb.

Elizabeth showed no desire or aptitude to fall into the Cordelia-mould. It was her ambition to become a painter. After her quarrel

[1] Some versions of the story extravagantly claim that she went to the ball dressed as a nun, but this is not true.
[2] *Testimony to Hilaire Belloc* p. 13
[3] Speaight p. 507

with Eleanor, she avoided the family circle. But Belloc kept in touch. Meetings, and money, were arranged. She spent much of the time abroad, and her gay and frequent letters to her father show the extent to which she was keeping his prejudices at bay. From Château d'Oex in Switzerland, for instance, she once wrote, 'I go down into Lausanne tomorrow – a bore, but it's a case of must! I am sorry to hear it is a hellish place. I had heard it was lovely . . . However I will see for myself if I like it or no. The foulness of Protestantism is enough to destroy any town.'[1]

Elizabeth Belloc was never to find a satisfactory place in the world. In looks, and in emotional terms, she froze, at this crucial moment of parting from her family, and remained like an emaciated ghost of the early 1920s, drifting about London, clad invariably in a dark blue cloche hat, until the end of her days. Months would pass when no one knew where she was. Quite often she slept on the Embankment 'underneath the arches', making occasional forays into the kitchens of her rich friends for sustenance. One night, Lady Diana Cooper heard a scuffling sound at the back door of her London house and dispatched her husband to see what it was; if a tramp, to be fed, if a burglar, to be arrested. Pyjama-clad, Duff Cooper opened the back door, and the skinny little form of Elizabeth Belloc darted past him into the kitchen. She did not want tea, she did not want alcohol, she wanted food. By this stage, Diana Cooper had made her bare-footed progress into the kitchen, a loaf had been placed on the table, and Elizabeth's anxious hosts were drifting about in search of eggs. She was not responsive to their conversation; nor did she wait for a plate to be put before her, still less for the loaf to be sliced. With long and unclean nails, she scratched into it, tugging away the soft bread from the crust in lumpish handfuls. Then, like a stray dog which had satisfied its hunger by scavenging in a dustbin, she arose and left them without a word: 'On with my coat and out into the night.'[2]

Wanderlust was what all the Bellocs had in common. Peter, by far the sanest of the children, left the Oratory School as soon as he could, aged seventeen, and spent a year at sea, on a Spanish boat going to South America. He then came back to Europe and got a job in Barcelona working for an electrical company. His elder brother Hilary, who had gone up to Balliol in his father's footsteps, had not made a success there, from the academic point of view. There had been disciplinary troubles. Like his father, he had a desire to explore the world, and in the course of 1923, Belloc fixed Hilary up with a job in a New York publishing house.

[1] BC April 24, 1925
[2] Story told to the author by Lady Diana Cooper.

I do not believe in his going on another two years at Oxford, as he has to earn his own living. If he were to have a considerable independent income, it would be another matter, but short of that, or of the great capacity in examinations, so as to have a chance of taking a high place in the Civil Service, the function of Oxford is to get to know one's generation, and two years are quite enough for that. He is very intelligent and well read, and has met a very great many people through my connection and through the University, and I think that when he got to understand what the publishing business was, and what kind of work was required in it, he would make good.[1]

Belloc wrote these things to Hoffman Nickerson, a rich New York gentleman-historian who was indeed able to provide the necessary accommodation and connections for Hilary when he crossed the Atlantic.

Belloc had first begun to receive letters from Nickerson (invariably beginning 'Dear Master') towards the end of the First War, and when he came to Europe as he frequently did, there were various abortive attempts to meet. Hoffman Nickerson though never a Catholic was *plus royaliste que le roi* in his attitude to 'The Master', and was anxious to arrange a meeting between Belloc and Charles Maurras in Paris in 1920. Although Belloc in general was irritated by disciples and impatient of those who adopted the *cher maître* attitude towards him[2], he became fond of Hoffman Nickerson and stayed with him and his wife in the spring of 1923 in their apartment in West 54th Street, New York City.

It was his first visit across the Atlantic for nearly a quarter of a century, and he had been resisting making it ever since 1919, when he was approached by a New York lecture agency, William B. Feakins Inc. Although he had, as we have seen, a very great need of the money, he had replied,

It is not now worth my while to come over for less than £2000 nett [sic] over and above my expenses and any commissions. Nor is it worth my while earning that sum in more than 3 months at the utmost of absence from England, which means under present conditions not much more than 2 months of my presence in America. When you add to this the fact that more than a certain number of lectures would be a task beyond my capacity – say 30 at the most – I think you will agree that the chances of my earning

[1] BC August 20, 1923
[2] JSN

such a sum by lecturing in such a time are slight. It would mean a guaranteed (not speculative) average of between £65 and £70 a lecture, and I am sure you will again agree that my name and the public knowledge of me in America would not carry so high a fee.[1]

Rather disconcertingly, William B. Feakins Inc, had written back to say that all these terms were acceptable. That still did not tempt Belloc to make the tour for another four years. Crossing the Atlantic would open too many of the old wounds, the memories of his first journey in 1891, when, as a radical young ragamuffin, he had made the great adventure in pursuit of the woman he loved. Now, a prematurely aged fifty-three-year-old personage, comically stiff and formal in his manners, clad in black fustian and stiff collars, he did not feel quite equal to New York. He liked to say that Europeans had more in common with the Hottentots than they did with the Americans, and in his case it was probably true.

But the main reason he did not want to cross the Atlantic was that he knew he would be lonely. Belloc was so persistently gregarious that it would be impossible for a narrative of this kind to chronicle all his friendships, which were kept in such vigorously frequent repair. To sail across the Atlantic and to lecture to strangers about the contrast between Europe and the United States would be purgatory even for £2,000. For he depended for his happiness on the constant company of the men and women he loved and trusted. It is impossible to imagine Belloc's existence without G.K. Chesterton and Maurice Baring, his ceaseless companions; without Mervyn and Aubrey Herbert, their wives Elizabeth and Mary; without Charlotte Balfour and Katharine Asquith and Laura Lovat; without Phil Kershaw, Duff Cooper, H.A.L. Fisher; without Juliet Duff. Moreover, his mother, who was now ninety-three, remained very dear to him, and he knew that, if he crossed the Atlantic, he might never see her again. The journey would also emphasise the extent to which his children were growing up, and growing away from him. And, in turn, they had brought him many new friends, of the younger generation, with whom he liked to laugh and sing and drink. J.B. Morton had first been brought to King's Land in 1922 by Peter Belloc, the same year in which Hilary introduced his father to Bonnie Soames. It was about this time, too, that Belloc first met such figures as Arnold Lunn, Douglas Woodruff and Christopher Hollis, who were to prove such imitative propagandists in the years ahead.

Belloc, in taking up with new friends, never dropped the old. When

[1] BC April 22, 1919

one looks at his engagement books, the wonder is that he found any time to write at all. It is one of his most striking characteristics, that he lost almost no friends, in the course of his life, except through death. The fact that he wanted to sit up until three in the morning with Peter Belloc and 'Beachcomber' in no way diminished his desire, the next day, to drink for hours with Chesterton or dine with Mervyn Herbert. Equally, dinner engagements four times in one week with Juliet Duff did not diminish his appetite for seeing old friends like John Phillimore (when that was possible); or making continental journeys with ancient friends like Edmond Warre or Charles Somers Cocks. If, in the course of this story, I have failed to emphasise that every week of Belloc's life was crammed with company, new and old, young and aged, pious and protestant, raffish and grand, that is simply because it is necessary to take it for granted. It is only when we picture him alone on a transatlantic liner, as he was in February 1923, withdrawn from the lifeline of constant merriment and company, that one is reminded once more of his fundamental loneliness and melancholy. 'I am now a days always homesick for distant faces instead of my home,' he had complained to Juliet Duff as long ago as February 1921[1] and, as he steamed towards New York harbour, he was absenting himself from both.

Moreover, he was understandably nervous about the reception he would get in some quarters. As he confided in a letter to his former secretary and old friend Ruby Goldsmith, now living in California,

> I am rather afraid the Jews may attack me, because apparently one thing they cannot bear is a work seriously dealing with their problem. They do not seem to mind being violently abused nearly so much as a severe analysis of the situation. I regret this. I think that the security and happiness of the Jewish community in the future depends almost entirely upon their facing the facts. Nearly every one I know has got one or more intimate Jewish friends – that proves that the differences between the two races need not lead to hatred or bitterness . . .[2]

'Goldie' had been such a friend in his life, close to him at the moment of his most shattering desolation. To her, he spelt out more of his feelings about the American journey:

> I am not at all cheerful about my trip to America, though I am very fond of the people. I am now so well-known that there will be any

[1] *Letters* p. 105
[2] BC January 30, 1923

amount of interviewing and newspaper fuss as you say. The thing to do will be to praise them wholesale – they like that; they have the great virtue of simplicity. I rather think that the educated European classes will travel less and less to the United States partly because of the difference of conditions, which they find trying (and especially the prohibition of wine) and partly because the expense is so high.[1]

The trip was long, and hard work. From New York, he went to Cincinnati. Then on, two days later, to Chicago. After that, as his agency informed him, 'You can leave Chicago on March 21 at 10.00 A.M. Via the Chicago, Rock Island and Pacific R.R., reaching Des Moines at 6.50 P.M, the lecture being at 8.30 P.M.'[2] His theme, written up as a book in *The Contrast*, was the difference between Europe and America. Some of the generalisations are silly. How can he know that 'the Americans are much happier' than Europeans? 'They are the happiest people in the modern world.' At other times, the contrasts which he drew are masterly:

Wealth and opportunity in America connote the very opposites of what they do in Europe: extreme neatness, rarity of detail, an hospitable cleanliness of bath, drains, sinks; facile communication, plenty of noise and metal – and no seclusion. With us wealth, especially wealth long possessed, is marked by an extreme of seclusion; a horror of noise; a carefully acquired distance from communications; a good deal of dust on old books and furniture; a mass of detail in every kind of reading and picture and chance; inherited or picked-up what-nots by the hundred; repose and (especially with the English gentry) what they call Froust – which some of them also call Fug.[3]

Politically, he rather preferred what he found in America to the decaying democratic systems of Western Europe. And he noted with pleasure

the resurrection in America and its rapid growth into what is now a dominant place of a certain principle which Europe has for the moment lost, and without which Europe remains politically stricken. That principle is the principle of *executive reponsibility vested in one man*: the principle which must be called, if we are to be accurate (in spite of false connections which we have gathered around the word), the principle of *Monarchy*.[4]

[1] Ibid.
[2] BC February 27, 1923
[3] *The Contrast* (1924) p. 50
[4] Ibid p. 84

Moreover, it was Belloc's conviction that the Americans had a better understanding than the Europeans of the Jewish Problem. He noted with rather gleeful approval that 'there are I know not how many hotels in America which refuse to receive Jews. As I have already said, the principle clubs refuse to receive them; the Universities, notably Harvard, have openly organised a defence against the invasion of further Jewish students.'[1] He mocks at the English public men who come over to New York 'and make their first stay in some Jewish banker's house' and think that they are meeting a representative of American society.

> In one notorious case an English professional politician enjoyed a sort of triumphal march through the New York ghetto, from the landing stage to the Town Hall, and our newspapers religiously noted it as an expression of American opinion. The intermixture of the Jew with the wealthy governing families, which has gone so far in England that it is the note of all English society today, is quite unknown in the United States. In the Oxford and Cambridge colleges, the great clubs, the crack regiments, the Public Schools, in all the bodies associated with wealth in England, the Jew has now an established and honoured place . . . But the Jew has no such place in the United States . . . In our great families intermarriage with Jews has become so common, or even so necessary, that, as I have said, nearly all of them now show Jewish blood. Not so American great families . . .[2]

It is hard to know to what extent these reflections owe to conversations with Hoffman Nickerson, the dedicatee of *The Contrast*, the disciple of Charles Maurras, and Belloc's host in New York. Nickerson himself was of Dutch origin. Belloc was probably right to suppose that such figures as his friend Miss Lansdale, or Mrs Willard, the mother of Elizabeth Herbert, were not of Jewish blood. But the taste left by these comments is bitter. He is parodying himself, here. He has moved on from the position of recognising, quite sanely, to Ruby Goldsmith, that 'the differences between the two races need not lead to hatred', to a basely anti-semitic pleasure in exclusively Gentile clubs and hotels. Why was he anxious to be so publicly offensive? Secure in private friendship, he needed public enemies. It is a psychological quirk which grew increasingly dominant with the years.

Hoffman Nickerson certainly provided him with generous hos-

[1] Ibid p. 175
[2] Ibid p. 172–3

pitality, and helped him out of his financial difficulties by settling his debts. And he arranged that Belloc's son Hilary should come over later in the year and try his hand as an apprentice publisher in New York.

For the most part, however, Belloc spent a truly penitential Lent on his lecture tour. He hated never being left on his own. He complained to Katharine Asquith:

> No one between the Arctic and Mexico does anything consecutively and no one thinks of time by paces of one hour's leisure any more than we think of it by one year's. They cut the day into 10-minute snippets and spend them one after the other in moving from place to place (half the time) and talking very slowly with a very small vocabulary the other half. And as they don't know of any other way of dividing the day, a man trained in another world is lost. No lie – or hardly any – is of avail. If you sit down to write a man at once sits down beside to talk – very slowly, heartily, full of good heart and with a limited vocabulary. If you are in a house it is your host. If you are in a public place then any stranger. As this talk (to a foreigner) is mostly of simple questions (Do you think Lloyd George will come back? Is the Duke of Connaught loved in England? Will the French stay in the Ruhr? When did you land? Was it rough? Ought the United States to do this or that?) there is no shutting one's ears.[1]

The standardised food depressed him as much as the absence of proper conversation.

> Life is reduced to a few activities, each served on a plain and simple model – not of necessity but of choice. Thus there is no toast, though they have inherited a toast tradition from Colonial times. All they tolerate is grilled bread. They slice bread with a machine into pieces which are of the same thickness in all towns, hotels and private houses all over their vast area, and every slice is grilled in a little electric heater.[2]

One thing was deeply moving to him, and it was what the Americans had in common with Europe, that is the Faith. 'In Chicago,' he told Maurice Baring, 'I shook hands, all at one go, with 22 nuns of the Immaculate Convent and 74 girls of the elder class. I said to each one "Pleased to meet yer", which is the formula.' When this charade was over, he was able to shuffle into church and be quiet. There only, he

[1] *Letters* p. 136
[2] Ibid. p. 139

could be completely alone with memories of his first visit to the United States, and recall the postulant manquée, whom he had crossed the continent to woo and to marry.

> Mass is said quickly in the churches, all the Latin and the English prayers and the sermons and the hymns of the Children are American:
>> 'Stairbait Mairturr Dorlawrawser
>> Juster Crutch'm Lackrimmawawzer'
>
> It moved me to tears of tenderness for I felt then the Faith to be truly universal.[1]

The next day, having lunched with the Chicago Medievalists, presided over by a Monsignor Kelley, he had to go back to New York for 'a huge "do"' to celebrate the landing of the Catholic Pilgrims in Maryland in March 1634, and to rejoice in the *Motu Proprio*, the twentieth anniversary of the Promulgation of Pius X's assault on the Modernists. Entertainments included an Ambrosian Gloria sung by the Children's Choir of the Pius X Liturgical Institute and the College of the Sacred Heart (Miss Mary Downey at the Organ) and a speech by Belloc on The Press and the Modern World. After this, he withdrew, not to the Nickersons' apartment, but to the Devon Hotel, on 55th Street at Sixth Avenue and penned his sonnet, 'O my companion, O my sister Sleep'. A few days later, Hoffman Nickerson arranged for him to meet Ralph A. Cram, architect of the splendid episcopalian cathedral of St John the Divine, and on April 3, sponsored by the Knights of Columbus, Belloc addressed the Public Speaking Class of St John's College, Brooklyn. After this, he went north to Boston, where

> 'I talked in a private house to an Anglican Parson who had, really and truly, *recently*, been tarred and feathered. He was a dull young man. The feathers, a woman told me, were for "modesty". It happened in Florida because he told negroes that God held them as equal to whites.'[2]

Shortly after this conversation, he looked about for a boat to take him back across the Atlantic. Greatly to his chagrin, it was impossible to get on a French liner and he was obliged to return in what he considered the barbaric conditions afforded by the Cunard line. 'I shall be back in May,' he announced to his friends, 'when by the

[1] *Letters* p. 141
[2] Ibid p. 141

way I am starting a new magazine entitled "The Illustrated Review".'

*　　*　　*

In the latter months of 1922, a Major Crosthwaite conceived the ambition to 'establish the first Catholic secular newspaper ever attempted'.[1] It is hard, from the major's letters, to understand precisely what is meant by this phrase, but, when he and a friend called G. Orford Smith had talked a bit about it, they decided that the periodical should be called *The Illustrated Review*. They approached Belloc a few weeks before he set out for America, in January 1923, and asked if he would like to become a shareholder in the paper, a director of the company, when it was formed, and, most important of all, the editor.

Taking a very charitable view of events, one might think that there had been 'misunderstandings' on both sides from the outset. But a serious historian of the episode is bound to point out what those misunderstandings were. Crosthwaite and Orford Smith did not understand that they were a pair of manifest gulls whom Belloc decided, from the beginning, to exploit to the utmost. They did not understand that, in their editor's opinion, the world owed Mr Belloc a living, in compensation for having failed to get a Fellowship at Oxford and for having failed to inherit the Parkes fortune. They did not understand that he had never been able to hold down any appointment which required of him regular attendance at an office, the keeping of hours or the satisfactory fulfilment of contracts.

They did not understand because they had not studied his journalistic career. *The Paternoster Review*, started with such enthusiasm in his late teens, had held his attention for less than its six months of life. *The Eye Witness*, which had been the most exciting journalistic venture of the Edwardian period, and a show of which Belloc was undoubtedly the star, had quickly come to bore him. His editorship of that paper had lasted six months, even though he could run it exactly as he chose, and even though it practised a style of journalism which, though popular on the Continent, had not been seen in England since the iconoclastic days of the 1830s.

Subsequent employment in Fleet Street – as when he was Literary Editor of the *Morning Post* – had ended in ferocious quarrels when Belloc had demanded a full salary in return for virtual non-attendance at his office. These things Major Crosthwaite and G. Orford Smith failed to understand.

They further failed to understand, and so did Belloc, the extent to

[1] BC November 16 1922

which the editor-designate of *The Illustrated Review* had come to be disliked in certain influential quarters. It was always said that Lord Beaverbrook forbade Belloc's name to appear in any of his newspapers. That is, it was always said by Belloc, who liked to intone, 'Dam the Beaverbrook; Dredge the Rothermere!' in expression of his contempt for the great Press barons. One reason for this embargo was, certainly, that the opinions he expressed were unacceptable. His *Land and Water* articles, which had begun so well, had subsequently been shown up as wildly inaccurate. His reflections of the hopeless corruption and absurdity of democratic institutions, his contempt for Parliament, and his implication that all people in British public life had been bought by the Jews won him more enemies than friends. Moreover, the Catholic drum was beaten loudly and repetitively.

Belloc wanted to believe that he was not employed in Fleet Street because of this wide range of daring opinions. And it may have been so. But a much more obvious reason for editors and newspaper proprietors failing to offer him work is to be seen in the tiny example of *The Illustrated Review*.

They planned the first issue for June 1, 1923. Belloc had tried to get Crosthwaite and Orford Smith to agree that, in the event of the paper failing, the 'good will' and the title should revert to him and be his possession, while the debts and financial liabilities remained theirs. Even they drew the line at this suggestion. But they did hire a sub-editor called Michael Pope to do all Belloc's work for him, and a business manager called Ponsonby, who received no salary, but received a commission if he was able to attract advertisements and keep up the magazine's circulation. Ponsonby soon found that this was more difficult than he had guessed at first. On the one hand, many readers felt that they got all the Catholic journalism they needed by reading *The Tablet*, *The Universe*, and *The Month*. On the other, certain financial and industrial concerns, which might have given the paper backing, were uneager to do so when they found out that Belloc was to be the editor. One can view this in any of three ways. Either it verified his conspiracy theory, the view that all capitalist enterprises failed unless they were approved by the Jews; or – another way of interpreting the same set of facts – it could be said that there was no moral obligation upon businessmen to give away their money to people who insulted them; or, more damaging than either of these reflections, it would have been reasonable to fear that any business enterprise which relied on the regular co-operation of Belloc did not possess a very stable future.

Money, then, was from the beginning tight. Before Belloc sailed to

America, Crosthwaite had only received the vaguest suggestions from his editor of how he intended to fill the first issue. Advertisers, who had been approached by Ponsonby, wished to see a 'dummy' of the paper. A thousand words on an unspecified subject had been promised by G.K. Chesterton. Belloc had promised, in addition to an editorial, to write a regular column on the Financial World. There was some talk of an article by Sir Philip Gibbs, and another by Maurice Baring.

While Belloc toured America, shaking the hands of nuns, and addressing the Chicago medievalists, Major Crosthwaite began to have his first misgivings. 'We are feeling (Pope and I) rather like a sheep without a shepherd,' he confided in his new editor.[1] Had Belloc really planned the first issue? Did he realise that it was to appear on June 1, and then be followed by *another* issue. 'I am quite sure we must produce the first number by Friday June 1st, and I am writing to beg you to bear this in mind and to do all you can to be back in England in time to oversee the production . . .'

It was good news for Crosthwaite, then, to learn that Belloc was to be back in England by May. Largely through Pope's efforts, they had almost collected enough material for one issue, but they were seriously in need of more advertisements, and were contemplating hiring another man, in addition to Ponsonby, to attract advertising revenue.[2]

Rather to Crosthwaite's consternation, Belloc, on his return from America, showed no particular interest in the new publication. After a token visit to the offices of the magazine (9, East Harding Street, off Fetter Lane), he announced that he was going off to France for a few weeks to recover from his recent debilitating exposure to American culture. Poor Crosthwaite scribbled off a letter:

Dear Mr Belloc,
I am exceedingly worried about the Illustrated Review – as you know we have no reserve of matter in hand, whereas we ought to have the bulk of matter for two or three numbers. Also we have practically nothing for No. 2 although we were clear of No. 1 a week ago. I am sure it is quite impossible to continue thus and I do beg you to take the problem seriously in hand. It seems to me to require concentrated attention for the next fortnight . . .[3]

[1] BC February 7, 1923
[2] BC May 15, 1923
[3] BC June 1, 1923

Belloc returned. He evidently got on well with his sub-editor, Michael Pope, but the poor quality of the *Review* embarrassed him, and he wrote to Crosthwaite insisting that his name be removed from the cover. Crosthwaite meekly stood down. 'Orford Smith and I both think that having regard to your view of the matter it would not be playing the game to press our request for your name on the cover of the I.R.'[1] Belloc had now forced them into the position where they paid him a full editorial salary for work done by Michael Pope, and were not even allowed to use his name. Pope enjoyed doing the work of editor, valued the somewhat second-rate articles which he managed to collect, and liked the independence which Belloc's long absences allowed him. 'The paper appears to be forging steadily ahead,' he wrote in July.[2] The letter was forwarded to Belloc in Barcelona where he had gone to persuade his son Peter to come back to England for the summer.

Crosthwaite was by now less sanguine. He had sunk £5,000 of his own capital in an enterprise which he now saw was 'fore-doomed to fail', and he complained to Belloc, 'I feel sure that there is every chance of success given the right management but it is not a thing that can be worked at odd moments nor can a decent production be hustled out at the last moment. I am sure with your genius we can succeed but genius without enthusiasm and direction is as useful as a motor-car without a driver'.[3]

Belloc was already in Barcelona by the time he read these school-masterly similes, and they do not appear to have touched his conscience very deeply. He rejoiced, after his lonely spring in the United States, to be revelling in the companionship of old friends and family. Much of August was spent sailing with Peter Belloc and his friends. In September, he, Peter and Elizabeth Belloc went to visit the Herberts in Somerset: Mervyn at Tetton, near the Quantock Hills, and Aubrey at Pixton.

When he reached Tetton, Elizabeth Herbert, daughter of his American admirer, Mrs Willard, rashly proposed that he took her out for a spin over the hills in her little Ford. He was a careless, over-confident driver, and was so deep in conversation with his hostess that he approached the first steep slope in far too high a gear. 'Mrs Mervyn got out (luckily) and I tried to start the car again by letting it slip down the road, but it got out of hand and swerved over the bank. Luckily it was held by a post which was

[1] BC June 7, 1923
[2] BC July 30, 1923
[3] BC July 15, 1923

there, but I got thrown and began to develop very bad pains shortly after.'[1]

From Tetton, he went on to stay at Pixton and found his old friend Aubrey Herbert far from well. Herbert had been, with Maurice Baring, Raymond Asquith and Edmond Warre, one of the crowd of undergraduates who had flocked into Elodie's parlour in Holywell Street, Oxford during 1898 and 1899. For the last twenty-five years, Belloc had been an intimate family friend of the Herberts, staying either in their houses in the West Country or in their villa at Portofino, first visited in 1900 to coach Aubrey for History Schools.

Three days after Belloc left Pixton that September of 1923, Aubrey Herbert died, having been rushed to a nursing home for an emergency operation. 'It is a most tragic and terrible business, and God only knows what his wife will do; she was so devoted to him, and she is left now with all those young children and an empty house: it is as tragic a thing as ever happened, especially as it was totally unexpected.'[2]

The motor accident, and the death of one of his oldest friends, drove thoughts of Major Crosthwaite out of Belloc's head, but when he returned to London, he found that things had gone from bad to worse on *The Illustrated Review*. On October 5, a letter reached him at the Reform Club from the major. It stated it as 'a practical certainty that to continue as we are doing at present must mean a complete failure'.[3] Crosthwaite recognised that Belloc was contracted to be editor of *The Illustrated Review* for seven years, of which only six months had passed. But he saw only two alternatives facing the paper.

First we can close down at once and save about £2000 losing about £4000 – or, in the alternative we can attempt to run the paper on an economical basis. Our ability to take the latter course depends on your generosity since by agreement you have the right to continue as Editor for another 6½ years or until the cessation of publication should this happen before that period expires if you will waive your agreement we believe we can pull the venture through and save our shareholders' money – quite possibly make the enterprise remunerative.

Crosthwaite showed his hand too clearly here. He could scarcely disguise his disappointment that Belloc, in addition to being a bad and ineffectual editor, had repelled the support of certain key figures in the world of advertising and journalism. In January, it had seemed to the

[1] BC September 29, 1923
[2] BC Ibid.
[3] BC October 4, 1923

pious major that the name of Hilaire Belloc, Catholic genius, would crown and decorate his enterprise. By October, he had come to feel the name was like a curse. But it was foolish of him to hurt Belloc's feelings by saying so; and it was even more foolish to expose the deeply precarious nature of the paper's finances.

Belloc expressed astonishment that the worm had turned. He declined Crosthwaite's offer of a meeting, saying that it was essential for him to have time 'in which to consider this quite unexpected turn of affairs'. Having done so, he considered that Crosthwaite was obliged to do one of two things: either sell *The Illustrated Review* to Belloc who, as a shareholder was not obliged to relinquish his interest in the company; or, to buy Belloc out, as editor and shareholder. The sum he suggested was £1,000.

Crosthwaite got the letter at lunch-time on October 9. By the afternoon post, he set out for Belloc the extent of the losses involved. He pointed out that *The Illustrated Review* had run for four issues, and that its circulation had declined ruinously. (The first issue sold 13,960 copies; the second 11,252; the third, 9,420 and the fourth 6,437.) The company was losing something in the order of £400 each month. A large part of the responsibility of this was Belloc's. He had not made efforts to produce the paper regularly. Nor had he bothered to attract interesting contributions to the paper. Belloc chose to disregard these facts and figures and, when he bawled Crosthwaite out on the telephone the next morning, he had added all the numbers together to produce a quite respectable circulation:

> He next told me that my connection with the 'Review' had made it difficult to get advertisements, a thing against which I had myself warned him. But I told him that I did not think that would account for the ridiculous total of £27 on a total circulation of between 30,000 and 40,000 copies and actual sale of 25,000 in nearly five months. I told him further that the responsibility for everything connected with the 'Review' apart from the editorial, was his, and his alone, and I could not be bothered with reproaches upon it, though I heartily agreed with them; for he and his had thoroughly mismanaged the whole affair.[1]

This is a very characteristically Bellocian way of conducting an argument. Crosthwaite complains that, under his editorship, circulation has sunk to 6,437. Belloc retorts that it is all Crosthwaite's fault if, with a circulation of between thirty and forty thousand, he only

[1] BC October 11, 1923

attracted £27's worth of advertising. He further demands that Crosthwaite should pay him £1,000 at once in compensation for loss of shares, status and salary.

Crosthwaite replied that, of course, they were unable to pay £1,000. They offered him £250. If he was unable to accept this and if, as he threatened, he went to law about it, the company would be forced to go into liquidation.

At that point, Belloc panicked, and showed his fundamental naivety about money. He had already confided to Pope that he did not hope for more than £500 compensation[1], but on October 15 he realised that his bluff had been called. 'I am advised that the company has power, which I never realised before, to liquidate, and by so doing to render my rightful claim for compensation for the injury to be done me nugatory. Had I known that the contract I signed could thus be rendered worthless, I would never have signed it.'[2]

He therefore proposed that Crosthwaite paid Pope his monthly salary of £75 and sent £350 at once to himself at the Reform Club. This was something of a come-down for a man who, only four days before, was shouting for '£1,000 in cash. I will accept no less'. In the event, he settled for £250, the company went bust, and *The Illustrated Review* and Major Crosthwaite were never heard of again.

Meanwhile, a *fracas* of an altogether more absorbing nature was making claims on Belloc's attention. 1924 was the year in which Lady Diana Cooper was enrapturing audiences in London and New York with her speechless role as the Madonna in Max Reinhardt's *The Miracle*. The ancient Catholic trappings of religion enjoyed a great vogue during the 1920s in the Established, as well as in the recusant churches. In Farm Street and Graham Street in London, the faithful flocked to Marian devotions, just as the New York audiences crowded into the Century Theatre to see Lady Diana. Nowadays, if one gazes at some characteristically 1920s handiwork, such as the lovely Madonnas carved by Martin Travers, it is hard to tell whether their resemblance to Lady Diana is accidental.

For Belloc, the profanity of the overlap was troubling and offensive. His devotion to the Blessed Virgin had been unwavering, as was made clear years before G.K. Chesterton joined the Church and Belloc wrote to him,

If we differed in all main-points I would not write thus, but there are one or two on which we agree. One is "Vere passus, immolatus

[1] BC October 8, 1923
[2] October 15, 1923

in cruce, pro homine." Another is in looking up to our Dear Lady, the blessed Mother of God.

I recommend to you this, that you suggest to her a comprehension for yourself of what indeed *is* the permanent home of the soul . . . She never fails us. She has never failed me in any demand.[1]

Much later in life, he was inspired to write one of his most moving Ballades when he read of an Anglican Bishop, (Barnes of Birmingham) 'who wrote to the Incumbent ordering him to remove from the Church all Illegal Ornaments at once, and especially a Female Figure with a Child'.

The 'Ballade of Illegal Ornaments' moves from blustering satire to the completely poignant *Envoi*:

> Prince Jesus, in mine Agony,
> Permit me, broken and defiled,
> Through blurred and glazing eyes to see
> A Female Figure with a Child.

It was natural then that, when he heard of Diana Cooper's theatrical representations of Our Lady, Belloc should have been disappointed. It was not necessarily any more blasphemous than the tableaux and dramas of Oberammergau. But he did not like it, and to Katharine Asquith, a new convert to Catholicism, he felt able to say so.

Katharine Asquith tactlessly passed on Mr Belloc's disapproval to Diana Cooper when they next met. The Madonna was upset. There was nothing, to her, profane in the tableaux. But she hated the idea of earning the disapproval of the man whom she regarded as a genius and a saint.[2] Belloc, equally, on hearing of her distress, was anxious to assure her that Katharine Asquith's account had been wildly inaccurate.

He composed an elaborate series of sonnets to smooth the trouble down. Like all his exercises in courtesy, there is a formality and courtliness about this gesture in which embarrassingness is held in check by self-awareness (almost by self-parody) and absurdity is balanced by the manifestly genuine nature of Belloc's *politesse*. Accordingly, the poems were bound up in red leather, stamped in gold and covered with marble end-papers: 'Six sonnets Addressed to Lady Diana Cooper and to be given her by Mrs Raymond Asquith, Laudata Laudatae, from the curious hand of her well-wisher, H.B.'

[1] Maisie Ward p. 400
[2] *The Rainbow Comes and Goes.*

That I grow sour, who only lack delight,
That I descend to sneer, who only grieve;
That from my depth I should condemn your height,
That with my blame my mockery you receive –
Huntress and splendour of the woodland night –
Diana of this world, do not believe.

Most of the poems were published, though in the printed text the word *Pheme* had been substituted for *Katharine* throughout, in such couplets as

Believe Sir Henry Judkin K.C.B.
But don't believe what Katharine says of me.

One of the more spirited poems was suppressed, because of its use of the word *Yids*:

Believe that Pegasus has great goose-wings.
(Young Pegasus, which in my stable stands!)
Believe Briareus had a hundred hands,
Believe that Helicon had springs and springs.
Believe that Argus had a hundred eyes;
Believe that Priam had a hundred sons;
Believe whatever's said, wherever runs,
Whatever falsehood, of whatever size.

Believe in every stupifying tale
Of Yids from Genesis to Malachi.
That sun and moon were halted in a vale,
That iron floated and the sea ran dry.
Believe in Jonah and his bloody whale –
But don't believe dear Katharine's dreadful lie.[1]

The poems reflect the almost ludicrously formal *courtesy* with which Belloc treated all his friends. But the incident of *The Miracle*, though resolved in good humour, showed the underlying core of his seriousness.

They show him, furthermore, to have been serious about his poetry. For, in that crowded year of 1923, he published his first collection of poetry for thirteen years. *Sonnets and Verse* contains many of his finest lyrics, such as 'The Winged Horse', 'Ha'nacker Mill', 'O my companion, O my sister sleep', and, the lyric poem for which he is perhaps most famous, 'Tarantella'.

[1] From the MS in Lady Diana Cooper's possession.

> Do you remember an Inn,
> Miranda?
> Do you remember an Inn?
> And the tedding and the spreading
> Of the straw for a bedding,
> And the fleas that tease in the High Pyrenees,
> And the wine that tasted of the tar?

The poem's flavour is only caught if it is *sung* to the rapid air of Belloc's composing. It provides an interesting counterbalance to what he wrote in his book on *The Pyrenees*, about inns. 'El Plan has a Posada called the Posada of the Sun (*del Sol*), but it is not praised; nay, it is detested by those who speak from experience'. Obviously, from his chapter on the subject, Belloc had wide experience of Pyrenean inns, both French and Spanish. But who was Miranda? When asked about it in later life Belloc would always say that he chose the name merely for its rhythm and sound: but I do not think it is often recognised that the person apostrophised in the lyric is almost certainly *male*. Belloc was loosely acquainted with the Duke of Miranda (a diplomat in London and a minor courtier of King Alfonso XIII); and, although he never travelled with the Duke, it is almost certain that he suggested the name. Belloc did not go for his roughest rambles, dossing down in flea-ridden straw beds, with young women. It is a lyric which celebrates male friendship, and the excitement of foreign travel. Celebrates? It elegizes them. When he addressed Miranda, he could have been addressing a dozen dead companions, who would go walking and drinking with him no more.

> Never more;
> Miranda,
> Never more.
> Only the high peaks hoar:
> And Aragon a torrent at the door.
> No sound
> In the walls of the Halls where falls
> The tread
> Of the feet of the dead to the ground
> No sound:
> But the boom
> Of the far Waterfall like Doom.

✴   ✴   ✴

After the fiasco of *The Illustrated Review*, what was Belloc to do next? He, or his children, continued to 'howl for pearls and caviar'. Beyond writing a short handbook on economics for Katharine Asquith's daughter Helen (then aged sixteen)[1], and a short account of Napoleon's 1812 campaign, he did not have many books on hand. There were no novels this year, no biographies and no major historical studies. America had exhausted him. Since writing was his only means of livelihood and he had quarrelled with most of the Fleet Street editors, the outlook was bleak.

For the latter months of 1923 and the early months of 1924, Belloc was kept on a 'retainer' by the *Philadelphia Public Ledger* as a European correspondent. The work was easy, well-paid, and precisely suited to Belloc's mood at the moment. He had no desire to belong to any of the major British political parties. He had cut himself off from all possibilities of political power, and could write, with wistful satire:

> Winston Churchill is again going through the weary round and Punch-and-Judy show of trying to get back into the House of Commons. It is astonishing to me that men of any capacity should still care for that kind of thing; it is such a waste of time, and not real power attaching to it, only a sort of newspaper reputation.[2]

Real power are, here, the crucial words. Belloc, in leaving the House of Commons, had not renounced the idea of exercising power in the world. But he did not wish to do so in a moribund political system. He was jealous, to the end of his days, of successful parliamentarians. But he had long ago ceased to believe in their system. In four or five clear political treatises, he had spelt out what he wanted. He wanted a system of government in which the power was vested in one man, whom he called a monarch. Only such a figure could purge the body politic of corruption and put into practice the rest of Belloc's programme. He wanted the elimination of capitalism, not by socialism but by a system of distributism. He wanted the power, and the money, of the rich, to be instantly curtailed. He wanted a return of the poor to the *land*. He wanted a restored sense of the old European unity, a unity which stretched back, and owed its origins, to the Caesars.

In such a scheme, Belloc felt that he had more potential power as a writer and a journalist than he had possessed as the Honourable Member for South Salford. In October 1923, the Italian Prime

[1] *Economics for Helen*
[2] BC March 18, 1924

Minister, whose public career had begun as the editor of a periodical far more obscure than *The Eye Witness*, made a speech to an assembly of journalists, in which he said that perhaps all newsmen carried a marshal's baton in their knapsack.[1] This was language that Belloc understood. Everything he heard of the Italian leader, Benito Mussolini, filled him with admiration. It was therefore a great joy to him when his American employers suggested that he should go to Rome, 'where I am going to write about the new Italy for them'.

[1] Denis Mack Smith: *Mussolini* (1982) p. 164

THIRTEEN

A LIGHT-HOUSE
1924–1930

1923 had seen the publication of a book called *Some thoughts of Hilaire Belloc* by Patrick Braybrooke. 'Lately, it has been evident to any student of Belloc that he has been going under a complete change. From being in the true sense a literary man, he has gone round to the position of a political propagandist, or rather he has acquired sudden and severe attacks of panic.' Braybrooke regarded Belloc's political despair as not only 'mistaken, but dangerous'. He found no evidence to support Belloc's view of the Jewish problem, no reason to think dictatorship, named monarchy, would be preferable to the House of Commons, and no reason to suppose that the British press would be freer if it were owned by industrial magnates rather than by the 'press barons'. 'Belloc,' concludes the study, 'is a man of middle age, he has done great things, but if he is to retain a place amongst the great, he must cease interfering with politics and turn to the better and nobler task of writing more books on "Everything" except questions that do not concern him.'[1]

Belloc, of course, had been 'interfering with politics' ever since he had left school, and Braybrooke's book was not going to deter him from doing so in his fifty-fourth year. He set off for Italy with a happy heart in February 1924. Already, in the previous year, he had been predicting to the Americans that 'we of Europe shall solve our own problems; probably by the restoration of the civilised South and West to its proper headship over the rest of European unity. Things return to their origins and our Roman unity should revive'.[2] And he had little doubt that the Italian *Duce* was the new Caesar who could bring this imperial ideal to pass.

At first thought, Mussolini might seem a strange hero for a man of Belloc's temper. The *Duce* was, for one thing, an atheist, who had condemned Christianity as 'detestable' and called on the Pope to leave Rome with the rest of his clergy, whom he described as 'black

[1] *Some thoughts of Hilaire Belloc* by Patrick Braybrooke p. 123
[2] *The Contrast* p. 267

microbes'.[1] His new fascist calendar dated events not from the birth of Christ, but from October 1922. Nevertheless, Belloc was not unique in his admiration of the Italian dictator. Mussolini's enemies could point out, truthfully, that he was a failed primary school teacher of dissolute life. Friends and enemies alike were obliged to recognise his dynamism, his Napoleonic capacity for hard work, his ability to get things done. In spite of his manifestly anti-Catholic origins, he soon realised that, for the success of his movement in Italy, a Concordat with the Papacy was essential. In the year before Belloc met him, Mussolini had married one of his mistresses in a religious ceremony. The future of the Vatican, and of the Papacy in Italy, was reassured in exchange for recognising that this diminutive lecher was the 'sublime redeemer in the Roman heavens'.[2]

Belloc was not disappointed when he met the man in the spring of 1924.

> I made a sort of pilgrimage to see Mussolini . . . I had the honour of a long conversation with him alone, discovering and receiving his judgments. What a contrast with the sly and shifty talk of your parliamentarian! What a sense of decision, of sincerity, of serving the nation, and of serving it towards a known end with a definite will! Meeting this man after talking to the parliamentarians in other countries was like meeting with some athletic friend of one's boyhood after an afternoon with racing touts; or it was like coming upon good wine in a Pyrenean village after compulsory draughts of marsh water in the mosses of the moors above, during some long day's travel over the range.[3]

This was not a judgment which Belloc ever felt much reason to revise. Nor, of course, was he alone in his estimation of the *Duce*. When Winston Churchill met him a few years later, he said, 'If I were Italian, I am sure I would have been with you from the beginning to end in your struggle against the bestial appetites of Leninism.' Thomas Edison thought him 'the greatest genius of the modern age'; Mahatma Gandhi described him as a 'superman'; the British Foreign Secretary, Austen Chamberlain, took the Duce yachting, and the Archbishop of Canterbury, Randall Davidson, regarded him as 'the one giant figure in Europe'.[4]

But, in almost all these cases, enthusiasm for Mussolini faded when

[1] Mack Smith p. 44
[2] Ibid. p. 163
[3] *The Cruise of the Nona* p. 164
[4] Richard Collier: *The Rise and Fall of Benito Mussolini* p. 92

the extent of his cruelty was unveiled. The fascists thought nothing of butchering their enemies in hundreds. In a fantastical way, this might actually have appealed to Belloc's imagination, for, from the beginning, he had revered the most bloodthirsty heroes of the French Revolution. In general, it is hard to resist the feeling that in Mussolini he saw an image of himself. Early photographs of the *Duce*, a stocky figure in a bowler hat, butterfly collar and black tie, bear a distinct resemblance to Belloc himself. Mussolini had in fact modelled this style of dress on that of his favourite film-stars, Laurel and Hardy, whose sartorial distinctiveness he regarded as the embodiment of transatlantic chic. He only abandoned it when he was informed that Laurel and Hardy were generally appreciated, not as models of sophistication, but as clowns.[1]

But the clue of Belloc's fascination with 'the divine Caesar' was not to be found in any accidental similarity which might have existed between the bowler hats and black fustian which both men affected. In the year that Belloc met him, Mussolini was hailed as 'the divine Caesar'. Only five years before, he had been an unemployable journalist, trying to propagate his own scurrilous little newspaper, *Il Popolo*, a periodical which, like *The Eye Witness* in Edwardian England, struck political attitudes and printed stories which the other papers would have been too timid to touch. In defiance of all the laws which appeared to govern Westminster and Fleet Street, the pugnacious Italian journalist, independent-minded, feared by conservative parliamentarians and by socialists, had swept to power in the city of the Caesars, promising, and very quickly achieving, a real cleansing of the system. Disregarding all economic rules, Mussolini made it illegal for food prices to rise. He attacked the big industrial magnates and confiscated the property of international financiers; at the same time, he severely limited the Unions and waged successful war on the bolsheviks. Industry and agriculture were temporarily revitalised. Farmers, whom he initially terrified – anyone who did not reduce the price of eggs and milk would be shot – began to benefit from food subsidies for the poor. The idleness and corruption which develop in all Civil Service departments all over the world, always and everywhere, were ruthlessly attacked by the new Caesar. Ministers arriving at their office after half past nine in the morning were greeted with sarcastic inquiries after their health, and then sacked. 'What is this bourgeois habit of going to lunch?' the *Duce* roared down the telephone, when told that one of his Ministers, at

[1] Mack Smith p. 108

two in the afternoon, was still not back in his office after his mid-day repast.[1]

Belloc, with his vast energies, his habit of working secretaries without a break until three in the afternoon, while he nibbled bread from his pocket, would have liked these stories. Mussolini was the journalist-dictator, and, as such, was the perfect self-image for Belloc to admire. Nor was this wholly ridiculous or contemptible. Belloc's earlier heroes, authors of the reign of terror like Danton and Marat and Robespierre, had not been afraid of shedding blood. Mussolini would not have been diminished in Belloc's eyes by stories of how ruthlessly he dealt with his enemies. Poverty, injustice, inequality and inefficiency deserved, in Belloc's view, to be dealt with ruthlessly. Mussolini was a man who genuinely appeared to be able, as well as willing, to do something for the poor; and this was the reason that he was so widely loved throughout Europe. 'Democratic' countries, such as England, by refusing to interfere with the inexorable processes of capitalism, allowed the fate of the poor to be decided, very largely, by factory owners, bankers and the magnates of industry. In the 1920s, if you could choose to be poor in Milan or poor in Middlesbrough, you might well have chosen to abandon the illusion of democratic liberty in order to live in a country where the rich were not *allowed* to exploit the poor.

The economic system which Belloc had been propounding for a decade now came to be known as Distributism, and it attracted a wide range of idiosyncratic support. His friend and counsellor Father Vincent McNabb was an enthusiastic supporter who believed that 'there is no hope for England's salvation except on the land. But it must be the land cultivated on a land basis and not on an industrial basis. Nothing but religion will solve the land question. And nothing but a religious order seeking not wealth but God will pioneer the movement from town to land'.[2]

Inspired by such thoughts, Eric Gill and H.D.C. Pepler retired to Ditchling Common in Sussex, where hand-printing and hand-weaving were cultivated, together with 'three acres and a cow'. These shaggy William-Morrisy idealists might seem at first glance to have had little in common with Belloc, from whom they derived their inspiration. And it was always a source of regret to him that the movement from town to land, of which Father McNabb wrote, was something undertaken not, as they had hoped, by the urban poor, the

[1] Collier p. 64
[2] Quoted *G.K. Chesterton and Hilaire Belloc: The Battle Against Modernity* Jay P. Corrin (1981) p. 99

exploited victims of the Industrial Revolution, but by artists, writers, potters, and other non-agricultural workers who were bold enough, and eccentric enough, to opt out of the modern economic system.

The mouthpiece of Distributist opinion, *The New Witness*, Cecil Chesterton's old paper, had folded in 1923, but two years later Cecil's brother kept the torch burning with the establishment of *GK's Weekly*, a periodical which gave voice not only to Distributist opinion among Catholics, but was widely supported by Chesterton's former co-religionists in the Church of England. Maurice Reckitt, a regular contributor to the paper, was deeply representative of the type they attracted. At Oxford he had been a Fabian socialist, but H.A.L. Fisher had pointed out to him the loopholes in the socialist point of view in the course of tutorials about medieval history. The *personal* structure of medieval society, as opposed to the functional collectivist programmes of the socialists, appealed to Reckitt. Here was a world where workers were protected by guilds, where merchants were under authority to the king, and the king under authority to God, in whose eyes all men, though hierarchically arranged, were equally distinctive and precious. The contrast with modern industrial society was obvious. Such a system, as Eric Gill observed, 'makes good mechanics, good machine-minders, but men and women who in every other respect are morons, cretins, for whom crossword puzzles, football games, watered beer, sham half-timbered bungalows and shimmering film stars are the highest form of amusement.'[1]

Before long, readers of *GK's Weekly* were anxious to be formed into a coherent political group, and at the first meeting of the Distributist League, in September 1926, they were able to see what a wide variety of ages, social classes and economic groups the ideas of the League had attracted. Here was a view which could inspire traditionalist Tories (like Ruskin, Tories 'of the old school; – Walter Scott's school that is to say, and Homer's') who hated the destructive ugliness of modern industrialisation; and leftists who were enraged by its injustice and inequalities. They heard speeches from Belloc, Maurice Reckitt and William Blackie. But the speech which encapsulated the Distributist point of view most wittily was G.K. Chesterton's. The people who wrote for *GK's Weekly*, he explained, 'his funny little paper',

> believed in the very simple social idea that a man felt happier, more dignified and more like the image of God, when the hat he is wearing is his own hat; and not only his hat, but his house, the

[1] Ibid. p. 95

ground he trod on, and various other things. There might be people who preferred to have their hats leased out to them every week, or wear their neighbour's hats in rotation to express the idea of comradeship, or possibly to crowd under one very large hat to represent an even larger cosmic conception; but most of them felt that something was added to the dignity of men when they put on their own hats.[1]

It was not all words. In something which now reads like an episode from *The Napoleon of Notting Hill*, one of their earliest campaigns was the London Omnibus War. The Distributists were furiously in favour of the private bus companies who were being driven from the London streets by the omnibuses of the monopolist Lord Ashfield's London General Omnibus Transportation Company. The issue was hopeless: the 'pirate' buses were bound to lose. But, quixotically gallant to the last, they took to the streets, and, egged on by Belloc and Chesterton, they raced the official L.G.O.C. vehicles. For the purpose, the privately-owned conveyances were brightly painted in distinctive colours – their scarlets, greens and blues summoning up the colours of a mediaeval tournament. They were labelled with names which could have come from a fantasy of William Morris: 'Vanguard', 'Pro Bono Publico', 'The Silver Bell', and 'Mountain Daisy'.

This owed much, doubtless, to the whimsy of Chesterton. But the aims and principles of the Distributists, if childishly simple, were far from being remote from the economic realities of the hour. The poverty of working people in the 1920s wrung Belloc's heart and excited his fury. Even though he regretted the socialist ideas by which they inevitably allowed themselves to be led, he was always on the side of the Trade Unions against the Government at this time.

The Distributist view, of course, was that the Unions, instead of merely begging for wages, like children clamouring for more sweets, should demand, as of right, joint ownership of the industries in which they served. To be shareholders in a common guild was the only way in which they could be liberated from the Servile State of Capitalism. Socialism was but the same Servile State given a different name. For a wage-earner, even if his wages became high, remained another man's property, his creature, his slave. Only by joint-proprietorship could the human dignity, destroyed by the Industrial Revolution, be restored. In 1925–26, the Union leaders felt triumphant for, in the face of the Samuel report which proposed cutting the miners' wages, they achieved an agreement with the bosses by which they settled for a

[1] Ibid. p. 107

minimum weekly wage. Belloc's view was that they should dispute the mine-owners' right to determine wages at all; they should have demanded a workers' co-operative there and then. The collapse came, not many years later, in 1928, with the publication of an agreement between Sir Alfred Mond, chairman of ICI, and Ben Turner, Chairman of the TUC. Mond and the employers 'conceded' that the workers had the right to negotiate their wages provided they did so through a Trade Union. In one stroke, the liberty of the working man in Great Britain was destroyed on both sides. On the one hand, the Unions abandoned the struggle for joint ownership and consigned their members to the status of wage-slaves. On the other, by insisting on Union membership, they deprived the wage-slaves of the power to struggle for liberty on their own. We are still living with the consequences of this disastrous agreement. After 1945, of course, the Labour movement, and the TUC with it, went headlong down the path of State Ownership – a Bolshevik principle held in abhorrence by the Distributists – and the principle of individual liberty for the British working people was lost, probably forever. The attempts of the first administration of Mrs Thatcher to 'privatise' various sections of publicly-owned industry smack more of the skulduggery of the Duke of Battersea than of Belloc's political theory; but Distributists would probably have welcomed the sale of council houses to tenants who wished to buy them.

1926, therefore, the year of the General Strike, found Belloc profoundly absorbed in the problems of the nation. The Strike itself, he saw as 'an exceedingly grave moment, in my opinion graver than the worst moments of the war; and its gravity lies in the inability of men to perceive the nature of the problem'.[1] He saw it as a spiritual problem. 'When a nation is divided against itself, settlement is the duty and not victory,'[2] he believed. As it was, the Rich managed to buy the Press, the Archbishop of Canterbury and the Leadership of the TUC. 'Yes, the Miners have lost the Strike all right,' he lamented in November, 'principally through the treason of a so-called Labour-leader called Thomas.'[3]

In a poignant way, the General Strike 'renewed his youth'. It put him in mind of the Dockers' struggles of the 1890s, and reminded him of Manning's assertion that *all human conflict is ultimately theological*. In the case of the 1926 industrial conflicts, the worship of

[1] BC May 13, 1926
[2] Ibid.
[3] BC November 11, 1926

Mammon blatantly overrode any questions of justice, fairness or human kindness.

> We are in a state of permanent and sullen civil war, modified by general patriotism and terror of the police and the troopers. The rich are seeing to it that these divisions shall grow more acute. God has blinded them. I have not met one single gentleman or lady on the side of the poor in this crisis. That's ominous![1]

At the height of the strike, in May, he expressed very clearly what he saw as the issue: a clear conflict between Dives and Lazarus, in which the wealthy man, far from allowing the poor to catch the crumbs from his table, drove him out further into destitution, on the pretext that to relieve his poverty would be to concede to Communism. Belloc deals with both sides of the matter very trenchantly:

> The Mind of Big Business is deplorably manifest in the Press. Every one of the little news sheets is crowing over the victory, and assuring the workmen that they must have their faces ground and must return to their old conditions or worse. The exception is the Daily Telegraph. The Jew man who owns that paper has behaved with more sense than his colleagues throughout the crisis.
>
> There was an interesting moment the day before yesterday when the Communist group, small but highly organised, approached the Parliamentarians and offered to take over the strike. It was really in the nature of a threat. But it came to nothing. There are no Communists to speak of in the country outside the little organised group of a few hundreds. If this were due to a public acceptance of right doctrine I should rejoice, for Communism is a detestable heresy. But it is not. It is due to stupidity, and the practice is much worse than ideal Communism, for the practice is a demand for practical communism without so much as knowing that it is communism.[2]

Throughout the crisis, he deplored the feeble leadership given by his own church. Cardinal Bourne was 'a good but very commonplace man', and Belloc realised that 'had Cardinal Manning been in Cardinal Bourne's place he would have stated the issue more exactly'.[3]

The division in the nation, and the blindness of the Rich, derived from their wrong-headedness, their heresy. For Belloc, the Catholic faith was not merely an ossified system of thought; it was an instru-

[1] Mells, October 28, 1926
[2] BC May 13, 1926
[3] BC May 10, 1926

ment, he would have said the only instrument, which makes clear thinking possible. Like his friend Chesterton, he believed in God in the same way that he believed the sun had risen; for it was by the light of the sun that he was able to see everything else that was.

*   *   *

It was the simplicity of Belloc's attitudes which made him such a distinctively indomitable controversialist. The complex issues of the General Strike were seen quite simply as a conflict between the rich and the poor. No one whose God *esurientes implevit bonis* could conceivably have been on the side of Big Business.

In historical controversy, Belloc approached his adversaries with the same clear-cut certitudes. In the same year, 1926, that he was attacking the callous indifference of the Rich to the plight of the under-paid and the unemployed, he was also waging one of his fiercest theological conflicts. The enemy on this occasion was H.G. Wells. The two writers had been acquainted since the beginning of the century. They both belonged to the Reform Club, and their relations had always been amicable, even – or especially – when they found themselves sparring over political issues. In the days before television 'chat shows' and programmes of political comment on the wireless, the rather mannered political controversies staged by such as Shaw and G.K. Chesterton were one of the only ways in which issues of the day could be drawn to the attention of the public. Wells, Belloc, Chesterton and Shaw often found themselves engaging in platform debates or writing conflicting articles in the papers, about the rival merits of Fabian Socialism and Bellocian Distributism. Both Wells and Belloc had begun as Liberals on the Radical wing of the party. They had developed differently: one as a staunch defender of human liberty and independence, the other as a believer in the New Dawn, and a political Utopia brought to pass already in Leninist Russia and soon to be forced on the unwilling democracies of the West. Wells was always an admirer of Belloc as a professional writer, and wrote to him, praising an article in the *Morning Post* in October 1908, 'You write wonderfully. I think indeed you write English as well as any man alive.'[1]

At the end of the First World War, Wells, having written a brilliantly funny novel called *Mr Britling Sees It Through*, announced that he wanted to write a 'serious' work of historical analysis. His English and American publishers reluctantly agreed, having no idea

[1] BC October 12, 1908

how successful, commercially, *The Outline of History* would become. The finished work, of some 750,000 words, was written at great speed in little over a year. Wells was not by training an historian; and, as his modern biographers tell us, he did not have time to read widely. Most of the material for his survey of world history came from the *Encyclopaedia Britannica* and Holt's *World History*. Now and then, he dipped into a book called *Medieval and Modern Times* by Robinson. *The Outline of History* is not informative, it is discursive. It is peppered with generalisations, and it makes no secret of its Evolutionary Utopianism. It presents a Human Race, not as Catholic theology understands that species – souls made in the image of God, but condemned by original sin. Rather, we meet an ever-progressive figure in Wells's pages, marching away from the repressive darkness of the past, onwards and upwards towards a classless world, rid of its superstitious religious systems and its sexual taboos, state-educated, enlightened and free. He concluded the revised edition with an inaccurate prophecy that 'the day may be close at hand when we shall no longer tear out the hearts of men, even for the sake of our national gods'. He gazes optimistically towards the future, convinced that 'clumsily or smoothly, the world, it seems, progresses and will progress'.

Since he chose to write the history of everything and everyone everywhere, we may marvel not as Wells's friend Arnold Bennett did, that *The Outline of History* is so long, but that it is so short. And, invariably, its accounts of specific historical events, movements or characters – science and religion in Alexandria, the Ottoman Empire, the rise of Christianity, the wars of Genghis Khan (spelt by Wells Jenghis) – are thin and sketchy. Nevertheless, as a commercial venture, it could not have been better judged, and he sold over 100,000 copies of the book within the first year of its publication. When it first appeared in 1920, Belloc reviewed the *Outline* in the *London Mercury*. In 1925, however, Wells reissued the book, somewhat revised, in fortnightly parts illustrated with pictures and maps.

No author can avoid feeling jealous when fellow practitioners achieve a huge commercial success. Belloc's historical work undoubtedly became very slapdash as he turned out his potboilers. But he had, as an undergraduate, been esteemed by the dons of Oxford as a first-class historical mind and he felt that his volumes, at least, of French history, were of considerable vitality and originality. While Wells was enjoying his prodigious success with one hastily-composed volume, Belloc, with his much more solid achievements, failed to make much money at all; and was therefore obliged to write more and more in order to keep up his income. In the year of his quarrel with Wells, he had begun to write a comprehensive four-volume history of England; but it was never to achieve anything like Wells's commercial success.

It would be naive, then, to discount the element of commercial jealousy which Belloc felt when *The Outline of History*, having made Wells hundreds of thousands of pounds, was reissued in popular fortnightly instalments. But envy was not his only reaction. For he knew that the writing of history was not a mere compilation of facts so much as it was the presentation of those facts in order to substantiate a point of view. And Wells's point of view, in Belloc's eyes, was simply wrong. Above all, it was wrong in the extent to which it distorted and assailed the Christian orthodoxies. Wells was a simple Darwinian. He did not believe in the Fall of Man. He believed that, through enterprise and aggression, the human race had dragged and fought its way out of the jungle by a process of natural selection. It was hampered in its progress onwards and upwards by the absurdities of religion; and no religion was more absurd or misleading in the whole *Outline* than the religion founded upon the Twelve Apostles with Jesus Christ as the chief cornerstone.

Wells had swallowed whole the view of certain German biblical scholars that Christianity had very little to do with Jesus Christ. Our Lord, for Wells, was a poverty-stricken idealist who, after death, had been badly misrepresented by his followers who wanted to add a lot of ideas from the old mystery religions and the Greek philosophers to an essentially simple moral code. He saw no evidence in the Scriptures, for instance, that Christ had instituted the sacraments. Like many before and since, Wells felt capable of distinguishing, in the Gospels, between the sayings which were 'authentically' those of Christ and those which were not. The attacks on worldly riches, and the parables of the kingdom of heaven were authentic. The institution of the Eucharist the night before He died, the command to baptise all in the name of the Trinity, the choosing of the Twelve, the promise of the keys of the Kingdom of Heaven to Peter were all 'interpolations' just as all elements of the miraculous were 'added' later.

If its commercial success was what primarily angered Belloc, he soon came to see that *The Outline of History* represented an assault on the Faith. The very fact that hundreds of thousands of people were buying Wells and reading him meant that he must be answered; and that, not in a short review in *The London Mercury*, but in a fortnightly commentary on the instalments as they were published. Belloc wrote this commentary for the Catholic paper *The Universe*, and his aims were simple. He wanted first of all to establish that Wells was not writing, as many people supposed, a dispassionate history. He was writing a tract. Secondly, much of what he said was ignorant and false. The Faith itself was under attack. And, like a doughty Crusader riding to war against the infidel, Belloc did not consider it his duty to be mild or polite. He represented Wells's view of history as provincial and narrow. He saw it entirely from the point of view of his own time, and assumed – without much foundation – that the post-Darwinian, early twentieth-century brain was superior to the brains of Erasmus and Aquinas. Wells was limited in his time – and imprisoned in his Englishness. Belloc, true to his intention to write anyone down as suburban who did not accept the Faith, suggested that Wells was a sort of Pooter among historians, who did not understand the Faith of Europe because he was not *of* Europe. 'Mr Wells means to say all that is in him, and if there is not very much in him, that is not his fault.'

Wells was baffled and hurt by the mercilessness and power of Belloc's fortnightly attacks. They came at a time of personal unhappiness in his own life and, in many accounts of the controversy, Belloc has been represented as a callous sadist, bullying and kicking poor little Wells when he was down. It has even been suggested that, since Wells was a notorious libertine, and Belloc obviously repressed, the bitterness of the attacks had something in them of sexual jealousy. All this is to discount the obvious explanation for Belloc's vigour. He enjoyed controversy, because he knew that he was good at it. But his reason for fighting was simple. He believed that he was right. He believed that there was only one 'household' where 'the human spirit has roof and hearth. Outside it, is the Night'. The apparently well-meaning utopianism of *The Outline of History* was intent on the extinction of that flame and the destruction of that hearth. Wells thought that the Catholic faith was one of the last bastions of a blind, unhappy and repressive past. Belloc thought it was the one bright light in a dark world, and that its destruction would usher in a new age of barbarism, an age darker than any we call the dark ages. So, tooth and nail, throughout 1926, they fought.

Wells, reeling from his fortnightly fisticuffs, published a short reply called *Mr Belloc Objects to 'The Outline of History'*. He was unable to conceal, and therefore chose openly to confess, that he had been bitterly hurt by the personal quality of Belloc's attack. 'What seems to make Mr Belloc feel brave and happy would make me feel sick . . . But there is nothing in his career and nothing in his quality to justify this pose of erudition and insolent superiority he assumes towards me, and which he has made an integral part of his attack . . . . He has thrown ordinary courtesy and good manners to the winds because only in that way can he hope for a controversial advantage over me.'[1]

It was true to say that Belloc was unnecessarily caustic in his tone towards Wells; equally true, perhaps, that beneath the 'insolent posturing' of Wells's opponent was a figure more vulnerable than might have been supposed. But, apart from these personal matters, what of the truth? Wells rallied his objections quite lucidly and clearly. Of the Fall of Man, for instance, he had this to say:

> Was and is the Eden story merely symbolical, and has the Church always taught that it is merely symbolical? And if so, what in terms of current knowledge do these symbols stand for? Is it symbolical of some series of events in time or is it not? If it is, when and what were the events in time? And if it is not, but if it is symbolical of some experience or adventure or change in the life of each one of us, what is the nature of that personal fall? What is the significance of the Garden, the Innocence, the Tree, the Serpent? To get anything clear and hard out of Mr Belloc's papers is like searching for a diamond in a lake of skilly. I am left with the uncomfortable feeling that Mr Belloc is as vague and unbelieving about this fundamental Catholic idea as the foggiest of foggy Protestants and Modernists, but that he has lacked the directness of mind to admit as much even to himself. Yet surely the whole system of salvation, the whole Christian scheme, rests upon the presumption of a fall. Without a fall, what is the value of salvation? Why redeem what has never been lost?[2]

Belloc made no secret, when talking to his Catholic intimates, of his regret that the Church was lumbered with so much 'Yiddish folklore'. He regarded the Old Testament, for the most part, as an unedifying piece of tribal mythology, but it did not appear to trouble him – as Wells thought it should have done – that the Catholic doctrine of the Fall was derived from the old Jewish tale. In reply to *Mr Belloc Objects* (which had sold 20,000 copies in one month of its publication in September 1926) he wrote a counterblast: *Mr Belloc Still Objects*.

> Mr Wells . . . envisages the Catholic Church as teaching an inchoate heap of doctrines, each of them highly concrete, each of them flagrantly impossible, and the chief of them an historical statement that in a particular place and at a particular time, to wit, the

[1] *Mr Belloc Objects* p. 7
[2] Ibid. p. 44

neighbourhood of Baghdad 5930 years ago, there took place the Fall of Man.[1]

With this *reductio ad absurdum*, Belloc abandoned the question of whether the Genesis story was taken by Catholics to be literally true; and he made no attempt to explain whether he believed it. He contented himself with listing a number of continental professors of biology who had rejected the Darwinian theory of Natural Selection in its simplest form. 'Do let me fire one more shot at Mr Wells – it is such fun!'[2]

It was fun, but *Mr Belloc Still Objects* did not demolish the enemy. It merely showed that Belloc and Wells inhabited different universes. From this distance, one cannot say that either of them emerged from the contest victorious. Belloc perhaps crowingly spotted a few more howlers in *The Outline of History* than Wells managed to pick out of his antagonist's commentary. That is not to say that the controversy was not important. A modern, sensual, secular-minded man had been confronted with the ancient orthodoxies. Belloc thought he knew what Wells was talking about. Wells certainly had no understanding of Belloc's position. For all he learnt from the quarrel, it might have been conducted in two different languages. Wells's vague notion that all religions were ultimately one, and that there would come a dawn when the more agreeable aspects of Buddhist and Christian morality would be embraced by a secular society which had discarded the troublesome doctrines of the supernatural, was such nonsense that Belloc had no trouble in demolishing it. But he did so with such gusto and vehemence that his public regarded him as a harsh, baying bully. Wells, for the time being, had a great deal of educated opinion on his side. And, to this day, those who equate Christianity with 'niceness' and mild words will feel that Belloc's vigorous assaults on a popular comic novelist did little to further the Kingdom of Heaven.

*   *   *

'There is a frightened thing at the heart of all this burly insolence,' Wells had written of his doughty Catholic opponent. 'He is a stout fellow in a funk.'[3] This view of the heart which lies when it claims to go right as a ribstone pippin, is buried in much of Belloc's mournful, carefully-executed verse:

[1] *Mr Belloc Still Objects* p. 22
[2] Ibid. p. 17
[3] *Mr Belloc Objects* p. 7

And I fear I shall be all alone
When I get towards the end.

In 1925, his old mother finally died. Only Eleanor, of his four
children, was in England when it happened. Peter was in Spain,
Elizabeth in Switzerland and Hilary in California. There was no one,
quite, with whom he could share the experience. From his sister, he
felt estranged. His wife was eleven years dead. He had been
accustomed to share all family news, all joys and griefs, with Bessie.
And, with her passing, he was alone in the world, alone in a sense he
had never been alone before. The fact that she was of great age did not
diminish his grief. Belloc wrote to Hilary in California:

My dearest Boy,
   You will have had my cable a fortnight before this reaches you I
suppose. Dear Grannie died quite peacefully and without any pain
at 8 o'clock of Monday the 23rd March. She was within ten or
eleven weeks of completing her ninety-sixth year having been born
on June 16th 1829. For about a couple of months past she had failed
rapidly, recognising people but soon losing the thread of what was
said to her. She was perfectly happy but at last unable to sit up and
lay in bed. She became unconscious like someone falling asleep on
the afternoon of Friday the 20th, and on Saturday and Sunday Aunt
Mary and I were with her at Slindon. She did not recover
consciousness, and the end came simply by her ceasing to breathe,
and the pulse dying down to nothing. She was anointed. The
funeral will take place at 10.30 on Thursday the 26th. She would
not have wished any elaborate mourning, and I think it will be quite
enough if you will put a black band on your arm for a couple of
weeks or so. I will send you out the obituary notices when I have
them.

This flood of detail, of sick-bed narrative, is precisely the kind of thing
with which Belloc and his mother filled their correspondence to each
other. Now that she was dead, and the almost daily correspondence
had ceased, he wanted to share the details of his mother's death with
his eldest surviving son. Bessie retained, to the end of her life, the
ability to hold, not only the affection, but also the attention, of her
children. Belloc and Marie Belloc-Lowndes quarrelled about who
was to pay Bessie's debts, and who was to engage her maid. They
worried about her health, and, very naturally, objected to her bossy
intrusion into every aspect of their lives. But they allowed her to be a

dominant and possessive mother. She never lost their respect, or their love. Belloc, on the other hand, before he was sixty, could feel his children slipping away from him. One child was dead; three were abroad. In their own fashion, they all loved him, but he was not certain of their love, and he was quite sensitive enough to know that his insatiable demandingness drove them away. As he contemplated the lifeless, hag-like, heavily bearded form of his old mother, he not only mourned for her; he envied her.

> I am exceedingly grateful that the end of her life should have come so naturally and so easily. Indeed during all the last thirty-five years things have gone as she would have wished them. She was and did all that she wanted and was I think completely happy. It is very rare indeed for a human life to have so long and comforting a passage especially in the last years. She spoke to me of you the last time I saw her, and knew that you were in Mamma's country. She herself had never seen California. I rather wish she had, for its great beauty and wholly separate character would have pleased her, and the considerable strength of the Church there. She went to America with me thirty years ago, but never saw anything except the East, and this, though she had cousins there, she found appalling, as all educated English people do.[1]

It is not known whether Hilary wore black arm bands in mourning for his grandmother, as instructed. He seemed to some who knew him almost like a parody of his father, addicted to travel and to quarrels in almost equal quantity. But there were differences. Having left New York to live with his mother's family, the Hogans, in San Francisco (one of whom he subsequently married), he no longer even kept up a show of politeness about his father's religion. Whatever else attracted him to California, it was not 'the considerable strength of the Church there'. It was partly this severance between father and son which led to their having separate lives, separate existences in separate continents. But Hilary could still write home a vigorous piece of Bellocian prose, as he did in reply to hearing of Bessie's demise:

> I have at last got to the top of Tamalpais and find the view to the northward even finer than I expected. The fold upon fold of hills that finally are lost in the mist gives one that wonderful feeling of elbow-room.
>   On Wednesday I fight a South African jew called Levine. It is all

[1] BC March 24, 1925

very amusing. I found it necessary to kick him for insolence last night. Later I caught him by the feet and dragged him down the street on his back. He is about 15 pounds heavier than I am and certainly four inches taller. But he is clearly a rat as he refused to bear [sic] fists last night and his morality will make it impossible for him to be physically fit on Wednesday, so I sincerely believe that he is going to get a genuine beating. No matter what the result I am greatly enjoying the business as it breaks the monotony of routine life.[1]

For Hilary's father, however, the monotony of routine life would have been a novelty. He had never had a regular profession, never been obliged to keep hours, never spent very long in the same place, and never been still. It was appropriate that the book which comes closest to being an autobiography in his vast *oeuvre* is the story of a voyage in his old boat, the *Nona*, tossed on the uncertain waters of the Irish and the English Channels.

Belloc is a figure analogous to Doctor Johnson in so far as the power of his personality and the force of his conversational presence – attested by innumerable friends – are never quite lived up to in his work. The books which seem most successful are those – like *The Four Men* and *The Path to Rome*, or essays such as those in *Hills and the Sea* – which reflect his conversational self. *The Path to Rome* was a self-portrait by a young man; and it was a journey through Europe. *The Cruise of the Nona* is a haphazard voyage by a man in his middle age, gazing back over a full life. It is only in part the story of a sailing trip. At every point of the voyage, the author turns to the reader to *talk*; and, reading it, one captures some of the quality which Belloc's friends enjoyed in his conversation. It is wise, and at the same time outrageous. It is bubbling with jokes and wit; but its underlying feeling is elegiac and sad.

The cruise which it describes was undertaken by Philip Kershaw and Belloc in the months after the death of Elodie. But he has conflated this journey with several other voyages, and punctuated it with references to some of his most cherished memories, ranging from conversations with his French grandmother's *amie de la maison*, Mme de Montgolfier, whose memories stretched back to the French Revolution, to his own conversations with Mussolini. Thus, as the little boat bobs about on the waves of the Irish or the English Channel, we have a sense of modern European history passing before us, just as its older history passed before us in *The Path to Rome*. It is one of the

[1] BC April 12, 1925

most enduringly re-readable books in English. Like Boswell's *Life of Johnson* or *The Life and Letters of Father Andrew SDC* it is the perfect bedside book. The adamantine and the playful Belloc are both present in it, infusing every page with wisdom. As in the case of Dr Johnson and Father Andrew, one confronts a man who appears much of the time to be doodling, but who has never lost sight of what he stands for.

> A man who knows that the earth is round but lives among men who believe it to be flat ought to hammer in his doctrine of the earth's roundness up to the point of arrest, imprisonment or even death. Reality will confirm him, and he is not so much testifying to the world as it is – which is worth nothing – as to Him who made the world, and Who is worth more than all things.[1]

Such testifying is a lonely business, and *The Cruise of the Nona* is the autobiography of a lonely man. Ten years later, Father Vincent McNabb was to penetrate this loneliness in metaphors which recalled *The Cruise of the Nona*:

> You have been a light-house for almost more than the run of life-times. It has brought you a certain loneliness amongst the sea and winds.
> But your moments of conscious loneliness can hardly be more than moments when you know – as we must make you know – how many your light has guided and how many your heroism of accepted loneliness has heartened.
> What I personally owe to the light-house that you are I can only dimly discern but can never repay.[2]

And this echoes a letter Father McNabb had written in 1919, when he said, 'I often ask God to further you in your great battles for the poor and for their Master.'

The solitude which came to a man who knew, in a society of flat-earthers, that the world was round, was increased by the perpetual toll of bereavement during the 1920s. *The Cruise of the Nona* was dedicated to the memory of 'Philip Kershaw, my brave and constant companion upon the sea: but now he will sail no more'. Within a few years he had also lost his great friend Jim Allison, who joined Kershaw, Cecil Chesterton, George Wyndham, Mervyn Herbert, Raymond Asquith, Edward Horner, Bron Lucas, together

[1] *The Cruise of the Nona* p. 51
[2] BC June 2, 1936

with his mother, his wife and his first-born son in the company of those whom he had loved since and lost awhile.

Hundreds of other friends, of course, lived on. And Belloc was a constant party-goer and diner-out. But like all frenzied lonely people, the more company he had, the less he was able to tolerate a single moment of solitude. His surviving letters reflect a fevered attempt to fill every waking second with human company. It was not enough to have engagements for luncheon and dinner, with perhaps a party in between. He had to arrange a companion for an afternoon walk, for a chat in the morning; and even writing – for most practitioners an essentially solitary task – was something which he did in the company of a secretary to whom he could dictate.

He was tied to the treadmill of ceaseless literary activity, not because he particularly wished to turn out a stream of historical biographies, but because his sources of journalistic income had dried up, and because he was always short of money. Sometimes, he could take himself off and write a book at great speed, on his own. *James II*, for instance, was scribbled in eight days while staying in a small hotel at El Kantara, on the edge of the Sahara desert.

> I wake at six. I get down by 6.30. I write this mud from seven, after coffee, till twelve. I eat at 12.30 (oh! the vile food!) very little and read articles in old magazines left behind by tourists of the flood: especially the Revue Hebdomadaire of 1922. I then drink coffee and brandy and smoke. At one I begin again the horrible sing-song of the tenacious and the brave – but ill judging – Jacobus. It goes on till four. I then take the air for half-an-hour. Then I write again till seven. Then I eat an ounce or two of nauseating food; then I do nothing for an hour but read or write a letter – as I do now – with *empressement*. Then by 8.30 I go to bed and pass the night in dreams of trying to telephone and not getting through, or of trying to read small print by bad light. Then I wake at six and begin all over again. What a book poor old James will have! He was dull. He never smiled again. But he deserves a better book.[1]

Belloc was not under any illusion about the quality of his pot-boilers. *James II* is a spirited, ludicrously biased book, designed to counterbalance the Protestant historians who saw the expulsion of the last Catholic monarch of England as a Glorious Revolution. He therefore painted up James's attractive qualities – his personal courage, his understanding of sea-power, his rebuilding of the Navy, his patriot-

[1] Mells, October 25, 1927

ism. His sadistic delight in watching people being tortured, and his fundamental dishonesty, are suppressed, and his imprisonment of the Seven Bishops, and his tyrannical deposition of the heads of the Oxford colleges, are seen almost in the same light as the good-humoured biffing of dons and Protestant clergymen which Belloc himself enjoyed.

In England, he could never have imposed upon himself the régime which solitude in the Sahara made a necessity. His work was endlessly interrupted by his quest for human society. When in London, he continued to see Lady Juliet Duff. It was widely known that he loved her, and she would refer to him as 'poor Hilary' when mentioning him to her friends. But marriage, even had she not been a divorced woman, would have been out of the question. She recognised that his consuming demands on her time would have been insupportable had she yielded to them altogether. He was so demanding of company that one person could never have satisfied him. He needed the wide circle.

Nevertheless, an evening spent on his own at the Reform, with a sleepless night in prospect, was torture to Belloc. It was characteristic, when writing to Katharine Asquith from Africa, that he should have had nightmares about 'trying to telephone and not getting through'. The telephone was always extremely important to him. He would not have it at King's Land, because he hated the idea of his own life of quietness being invaded by other people. But he did not feel the same about the solitude of others. It was part of his regular practice, when calling at the houses of his friends, to ask if he could use the telephone. Complicated arrangements would then be shouted down the receiver; 'plans' would be settled or altered; the next piece of social life would be arranged before he settled to the one he was having at that moment.

One of his most poignant epigrams was addressed to Lady Juliet Duff, and was called 'The telephone'.

> Tonight in million-voicèd London I
> Was lonely as the million-pointed sky
> Until your single voice. Ah! So the sun
> Peoples all heaven, although he be but one.

His addiction to ringing people up got the better of him even at the most sacred or inappropriate moments. Those who do not under-stand the nature of Belloc's matter-of-fact piety would be scandalised by the story of his son-in-law being received into the Church. The ceremony was of solemn significance, not merely of its essence, but for what it signified in Belloc's own life. All his children now had lives of their own. But it was to his daughter Eleanor that he remained closest, not least in a geographical sense. The young Protestant schoolmaster whom she had married was now to be of the household of the faith, creating a bond of reconciliation between himself and Belloc which was to be of deep importance in the coming years. Yet the atmosphere which Belloc brought with him to church that day was one of restless social bustle, rather than of prayerful awe. While Rex Jebb recited the Apostles' Creed in Latin, to signify his acceptance of the Catholic Faith, Belloc leaned forward to Father Vincent McNabb, who was conducting the ceremony and said, in a loud voice, 'Excuse me, father, is there a telephone in the sacristy?'

The tale suggests an absence of personal piety. It is necessary to reiterate that this is a false impression. Belloc did not bother to come to see his friend G.K. Chesterton received into the Church. He talked through the reception of his son-in-law. This was not a sign that he was insensitive to the importance of these ceremonies. But he had no way of displaying his emotions to men, and so he made no attempt to put on a sham piety for these occasions. The processes of God, at the hands of His priests, were so completely real to Belloc that he took them for granted. But he did not undervalue them.

An example of this can be seen in the case of a new friendship which he made in 1928, when he met the diplomat Eric Phipps and his wife Frances. Charmed by him, the Phippses asked Belloc to stay at their house in Wiltshire, and on Saturday night he enquired where he could hear mass in the morning. Sir Eric was unsympathetic to the Catholic religion, but Lady Phipps said that the nearest Catholic church was in Devizes, and asked if she could accompany her guest. He took with him to church, as was his practice, a large altar missal with which he was accustomed to follow the mass as it was being muttered silently at the altar. On this occasion, aware that Lady Phipps was not familiar with the order of mass he lent her the great book, occasionally pointing to the place if she got muddled. She had recently suffered a great bereavement, and was in a state of bewildered grief and muddle about death, and God, and suffering. As she heard mass that morning in Devizes in 1928, following it in Belloc's missal, with its large illustrations of Christ's passion, she felt that she had a little glimmering, for the first time, of the core of the Catholic religion. She had supposed, as most Protestants do, that it began with a lot of improbable historical claims; or that it was largely a matter of accepting the authority of the Church, in the way that men and women decide to obey the manifesto of a political party. She saw then that the centre of the Catholic religion was the mass, and that human suffering and our knowledge and fear of death were contained in its mystery, and that it bore a direct relation, too mysterious for any superficial or immediate understanding, to the Crucifixion of Christ.

People afterwards said that Belloc had been 'getting at' her; that he had 'talked her into' becoming a Catholic. This was not how it was. She made that journey alone and over a long period. But she was helped to it, not by Belloc's apologetics, but by seeing him at his devotions.[1]

Vincent McNabb, who had few illusions about human nature, and was not a sentimentalist, had seen long before that the whole direction of Belloc's life was bound up with his religion. All his political standpoints sprang from his conviction that the Incarnate Christ had founded a Church, and that it was by divine providence that this Church had been established in the heart of the old Roman Empire. 'The faith is Europe and Europe is the Faith.' From this conviction sprang, on the one hand, his incredibly *naif* notion that Mussolini was a model of ancient imperial virtues; on the other, his detestation of the materialism of capitalists and bolsheviks, and his yearning for a political system in which the dignity of the poor was recognised; in which they were neither as children in a socialist nursery, nor as cogs in a capitalist machine; but as souls made in God's image and likeness, who in a sane world would lead free and independent lives with property of their own. Belloc could not, like Charles Maurras, urge the acceptance of Catholicism merely as a political idea. He urged it because he believed it to be true, and this belief made him ruthlessly belligerent with those whom he believed to be in error.

> Heretics all, whoever you be,
> In Tarbes, or Nimes, or over the sea,
> You never shall have good words from me.
>   *Caritas non conturbat me.*
> Oh, he thwacked them hard, and he banged them long,
>   Upon each and all occasions,
> Till they bellowed in chorus, loud and strong
>   Their orthodox persuasions!

The absence of *caritas* in his dealings with such as H.G. Wells has led many Catholics of a milder generation to disown Belloc. They have forgotten perhaps that Belloc himself seems mild when read beside the controversial writings of Thomas More, not to mention St Jerome or Tertullian. In all cases, the natural belligerence of the man, his

[1] Lady Phipps. Conversation with the author.

delight in a battle, has been harnessed for what he genuinely believed to be, not merely a good cause, but the only cause.

It is in his private dealings with individuals that we see the other side of the noisy, public, posturing Catholic apologist. Katharine Asquith found that Belloc alone was approachable in her grief. Frances Phipps found the same. And it is noticeable that he had, on the whole, more conversational sympathy with women than he did with men. Charlotte Balfour, Bonnie Soames, Mary and Elizabeth Herbert could all have given very similar testimonies.

* * *

It is impossible to write a coherent narrative of days which were so prodigally *crammed* as Belloc's were in the late 1920s. Amusing as his friends found him, his companionship was exhausting, and they appear to have spread the burden widely. Now at Pixton, now at Mells, now back in London, now on to Sussex, Belloc was no more tranquil as he approached his sixtieth birthday than he had been as a boy of nineteen. Glimpsed in the streets of London, as he often was at this date, he appeared to carry an air of bustle along the pavement with him. His broad black hat on his head, a cape or overcoat billowed about the stocky form, from which burst, in exaggerated profusion, torrents of sound, pocketsful of newspapers, a busy air of being on the march, with no particular sense of his destination.[1]

Much of the day was given to conversation – with Chesterton and Baring, who were still constant companions, with Douglas Woodruff, J.B. Morton, Edmond Warre. Warre was an architect, and one of Belloc's most amusing cronies. During 1929, Belloc abandoned his habit of staying at the Reform Club when in London and took rooms in Warre's house in Little Stanhope Street.[2] The arrangement did not work. One of the reasons why Belloc wanted a private apartment, rather than a bedroom at his club, was so that he could be visited in the mornings by a secretary to whom he could dictate. He had not reckoned on Warre's formidable servant, Mrs Forster, who guarded the house like a fortress, and certainly refused to admit young women unchaperoned. On other occasions, Belloc would himself be refused admission; when he came home after dinner at ten o'clock one night, he found that Mrs Forster had chained and bolted the front door against his entry. Defeated by the ogress, he moved back into the Reform, receiving from his literary agent, A.D. Peters, permission to use a room in his offices in Buckingham Street where he could pace

[1] Margaret Stephens to the author.
[2] BC Letters March–September 1929

about and dictate his books at the odd hours he was able to snatch from the social round.

Peters, who was Belloc's last agent, was far from being his first. In their time, all the well-known early twentieth-century agents had worked for Belloc, many of them simultaneously: A.P. Watt, A.M. Heath, Curtis Brown. If possible, he tried to evade paying them the customary ten per cent of his earnings from whatever publisher they had engaged on his behalf. It was only when his relations with other agents had become impossibly acrimonious, when he had taken on far more work than he could manage, and when his affairs were, to say the least, disorganised, that he turned to Peters.

He did not write a letter. A secretary at Peters's office in Buckingham Street admitted him one afternoon at about three o'clock. He did not say who he was, nor did she recognise him, as she peered askance at his well-filled black fustian suit, at this date an even dark mass, comparatively clean, but bulging at the pockets with newspapers and a bottle of white port. She assured him that Mr Peters would soon be back from his luncheon. And for an hour the semi-shaven stranger, hair *en brosse* and eyes aflame with suppressed impatience, sat on the sofa in the hall. When A.D. Peters arrived back, Belloc rose to his feet, and, with a courtly bow, shook his hand.

'My name,' he said, 'is Belloc, and I wish to put my literary affairs into your hands.'

It was the beginning not merely of a business association, but also of a friendship which was to last until Belloc's death. The work involved in taking on Belloc as a client was considerable. Peters dealt with him 'personally', going to stay in Sussex from time to time, taking him out sailing, and travelling on the still frequent jaunts to the Continent. Sometimes they were joined by Peters's colleague, W.N. Roughead, a large burly man who looked like (and was) a University rugger blue. It was Roughead who did most of the paper-work for Belloc, drawing up his contracts and paying his cheques. A third member of A.D. Peters's staff was required to produce the books themselves. For, during the periods when his regular assistant, Bonnie Soames, was escaping to do her own work, he required the assistance of a young woman to whom he could dictate. Peters provided him with a young secretary called Margaret Stephens. They quickly established a professional *rapport*. He would ring her up at strange hours (having established her private telephone number) and ask her to appear, sometimes on a Saturday afternoon, sometimes on a Sunday morning, if not during office hours in Buckingham Street. He expected a neat typescript to be delivered the next day at the Reform

Club. The dictation was rapid, in a growling voice which struck Miss Stephens as very French. In particular, she was struck by the wholly unEnglish quality of his 'r's. The only real pauses would come when he would splutter 'VERIFY' or 'SPATCHCOCK! I want this spatch-cocked in before that last sentence about Louis XIV' While she turned back in her notes to find the sentence he meant, he would have raced ahead again with the dictation, giving her little time to catch up.

His demeanour on these occasions was exaggeratedly courtly and chivalrous – much bowing – but there was no personal chit-chat of any kind. He had sporadic professional dealings with Miss Stephens lasting over a dozen years, during which time she befriended his daughter Eleanor, and visited other members of his family. But, during the dictation sessions, he never made any personal comments at all – no reference to his family, no inquiries after her health, no allusion to anything except the matter in hand.

Bonnie Soames had the same experience, during work-hours, of this almost trance-like absorption. Once, when she had come over to Pixton to help him finish a book, they sat alone together in the library. All the Herberts were out hunting, and there appeared to be no servants about either. Belloc began to dictate, as usual, firing words at her more rapidly than any pencil could scribble short-hand. After an hour or so of this, Miss Soames became aware of a hideous screaming noise from the next room, and she at length felt constrained to mention it.

'Mr Belloc, can you hear that noise?'

'Noise, my child?'

'It sounds like a boy screaming.'

Pause, after which Belloc said, 'It is a boy screaming.'

'Well, Mr Belloc, don't you think we should investigate it?'

They paced about the house, but the noise had died down. It was only when they returned to the library that the banshee-shriek once more assailed their ears. It began to dawn on Miss Soames that this was a case of the supernatural; they were not listening to a live gardener's boy being whipped; they were hearing something spectral. Once more they paced the house, and checked every room. It was only in the library that the screams could be heard, and yet no child was visible.

Miss Soames sat in her chair, shaken and alarmed.

'I don't think there is anything we can do about this,' said Belloc, who promptly went on with his dictation, his own voice drowning that of the child's soul in torment. It provides a perfect example of his concentrated absorption in his work; and also, of how much for granted he took the absolute reality of the supernatural.

Miss Soames, when she dictated for Belloc, would firmly insist on stopping for luncheon. Miss Stephens was less forceful in this respect and would allow him to work until she wilted with hunger. He would arrive for sessions with her having heard mass and eaten a large 'meat breakfast' – by which he meant a plate of bacon and eggs. This was consumed at about ten in the morning, several hours after Miss Stephens had left the house for work, so that when Belloc was getting into his stride at half past one, she was starting to feel faint. When this fact dawned on him, he started to bring a picnic; and, after an hour or two's dictation, he would produce a loaf of bread and a bottle of wine and a single glass from his pocket. Miss Stephens would drink from the glass first, on his insistence. He was incapable of drinking from a glass without leaving a creamy-coloured smear around its rim, and inadvertently spitting crumbs into the wine itself. After such a collation, they could continue work for another few hours.

Once, in Buckingham Street, the flow of words suddenly stopped, and Miss Stephens looked to see what had struck Belloc dumb. He was fumbling in all his pockets, his face taut with anxiety.

'What is the matter, Mr Belloc?'

'I thought I had a bottle of white port in my pocket, but it appears not to be there.'

'But I can go over to the Adelphi Hotel and buy a bottle.'

'Surely, Miss Stephens, it is not *rrr*ight for a woman' . . . (pause) . . . 'to enter a hotel on her own and buy *port*.'

Realising that his happiness depended on being able to consume this sweet white wine, she insisted on going; and, when she reached the bar, she remembered to buy a corkscrew with which to open the bottle. When she got back to the office, Belloc was shouting, 'Calamity! Disaster!'

'What is the matter, Mr Belloc.'

With great fumblings in his pockets, producing handfuls of crusts, cheque-stubs, fluff, newscuttings, he said, 'I have forgotten my cork-sc*rr*ew!'

Her foresight in having remembered to buy such an article was highly commended.

*   *   *

Needless to say, the work produced under such conditions was of a very uneven quality. In order to pay for the pearls and caviar for which Belloc himself, if not his children, howled, he allowed himself to be signed up for far too many books. Most of them were dictated with no previous research or preparation and, although they are tributes to his almost preternatural fluency and eloquence, they are inevitably patchy. Nevertheless, even in his work of a later period, the *breadth* as well as the quantity of his written *oeuvre* is remarkable. Consider the books he wrote in 1928 and 1929 alone: two more fattish volumes of his *History of England*; biographies of *James II* and *Joan of Arc*; as well as three or four novels, a travel book and several works of apologetics – *How the Reformation Happened* and *Survivals and New Arrivals*. This last is one of Belloc's most successful assertions that 'the line of cleavage throughout the world lies between what is with, and what is against the Faith'.[1] It is a book which deserves to be much better known. Its vision of Europe, and of modern religion, might have seemed bizarre at the time of writing; but almost all his prophecies have come to pass.

A completely different work, and published in the same year, is an extraordinary romance entitled *Belinda*. It is penned entirely in the idiom of the early nineteenth century and tells the story of how Horatio Maltravers and Belinda Montgomery, young people of gentrified stock, fall in love with one another, are frustrated in their union by the opposition of the grown-ups, but are ultimately united in wealth and happiness. To Maurice Baring, he wrote, 'I have finished *Belinda* – a fearful sweat – like sawing marble – but worth it. It is the only thing I ever finished in my life and the only piece of my own writing that I have liked for more than 40 years.'[2] Certainly, it is a delightful thing. At times, the pastiche is so good that one would not know it was not the work of some hitherto undiscovered contemporary of Peacock, Jane Austen and Miss Edgeworth. At times, however, it has a flowery 'Georgian' sentimentality which recalls the stories, like *Orpheus in Mayfair* or *C*, of Maurice Baring himself.

In the light of all that has gone before in this chapter, the appearance of *Belinda* seems surprising. The thunderous defender of Mussolini, the violently scornful religious apologist, the fat old man in fustian, dripping crumbs and odours wherever he carried his smelly old bundles of laundry and luggage, these masks seem to have no imaginative kinship with the sentimental scenes of *Belinda*. True, it is a sentimentality which is deliberately arch, and semi-comic. But, like his own manners with women, the exaggerated courtliness was only tinged with comedy. He slaved and worked at *Belinda*, extolling the manners and customs of the English gentry before the Reform Bill and celebrating the joys of romantic love. This, and not his works defending the Catholic faith or the Catholic view of history, was the book that he endlessly rewrote with his own hands. 'I go over it word

---

[1] *Survivals and New Arrivals* p. 15
[2] July 20 1928, quoted Speaight p. 500

for word, like a mosaic; changing, fitting in, adapting, dictating, erasing, spatch-cocking, caressing, softening, glamouring, suppressing, enhancing and in general divinising this my darling treasure.'[1]

The deep vein of nostalgia and romantic sentimentality which was buried in Belloc's nature shines out, not embarrassingly, but beautifully, in *Belinda*, and it was soon to attract a discerning band of admirers. Father Waggett, for instance, the Anglican monk who had gone to Cambridge to persuade Protestants not to listen to Monsignor Benson, was ecstatic about the book.

> My dear and dearest Belloc, Your *Belinda* is unspeakably beautiful. I thank God for a fresh unfolding of your genius, a fresh date for the life of our prose exquisite in spirit and in form. Every word is lovely. The humour of the convention moves within the limits of an accomplished harmony. And what you give us in your music is a deep consolation. We have had too much of affection that is hindered & crippled, moving between rash impulses and nameless regrets. In the delicately tinted image of Belinda, now the owner of my devotion, you have shown the love, hindered by circumstance, but in itself at once free and safe; a little sister of the Love that casteth out Fear. If this is what our grandparents knew how worthily you have reminded us of what they knew.[2]

Waggett's letter goes to the heart of what is remarkable about Belloc's romanticism. He cared deeply for women. He had a high view of his own emotional attachments. But it was a view which obliterated any trace of eroticism. The post-Freudian glorification of sex was something which disgusted him. His devotion to Elodie had not been primarily sexual; nor, however much he had been 'in love' with Juliet Duff, could the memory of that greater, and earlier, devotion ever fade.

As he approached his sixtieth birthday, there are two surviving visions of Belloc which need to be remembered together. One is the rampaging, gregarious, noisy figure, on the march with his friends. Another is a solitary figure, whose broken heart has never been mended, and who gazes towards death with lonely longing. Many illustrations of both sides of Belloc's nature could be chosen. I choose two. In the first, we read in the memoirs of 'Beachcomber' an account of travelling abroad with Belloc, rushing from cheap hotels to early mass; and then, without breakfast, to the nearest station, always on the move, always grumbling, always late, always angry.

[1] Ibid.
[2] BC February 1, 1929

'Bear' Warre, Peter [Belloc], he and I were once walking (against time of course) through a Norman forest. All the while he kept up such a running fire of high-spirited grumbling, with sudden invective against the whole lot of us, that we were exhausted with laughter. Then, without warning, he began to talk about the evolution of the wheel, and we were listening interestedly when the cursing began again, much louder, much more violent. We three rolled about and the din was terrific. Anyone meeting us would have taken us for a party of lunatics. But we met nobody, and in the boiling hot weather we blundered on through the forest, howling with laughter.[1]

This splendidly inconsequential anecdote brings Belloc vividly to life because it shows how much he needed, temperamentally, to be much of the time on the warpath. When we see him rumbling through the forests of Normandy like a wild animal, lecturing his companions, many of his more baffling public posturings fall into place. H.G. Wells, like so many others, recoiled with wounded horror at his snarlings and grumblings. His friends, hurrying along behind him to keep up with his exhausting pace, were howling with laughter.

But another Belloc was the man whom Juliet Duff called 'poor darling Hilary', whose courtly good manners, whose profound courtesy towards women, and whose sad eyes provoked, particularly in his feminine companions, a deep sympathy. This was the self he dramatised in his sad little poem, 'Farewell to Juliet', in which all his devotion to her cannot blot out the memory of Elodie, and the great love of his youth.

> How shall I round the ending of a story,
>   Now the wind's falling and the harbour nears?
> How shall I sign your tiny Book of Glory,
>   Juliet, my Juliet, after many years?
>
> I'll sign it, One that halted at a vision:
>   One whom the shaft of beauty struck to flame:
> One that so wavered in a strong decision:
>   One that was born perhaps to fix your name.
>
> One that was pledged, and goes to his replevening:
>   One that now leaves you with averted face,
> A shadow passing through the doors at evening
>   To his companion and his resting place.

FOURTEEN

ADVICE
1930–1935

There is a story of Belloc, during the 1930s, encountering a man in a railway carriage who was reading a volume of his *History of England*. Belloc leaned forward and asked the man how much he had paid for the volume, and, being informed of the price, fished the sum out of his pocket. He then gave the money to his companion, snatched the book from his hand, and tossed it out of the carriage window.

Even if this story is untrue[1] it enshrines a rather sad fact about the last years of Belloc's active life. And that is, that he felt constrained to devote nearly all his professional and intellectual energy to churning out historical 'pot-boilers'. The reason for this was that he could no longer secure an adequate income from journalism. There can be no doubt that, in his persistent assaults on the political framework by which Great Britain and its Empire were governed, he had made enemies among the newspaper proprietors. They did not want articles in their papers which suggested that parliamentary democracy was no more than a cloak for the corruption of capitalism in its last decay. Some of the things, moreover, which he wrote about the Jews were calculated to cause offence, and succeeded in their calculation.

Belloc probably exaggerated the extent to which he was cold-shouldered by the Press Barons. Other things need to be taken into consideration, before one accepts the idea of a plot to exclude right-thinking Catholics from the columns of the *Daily Express*. The fact that Belloc was an unreliable columnist, frequently late with copy, and given to disappearing without warning to the Continent for weeks at a time, probably had as much to do with his failure to secure employment as a journalist as did his allegedly intolerable ideas. He was therefore stuck with writing books, and this is a pity, not merely because it worried him and wore him out, but because very few of the last thirty-five or so in the Belloc canon are any good.

Belloc is always at his best over a short distance. Essays and verse

---

[1] I have heard it from several sources, but never seen it substantiated.

are his best mediums. He very rarely wrote a biography of extended length, after the First World War, which gives a picture of his subject in the round.

There are occasional, brilliant vignettes. The deaths of all his subjects are well-told: Milton, 'no longer believing the omnipotence of his Creator, the Divinity of his Saviour and the native immorality of mankind'; Cromwell who 'had gone to discover whether there were beatitude for his reward who had hewn to pieces the enemies of Jehovah; or whether he should fall shrieking into the hands of an angry God; or whether Death be indeed no more than a mighty sleep'. The deaths of Napoleon and Cranmer are equally good. So, too, are nearly all the battles Belloc described. And there are delicious epi-grammatic touches, as when he writes of William Cecil as 'one of the greatest and certainly one of the vilest men that ever lived'.

Yet Belloc's last books are not as interesting as they deserve to be; certainly they are less interesting than these flashes, if excerpted, would suggest. And the reason is their monotony of tone. For the most part, the flood of books which he published in the 1930's are not, as they claim, essays in biography or portraiture. They are expositions of Belloc's view of history; and, from that point of view, to have read one of these later books is to have read them all. For whether he purports to write about Wolsey, or Cranmer, or Charles II, or Milton, or Richelieu or Oliver Cromwell or Louis XIV, he tells the same old story. That is, Catholic Monarchy is alone capable of protecting the interests, freedom and property of the private citizen. The enemies of Catholicism at the time of the Reformation were in cahoots with the powerful new bourgeoisie, the money power repre-sented by families such as the Cromwells and the Cecils. Charles I was the last monarch in England who was able to preserve the freedoms of the common man. The Rich, represented by Cromwell, took over the running of the country when they chopped off King Charles's head, and they have, in effect, been running it ever since. There were attempts (the 'last rally' of Charles II, the heroic James II) to suppress the Rich, who had of course invited the Jews to settle in London almost as soon as the King's head was severed from his body. But they failed.

England had a weak dynasty, that of the Stuarts. France in the seventeenth century was rescued by the combined genius of Richelieu and Louis XIV who both asserted the ancient medieval Catholic absolutism. They persecuted the Rich, and they were therefore able to rule effectually. It was only when the French monarchy became corrupted by the Rich, in the eighteenth century, that the ancient rights of the people had to be reasserted by the Revolution. Belloc therefore could with logic remain a supporter of the Revolution while being passionately loyal to the principles of European Catholic monarchy.

There are so many flaws in this general view that they are hardly worth mentioning. There is, for instance, no evidence that James I or Charles I – or for that matter his sons Charles II and James II – were any more anxious to protect the private property of private citizens than was Oliver Cromwell. Moreover, there were plenty of facts that Belloc chose to ignore when he was arguing a case. So, his James II emerges as a brave patriotic figure with a love of the sea; but we are not told of his perverted love of torture. Louis XIV was a great Catholic absolutist, a defender, like Thomas Aquinas and *GK's Weekly*, of all the things which Cardinal Manning had expounded in his sermons and political writings. So it does not suit Belloc to remind us that the pope (Innocent XI) so disapproved of Louis XIV that he caused the bells of the Vatican to ring out to celebrate the victory of William of Orange over the Catholic forces of James II and Louis XIV at the Boyne. Indeed, the only allusion to that battle Belloc makes is to 'William's bungling at the Boyne'.[1]

It is not my purpose to criticise Belloc as an historian. His inaccuracies, and his defects, are obvious. They should not be laughed at too smugly. For, in his way, he was a pioneer, in exposing the fundamental absurdity of the 'Whig view of history'. When he died, Hugh Ross Williamson wrote the following tribute:

> Twenty years ago I found it difficult to read him without anger. If my masters, Pollard and Gardiner, were right, Belloc was an inaccurate and tendentious crank . . . My mind was changed not by reading Belloc but by studying sources, which revealed not only the consistent and conscious dishonesty of Pollard and Gardiner but the general rightness of Belloc . . . One example may suffice. In the fourth volume of his *History of England*, published in 1931, he said that Elizabeth I's ecclesiastical policy did not represent her own religious wishes but showed her the prisoner of Protestant extremists. This year – 22 years later – Prof. Neale has published a book which is welcomed as a major (and even revolutionary) historical work because it arrives at the same conclusion.[2]

It is rather a distorted view of John Neale's great biography of Queen Elizabeth to suggest that its reputation rests entirely on a coincidence of view with Belloc in the matter of the Queen's religion. But the

[1] *Monarchy* (1938) p. 346
[2] *The Catholic Herald* July 24, 1953 p. 5

general point is a fair one. If Belloc is occasionally absurd in his implication that all the papists in English history were good and all the protestants were bad, he was contradicting absurdities which were quite as gross. The sad thing is that, by the time he wrote most of his English history, he did not have the time, or the money, or the inclination to do any of it properly. With sufficient leisure and incentive, he could have written some supremely great biographies. It is a great loss to the world, for instance, that he never wrote properly about Napoleon. And, had he been caught at the height of his powers, he could have written the most superb biography of St Thomas More, for there is much that More and Belloc have in common, both as controversialists and humorists.

What makes the books which he *did* produce during the 1930's depressing is their repetitiveness. Even in his undergraduate days, it had been noted that he was happy, in his speeches to the Oxford Union, to make the same points over and over again. If he believed a thing to be true, it did not embarrass him to publish it in book after book, to repeat it in speeches, articles and conversation. Since his income now depended upon filling up books somehow; and since no one, not even Belloc, has an inexhaustible range of things to say; and since he had long since grown bored with his own art, he subdued his distaste for the poor quality of the work so as to pay for the 'pearls and caviar' for which his children still allegedly howled. 'I sit here all day long grinding out hack work at a prodigious rate' is a characteristic comment from this date.[1]

Very few of these final thirty-five books, dashed off during the 1930s, were composed by Belloc's own hand. He dictated almost all of them; and the memories of his son-in-law, Reginald Jebb, show the extraordinary extent of Belloc's natural eloquence. For, though they may be repetitive and inaccurate and capricious, it could never be said of any of his books that they were wholly inelegant or badly made.

It seems likely that the ability to fix his mind on a subject to the exclusion of what was happening around him was a big element in his fluency when lecturing or dictating an article. He told me once, when I had been trying to keep up in long hand with his flow of words as he dictated an article, that as a subject took form in his mind it fell almost automatically into paragraphs, and once he had begun to dictate he could see the structure of his sentences and rarely had to hark back and rearrange them. None the less, when he was writing a book he usually wrote down with his own hand a

[1] Mells 1933.

number of passages of special importance, which he would introduce in their places into his dictation. Nor was it only the structure of what he had to say that he mastered in dictating. The words he used and his style adapted themselves (without effort, it seemed) to his subject. One afternoon, after a bout of influenza, he came down in his dressing-gown still quite knocked out by his illness, and from an arm-chair asked me if I would take down one or two notes for the paper he was editing. We rushed through several of these at top speed, and then he said, if I could spare the time, he would like to write a short article. The words poured out with the same rapidity but in a style quite different from the staccato of the notes. This finished, I thought he must be exhausted and suggested a rest on the sofa. Instead, he told me that it was his habit to write at least 1,000 words of his history each day, and that day he had not done so, so if I was not tired . . . And off he went again, his style once more entirely changing. It was a remarkable achievement for a sick man and it would have been impossible unless his mind had been able to department and store up, not only a number of quite separate trains of thought, but the shape of the sentences and the style in which they were to be expressed.[1]

Inevitably, this method of work involved a little entourage of servants, amanuenses and assistants, and the burden for producing the greater part of these books fell heavily on the shoulders of Bonnie Soames. It was work which she did lovingly and joyfully, but it involved considerable sacrifice. He exploited her devotion to the point where she was scarcely able to pursue her own career as a writer and journalist without periodic escapes. For, when she was at King's Land, she was expected to be absorbed completely in Belloc's literary activities. This was not to say that his company, and conversation, and the movement, even at this date, of his mind and tongue, were not exceedingly stimulating. Miss Soames regarded her position as one of great privilege. But her family and friends noted that Belloc's demands upon her energies would leave her not infrequently drained and exhausted.

It was no mere matter of copying out what he chose so rapidly to dictate. He dictated his Milton book to her over a space of ten days in the study at King's Land. As usual, she could barely keep up with the speed of his sentences; and, since the next day the *dictée* would start again with equal speed, there was no time to type up what she had scribbled down in shorthand the day before. At the end of the ten

[1] *Testimony to Hilaire Belloc* p. 19

days, she had a mountain of short-hand notes, but the first stage of the book was done. Belloc said to her, 'My child I am going to Paris. Make sure that the book is sent off to Cassell.' 'But do you not want to read it through before you send it to the publishers?' 'Oh, no, no, my child, I am sure it will be quite satisfactory.'[1]

Can any author have ever behaved with less dedication? And yet the Milton book is a very good one. Belloc excelled both at literary criticism and in the exposition of theological error. His favourite English poet gave him ample opportunity to spread his wings in both capacities. *Milton* is one of the best books of the final phase. Much of this fact derives from the perfect blend of sympathy and antipathy which Belloc felt towards his subject. How much of it depends upon the industry of Miss Soames, who typed the book up in Belloc's absence and sent it to the publishers, will probably never be known.

Belloc's exhaustingness stemmed only in part from his great prose output. He left his helpers and intimates *drained* because they were all caught up in his tempestuous restlessness, his ceaseless travel, his bursts of song and hilarity, his passionately expressed opinions, the air of bustle which he carried with him everywhere. He confessed to Elizabeth Herbert in 1930 that he was 'tortured by lack of sleep'[2], and this affliction – a familiar one to all depressive and restless minds – was to be with him to the end. But one can exaggerate the picture of Belloc's melancholy, sleepless in the Reform Club, or manically dashing off by a night train to the Continent for yet another breath of Catholic air.

He was, if possible, more social during his sixties than in any other decade of his life. For his sixtieth birthday itself, a great dinner was organised, with G.K. Chesterton in the chair at the Adelphi Hotel. Forty friends attended, and Belloc was presented with a goblet inscribed with a tag from his own heroic poem in praise of wine.[3] Chesterton has told the story in his autobiography of how it was impressed upon him that there were to be no speeches. 'I merely said a few words to the effect that such a ceremony might have been as fitting thousands of years ago, at the festival of a great Greek poet; and that I was confident that Belloc's sonnets and strong verse would remain like the cups and carved epics of the Greeks. He acknowledged

[1] JSN to author.
[2] BC January 18, 1930
[3] G.K. Chesterton's *Autobiography* tells us that the lines were 'And sacramental raise me the divine/Strong brother in God and last companion, wine'. Robert Speaight's biography of Belloc records that the lines were 'Open, golden wide/with benediction graven on the side'.

it briefly, with a sad good humour, saying he found that, by the age of sixty, he did not care very much whether his verse remained or not. "But I am told", he added with suddenly reviving emphasis, "I am told that you begin to care again frightfully when you are seventy. In which case I hope I shall die at sixty-nine". And then we settled down to the feast of old friends, which was to be so happy because there were no speeches."[1] As is well known, all forty men at the dinner eventually rose to their feet and made a joke oration of some kind or another: A.P. Herbert pretended to be addressing some sort of Workmen's Benevolent Society, Duff Cooper pretended to be a Lloyd George Liberal, Jack Squire praised 'Beachcomber', and 'Beachcomber' praised Jack Squire, and D.B. Wyndham Lewis, who thought he could avoid making a speech by hiding under the table, was dragged out in schoolboy fashion and made to speak like the others. Read in sober prose, it sounds a most excruciating evening. It was obviously one of those occasions which no description can capture, but which was not merely riotous and hilarious, but in some way very moving. There were old friends there stretching back to undergraduate days – E.S.P. Haynes and Maurice Baring; T. Michael Pope, Belloc's assistant on the ill-starred *Illustrated Review* was there, together with E.C. Bentley, Christopher Hollis, Douglas Woodruff and the rest. The memory of the evening prompted Chesterton, with characteristic exuberance of heart, to conclude his 'portrait of a friend' with a quatrain of Sir William Watson's:

> Nor without honour my days ran
> Nor yet without a boast shall end;
> For I was Shakespeare's countryman,
> And were not you my friend?[2]

Most of the published memories of Belloc are by his male acquaintances, and so we tend to think of him as belonging to a predominantly male society. But, in fact, the majority of his close friends during the 1930s were women. In the same year as the Adelphi dinner, he spent two months in London during which he received at least sixteen invitations from Sibyl Colefax.[3] He dined, whenever he could – often every day in a week – with Lady Juliet Duff; and, even on days when they had met in the morning, he might receive letters from her by the afternoon post. And he would reply, 'Darling, darling, darling

[1] Ibid. p. 306
[2] G. K. Chesterton: *Autobiography* p. 306
[3] BC Many examples e.g. April 26, 1933

Juliet – three darlings one in three.'[1] He maintained a constant correspondence with Katharine Asquith, and he saw much of Diana Cooper. In March 1933, he dragged himself all the way up to Leeds to watch her perform on stage. 'I don't like the theatre much any more than you do,' he confided to Katharine Asquith, 'but I'm so fond of Diana and Leeds isn't awfully far from Ampleforth'.[2] When in London, he would entertain Lady Diana by taking her and her husband Duff Cooper to the Music Hall, whose songs he always enjoyed.

But perhaps his closest bond outside his own family, as he began to totter towards old age, was with the Herbert family, and particularly with Mary Herbert at Pixton. They are immortalised in the epigram 'On the ladies of Pixton':

> Three Graces; and the mother were a Grace,
> But for profounder meaning in her face.

One of these Graces, Laura Herbert, was to become the second wife of Evelyn Waugh. Belloc had encountered Waugh in the summer of 1933, at an early stage of the novelist's involvement with the Herbert family. The young man had been on a Mediterranean cruise with Alfred Duggan to the Herbert family villa, Altachiara, at Portofino near Genoa. Belloc frequently went there. He happened to be staying there with Mary and Laura Herbert when Duggan introduced his remarkable guest. Mary Herbert afterwards remarked that Waugh had been on his best behaviour. He was polite to the point of smarminess; and, as a quite recent convert to Catholicism, anxious to ingratiate himself with the great Catholic man of letters. However, when he was gone, and Mary Herbert asked Belloc his opinion of the young convert, she received the surprising reply: 'He has a devil in him.' When she discovered, to her alarm, that Waugh was in love with her daughter and intended to marry her, she frequently was given reason to remember Belloc's prescience. It is a good example of the slightly peasanty, witch-like quality of Belloc's nature, something he had possessed in common with Elodie. He saw through people very easily. He lived by hunches, whims, and funny little superstitions, such as his insisting that his children and grandchildren went to tell the bees at King's Land when anyone died.

In the case of the encounter with Evelyn Waugh, few would deny that there was some truth in Belloc's insight; though no one in the

[1] e.g. BC October 10, 1933
[2] Mells March 23, 1933

Herbert family was able to guess it at the time. The recognition of the devil in Waugh did not, of course, blind Belloc to his skill as a writer, as a generous letter about *A Handful of Dust* makes clear:

> Dear Waugh, I don't know where you are so I send this to your publishers to forward. It is to tell you my admiration of your book which I have just read. It is worth expressing, because I can read hardly anything nowdays: and when a friend gave me the Handful of Dust to read because I had nothing for the train journey back to town I was sure I shouldn't get beyond 3 pages. I never do. Its a curse on me. But I could not let it go & I took it with me in Cabs, food places, busses [sic] and everywhere till I had finished it at a go. It is really a remarkable thing, and it owes its quality to *construction* – which today is, in prose, as rare as virtue. Every word is right, and in its right place: so that the effect is a maximum for the material employed. You really are to be congratulated.
>
> I think you will write great tragedy. But I'm a bad critic. Only a good taster – when I can eat at all. Yours always, H. Belloc.[1]

It must have been a very gratifying letter to receive, not least because it encapsulates so precisely a view of art – that it depends on construction – which is coincident with Waugh's own.

*   *   *

In 1935, two years before Waugh married her sister Laura, Bridget Herbert got married to Edward Grant, and Belloc gave her as a wedding present a manuscript book entitled ADVICE and containing all manner of information – largely about wine, a little about food – which a young wife and hostess ought to know. In 1960, the book was printed, with a preface by Evelyn Waugh, who wrote that Belloc's 'interest in food, wine and domestic economy was strong and idiosyncratic to the verge of perversity. He believed that in those matters the rich were ready dupes; that excellence was rare and found in obscure and humble places. Some of the information given in the book is already obsolete; some of it expresses crotchets; but the bulk is a garnering of wisdom and in every turn of phrase may be heard the unmistakable authentic tones of the great man'.[2]

That is a very fair comment. *Advice* deserves a wider audience than it has received. For, even where its counsels can no longer be followed, they are always entertaining. Few young women setting up house nowadays would be rich enough to heed the advice:

[1] Ms. in the possession of Mr Auberon Waugh
[2] *Advice* p. 36

Always get silver – never plate:
whether you are buying, or choosing for yourself a present given to
you, or stealing, *always* buy silver.

Plate does not last – especially electro-plate – modern plate powders
destroy it; it never looks right and it doesn't pawn or sell or make a
gift for your descendants. At all sacrifices have silver: all silver, and
the thicker and heavier the better.

And this I say having myself sinned horribly the other way a
thousand times, but now converted in age I know the truth. Silver
is good to eat off and to look at and to drink out of. Plate is a fraud.
You will never regret the silver you will accumulate in a long life. It
goes with white hairs.[1]

The culinary advice, like the works of history which were engaging
his professional attention when he wrote it, is made up more of
vigorous general views than of particular receipts. ('There are two
kinds of cooking: Hot and warm. They are quite distinct, and the
mixing of them up ruins life.') But there are specific injunctions about
the right sort of salt (sea-salt: 'If you use processed salt you do so at
your peril. It does not even taste like salt, and it leaves a sediment: it
does not fully dissolve. Avoid it like the plague') and instructions
about how to make salad:

To make good Salad: use a spoon – a big spoon (and a fork) of Horn
or Wood. Never use metal. Pour in $\frac{3}{4}$ full of wine and vinegar (called
Orleans) (Malt Vinegar is death). Into this put salt, a goodish lot,
and a *little* pepper – not essential. Dissolve them thoroughly in the
vinegar by stirring with a fork. Then, and not till then, *scatter* (not
pour) the vinegar over the lettuce turning the lettuce as you do so. If
you pour instead of scattering, or fail to turn the leaves as you
scatter, the vinegar will all lie in one place and most of the salad will
be tasteless.

When the vinegar is thus scattered turn the whole vigorously
pressing the leaves against the sides of the bowl gently as you stir. In
this way the vinegar gets right into the whole thing. Then add not
less than 2 spoonfuls of olive oil and as many more as you like. The
amount after the first two spoonfuls makes no difference.

Then eat the salad with your fingers. A man who cuts salad is I
know not what.'[2]

[1] Ibid. p. 34
[2] Ibid. p. 13

But, for the most part, the treatise is taken up with drink. How to serve it ('Never warm Red wine' are the opening words of the little book), how to bottle it, uncork it – 'Many waste their lives in dealing with the corks of fizzy wines . . . The rule is to take a sharp knife and cut off the excrescence leaving the rest of the cork flush with the top of the bottle. Then pull it out as you would an ordinary cork';[1] how to store it, and even how to transform it. The volume ends with a superbly optimistic and self-confident Post Script.

To make good old Brandy out of Vile Stuff

(1) Pour it through the air into a large receptacle, e.g. from the top of the stairs into a bath below.

(2) Put it into bottles, with a plum in each bottle.

(3) Stand it up *with no corks in the bottles*, for some 2 or 3 days, even a week – or 3 weeks.

(4) Put in a *drop* of Maraschino into each bottle.

The bottles are now old Brandy, and you can give them funny names and drink the stuff out of big glasses and roll it around, warming it with your hands and smelling at it like a dog.

FINIS[2]

Alan Pryce-Jones recalled how Belloc himself had been the victim of a similar trick in the early 1930s, but accepts, perhaps a little too readily, the idea that Belloc could not tell the difference between good drink or bad.

> I remember one evening in Sussex . . . staying at a house near his own at which he was coming to dine. Just before dinner our host, Lord Rosslyn, remembered, too, that Belloc liked port. At the end of dinner, therefore, after someone had gone to the village and brought back a bottle of three-and-sixpenny port from the local off-licence, the wine was decanted and brought up with ceremony. 'This', said Lord Rosslyn, 'is all I have to offer. I have kept it as a historical curiosity. It is the last bottle of my father's port laid down for me' – and here he went into elaborate details of place and date. 'It will probably be undrinkable by now. It may be sugar. It may be vinegar'. And he poured a glass out. Belloc drank it slowly. 'A remarkable wine', he said at last. 'An admirable wine. There is no

[1] Ibid. p. 12
[2] Ibid. p. 37

reason to waste it on these young people'. And while he kept the decanter by him pausing in his talk occasionally to refill his glass ('No, no' Lord Rosslyn would expostulate, 'No more for me. I have only brought it up for you') I felt for him my one moment of true affection. There is nothing more endearing than to catch a great man in the middle of a huge mistake.[1]

But, of course, an equally plausible explanation for Belloc's behaviour is that he saw through the tease, but chose to behave with the solemn mock-politeness which was his wont. So long as he kept the decanter by him and had plenty to drink, he would not much have minded whether it was good and old or whether it was 'vile stuff'.

* * *

Belloc had always struck his contemporaries as being older than he actually was. He seemed ancient with wisdom and experience when he went up to Balliol as an undergraduate; and Lady Diana Cooper, meeting him for the first time during the Great War, had thought of him as a very old man. Now at last, as the 1930s advanced, he was becoming old in truth, even a Grand Old Man. He and Chesterton had been caricatures of themselves for a generation, as far as the general public was concerned; and they did little to alter their 'image'. People believed them to be overweight, Catholic drinking men, whose political views harked back to issues which were more alive in the days of the Boer War and of Dreyfus than they were in the 1930s. People knew them as a curious blend of laughter and anger, of clowning and controversy. And, in their public appearances, neither Chesterton nor Belloc did anything to disappoint the public view. For three shillings, every Thursday in the earlier part of 1934, you could go to Gatti's restaurant in the Strand at 12.30 for 1.15. There you would be entertained by 'Good food, Music, Social Intercourse, Wit and Wisdom',[2] the latter provided by Belloc, Chesterton and their cronies Ben Tillett or R. McNair Wilson.

Much of Belloc's life had been spent on platforms. And yet, in spite of his very public defence of all his opinions, particularly his religious opinions, he resented the idea of being a professional or 'official' Catholic. In the course of a long life, he opened innumerable Catholic fêtes, presided at the speech-days of innumerable Catholic schools, sent cheques to convents and churches all over the country when they appealed to him for help, and was then obliged to turn up and make a

[1] *The Listener* March 21 1957 p. 481
[2] Leaflets survive at BC.

speech at the official opening of the (usually rather ugly) building. All this he did, grumblingly, but not without humility. What he did not desire was 'official' recognition from his church.

Early in 1934, he and Chesterton were appointed by the Pope Knights of the Order of St Gregory the Great. The honour pleased Chesterton hugely, appealing to the side of his nature that had written the 'Ballad of the White Horse' and 'Lepanto'. But the news of Belloc's honour lay unanswered on his desk at King's Land for day after day.

'Aren't you going to answer your letter from the Pope, Mr Belloc?' Bonnie Soames asked him. 'You will have to say something in reply. Mr Chesterton has already accepted his medal, and regards it as a very great honour.'

Belloc appeared not to have heard, and then said, 'Why should I accept an "honour" from some greasy monsignore?'[1] Such an attitude to the Papacy would have surprised many of his co-religionists. It could be said that there was nothing incompatible in holding the apostolic *office* in high regard, while despising the more absurd trappings of the papal court. But the rebuff reveals a deeper and harder cynicism in Belloc's nature which he found it hard to conquer. With a part of himself, he was perhaps always a pagan, a noble old Roman pre-Christian. With another small part of himself he was a sceptic of the French revolutionary school, a devout reader of Rousseau's *Contrat Social*. These sides to his mind and imagination were held in check by a strong habit of piety. They were subsumed and Christened. But, every now and then, they would burst out in some irreverent, or even blasphemous, inconsistency. As he grew older, in fact, the rather juvenile desire to 'shock' grew stronger and not weaker.

Hugh Kingsmill, writing to a friend, recorded that his brother Arnold Lunn 'was dining with [Edward] Shanks the other day and Shanks said that at a recent dinner with Belloc, Belloc somewhat tight opened up about Christ. "I revere him because I am instructed to by the Church but personally I find him repellent. The fellow was a milksop."[2]

Although this (confessedly third-hand) story feels as though it has been 'improved' in the telling, Belloc is certainly recorded as saying quite similar things. Though he is not known, on any other recorded occasion, to have referred to his Saviour as a milksop, he did say,

---

[1] JSN. Pronounced grreazy.
[2] Edward Shanks to Hugh Kingsmill

often, that his only reason for revering Christ was that the Church told him to. Since the Church *did* so decree, Belloc was happy to 'pray detestable drink to them/That give no honour to Bethlehem'. There is a sort of madness in this point of view, since one presumably only believes in the Church if one thinks it was founded by Our Lord. But it is the kind of madness which appealed to Belloc's sense of humour, precisely because it was shocking to the pious.

* * *

In 1934, an almost farcical quarrel with a servant led to a great change in Belloc's life. On a wintry day, he asked his factotum George Rance to drive him to Oxford, and, to his amazement, George refused, claiming that the roads were icy and impassable. Tempers ran high and, when Rance became adamant, Belloc dismissed him. This calamity meant the departure of George's wife Edith, who had been Belloc's cook for thirty years. Rance maintained that Belloc had been killing her with overwork, but she was devoted to her master and the times when she had to cook meals at King's Land were heavily outweighed by the periods of Belloc's absence. True, he could be an exacting employer. Great fuss was made about the food. Edith would be nagged about buying perfect Dover soles for his luncheon of Friday. He would lecture her about how to cook them in the best French manner, and tell her, who had been cooking for over fifty years, how to gauge that the butter was exactly the right temperature. When the magnificent fish finally reached the dining-table, Belloc would be drunk, and having forked up a few mouthfuls, he would declaim, 'I am like the wild elephant: I spoil more than I eat.'

With Edith's departure, a new phase of Belloc's life was to begin. Although, for the first thirty years of this century, he was very rarely there, King's Land always played a most important part in his personal mythology; and it was home. He had given up his flat near the Oratory. Life in 'Bear' Warre's rooms in Stanhope Street had not been practicable. Much time was spent at the Reform Club and in other people's houses. But, as he grew older, Belloc felt increasingly the need of home.

It was then that his daughter Eleanor, and her husband Reginald Jebb, made the decision to go to live at King's Land to keep house for him. It was a brave move; some would maintain that it was not a wise one. Eleanor was, to put it mildly, not particularly house-proud; nor was she a gifted cook. But she bravely undertook the task, knowing that somebody had to do it. Doubtless, the Jebbs found that they were helped in their decision by the fact that their various educational enterprises had begun to founder. After Reginald Jebb became a Catholic, he had tried to set up a Catholic prep-school of his own – St Louis's, near Rugeley; and Belloc had written to every papist family he could think of, imploring them to send their men-children between the ages of seven and thirteen to this establishment. Somehow, they never succeeded in attracting an economic number of children. And, by 1934, there was only one boy left in the school, Auberon Herbert. His mother, Mary Herbert, was doggedly loyal to Belloc, and would doubtless have left him at St Louis's, had not the Jebbs moved to Sussex.

'I have now', Belloc wrote in January 1935, from King's Land, 'not only all my grandchildren and the added bunch of Eleanor's servants here, but five cats also under my roof – by name Tom, Bogles, Nicky, and the two little kittens who are useful for the young grandchildren. Kittens and children go together like strawberries and cream. Or any other pair of twins. That again is innocence, on which for my part I lay great store. I have always wanted to recover my own and I understand that that is done by drinking Lethe, which cures remorse as the springs of Vittel cure gout.'[1]

In February 1935, Belloc set out for one of his most extended journeys since the First World War. It began with a lecture tour of the Eastern Seaboard of the United States, and was to involve a journey home in the fullest sense of the word; for his return voyage took him, via Cuba, to Spain; and, from Spain, across the Mediterranean to the Holy Land, which he had never visited, and which was to inspire his last truly considerable work of prose. He confessed in a letter to his son Hilary before setting out for the States:

People ought not to write unless they have independent means on a scale sufficient for an educated man and his wellbeing. For to earn one's bread by writing is not only unnatural but servile. I am exceedingly grateful for the amount of leisure I have had which has permitted me to write perhaps ten books, possibly a dozen, after my own fashion and freely. The sort I would have written if I had been independent. There is 'The Path to Rome' and 'The Four Men', a few essays, especially in 'Hills and the Sea', 'Belinda', and 'The Servile State'; also my big History of England. I should like all my friends to pray that I may be able to finish that boa-constrictor of a self-imposed task. I am going to tackle volume five this year. It could à la rigeur be wound up in that volume which will take it

[1] Mells March 17 1935

to the end of the Stuarts. But I would like to do volume six, the 18th century, and volume seven, the 19th, before I die or get past work.[1]

After three weeks staying with the Herberts and with Katharine Asquith in the West, he set out from Southampton by a French ship, the M.S. *Lafayette*. When he was within 200 miles of New York. he wrote back to Mrs Asquith,

It has been an easy voyage except for (a) the intolerable vibration (b) the intolerable expense. There are few people on board and the weather has not been more than entertainingly rough. Today it is quite smooth. Also the quiet manner of the French ship makes things less detestable than they might be. But all liners are detestable. They want to be cosmopolitan hotels – and that on the sea! The best thing on board is Sunday mass, & the worst is occasional music. But the cinema runs it close.[2]

Sailing into New York harbour awakened ancient memories. He remembered his journeying there in youth, and with memories of that voyage came back in the most acute form recollections of his lost Elodie. But this time, his grief, which for twenty years seemed as though it could not be assuaged, received a glimmering of consolation. And, if it had not happened to Belloc who was repelled by St John of the Cross and all this 'union with God' business, one might say that the experience was mystical. He expressed it, however, to Mrs Asquith, in characteristically materialist terms:

There is a thing I must tell you, dearest Katharine. It is a thing I have spoken of to you perhaps twice, perhaps three times, & certainly to no one else. Do you remember that I wrote to you seventeen years ago, that the Resurrection of the flesh was true? That also can be experienced as well as believed: experienced as rarely as visions, but experienced.

I came through Sandy Hook & the Narrows into New York harbour, by that same February edge of mortal cold that I came through first, when I was a boy: not yet of age: on a perilous journey, seeking and making for goal. Often have I remembered that voyage. But this time – with a life-time in between, all the derelictions, all the despairs – the original matter returned completely, armed with life, unaffected in any way by time, easily unconquerable. Certain. Fully existent. These are those flashes which reveal all the truth of doctrine as a lightning shows the very

[1] BC January 28, 1935
[2] Mells February 13, 1935

rain drops on a stormy night & the edges of the leaves. It is essential to believe, & the Faith is all in all: sufficient. But one such experience, granted for a moment, confirms the soul of man. Do you remember that I wrote to you the phrase 'All will be restored to you'? And so it will. These eternal things are easily the masters of time.[1]

Armed with this renewed vision and faith, he disembarked in New York. The tour itself, though tiring, was successful. Those who were intimate with Belloc were sometimes embarrassed by his platform manner. But the number of such intimates was now diminishing with the years. His formal, courtly and rhetorical modes of address had hardened about him like a shell. There were few, meeting him for the *first* time from now onwards, who felt capable of *closeness* with him. But, if this was a handicap in social relations, it was perhaps a positive advantage in his public persona. His analysis of the world situation, his version of history, his verbal mannerisms and his habits of over-expression might have been all too familiar to his band of family and friends who, from now onwards, loved him almost in spite of, rather than because of, what he said. H.A.L. Fisher, meeting him again after a gap at about this date, remarked on how crashingly *boring* Belloc had become.[2] On a public platform, addressing an audience who had never heard him before and would probably never hear him again, none of this mattered. And it had the rather moving, and liberating effect of making him less boring; as is shown both by his letters, and by the book he wrote after his long voyage, *The Battleground*. He addressed large audiences in Boston, New York and Washington, and on each occasion he felt that his speeches had gone well. To Lady Phipps, whose husband was now British Ambassador in Berlin, he wrote, from New York,

I do not find this place greatly changed. Indeed I have found that it is in this case, as it is in almost all others – the newspapers and print in general give a false idea of life. The depression is obvious, but I think we are in a worse way in England, and everybody here is hospitable and kind, as they have always been to me in the past. I am glad I came back. It may be for the last time, as the journey is a great strain and I get neither richer nor younger.

Of my blood relations over here, who belonged originally to Pennsylvania, I find that all are scattered or dead, and my connec-

[1] Mells March 17 1935
[2] Mrs Bennett to the author

tions far off in California, among whom my son, who lives there, is married, are at a distance I cannot reach.

It is forty-four mortal years since I first came to this city, and that is pretty well all the active part of my whole life. I am glad to have seen it again. I seem to be the only Englishman who feels at home in spite of the incredible difference between the United States and England. I have had to touch upon the fringe of the smart, which is very fatiguing and futile, but I am very glad I came over. One thing I did put down my foot upon, and that was going to dine at the Vanderbilts. There is no conceivable reason why I should do such a thing, so I refused point blank.

But I was particularly glad to get to Boston again, and see the Unitarians. There is one trouble about them, and that is the imitation of England, especially at Harvard. It doesn't suit them, and it is irritating. The old, well-rooted Boston people have a great attraction for me. They resolutely shut their eyes to the fact that Boston is the most Catholic city in the world. They live in a little false memory world of their own. They are good people, mostly Unitarians like my mother's family, and are persuaded that Oxford and Cambridge adore them. Trevelyan has been over here telling them so, I suppose he thought it patriotic. What is more, he has, like the King of Moab, sacrificed his son, for I understand he has sent his son to Harvard, which is really going rather far. I am afraid, however, that no gesture would make Americans come in again to help England in case of war, and the most desperate efforts at friendship will ultimately fail.[1]

Another historian, A.L. Rowse, has commented upon Belloc's 'summary ill-considered judgments, such as – "Trevelyan, a typical product of the highly anti-Catholic English universities and governing class". Actually, as I know, Trevelyan was very pleased to have a good Catholic historian, a monk to boot – Dom David Knowles – to succeed him as Regius Professor at Cambridge'. And Dr Rowse goes on to quote a Frenchman's judgment of Belloc which seems, in its savage truth, to describe nearly all his utterances in this final phase of his existence – the assertion that the Americans would never enter a European war on Britain's behalf is typical of all his political predictions in the 1930s: 'J'avais l'impression d'un prophète qui se trompe toujours.'[2]

---

[1] BC February 27 1935
[2] A. L. Rowse: *Portraits and views* p. 86

By March, his American tour was getting him down, and he wrote from Miami:

> I have not been allowed one instant's privacy or leisure. It has been something infernal. The inhuman strain was due to three things. First it seems I am a great deal better known than I was 12 years ago: Next America has got appreciably further from Europe in manners & more intense in its publicity and promiscuity – and on top of all that I am much older & at last really feeling age: the thing was too much for me (and still is. I feel myself breaking under it).
> 'Still', I said to myself, 'when the actual yelling and bawling is over & I get down to the half tropical south, where I am to meet friends I shall have leisure to be able to sit down and write: – I mean to write seriously, not notes – but it was not so. The incredible conditions continue, & I shall escape – if I do – only just in time.[1]

In Miami, he managed to have a few days respite staying with his old friends the Nickersons, writing a characteristically authoritative 'Collins' to the wife of the man who always addressed him as 'Dear Master':

> Dear Mrs Nickerson,
> You will find that in the matter of the omelette the whole art consists in having the frying pan really hot, and quite a little butter. Also try to turn it over before it is quite finished; it then goes on cooking itself. One gives the frying pan a shake or two at the last minute, and then turns over the omelette on a flap. You want to stop stirring it about half a minute before giving it the last shake and turning it over . . .[2]

After Miami, he managed to get a boat to Cuba, and from Havana he sailed to Spain, a long rough voyage; but to Belloc the sea was always consoling and restorative. Moreover, he was moving back towards the Old World, where he was at home. America, he concluded, 'is as foreign as the moon. A completely other thing, not only from us, but from all the mass of what is mature and full of ancient savour in the old world'.[3] 'It was', he concluded, 'imprudent to risk this journey but I am glad I did it & I think the money I have earned will pay for *all* the expenses including the journey to Syria – where I shall recite my favourite passage from the Iliad and all the Heliodora: one of the few things I know by heart.'

[1] Mells March 17, 1935
[2] BC May 28, 1935
[3] BC June 4, 1935

'Syria' was Belloc's word for the strip of territory commonly called the Holy Land, and which takes in modern Israel, Syria, Lebanon and Jordan. Another word he had for it – the title of his book about the place – is *The Battleground*. It is one of his finest books: a surprising late flowering of the genius which had shone out in *The Path to Rome* and *The Four Men*. He chronicles the history of that place from the earliest times until the present.

> Here the gods of Egypt appeared, not without majesty, but disdaining to plant their worship; here in the Syrian belt the very evil gods of Lust and Torture were to await the proclamation of Israel and to be locked in battle with the God of Israel – and One Jehovah – and to succumb; Moloch and Ashtaroth and Baal. Here the Spirits of loveliness were to waft in from the West in the wake of the Greek armies, and here Aphrodite mourned for Adonis dead. Here in the fulness of time came the flower of our Revelation, the kindling of the Gospel, the founding of the Church, the violent, obscure, creative tragedy whence our civilisation arose. Herein arose the Main Challenge: whether the Christ had come indeed or not.[1]

To be sure, there are passages in *The Battleground* which are likely to be read with embarrassment by any liberal Catholic today. Some of his readers might wish that Christ still slept in His tomb when they read such passages as this:

> After the Crucifixion, Death and Resurrection of Our Lord, two things happened at once: each destined to dominate the whole of future history. The first is the immediate appearance of the Church; the Church was founded at a stroke, in the first days after the Ascension. The second is a violent antagonism between the Jews and the people among whom they are destined or condemned to live – the Roman and Greek worlds and their descendants.[2]

This rather makes it sound as though the most important consequence of Our Lord's resurrection was the emergence of hard-line, old-fashioned Roman Catholic anti-semitism on the French model. And anyone wishing to make a harsh comparison between Chesterton and Belloc would recall the moving meditation in *The Everlasting Man* on the Garden of the Resurrection. 'On the third day the friends of Christ coming at daybreak to the place found the grave empty and the stone rolled away. In varying ways they realised the new wonder; but even they hardly realised that the world had died in the night. What they

[1] Ibid. p. 241
[2] Ibid. p. 246

were looking at was the first day of a new creation, with a new heaven and a new earth; and in a semblance of the gardener God walked again in the garden, in the cool not of the evening but the dawn'[1].

But it would be unfair to dismiss *The Battleground*. It succeeds, like the best of Belloc, where he conveys his rich sense – stronger in him than in any author I know – of a history of peoples growing out of the exact landscape and surroundings in which they lived. Nor should the bluff expression of certitudes make us imagine that the question – whether the Christ had come indeed or not – was not a matter of the highest personal moment for Belloc. He was moved by holiness in others. He knew that in the accepted sense of the term he could not aspire to it himself. He therefore disliked giving an impression of himself as more 'pious' than he actually was. He would rather shock people by saying that he found Christ 'repellent' than be thought 'pi'. Nevertheless, after his strange experience sailing into New York harbour in February 1935, followed by setting foot in the Holy Land itself in May of that year, Belloc's piety deepened. He did not brag about it in his books. But there can be no doubt of it if we read his letters on this journey to Katharine Asquith, who was perhaps his closest confidante in religious matters. Here he writes of Gethsemane.

There are now left alive 2 or 3 very old olive trees – the tiny leaf of one of which you shall duly receive. Do not despise it, for it is a material link with the most sacred place of the earth: the place where God himself suffered. The Agony in the Garden is the core and height of the Passion. The near anticipation of a dreadful thing is the acme of its effect: when the falling of a blow is morally certain, the last awaiting of it is the master trial. The sequel is more exhausted; and that is why all those who know the significance of Christendom should revere – even beyond the rock of the Cross or the Holy Sepulchre itself, or the Altar of the Annunciation in Nazareth or the Grotto of Bethlehem – Olivet. 'Dieu même a craint la Mort'. That is great poetry and therefore, justly interpreted, sound truth: sound theology. Not that God Himself can suffer, but that God was so intensely, so intimately Man in the Incarnation, that the memories and experience of Divinity and Humanity are united therein: and through it, the worst pain of the creature is *known*, by actual experience of our own kind, by the Creator. We are, of all our miseries, much the most afflicted by Mortality: and that means not mere Death – least of all our own, which may be but a blessed sleep between the good troubled life and the good

[1] G. K. Chesterton *The Everlasting Man* (1925) p. 247

untroubled life of beatitude – but the impermanence of all things, even of love: the goodbyes and the changes that never halt their damning succession: the unceasing tale of loss which wears down all at last. *That* is mortality. *That* is the contradiction between our native joy and our present realities, which contrast is the curse of the Fall. But in truth it is altogether more and of a different quality from our miseries in general. It is the very air of desperation which the race must breathe, even that one more experience which so transcends all other affection in depth and habit so that it is quite other from the rest, even that snaps in the moment. The object of it vanishes utterly, nor can it be decided whether those are more despicable in intelligence or morals who pretend that Death can be tricked by the imagination. It is a curtain of Iron, a gulf impassable, an impenetrable darkness, and a distance as it were limitless, infinite. The miracle whereby such an enormity coming upon immortal souls does not breed despair, is the chief miracle of the Incarnation – and to work that miracle, the Incarnate – with what a supreme energy – accepted our pain, almost refused it, but accepted it; and it was greater than any pain of ours: physically beyond endurance and in the spirit a descent into Hell.

Nowhere is there meaning in prayer as at Gethsemane. Upon such a foundation, perhaps, the soul that prays shall lift into fulfilment and recovery. It is, that garden and its shrine, the very centre of man's world,

That is Olivet, dear Katharine; I wonder whether some day you will see for yourself that earth? surrounded today with all the turpitude that man can fall to, and all the baseness and betrayal that man when he revels in hypocrisy can attain. It has survived every other attack, the alternate neglect and assault of those twenty hundred years, and the light shines unchanged over it. Goodbye, dear Katharine; I have told you what I had to tell. Yours H.B.[1]

It is worth quoting this letter so fully, because there is so much of Belloc here, and so much of him which he normally kept carefully concealed. It shows more nakedly than anything he ever wrote, how close the very thought of Death brought him to Despair; and how the one thing that could rescue him from despair was the Passion of his Saviour.

[1] Mells May 3, 1935

FIFTEEN

THE BATTLEGROUND
1936–1942

In *The Battleground*, Belloc had written of the Crusades as the movement when 'our people, the West, Christendom, made a last rally of our race for the recovery of Syria from the men of the desert'.[1] Throughout the year of Belloc's journey to the Holy Land, 'our people' were arming once more against the desert people, not of Syria, but of Abyssinia. Mussolini secured an alliance with France against Germany in May, speaking of the necessity of 'destroying Hitler' if necessary.[2] He was unable to secure the alliance he desired with the British, and was worried that they might try to stop his African war. But, on the whole, he was advised, they were more preoccupied with the threat of Hitler than with the fear of anything the Italian army might do in Abyssinia. Neither calculation, in the event, turned out to be quite accurate.

From Berlin, Lady Phipps wrote to Belloc at precisely this moment to assure him that 'we have made friends with many of the "nazis". Some of them are not to be liked – But many of them are rather disarming and I like quite a number'.[3] This must have confirmed Belloc's view that 'Hitler is completely forgiven' by the English, anti-German feeling in England kept going entirely by a strange alliance of eccentrics such as Winston Churchill, and himself, and the Jews. In spite of the fact that Hitler had been brought up a Catholic, Belloc persisted in believing him to be wholly 'Prussianised' and therefore, like the Abyssinians, barbarian.

Mussolini invaded Abyssinia in October 1935. It is now thought that, by the time it ended, the war might have cost half a million Ethiopian lives.[4] There was an outcry in England against it, and Anthony Eden eventually persuaded the Government of Baldwin to introduce sanctions against Mussolini.

[1] *The Battleground*, p. 323.
[2] Mack Smith, p. 194.
[3] BC, May 29, 1935.
[4] Mack Smith, p. 201.

There was one English paper, however, which wholeheartedly supported Mussolini's invasion; and that was *G.K.'s Weekly*. It caused a split in the ranks of the Distributists from which the movement never recovered. G. K. Chesterton himself was not personally responsible for the issue of the paper in which the invasion of Abyssinia was celebrated. He later wrote articles trying to mollify its effects. But it was too late. The old 'guild socialists' like Maurice Reckitt[1] resigned from the board of the paper. Chesterton was by then too ill and too fuddled (though no one quite recognised this) to take any definite line. He deplored the loss of life, but told Reckitt: 'Very shortly, the mortal danger, to me, is the rehabilitation of Capitalism, in spite of the slump, which will certainly take the form of a hypocritical patriotism and glorification of England, at the expense of Italy or anybody else'.[2] On the other hand, there were those who felt that the Italians must be supported, more or less whatever they did.

Belloc, meanwhile, was having one of his extended European tours. In February 1936, he left a flu-ridden King's Land, urging Eleanor to make her husband drink more champagne. 'It is the one thing that conquers "flu".'[3] He went to stay with the Phippses at the Embassy in Berlin, he then visited Poland, though he failed to see Our Lady of Czestochowa; then to Vienna, and from Vienna to Burgundy and from Burgundy to Paris. 'This perpetual travelling is the devil – for me anyhow at the edge of age.'[4]

By March, he was back in London, where he was able to hear what the English, and the Americans, together with the League of Nations, thought about Mussolini's activities. He went to a grand dinner at Mary Herbert's on March 14:

> I wore a white waistcoat, and felt very odd. Theodore Roosevelt told long stories very slowly. That nice woman Lady Something Gore, said that the only people who objected to the League of Nations were Catholics, whereat I said that this was because Catholics were in touch with reality. I then added that I thought the League of Nations was Masonic rubbish.[5]

A few days later he lunched with Churchill and Raymond Asquith's old friend 'Bluetooth' Baker, now Warden of Winchester, and found, again, the same mysterious anti-Catholicism[6] in the matter of Musso-

[1] Maisie Ward p. 549.
[2] Ibid. p. 550.
[3] BC February 10, 1936.
[4] Mells February 26, 1936.
[5] Mells, March 14, 1936.
[6] Mells, March 31, 1936.

lini who had won 'a great diplomatic victory'; one so 'subtle' that the press had missed it, being blinded by 'suburban sentiment'. Reginald Jebb was simply parroting his father-in-law when he wrote to Belloc at that date: 'Every day Mussolini's policy and actions appear in a better light – he seems to make no mistakes – and our politicians look sillier and sillier.'[1]

In April, Belloc heard grave news of his friend Maurice Baring, and rushed to the bedside. But Baring recovered, and Belloc went off to Paris in pursuit of Bonnie Soames, so that he could dictate to her his book on the Crusades. When he came back, he went to see H. A. L. Fisher, and was distressed by how ill he seemed. He, and Baring, Belloc pronounced, were not long for this world. In fact, they both had some years to go; and the friend who was about to die was G. K. Chesterton. That vast hulk was separated from that childishly charming soul on June 14, the Sunday within the Octave of Corpus Christi; and the memorial card had printed on it the Introit for that day's Mass: 'The Lord became my protector and he brought me forth into a large place.'[2]

Belloc had, of course, continued to see Chesterton whenever they happened to coincide in London. He had contributed regularly to *G.K.'s Weekly*. And there had certainly been nothing in the nature of an estrangement between the two men. But that phantom 'the Chesterbelloc' was a largely Edwardian joke, and in recent years Belloc had seen far less of Chesterton than he had seen of the Herberts, 'Bear' Warre, Katharine Asquith or Duff and Diana Cooper. Nevertheless, at the great Requiem which was offered for Chesterton's soul in Westminster Cathedral, it was inevitably to Belloc that the newspaper cameras and reporters turned. In the course of the mass he managed to sell his exclusive obituary of Chesterton to no less than four different editors.

But this is not to say that Belloc did not feel Chesterton's death keenly. It represented the end of a vast chapter of his own life; and it was largely piety to the length and age of his friendship with Chesterton which made him accept the editorship of *G.K.'s Weekly*. The directors, meeting shortly after Chesterton's death, urged Belloc, and those concerned with the paper, to wind it all up. But he was adamant that it should continue.

One reason for this, most certainly, was that Belloc wanted to have a place where he could write exactly as he chose about the international situation. To anxieties about Italy and Germany, there was

[1] BC May 29, 1936.
[2] Ward, p. 552.

added the drama of Spain, now plunged into Civil War. *G.K.'s Weekly* or, as it became, *The Weekly Review* was, of course, very far from being the only English paper to support Franco. *The Tablet* did so, under the editorship of Douglas Woodruff; so did the *Daily Mail*, *The Observer* and the *Daily Sketch*. But the very strong body of support which existed in England for the Republic gave Belloc the pleasing sense that the English, were, as usual, idiotically misinformed; and that he was the only man who really understood what was going on. To the young Lord Oxford and Asquith, then an undergraduate at Balliol, Belloc wrote: 'It will be interesting to see whether anybody buys GK's weekly now that some trouble is being taken with it. The chances are that less people will buy it than before because the cranks will be put off, and the cranks are always the standby of papers of that sort'.[1]

By 'the cranks', Belloc meant the simple-lifers, the Guild-socialists, and the band of mildly eccentric hangers-on whom G.K. had done nothing about excluding from the office. One very distinguished figure in the Distributist movement whom Belloc had always dismissed as a 'crank' was H. D. C. Pepler, who had run the St Dominic's Press on Ditchling Common with Eric Gill. The rapprochement between Pepler and Belloc came about slowly, but the first glimmering of it occurred shortly after Belloc had taken over 'editorship' of the paper. This meant, in effect, turning up at the office once or twice a month to supervise what was going on, and to use the telephone. The staff, in spite of the quarrels which had existed among themselves, had all loved GK, and they found Belloc by comparison aloof and formidable. He made no effort, as Chesterton had done, to entertain them, or to make them laugh.

One day, Pepler sent word to the office that he had done a series of mimes for television, among them one based on a scene in *The Four Men*. Television sets were almost unheard-of in the 1930s, but Pepler told Belloc that arrangements had been made for him to see the programme at the electrical shop, specialising in gramophone records, in New Oxford Street. A taxi arrived, and Brocard Sewell, a young man destined for the monkish life, but at that stage a worker in the office, was delegated to escort Mr Belloc to see the television. The two men said little to each other in the back of the taxi. Belloc asked Sewell if he knew the best eating-house in London. He did not. He was told, 'It is that of the snail, which some call *l'Escargot.*' And there was silence until they got to the shop. When Belloc saw the television

---

[1] BC, October 17, 1936.

set in action, he was entranced, wanted to go on watching after the images had flickered from the cathode ray tube, and was moved that his own work had been used for one of the earliest television programmes.[1] One can easily imagine with what trenchancy he would assail the mindless vulgarity of the modern cult of television. Yet, had he had the chance, he would probably have enjoyed appearing on it; for loud, and repetitive, and strongly opinionated persons make more of a showing on T.V. than those who are drawn in subtler shades.

Needless to say, Belloc did not concern himself very much with the day-to-day running of the weekly. By the time it was publishing articles by such fascists as A. K. Chesterton (G.K.'s cousin), urging the British Government to form an alliance with Franco and Hitler against the Soviet Union, the editor was once more on the high seas, sailing to New York for another lecturing tour. He was tired and 'flu-ridden, and so it was a comfort to take with him Bonnie Soames, writing ahead to friends such as Hoffman Nickerson in an attempt to get her 'writing work'.[2] It was her first visit to America and she was never, except for visits to her family, to return. In time she settled on Long Island and married Hoffman Nickerson.

They travelled, as was Belloc's wont, on a French boat, the S.S. *Champlain*, a vessel which Belloc averred to Katharine Asquith was controlled ultimately by the Rothschilds.

Talking of Yids the swarm of Yids on board this sparsely populated craft is extraordinary: there are hardly 100 people on board and at least 81 are incredible: monsters of the deep. They always form the bulk of transatlantic (north transatlantic) travel; and as, today, they won't take German boats, they crowd into French, Dutch and English. There are two Americans on board – men, and one she-American. Now, Americans are vocally and loudly and simply and in child-like fashion Jew-haters. So I live in hopes of an explosion before we reach the beatitudes of New York. Wouldn't it be amusing if this next outburst of blind rage against the poor old Jews were to blow up in New York? The Oxford dons are still reeling under the blow of their beloved Prussia having attacked Israel and if their Anglo-Saxons (as they call the Yankees) were to follow up they would think the world had come to an end. If or when the New Yorkites rise against the

[1] Brocard Sewell to the author.
[2] BC, January 8, 1937.

Jews there will be a pogrom: for the Americans yield to none in promiscuous violence and bloodletting.[1]

As it happened, no such pogrom took place in New York, either while Belloc was there, or later. This visit, his last to America, exhausted him more than any of his previous visits. The newspapers noted his arrival with polite little articles. He told a reporter for the *Boston Globe*, on his arrival in New York harbour, that 'he would like to have been a banker but never have to work in a bank.' The reporter attributed his theological preoccupations to Dutch ancestry. Belloc, 'like those Pennsylvania Dutch theologians of 100 years ago, doesn't mind using a cannon when he's gunning for a gnat'.[2]

In the main course of lectures he gave at Fordham University, which he published as *The Crisis of Our Civilisation*, Belloc made it clear that he did not believe himself to be 'gunning for a gnat'. Two great systems – that of Western Capitalism and that of Soviet communism – were, between them, wiping out the last vestiges of civilisation. It was thus that Belloc saw the contemporary scene. 'There only remains as an alternative to apply the fruits which the Catholic culture had produced when it was in full vigour, the restriction of monopoly, the curbing of the money power, the establishment of co-operative work, the main principle of the Guild, and the jealous restriction of usury and competition, which between them have come so near to destroying us.'[3] They were all the old remedies which he had been proposing since at least as far back as 1912, and which anyone could have read in Leo XIII's *Quod Apostolici muneris* of 1878, or *Rerum Novarum* of 1891. The first of these encyclicals singled out for particular opprobrium and condemnation 'that class of men who, under various and strange names, are known as *Socialists*, *Communists* or *Nihilists* and who, spread over the globe and bound together closely by a criminal bond, no longer seek the friendly shelter of their secret conventicles, but come forth boldly into the daylight.'[4] The second and more famous encyclical condemns the mammon-worship of capitalism in equally forceful terms. Belloc, who had learnt his politics from Cardinal Manning, could see very clearly that the modern world was poised between two choices, to right and left, both of which denied the fundamental principles of the Catholic religion as defined by his nineteenth-century mentors.

[1] Mells, February 5, 1937.
[2] *Boston Daily Globe*, January 29, 1937.
[3] *The Crisis of Our Civilisation*, p. 62.
[4] Bernard O'Reilly: *Life of Leo XIII* (1887), p. 372.

New York wearied, and also revolted, him. He felt unable to stay with his hosts, the Jesuits of Fordham University. 'The moment you stay with a community in the United Stated they fasten on to you from the first hour of the day until bed-time, and never let you go.'[1] He was therefore obliged to put up at an hotel and this, combined with the expenses of Bonnie Soames's lodgings, diminished the profitability of the tour. The Hotel Devon, where he put up, was comfortable, but he could not sleep there, and moved to Long Island to stay with his friend Hoffman Nickerson.

> There all is quiet. I come into New York (by car, as a rule 40 miles, *hideous* landscape) to lecture twice a week at the big Jesuit College called Fordham University and I usually stop a night or two over in a room which Mrs Willard, who is as good as she can be, has lent me.[2]

It was a truly penitential Lent, and by Good Friday he was still complaining that the 'Jesuits for whom I work sweat me to death'. He was also accepting invitations to talk in Boston, in Washington, and Philadelphia:

> I am working myself to death. I fly about from town to town (from time to time – but with no Mrs Rhys, damn it: all alone) and jabber and jabber and jabber and jabber and jabber for 250 dollars, 300 dollars and even 500 dollars a shot. I will talk on anything and everything – it matters not what for no one understands anything here if it is said in the 'English accent' (which they detest) and even if it is said with a snarl (which I can affect very passably now) they don't understand it unless it repeats exactly something (false) which they have heard 48,376,277 times before: such as: that war is all wrawng and why cahunt everyone in Yurrup live peaceably same as us; that Religion don't count same as it uster 'cos there's morenlight'nment now.[3]

The longer he was there, the more he pined for home. 'With what tongue-hanging-out-and-panting do I await my re-entry to European things.' He was anxious about the Spanish war, and praying throughout May that Bilbao would be occupied by the National Army. It shocked him that the Basques were 'ranged with murderous Atheists and the Jewish International.' And the Anglo-American alliance,

[1] BC, January 8, 1937.
[2] Mells, February 23, 1937.
[3] Mells, April 15, 1937.

based on what he took to be a complete ignorance of European affairs, worried him even more.

There's no doubt at all about our being able to wangle the Americans to helping us *again* if need be – or even saving us. We teach them all. For instance, the Divine Right of Moses Rosenburg first and the second Jew (whose name I forget) to order the revolution in Spain, forbid the Mass under pain of death and torture and prevent little children being taught their prayers. We have also put it across that the French government is a noble democracy – like our own egalitarian land – and that Italy is ruled by a blood-thirsty monster. But there is this danger about our control of the poor old Yanks, that it's like being dependent upon an idiot innocent giant child. They will do their best for us but that best may be mortally dangerous.[1]

By the end of May he was on his way home, once more on a French liner, 'full of incredible noise':

There is a nigger jazz band with the niggers making loud animal barks and yelps at short intervals. There are some 319 passengers – nearly all Americans of the middle class who yell like brazen trumpets all day long and cut in with blasts of deafening metallic laughter at their own jokes – and all their fellow-citizens join in. There is the Hurrahing of the exultant sea and there is a fine vibration shaking the boat like a fiddle string.

The French (crew and pursers and waiters) are, as always, steeled to heroic endurance by the prospect of Games. They marched to Delphi, they took Rome twice at 2200 years' interval and have fought I suppose as many civil wars as could be crammed into 60 generations. Yet they still precariously survive – supported by the ardent love of money, in small but continuous driblets . . .

. . . It is an immense relief that the American bout is over. The tension accumulated until it grew unendurable and three separate times I thought I should have to give up in the middle of a lecture – the last only a few days ago. The utter foreignness of that mechanical life, even to me who knows the place so well and for so many years and who admires the simplicity and huge generosity of its strange people is a burden beyond bearing when it is accompanied by excessive work and travel and added to by the

[1] Mells, May 3, 1937.

weight of years. It is accomplished now. It may leave after-effects but it is at any rate the last of such efforts.[1]

*   *   *

If the foreignness of America exhausted him, he found the parochialism and narrowness of English Protestantism no less stifling on his return. Throughout 1937, he was engaged in acrimonious argument with the Cambridge historian G. G. Coulton.

Twelve years older than Belloc, Coulton had a tenacity and a love of quarrels which, if anything, exceeded Belloc's own. In his day, he was famous, not only as an historian and a conspicuous, cocoa-drinking Cambridge eccentric, but also as passionate controversialist. Time has obscured his reputation. An Anglican modernist by conviction, he had two obsessive themes as he careered furiously into old age: the wrongness of pacifism and the rightness of the Reformation. He plugged these themes relentlessly in reviews, public meetings and letters to the press.

Like Belloc, Coulton was greatly haunted by the encyclicals of Pope Leo XIII. For Belloc they had been his greatest single source of intellectual stimulation. For Coulton's analytical intelligence, they were obscurantist and intellectually dishonest. Repeatedly in his writings, Coulton returns to Leo XIII's Letter to the Clergy of France, of September 8 1899, in which he exhorted them to study history, but 'those who study it must never lose sight of the fact that it contains a collection of dogmatic facts which impose themselves upon our faith, and which no man is permitted to call in doubt.' This command, according to Coulton, 'poisoned the very sources of history'.[2] An historian's duty was to the truth. Roman Catholics, working under the shadow of Leo XIII's Letter, would inevitably feel torn in their loyalties: on the one hand to truth, on the other to the papal discipline. For Coulton, there could be no higher duty than the dictate of truth. Others have believed this, but he did so with the violence of a fanatic. In her memoir of Coulton, his daughter wrote of 'his attitude to lying. He loathed and detested it with a fury, an abandonment of fury which had much of emotion, little enough of reason'.[3] She describes how, as a child of five, she pretended to her father that she had seen a rabbit's nest in their garden at Shelford near Cambridge. 'I had just enough *nous* not to place it up in the branches – and the five dear little rabbits in it'. Coulton was not at all amused by what was obviously a childish

[1] Mells, May 28, 1937
[2] G. G. Coulton, *Sectarian History* (1937), p. 5.
[3] Sarah Campion, *Father, a portrait of G. G. Coulton at home* (1948), p. 26.

fantasy. He insisted on being taken to the rabbit's nest and, when he had established to his satisfaction that it was a figment of his daughter's imagination, he whipped her soundly.[1]

Coulton emerges from the memoirs of his daughter, as from his own rather humourless autobiography[2], as a Gradgrind who could not tolerate the slightest whim or fancy lest it toppled over into a position of intellectual dishonesty. If this were his attitude in relation to stories made up by a daughter of whom, in a savage Victorian manner, he was very fond, he naturally felt even more impassioned when writers appeared on the scene purporting to be historians, but actually constrained by loyalty to a party line. Throughout the first three decades of this century, Coulton had thundered and raged, often with great effect and always with passionate conviction, against the Roman Catholic historians. Cardinal Gasquet was a particular bête noire, for he continued to repeat and republish statements about the Wycliffites, the medieval bible and late medieval monastic life which Coulton had no less often proved to be false. In 1921, when the University of Cambridge had proposed to grant honorary degrees to Cardinal Bourne and Cardinal Gasquet, Coulton successfully opposed the motion, and they went without their doctorates.[3] Even without Belloc to torment him, Dr Coulton would have found plenty to occupy his declining years. When newspaper editors, for pure weariness, stopped publishing his voluminously vituperative letters, Coulton had pamphlets privately printed which, as he advertised, could be obtained by sending a stamped addressed envelope to his home at 90, Kimberley Road, Cambridge. There were a score of such pamphlets available in 1937 alone. They have titles like *In Defence of the Reformation*, *Sectarian History*, *Romanism and Truth*, *Infant Perdition in the Middle Ages* and *A Premium upon Falsehood, dealing with Fr H Thurston's attempted defence of Cardinal Gasquet*.

By the time of his greatest conflict with Belloc, Coulton had been aware of him for many years. Given Belloc's love of controversy and Coulton's obsession with the dishonesty of Roman Catholic historians, the two seemed made for each other. And, throughout the 1920s, Coulton wrote reviews of Belloc's books and did what he could to counterbalance Belloc's oversimplified views of the English Reformation.

On June 30 1937, Father Ronald Knox wrote to the *Daily Telegraph* challenging Coulton's assertion that the Roman Church had ever, at

[1] Sarah Campion, p. 27.
[2] *Fourscore Yoears* (1943).
[3] G. G. Coulton, *The Gasquet Scandal* (1937), p. 5.

any stage in its history, allowed divorce. The correspondence which ensued was extended. Belloc entered the fray on behalf of Knox. Coulton replied. Belloc retaliated. Eventually, the editor brought the correspondence to an end, and Coulton, who felt that he had not said enough on the matter, published the whole exchange as a pamphlet, *Divorce, Mr Belloc and the 'Daily Telegraph'.* The individual details of each swipe and sally need not concern us now; there is nothing deader than a dead quarrel. While they posted off their carefully-phrased insults and waited excitedly for the adversary to reply, Spain was being torn to bits by civil war, Mussolini was forming his axis with Hitler, the Germans were rearming and preparing the enactment of the *Anschluss* and the racial laws. There is something rather ludicrous about these two bad-tempered old men, one aged 67 and the other aged 79, wasting ink and postage on the subject of whether the Synod of Arles in 314 did or did not allow divorce, while all about them, creation groaned and travailed.

Belloc, in any case, did not know anything about the Synod of Arles. Coulton, who had devoted his life to the study of ecclesiastical history, managed to name, in the course of the controversy, three popes and three councils or synods who had spoken of the marriage tie as dissoluble in certain conditions. There was, of course, no answering Coulton on his own terms, for he was simply right and Belloc wrong. Coulton was infuriated that Belloc, instead of replying in the particular periodical where a challenge had been thrown down, would always, in return, attack Coulton in the pages of Catholic periodicals such as *The Universe* and *The Month* which refused to print Coulton's replies. Then, when the exasperated Coulton bombarded Belloc with telegrams, registered letters and other public challenges for a response to his irrefutable display of historical evidence, Belloc was silent.

Sometimes, as Coulton also knew, Belloc was simply dishonest. Dr. A. L. Rowse, an historian with a keen sense of Belloc's literary genius, recalls, 'I once described his variations on the Elizabethan age as "a farrago of lies". This of course was libellous (G. M. Trevelyan in conversation roundly called him a liar). That it was all the same true I knew from a mutual friend, Douglas Woodruff. Belloc was then having a controversy with that *enragé* Cambridge champion of truth, Dr Coulton; to close it Belloc came out with something devastating. Woodruff asked him, "But is it true?" Belloc replied blithely, "Oh, not at all. But won't it annoy Coulton?" I thought and still think that rather wicked.'[1]

---

[1] A. L. Rowse, *Portraits & Views*, p. 72.

Coulton thought it wicked too, and he had none of Dr Rowse's generosity of temper in dealing with Belloc's outrageous mendacity. Since Belloc refused to answer him point by point over the question of divorce, Coulton devoted eight scathing pages of his new pamphlet to 'Mr Belloc's Past Record'.

Nobody reading those pages would ever be able to take Belloc wholly seriously as an historian in the academic sense of the word. It is a list of simple blunders and howlers, published by Belloc over the previous twenty years. What shocked Coulton so much is that when the mistakes were pointed out to him, Belloc did nothing to correct them in any future statement on the same subject. Often he repeated errors gleefully. 'How many Englishmen know that Du Bellay's immortal sonnet was but a translation of Quevedo?' Belloc had asked, adding with typically insulting bluster, 'You could drag all Oxford and Cambridge today and not find a single man who knew it'. A dangerous boast, for Cambridge, once dragged, was found to contain Dr Coulton who was able, like dozens of others, to point out, 'Unluckily for Mr Belloc, Quevedo was born twenty years after Du Bellay's death; and the theft was, of course, the exact opposite'. Coulton takes almost equal delight in quoting Belloc's assertion that Newman's conversion had taken place 'a lifetime before' Renan's exit from the Roman church. In fact, they happened not merely in the same year, as Coulton points out, but within days of each other. Belloc appeals 'to Matthew Paris as an authority for the battle of Evesham which was fought after his death'. Again, Belloc claimed that the Black Death in Norwich alone claimed 57,374. Obviously it was a figure he had simply invented, for, when challenged by Coulton he was unable to prove that the population of Norwich had been greater than 50,000. 'He therefore slightly abandoned the embarrassing 7,374; who must too obviously be non-existent, and maintained only that 50,000 had died out of those 50,000 who were the most his fancy could create'.

As the catalogue proceeds, however, we find that Coulton has abandoned points of historical inaccuracy and descended to mere abuse. 'The unpopularity of Mr Belloc's church, in so far as it exists, is mainly created by him and others like him; men who are not only bullies but cowards. Mr Belloc knows perfectly well that he would not dare to discuss publicly with me, here or in London, to be reported verbatim and printed, such subjects as Papal Infallibility, Roman Catholic and Protestant Intolerance, or the Causes of the Reformation'.[1]

[1] *Divorce, Mr Belloc and 'The Daily Telegraph'*, p. 16.

Coulton's dedicated humourlessness was only fuel to Belloc's flame. Ever since his failure to be elected as a Fellow of All Souls College, Oxford, he had been consumed with a hatred of dons. Many people imagined that Coulton was the object, years before, of the 'lines suggested by the reading during a solitary lunch at the Holborn restaurant of a criticism written by an Academic fellow upon the literary works of my friend Mr Gilbert Chesterton'.

> Remote and ineffectual Don
> That dared attack my Chesterton,
> With that poor weapon, half-impelled,
> Unlearnt, unsteady, hardly held,
> Unworthy for a tilt with men –
> Your quavering and corroded pen;
> Don poor at Bed and worse at Table,
> Don pinched, Don starved, Don miserable . . .

and so on. In fact, the Don of the poem became a composite figure of Belloc's fantasy life. But then, so, in a remarkable manner, did Coulton. Back in 1929, Belloc had felt constrained to write an article in *The Universe* in which he commented on Coulton's fanatical anti-Catholic prejudices. After the rumpus in the columns of the *Daily Telegraph* concerning the Synod of Arles, Belloc returned to the attack by writing two articles in *The Month* which appeared in November and December 1937. Predictably, he writes *de haut en bas* and emphasises that Coulton's methods of controversy are 'deplorably suitable to the time and place in which we live. Their strength and weakness both attach to a hurried urban generation formed by what is called "elementary education"'.[1]

This posturingly snobbish innuendo does not answer Coulton's major charges: that Belloc was not merely a tenth rate historian, but also a bully, a coward and a liar. But, while being unable to cast out the mote in his own eye, Belloc was clever at exposing the beam in Dr Coulton's. His main criticism of Coulton as an historian is that he was an advocate and not a judge. 'History should be written not from the Bar, but from the Bench'. This might be considered 'ripe', coming from Belloc; but he moves on to a fundamentally powerful attack on the fallacy inherent in Coulton's writings: viz. that good history consisted entirely in freedom from factual errors. Freely acknowledging his own appalling inaccuracy, Belloc goes on to say that the illusion of 'accuracy' does not stop historians with no judgment from

[1] *The Case of Dr Coulton* (1938), p. 6.

leaping to the most absurd generalisations. 'A cultivated knowledge of the main causes is neglected: precise dates and conventional spelling count for more than a right appreciation of the past, while misprints and slips of the pen are the only things thought to be errors. It is excusable to call Napoleon a second-rate bungler: but it is not excusable to print Monday for Sunday as the day of Waterloo'.[1]

The point is well made. In the debate about marriage and divorce, for instance, there can be no doubt that although right in every detail, Coulton was wrong in general principle. There never had been a period in history when the Latin Church at large approved of divorce, nor one when the ordinary laity could obtain divorces except in the most extraordinary circumstances. The 'three councils and three popes' whom Coulton advances as advocates of divorce were all very obvious exceptions to a general rule. But, because Belloc was an apologist before he was an historian, he had to spoil his case by lying. It was only when he came to give a considered view of 'The Case of Dr Coulton' that he was able to come to the sensible view that Coulton

> does not appreciate the weight of a whole stream of tradition, supported by a parallel stream of documentary evidence. If these combined make for a certain conclusion which no rational man can doubt, he would think it sufficient to bring out against it one isolated exception. Many generations hence there will be a broad stream of tradition and document to shew that Englishmen in the nineteenth century did not eat human flesh, but I am sure that if Dr Coulton were on the other side he would triumphantly quote the shipwrecked mariners of the *Mignonette* and continue to say that the Victorians were cannibals.[2]

This is fair criticism of Coulton's methods, but it is only fair up to a point. The truth is that an historian needs *both* good general judgment and a willingness to submit to what Matthew Arnold called the despotism of fact. Many people, surveying the evidence of English 16th century history will believe that Belloc, following Cobbett, was fundamentally right in his account of the sacking of the monasteries. The monasteries were dissolved, not because men like Thomas Cromwell were consumed with Protestant zeal, but because of their greed. But Belloc, who had such a strong case here, repeatedly spoilt it by insufficient research, by blustering denials that there were *any* religious houses in England which deserved suppression, and by simple dishonesty. Nor, having exposed the worldliness and the sheer

[1] Ibid.
[2] *The Case of Dr Coulton*, p. 11.

avarice which led to the dissolution of the monasteries, was Belloc ever able to do justice to the subsequent achievements of the Tudors; particularly of Queen Elizabeth. 'History should not be written from the bar but from the Bench'. He had such a bee in his bonnet about the absolute evil of Protestantism and of 'the Money Power' that he was unable to see that good things came about as a result of the cultural and economic expansion of Elizabethan England; and that these things would not have happened without the Reformation.

On the whole, it can not be said that Belloc or Coulton emerge from their slanging-matches with much dignity. Coulton was notable only for his rudeness. Most other professional historians, then and now, Catholic and Protestant, have been unable to regard Belloc as an historian in the serious sense of the word. For Belloc himself, the existence of this point of view had nothing to do with his failure to check facts or verify sources, still less with his tendency to insult and generalisation. If he was regarded as a mere stylist who had long ago stopped writing proper history, that did not begin to puncture his self-confidence; for the fact that people thought in this way was merely evidence that they had been told to do so by the 'official historians' who were, very naturally, paid by the Rich to lie about the Past.

*   *   *

The Coulton controversy was really no more than shadow-boxing, a little revival of the old pleasures of the chase, when, in the days of his vigour, he had enjoyed baiting H. G. Wells. In so far as he still wanted to engage in public controversy, he more wished to discuss the state of Europe. On a personal level, he was tired, and wanted more time to amuse himself with his friends, and potter about in France or Sussex. 'I can't get through my work!' he complained in March 1938, 'It is old age and will get worse.'[1]

In February, Bonnie Soames returned to Europe to visit her family. She had been paying a very modest rent for a room in Paris, which she now handed over to Belloc, who took it for six months. 'It will be a great convenience for keeping clothes and paper and things permanent, so that I need not lug heavy handbags across the channel, and so that I shall have some centre at any rate, even if it is only for passing through during my travels and perhaps for a few days at a time.'[2]

Here he struggled on with his book on Louis XIV – *Monarchy* – which is in reality a book about Mussolini. And here he gave the

[1] JSN, March 17, 1938.
[2] BC, March 16, 1938.

occasional guilty thought to the book he had promised to write *On the Place of Gilbert Chesterton in English Letters*. In the great 'Chesterbelloc' days before the First World War, Belloc had celebrated his friend in verse as 'the only man I regularly read'. In fact, when he came to prepare to write about GK, he realised that he had read almost no Chesterton, apart from the poems commended to him by George Wyndham. It was not until 1938, for instance, that he flicked through *The Everlasting Man* for the first time. Chesterton's verbal mannerisms made him, in Belloc's eyes virtually unreadable. He found him whimsical and sentimental. Besides, these days, he read very little at all. 'The only man [he] regularly read' was P. G. Wodehouse, whose novels he devoured with admiration and enjoyment as soon as they appeared. He possessed them all and never tired of telling his friends that Wodehouse was the most distinguished master of modern prose. And, in June 1938, he read Evelyn Waugh's *Scoop*. It was a satire after Belloc's own heart. It is much funnier than Belloc's own novels, but it is precisely the kind of book Belloc had tried to write as a young man, with its absurd journalists, its gullible capitalist magnates, its thinly veiled portraits of contemporary figures.

> My dear Evelyn,
> I have just read 'Scoop'. It is very good! I have not read anything comic like that for heaven knows how long and I was grateful for it. It is even true that I laughed out loud eight or nine times. My opinion may be worthless or valuable according to two criteria. I read hardly anything outside that I have to read for my detestable hack-work. Therefore I am a bad comparer. On the other hand when I read anything I nearly always put it down again in two minutes because I cannot understand or value the things now printed in this country. Therefore if I not only understand but value your book it is an original emotion; and very strong . . . I hope it has sold like a mill-race. It deserves to! I am a little sorry there was no actual cannibalism. . . . I am going to Denmark where I hear the people are happy, if I find they are indeed so I shall be indeed enriched but I cannot believe that reputation to be true. I have known happy places in my life, but that was a long time ago and I thought that by this time they had all disappeared.[1]

He had last visited Scandinavia with Lord Basil Blackwood in 1893, in bachelor, undergraduate days. On this occasion, his companion was a friend who stretched back almost as far, 'Bear' Warre. 'His beauty is

[1] BC, June 13, 1938.

more dazzling than ever',[1] which was more than he could say for Denmark, and more than he could say for the British Government. He found it hard not to 'laugh about Eden. Ha! ha! The nonconformists are slobbering all over him. *His* foreign policy is simple – getting even with Mussolini for jeering at him when he tripped over the doormat and half fell. On such small causes do great events depend'.[2] Then, in the autumn, came the conference at Munich Eden had by then resigned. Chamberlain committed the British Government to accepting the partial German annexation of Czechoslovakia in exchange for assurances of peace. Chamberlain appeared at the British airport waving his notorious piece of paper and speaking of 'peace in our time'. Hitler sat down to contemplate which piece of territory he would next annex. And Mussolini returned to Italy, proclaiming that he had saved Europe and made Chamberlain lick his boots.[3]

Belloc's view of the event was sad:

> With every day that passes it is clear that England received an incurable wound at the hands of Prussia at Munich. The French may recover because they have a tradition of revolution and because everything is openly discussed but over here the shock has been such that no educated people know what has happened and are beginning to take it for granted that we must attach ourselves to the Prussian orbit even at the expense of future and perhaps rapid decline. We can neither build nor train for the air at the continental rate. We cannot compete with the slave labour of Nazi Germany, especially as its slaves like their slavery.
>
> I think it will take the form of Germany asking to go into partnership with us, having control of the trade unions and of the coaling and relay stations thereon. And as I have said in print that would mean that we should be junior partners only. The Italians will join in.[4]

There were doubtless those who took a very different view of events. And it is hard, from a post-war perspective, to believe that so many dons, politicians and other Bellocian bêtes noires were as passionately pro-German as he believed. His championship of Mussolini continued to shock readers of *The Weekly Review*. 'We get complaints from people who hate Italians and have an admiration as

[1] JSN, August 26, 1938.
[2] JSN, February 22, 1938.
[3] Mack Smith, p. 224.
[4] BC October 29, 1938.

well as a horror of Berlin.'[1] And this is the line he repeated again and again. The British Government, since the beginning of the Thirties, had been pro-German and anti-Italian. Whereas, if it had had the values of 'old Europe' at heart, it would have allied itself with Mussolini against Hitler. In this view Belloc was not alone. Churchill entertained it until a late stage of the 1930s.

It is not wholly absurd to speak of Churchill and Belloc in the same breath at this juncture. For Churchill, in 1938, was a political has-been, whose ideas counted for nothing and who was too old to be thought resuscitatable. I say this, not because Churchill and Belloc were identical in their political views; but to show that there were any number of old men, survivors of the Edwardian parliaments, who looked on with alarm at the impending peril. Lloyd George confirmed Belloc's view that the British were a fundamentally pro-Prussian people by echoing George Bernard Shaw's enthusiastic praise of Hitler. Belloc had a short column in the *Sunday Times* and he had the ruins of *G.K.'s Weekly*, now filled with articles by 'a host of second-rate cranks who will write their fingers to the bone for nothing'.[2] It is not to be wondered at that he felt a sense of impotence; but within the impotence there stirred, half fantastical, a sense that his voice might, after all, count for something. He would have loved political power; and there was never a moment he would have loved it more than on the eve of the Second World War. Like so many political journalists, Belloc had a highly developed fascination with power as a thing which he would have adored to wield himself. Now, as the end of his career approached, a full sense of his impotence came upon him; and, with his impotence, a near-despair. The closer the great European powers advanced towards conflict, the more certain Belloc became that Civilisation, which he had described as being in a state of crisis in 1937 (and in every previous year, stretching back to 1897), was now in dissolution. He was about to experience 'A Darkening and the end of it'.

In the middle of 1939, an article was to appear in the *Weekly Review* entitled 'What a Russian Alliance means'. It claimed that international Jewry was forcing Germany into a world war so that it might issue usurious loans, as it had done in the First War, to finance the whole affair![3] If these were not Belloc's views exactly, he did have a very great dread, as war approached, that there would be profiteering by the manufacturers of armaments. And he wrote from the Continent

[1] Speaight, p. 483.
[2] Ibid.
[3] Quoted Jay P. Corrin, p. 192.

to an old friend of his from the days of the First World War, Major General Guy Dawnay. Belloc's proposal was that there should be an international round robin, signed by a few 'weighty names', suggesting a detailed plan for eliminating private profit from armaments. 'You were listened to in the Great War. I think you would be listened to now. But the race is hot and a few days may decide it.'[1] Needless to say, the round robin was not drawn up.

This letter was written from Rome, where Belloc had been sent by the Hearst Press to cover the funeral of Pius XI and the new papal election. In March he watched the solemn coronation of Eugenio Pacelli as Pius XII. It was appropriate that Belloc should have been there. Born only nine days after the ninth Pope Pius had declared himself to be infallible, Belloc was almost a child of the First Vatican Council. The Catholicism in which he was nurtured, and of which he was the most eloquent champion, is unlike the Catholicism of the Second Vatican Council. It was 'triumphalist', baroque, certain, glorious and hard. Pius XII was the last Supreme Pontiff of the Church to maintain this Faith in its fullness, and with the supreme confidence of his five predecessors. After that, a very different order of things would come into being; an order which Belloc would, in many particulars, not have recognised as Catholic at all. At Pius XII's coronation, no one could have guessed that Europe, however scarred and changed, would more or less survive the coming conflict; that there would be some kind of visible continuity between the Europe of 1939 and that of the 1980s; but that the one thing which would be changed out of all recognition was the infallible and unchangeable Church. The ceremony itself made a deep impression on Belloc and, in writing to his son Hilary about it, he directly related its impressiveness to the current political crisis:

> It was an astonishingly fine sight, the finest I have ever seen in my life. Of course one expected it to be that anyhow, but it was especially magnificent on account of the enormous crowds. There were about a million people in St Peter's and outside all the way down to the Tiber and even across the Tiber on the other side. The least estimate was 750,000 and the highest one million and a quarter. Also the people showed the utmost enthusiasm. By far the most of them were Romans. I think the reason for this special excitement was that it was an opportunity for a genuine expression of emotion. Under these modern despotisms such opportunities are rare and every advantage is taken of them. The Italians as a

[1] Speaight, p. 517.

whole support Mussolini because he is against the money power and, to the average poor man, especially if he is a wage-earner, it does not make much difference what kind of government there is so long as he is regularly and sufficiently paid. And it pleases him to see the rich people subordinated to the power of government. But despotism is not a natural form of government, and it cannot last indefinitely.[1]

This is an interesting comment. For twenty years, certainly since he published *The House of Commons and Monarchy*, Belloc had been asserting that 'monarchy' – indistinguishable in his definitions from most reasonable definitions of 'despotism' – *was* the natural form of government. This is the first hint, in any of Belloc's letters, that Mussolini might be tainted by imperfection. Perhaps he realised that there was something a little fantastic in seeing Mussolini as a defender of 'Europe and the Faith'. The dictator's attitude to the late Pope's demise was to wish that the Italians could get rid of the Papacy for good. He knew that in so far as any of them went to church 'that was merely because they knew that the Duce wanted them to'. By now he was once again admitting that he was an unbeliever, and that if you had to be saddled with a religion, Islam was more 'effective' than Christianity.[2]

Belloc was shocked, too, by the 'injustice and folly of the anti-Jewish policy in Italy', which made his friend Max Beerbohm's position there uncertain. He wrote to Maurice Baring:

They had not even such an excuse for it as the Germans had. I am particularly sorry for Max Beerbohm, of whom I am very fond, and who was so well fixed at Rapallo where he had counted on finishing his old age in a good climate and at peace with his admirable wife. I have often told you about her. She was a Miss Cohen, a Jewish actress, high Anglican, I gather, in religion, like Max's own sister.[3]

Nevertheless, the crimes and excesses of Mussolini, even – or especially – when he started to imitate the Prussianized brutalities of his new Nazi allies, remained firmly the fault of Anthony Eden. The despotism of the *Duce* 'would not have lasted in Italy so long as it has but for the great mistake England made in trying to impose what are called sanctions. These rallied the people round Mussolini and excited

---

[1] BC, March 22, 1939.
[2] Mack Smith, p. 222.
[3] BC, March 25, 1939.

their patriotism. The recent outrageous conduct of Hitler has had the opposite effect'.[1]

Belloc left Rome, still feeling very ill with influenza, and stayed for a few weeks in Paris as the guest of Sir Eric Phipps, who had moved from Berlin and was now British Ambassador to France. He was convinced that what was needed to defeat Hitler was for the British Government to raise an army. 'That is the key point that I am always hammering at . . . Without an army we cannot exercise any pressure at all.'[2] The French have by now what is by far the best army in Europe, but it is not large enough to act alone against the Germans.'[3] 'All that is wanted is a comparatively small expeditionary force, but the trade unions refuse to allow that and the banks do not like the idea either. So we are reduced to making a quantity of machines, especially aircraft and of course ships, but the keystone of the whole affair, which would be a mobile armed force to be landed where we chose in support of this or that point, is lacking.'[3] When one considers the crucial part which German aircraft had played in winning back Spain for the Catholic faith, Belloc's rather Luddite attitude to the building up of the Royal Air Force is surprising. Within little more than a year, the 'best army in Europe' had been easily outmanoeuvred by the Germans; the British expeditionary forces had been crammed into pleasure steamers and fishing-boats at Dunkirk, and the whole survival of the free West was to depend, for a few hair-raising weeks, on the fact that the British had been 'reduced to making a quantity of machines, especially aircraft'.

But, throughout the spring and summer of 1939, he continued to pontificate on these subjects; and, rather surprisingly, the *Sunday Times* signed him up to write a series of articles, should war break out, on modern military strategy and tactics.

Half-aware, as everyone else was, that war was imminent, he spent as much time as possible abroad, and was for extended periods in Paris, where his friends – Duff and Diana Cooper, various Herberts, 'Bear' Warre and others – could come and see him. He only snatched a glimpse of Katharine Asquith in May on her way back from Lourdes.

> She could not stop because she had to be in command of the whole train, it seems, and all the poor people were dependent upon her presence. I do admire the trouble she is taking! How other people can manage to be so devoted is a standing mystery to me. For

[1] BC, March 22, 1939.
[2] BC, March 17, 1939.
[3] BC, March 22, 1939.

myself, it is with the very greatest difficulty I can manage to fulfil the most ordinary tasks and anything like self-sacrifice would appal me.[1]

By June, he had just about finished his very haphazard life of Charles II – *The Last Rally* – and asserted to Mrs Asquith:

> Writing for one's living (and other people's) is an abomination. Man was never meant to live by his (or her – car 'l'homme' est un mot collectif . . .) pen. 20 years ago I said that in a newspaper & Arnold Bennett wrote an angry letter to that newspaper saying, 'What did HB mean by the word "meant"? meant by whom? . . . Did I (asked Arnold Bennett – a good-natured man with a hare lip and a simple face otherwise) did I mean "meant" by a hypothetical God?' To this I answered by yet another letter saying 'Yes! But not "a" (or rather "an") hypothetical God, but by a real God full of beef, creator of Heaven and Earth et omnium visibilium et invisibilium.' This letter, as you may well believe, they wouldn't print. (What an extraordinary country England has become! Quite cut off from the world!) I'm going back to the lovely Island. I must once more bathe in the beauty of South England 'before I croak' as Oenone said to Mother Ida.[2]

The summer passed quite happily. He made his usual West Country tour, staying with Herberts in Pixton and Tetton, with the Asquiths at Mells, with the Phippses near Marlborough, and then down to Sussex where he spent a lot of time with Duff and Diana Cooper at their cottage near Bognor Regis. In August, he nipped over to Paris once more and sent to Bonnie Soames in America his view of the European situation:

> Mussolini is a very sane and well-balanced man, with a clear idea as to his own politics and the nature of other nations. He has made one big mistake, which is allowing himself to be moved by personal passion in his quarrel with the French freemasons. They would not allow an understanding with Italy, but he would have done well to have arranged one in spite of them.[3]

By now, Belloc appears to have forgotten Mussolini's open hostility to the Vatican, his Nazi-style persecution of the Italian Jews, and his alliance with the Germans, which in the spring had been giving him

[1] BC, May 26, 1939.
[2] Mells, June 10, 1939.
[3] BC, August 4, 1939.

pause. He probably did not know quite how parlous a state the Italian economy had reached under the *Duce*'s forthright condemnation of 'the money power'; and he had, of course, found reasons to justify the invasion of Abyssinia and the slaughter of half a million North African peasants in the course of being Europeanised. But none of these things seems to have diminished *Il Duce*'s greatness in Belloc's eyes. His only other fault would appear to be in his family relations:

> It is also rather foolish of him to allow himself to be so dominated by a violent and vulgar daughter, whose husband, Ciano, cannot have anything in him, but quite certainly all his weight of intelligence and his excellent diplomatic skill will be used to prevent the Germans from making fools of themselves . . . [1]

In the spring, Belloc had been afraid of an imminent war and wished that, instead of wasting money on aeroplanes, the British Government would organise a small expeditionary force to join that of the French — 'the greatest army in Europe'. But now, in August 1939, thanks to the diplomatic genius of Benito Mussolini, it appeared that the danger of war had been averted.

> Hitler himself, of course, is a danger because he is a revivalist, and unaccountable, like all people who are touched with lunacy, especially religious megalomania. Also he is quite ignorant, whereas the other conductors of Europe have some idea of the past and of the modern world as well. But I doubt whether Hitler or any of his surroundings will run the risk of a military adventure. [2]

He planned a little holiday for himself in the autumn. He would cross to Paris, and then go down to Portofino and stay with Mary Herbert. On August 24, he wrote to Lady Phipps that 'it seems to me not unlikely that Hitler will postpone any action until he has had the chance to make some further declaration and appeal, for he must know that if he goes to the full limit of insanity it will be the end of himself and all the new violence in the Reich'. [3]

Six days later, the Germans invaded Poland, and the war had begun. The blame of course was to be laid firmly at the door of the Jewish bankers, who had allowed Prussia to re-arm in the first place; and of the Oxford Dons, who had taught a whole generation the 'doctrine that Prussia, which they call Germany, is a kind of God, twin to our Glorious Selves'. [4]

[1] Ibid.
[2] BC, August 4, 1939.
[3] BC, August 24, 1939.
[4] *Letters*, p. 281.

Ronald Knox, assessing Belloc's life and career, was to ask, 'Why must he always be different, not thinking the thoughts of common men?' And he came up with the answer that 'Belloc's destiny was conflict and he did not love it. He was "a prophet lost in the hills"'.[1] But the truth of the matter is that Belloc plainly loved conflict; he delighted in the idea that everyone else was wrong and he was right. When calamity came upon the world, he knew that it was a safe bet to blame the financiers, the dons, the parliamentarians, the heretics, the whole world of the English, Protestant 'establishment' to which in some ways he would have liked to belong, but which he always regarded with the amused suspicion of an outsider. His comments on the approach and outbreak of the Second World War suggest less the prophet in the hills and more the famous *Punch* cartoon in which everyone was out of step except Charlie.

* * *

Belloc had two main concerns in the opening year of the war – France, and his children. He managed to visit France at the end of November 1939 and, in the company of Henri Massis, he went to see his old regiment in the Maginot line.

> At the front I found my old regiment and my old battery, which brought me to the verge of tears, especially when I met my old gun. It had just come out of the front line, and there were all the young men, looking as fresh as daisies and as muddy as an old-fashioned London street. The Colonel made a speech and assembled the officers, so I had to make a speech and then I stood the men huge masses of wine. The regiment gave me champagne, but I gave my piece nothing but gallons and gallons of red wine which they far prefer. It is an astonishing thing to come back to the same atmosphere and tradition after a gap of just on fifty years. It is the only pleasant accident to mortality I have known, and had an air about it of the immortal.[2]

Then he went on to Belgium where he had a long private audience with the King ('I took to him enormously'), and then home 'more dead than alive' with exhaustion,[3] and knocked up by his first experience of flying in an aeroplane. 'I got violent vertigo, as I

[1] Speaight, p. 536.
[2] Speaight, p. 519.
[3] *Letters*, p. 285.

always knew I should if I flew through the air in a flying machine. I shall probably never recover from that foolhardy experiment!'[1]

He was still very busy. He was toying with a book on England and France. He was writing his very scrappy essay on *The Place of Gilbert Chesterton in English Letters*. He was planning his *Elizabethan Commentary*. He was writing weekly articles in the *Sunday Times* on the progress of the war, and regular contributions to the *Weekly Review*.

Tiredness developed into violent influenza over Christmas, which he found hard to shake off; but, in the spring of 1940, he went off to Paris again. To his 'great joy', he coincided with the Duff Coopers and was able to dine with them on Easter Day. Meanwhile, he enjoyed frequent mass ('it is the essence of the Church to have a lot of low masses and no sermons'[2]) and got on with his writing, glad to be away from the 'Protestant ethos' for a while. ('Talking of which, I mean the Protestant ethos, look at Scandinavia! Oh! What a horrible comment on goodwill and peace and being kind to the cat and all!'[3])

But there was another reason for his being in France. He was looking for his daughter Elizabeth. The other children had, for the time being, ceased to worry him. Hilary had left the United States and was a Lieutenant in the Royal Naval Reserve, based at Halifax in Nova Scotia. Peter, through the influence of General Dawnay, had managed to get a commission in the Royal Marines. Eleanor remained at King's Land with her husband and children, keeping house for her father as best she could. It was many years since Eleanor and Elizabeth had been on speaking terms. So Belloc's journey was a lonely one. He managed to get a letter through to her address in Marseilles, and she replied at the end of May, apparently oblivious that there was any danger.

He returned home, grievously anxious. On June 10, the Italian *Duce* declared war on the Allies, an inevitable event which must have torn at Belloc's heart. By the end of June, the unthinkable had happened. France had collapsed. Marshal Pétain had been one of Belloc's heroes since the First War. He had proclaimed the virtues of *travail*, *famille*, *patrie*; he had restored the monarchical principle in public affairs. He was a man who appealed to Belloc, and whom Belloc did not hesitate to praise. [4] Now, this same Pétain had surrendered to the Boche. Europe was witnessing something much more ghastly than the legends of 1870 on which Belloc had been reared.

[1] Ibid, p. 286.
[2] JSN, March 13, 1940.
[3] JSN, April 6, 1940.
[4] Speaight, p. 521.

'We talk of a "stunning blow",' wrote Belloc's old friend J. B. Morton. 'The adjective is the only one to use to describe the effect on Belloc of the defeat and collapse of France after so short a campaign. He was too bewildered and dazed to talk about it much. It was difficult to accept the fact that it had really happened.'[1]

But, if it overshadowed the summer of 1940 – and there was no possibility of celebrating his seventieth birthday in the way that they had caroused on the occasion of his sixtieth – it is wrong to suppose that Belloc went into a complete decline. He blamed the fall of France on the 'refusal of the Bank of England and its New York associates to allow England to have any army'.[2] And there can be no doubt that it made him suffer. But he slogged on.

For one thing, he had the worry of Elizabeth to occupy his mind. Several months later, he discovered that she had got out of France, through Bayonne, just in time; and, from Spain, she managed to get back to England.

The change was at first imperceptible, but her father would 'never be the same' again. They waited for the Pope to speak out against the Nazis but they were disappointed.

The Pope continues to be mum and to confine himself to gener-
alities. He is to be blamed. He should speak out as he ought to have
done – or rather his predecessors – in the last war. That's what he's
there for, to act as the teacher of Christendom; but he continues to
be brow-beaten by people who talk of a large and powerful
Catholic body in Boche-land. There is no such thing. The Catholic
Germans were swamped and dowsed long ago in a flood of horribly
vulgar Paganism with Atheist architecture.[3]

He continued to work on his *Elizabethan Commentary*, and was thrilled to discover 'in the matter of true history, I have now implanted and established the term "bald as an egg" applied to Elizabeth Tudor: at the age of 30 all her hair fell off! It never grew again'.[4]

By the end of the year, he had come to realise that

the Fascist regime in Italy will not survive as it has been. And what a
pity! A strong civilised Italy is of incalculable advantage to Europe.
The wretched ass Eden was to blame of course – ignorant and vain

[1] Morton, p. 159.
[2] *Letters*, p. 294.
[3] JSN, July 22, 1940.
[4] JSN, November 11, 1940.

as a tart – but a man of Musso's calibre ought not to have let himself be provoked into folly.[1]

After a much-muted King's Land Christmas, he began 'a progress through Oxford and the West'. He stayed for a few nights at the Trout, a pub on the edges of Port Meadow, just outside Oxford, and made sorties into the town.

> 'Oxford is *crammed*,' he complained. 'One can hardly walk along the streets. The population has multiplied by 3. Half the addition is due to an exodus of East End Jews who have heard that the Germans won't bomb Oxford . . .'

The place inevitably awoke in him his ancient obsession with the dons.

> It is curious how the beastliness of dons increases on one's consciousness as one grows old. When one is young one takes them in one's stride, like bugs in a continental hotel, but after a certain age one recognises the full horror of them. What is it that makes them so beastly? I have often heard it discussed and never concluded. Some say that it is because they are able to patronise and lord it over young men who can't answer them. Others say it is because they eat such horrible food. Certainly Oxford food is beyond compare for horror.[2]

On his return home, he found that Josiah Wedgwood had sent him an 'anthology of freedom. I am very fond of him but it is monstrous of him to have done that. However he is a Member of Parliament, a very good fellow, several hundred years old; and his family and mine have been intimate for four generations so I forgive him'.[3]

Many of these jaunty thoughts were written to Bonnie Soames, now Mrs Hoffman Nickerson, homesick in America with two baby boys. They may be compared with his habit of bursting into song to disguise his sorrowful thoughts. But, equally, they can be seen as symptoms of that 'spouting well of joy within which never yet was dried', which he had celebrated in his song of the Winged Horse. Life was very sorrowful, and few have had a stronger sense than Belloc that our theological condition here is best defined by the Salve Regina which speaks of us 'mourning and weeping in this vale of tears'. But his natural exuberance could not be quenched. And,

---

[1] JSN, December 31, 1940.
[2] JSN, January 19, 1941.
[3] JSN, February 22, 1941.

even in the midst of heavy sorrows for Europe, he could be funny. Mrs Nickerson wrote to him that she was trying to find consolation in those dark days by reading the Scriptures; but that she found St Paul 'difficult'. He replied,

> If you find St Paul difficult, as you say, it's not your fault. The old Yid (saving His Holy Office) had a most turgid and muddly mind. But every now and then he squeezed out a fine lapidary sentence – sometimes Pantheist, sometimes Patriotic. One witness to Catholic Truth is the fact that it appears even in the writings of St Paul. Of him one may say as the Dominican said of St Jerome, 'If he is a saint, any one can be a saint'.[1]

* * *

But, to the Fall of France of the previous year, there was to be added another blow, more personally intolerable. Peter Belloc went out with the Fleet in the boat to which his battalion of the Marines was attached. He picked up a germ, apparently not serious, and was taken ashore to a hospital in the north of England. Septicaemia followed, and sudden pneumonia. He died in April 2, 1941. J. B. Morton, his closest friend, learnt of his death that day, and tried to get hold of the parish priest at West Grinstead to break the news to Belloc. But, by the time Father Riley had reached King's Land, Belloc already knew.

The body was brought south, and it was arranged that Peter should be buried at West Grinstead beside his mother and his brother Louis, who had died at the very end of the last war. As they were preparing to leave the house for the funeral, Eleanor helped her father on with his coat. 'My child', he said, with a troubled frown. 'Is it Louis or Peter?' 'It's Peter, Papa,' she said, realising with a jolt in her heart that his faculties were going.

A few days later, Belloc went over to Henfield to see the Mortons. He had not slept since his son's death, and he was shivering with cold.

> He said he would like to snatch a few minutes sleep. So he sat in a chair, muffled in his cloak, with his feet stretched out to the fire, and was silent for a little while. I do not think he slept. After a time, he opened his eyes. Suddenly he said, 'He was such a happy boy, wasn't he? Such a happy disposition always'. I told him that Peter had been my closest and dearest friend, and what that friendship had meant to me, and he said quietly, 'I know'.[2]

[1] February 24, 1941.
[2] Morton, p. 160.

For the remaining months of 1941, he continued his routine, as far as war-time permitted it, of rambling about, visiting his friends, and writing. In June, he rallied, for

> Eleanor has managed to buy 600 bottles of South African claret. How glad I am that the Dutch discovered the Cape of Good Hope and took with them a lot of French Huguenots who, in spite of their detestable religion, had retained the power of making wine. How merciful is God![1]

But his family, and all those who were close to him, were worried. He was evidently restless and miserable for the rest of the year. And then, on January 30, 1942, he suffered from a slight stroke in the Reform Club. The club servants put him to bed, but there was an air-raid that night and no one at King's Land was told until the next day. He was then brought home and by February 2 he had developed pneumonia.

Father Riley came over from West Grinstead on the 3rd. Belloc was conscious, but very weak, and Eleanor was convinced that her father would not live more than a matter of hours. The priest anointed him. Johnnie Morton arrived and was told the sad news.

A nun had been sent over from the Bon Secours sisters to nurse Mr Belloc through the night, should he survive the night, and Morton went upstairs to see his old friend, and to ask him how he was.

> He said in a weak voice, 'Oh, I'm all right', then after a moment: 'There was a fool called Coué – a Frenchman. He said "Every day in every way I get better and better". Well that's how it is with me'. We talked for a while, and then the Sister brought him a glass of milk, which he refused vigorously. 'Tell them', he said, 'to take that filthy stuff away and bring me a glass of wine'. I passed this on to the Sister, who did not like the idea at all. But my wife managed to convince her that a man who has been drinking wine all his life is none the better for having it suddenly cut off. So he had his glass of wine, and listening to his talk, I could not believe that he was going to die, ill though he was.[2]

Nor was he to die for another ten years, even though the whole condition of his life had changed irrevocably.

[1] JSN, June 10, 1941.
[2] Morton, p. 162.

SIXTEEN

A PRIVATE GENTLEMAN
1942–1953

'The business of human life turns, as I have heard that battles turn, not to tragedy but to agony towards the end.'[1] Belloc had written the words to Evan Charteris in 1914 when he was still shaken with the recent death of Elodie. Many of Belloc's friends and acquaintances would have thought that the words applied very well to him. And they might have thought of his unhappy poem, 'Discovery', which concludes:

You find that middle life goes racing past.
You find despair: and at the very last,
You find as you are giving up the ghost
That those who loved you best despised you most.[2]

But these are the reflections of Belloc gazing at old age from a dread distance. Prematurely, and at the age of seventy-one, he was thrust into a condition of incipient, but increasing, senility. But the decade which followed his stroke were not years of empty agony or bitterness. Nor was there any justification in his fear that those who loved him best would despise him most. For, almost the first, and very surprising, effect of his stroke was a quietening down of his relationship with his daughter Eleanor. In the six years previous there had been a great number of occasions in which there had been raised voices and slammed doors. Now, as he crept back to health, and rose from his bed, he was quieter.[3] Frustration was, very naturally, felt on both sides. For Mrs Jebb, there stretched ahead, she knew not how long, a period in which she was now to be responsible for her father. For Belloc himself, there was the unwonted stability which his feebleness imposed. Even had there been no war on, he would no longer have been able to lead his perpetually peripatetic existence. For the previous seventy-one years, he had been on the move, between England and

1 *Letters*, p. 61.
2 *Complete Verse*, p. 80.
3 Philip Jebb.

the Continent almost continually. School terms at the Oratory can have been the only spells when he was in the same place for more than three months in the space of his entire life.

Now, his travelling was curtailed. And, as the years passed, it was to be abandoned altogether. Living with him must have been a strain. If he escaped the cruel fate of his poem 'Discovery', it is less certain that he was going to avoid that of Mary Lunn in his poem 'The Example' who

> Died suddenly, at ninety-one,
> Of Psittacosis, not before
> Becoming an appalling bore.[1]

Anthony Powell glimpsed him on one of his pathetically rare visits to London in 1943 in 'the Allies Club (a wartime institution, the Rothschilds' house in Piccadilly, now no more, next to Apsley House). Belloc, who by then was very doddery and vague, had by no means ceased to drink. He was in charge of two of the Acton sisters, Mia Woodruff and Aelda (not yet married). At an early stage of the evening, with Belloc at the bar, Mia hissed to Violet as we passed: "I wish Douglas (her husband) would turn up – I've run out of money." Later after dinner we saw Aelda (who was very small) attempting to pilot the considerable bulk of Belloc up the stairs from the dining-room, and heard him constantly repeating, "There's a taxi at Hayward's Heath".'[2]

A similarly dilapidated Belloc was recorded by Evelyn Waugh when he met him on one of his last tours of the West Country in 1945. Waugh thought Belloc 'looked as though the grave were the only place for him'.

> He has grown a splendid white beard and in his cloak, which with his hat he wore indoors and always, he seemed like an archimandrite. He lost and stole and whatever went into his pockets, toast, cigarettes, books never appeared, like the reverse of a conjuror's hat. He talked incessantly, proclaiming with great clarity the grievances of forty years ago: that the English worshipped the Germans and respected only wealth in one another; that the rich enslaved the poor by lying to them; that the dons at Oxford were paid by the rich to lie . . . He is conscious of being decrepit and forgetful, but not of being a bore.[3]

[1] *Complete Verse*, p. 227.
[2] Letter to the author.
[3] Waugh: *Diaries*, p. 627.

The beard, thick, food-encrusted and patriarchal, was grown in 1942 to hide the slight distortion of his features which had remained after the stroke. Once it had grown, it would have been difficult enough to remove. He did decide to do so once, when being driven down the main street of Marlborough by Frances Phipps. The barber confessed himself unequal to the task and they ended up having it hacked off with surgical scissors at the local hospital.[1]

When he returned to King's Land, Mrs Jebb expressed horror at his appearance and, in the collapse of health which invariably followed one of his journeys then, the beard was allowed to grow, never to be shaven again. Belloc's less understanding friends felt that Eleanor was 'over-protective'. They did not realise that whenever he went away he drank and talked too much, and returned exhausted. In 1944 he had a bad attack of pneumonia from which he nearly died. Gradually, he was only well enough to be driven over to the Black Horse, a pub in Horsham. His companion on these occasions was J.B. Morton, now his dearest and most constant visitor. It was scarcely the sort of inn which would have inspired Belloc in the time of his vigour to write a drinking-song. The dullest of provincial hotels, it was also, in those days, extremely strict in its appliance of the abominated licensing laws. Nor would they bring a bottle of port to the table, so it was necessary, if luncheon were to be consumed without anxiety, to order rows and rows of glasses of port in advance against the moment when the waiter informed them that the hour of three was past and the bar closed. The respectable people of Horsham (which he invariably pronounced Horse-ham) must have been mildly surprised at the sight of these two, who had the drinking habits of Fleet Street and were, in any case, neither quiet nor inconspicuous. But even if the billowing black of Belloc's clothes, or the noise from his table, or the amount of drink he was consuming failed to catch the attention, the people at the neighbouring tables could not have missed his growing and obsessive desire for bread. It was an old habit, picked up no doubt in the army and maintained through a life-time 'on the road' when he never knew when his next meal was to be had. But, in old age, he took to stuffing bread into his pockets and leaving it there for several days. When the bread from his own table at the Black Horse had been stowed away, he would wander round the other tables and take the loaves from other people, muttering that lack of bread was the result of false religion.[2]

With old age, his formerly iron capacity to absorb any amount of

[1] Speaight, p. 527.
[2] Speaight, p. 527 and Philip Jebb.

alcohol left him. One night at supper, after drinking his usual bottle
of Algerian red wine, he staggered when rising to his feet and – an
habitual gesture – drinking the last of his wine while standing. He fell
backwards and held on to the window-curtains behind him, tugging
the fitting of curtain rod and rings to the floor. When he had been
helped to his feet and escorted off to bed, it was decided that he could
no longer drink a whole bottle. Henceforward his ration was half a
bottle of red wine, watered.[1]

From now onwards, he abandoned his habit of drenching himself
in Floris scent, and the black of his clothes became ever more thickly
encrusted with food and candle-grease. One of his grandchildren
recalled that he had 'a capacity to repeat himself in some crazy way
only now equalled by the technology of toys. He was like one of
those alarming dolls to which a string is attached which, when pulled,
will say one of five or six things regardless of the occasion'.[2]

The Jebbs – the parents in their forties, and four growing children,
all of whom had reached adulthood by the time of Belloc's death –
became accustomed to the almost ritual quality of these repetitions.
'Winston Churchill is a Yank.' 'Has the habit of boasting died out at
Balliol?' 'Do the dons still believe that the Saxons came over to
England in little boats?' He would revert to old figures from the past –
'Jowett of Balliol: a eunuch with a squeaky voice.' His old nurse,
'poor darling, she believed in every word of the Bible'; which was, as
everyone knew by then, 'a pack of lies', 'lying as only shameless yids
can lie'.[3]

One of the most striking features of the litany was its total arbitrariness, and a stranger who had never met him before would be
subjected to it without any introduction or preparation. It was at this
stage of his life that he first met Dom Aelred Watkin, subsequently
Headmaster of Downside, who recalls:

> I arrived on a dark winter's afternoon and it was about 4.00 when I
> was first introduced to Hilaire Belloc. He was sitting at the far end
> of his refectory dining-room table with his back to the window.
> He was drinking wine from a silver cup and, sitting there with his
> huge beard and black coat and rather faintly illuminated by two
> candles, he seemed to have strayed from another age. I was
> introduced to him – he had never met me before – and his first
> words were: 'And what is the news from London, father? Do they

[1] Memories of PJ, AJ and JJ.
[2] Julian Jebb.
[3] Ibid, Dom Aelred Watkin and Dom Philip Jebb.

still think Dreyfus was innocent? Poor darling, he was as guilty as sin.'[1]

This obsession with the 'news' – relating to the deeper and deeper past – did not diminish with the years. He was unhappy when his son-in-law Reginald Jebb was not about to tell him 'the news' and it was his invariable question to anyone who had come from London. His own visits to the metropolis were a very rare thing now, but even they partook of a wholly formulaic and repetitive character. He would be driven to London by car. The days of the train were over. And he would always sit in the front passenger's seat. When the vehicle was on the move he would half-turn and ask. 'Is Rex in the car?' 'No, Papa.' 'What an intolerable bore. I like someone to talk to in the car.' Minor irritations of this kind were 'an intolerable bore' and major ones were 'rather a bore' or a 'pretty good bore'. The same remarks would be passed at the same points of the journey. For instance, as they passed the bottom of Box Hill, he would say, 'That is the house of the Edwardian (Ed-wah-rr-djan) novelist George Méridith or, as some say, Merédith, who always spoke with respect of my beloved wife and thought in Welsh until his dying day.'

* * *

Such journeys were usually sad, and were made to attend the funerals, or requiems, of his friends. Father Vincent McNabb had died in 1943; Maurice Baring in 1945; and his sister, Mrs Belloc-Lowndes, died in 1947. Soon the journeyings stopped altogether, and he remained in Sussex.

King's Land was far from empty. As well as the Jebbs, and their friends, Belloc had the companionship of many visitors. The rituals of the King's Land Christmas were still performed. And, for all the repetitions, there was still laughter to be had. Even in his endless harping on ancient 'news' there was a kind of self-conscious irony. It would be quite false to suppose that he was shuffling about in a state of permanent disgruntlement with the Jews, or the Rich, or the Dons. Rather, he had long before become accustomed to habits of speech in which they were the butts of his ribaldry. And, if the gramophone needle was stuck, pathetically, compelling him to repeat the same old pleasantries, they remained jokes. The children, too, obviously laughed not at his wit, but at his farcical eccentricities, and at the stream of absurd grown-ups who flocked to the house to see him. Merriment could always be had from hearing the tones of Mr

[1] Dom Aelred Watkin to the author.

Sumner, the parson from Shipley, who called regularly about twice a week. Belloc appeared to like him very much, and they could have cultivated conversation of a sort which was rare among the clergy of Belloc's faith. Their conversation would invariably be punctuated by the parson being offered sherry by his host; and the young family would wait to hear his feigned refusal to accept the drink. 'No, no, no' – pause while the glass was filled – '*Thank* you, Mr Belloc'; a ritual which never failed to make them weep with mirth.

Their life, that of the young Jebbs, took place in the day nursery, the drawing-room, the kitchen and their bedrooms. King's Land is a perfect house for children, with its warren of corridors and out-houses, its farm, and its mill. Reginald Jebb, when he was not editing the *Weekly Review* with Hilary Pepler, was happiest when he was devoting himself to the farm. What the publican at Shipley had said to G. K. Chesterton all those years ago – 'Belloc? Farms a bit doesn't he?' – was true to the end.

Mr Belloc himself – and he was really now 'Mr Belloc' to everyone who did not feel entitled to call him 'H.B.' – shuffled about between the study and the kitchen, and the chapel, and his bedroom. His reading now consisted entirely of *The Diary of a Nobody*, his own works, and the novels of P.G. Wodehouse, which he would read with the satisfied intentness of an old priest poring over his breviary. When bedtime came, he would shuffle upstairs; into the chapel where he gabbled his night prayers, along the corridor, kissing Elodie's door as he went, the grease from his candle splattering on to his clothes, and into his room. Very occasionally, a grandson would take him more food in his room, for his need of bread, even at night, was insatiable. They would find him lying in darkness, propped up on one elbow, a novel of Wodehouse's held to the flickering candle-light on the bedside table. And sometimes he would mutter, 'Admirable, admirable,' at its perfection of phrasing. As he did so, house-mice scampered on the coverlet of his bed, and nibbled excitedly at the pockets of his scruffy camel-hair dressing-gown, spread out over the bedclothes, thick with appetisingly stale crumbs. He would seem as oblivious to them as to a midge in summer.

In the morning, if there were a priest staying in the house, he would shuffle in the mice-ridden dressing-gown the few yards along the landing to mass in the chapel, muttering as he did so, 'What we suffer for our holy religion.' Then he would dress, and, after breakfast, the quiet routine would begin again. If, as often happened, a cat were sitting in his study chair, he would say, 'Pretty pussy – lovely pussy – get out, damn you,' and push the animal to the floor. He might then settle to read. In the summer, if he needed to go to the lavatory, he would merely walk out of his study and use the lawn. In the winter, he shuffled along the corridor. He liked to go in hunt of leaves, prodding them with his blackthorn stick. He believed it was bad luck if they blew into the house. Foibles of a lifetime had now hardened into serious preoccupations. The matter of doors was one of the few which made him raise his voice in that draughty house. 'My darling, you must teach your children to shut doors' was a constantly reiterated phrase to his daughter, receiving the invariable reply, 'Yes, Papa.' But his curses were loud if the door were slammed.

Often, as he trundled back to his study after a meal, he said – imprisoned in the habits of sixty years – that he must do 'his work', a declaration which would provoke hoots of rather cruel laughter from the children when he was gone. The days of 'grinding out hack work' were over now. And, on the whole, this brought peace rather than frustration. After Sir Walter Scott had been incapacitated by a stroke, he asked his family to carry him to his desk, where he was propped up, and a pen put in his hand. But the pen fell from his fingers, and the stoical Scott fell back weeping upon the pillows, saying, 'No repose for Sir Walter but in the grave.' There are no such recorded scenes in the later days at King's Land. Belloc sat in his chair. No longer able to afford cigars, he smoked a pipe, a habit taught him by his son-in-law. He enjoyed lighting, and relighting, the noxious object before settling down to a happy re-perusal of his own books. Sometimes a child, dashing about the house in the way that children do, would come upon Belloc, not in his study, but pausing on the landing over the hall, where a shelf was kept, containing most, if not all, of his published works: over one hundred and fifty titles, counting pamphlets, biographies, essays, economic and political tracts, topography, military history, religious apologetics, comic novels and verse. And he would mutter, 'My child, when I survey these works, I think what a *fine* fellow I am!'

But he was by no means depressed to be released from the treadmill of having to produce any more 'work'. When Hugh Kingsmill and Hesketh Pearson visited the seventy-six-year-old Belloc, and plied him with Boswellian questions, it was inevitable that they should exact some Johnsonian exaggerations in reply. But there is no reason to suppose that he was being entirely dishonest in his teasing.

PEARSON: Are you going to give us an autobiography?
HILAIRE BELLOC: No. No gentleman writes about his private life. Anyway, I hate writing. I wouldn't have written a word if I

could have helped it. I only wrote for money. *The Path to Rome* is the only book I ever wrote for love.

PEARSON: Didn't you write *The Four Men* for love?

HILAIRE BELLOC: No. Money.

PEARSON: *The Cruise of the Nona*?

HILAIRE BELLOC: Money.

KINGSMILL: That's a wonderful passage in *The Path to Rome* about youth borne up the valley on the evening air.

HILAIRE BELLOC: Oh – yes.

KINGSMILL: I love the poetry in your essays, especially in the volume *On Nothing*.

HILAIRE BELLOC: Quite amusing. Written for money.

PEARSON: What profession would you have liked to follow?

HILAIRE BELLOC: I was called to the Bar. But what I wanted to be was a private gentleman. Lazing about doing nothing. Farm as a hobby, perhaps. Keep someone to run it.[1]

It hardly needs to be said that Belloc was playing a game with his two visitors; and that his memory, if it was a true memory, of being called to the Bar, was inaccurate. But there is something rather satisfying, and only partially fantastical, about his sense that the perfect life was one in which he lazed about doing nothing, and was simply 'a private gentleman'. For that is what, in the last ten years of his life, he became.

Often, he would break into song, sometimes for the amusement of visitors, sometimes on impulse: either music-hall songs such as 'Chase me, girls, I've got a banana!' or French airs, or ditties of his own composing. We still know what these were like from the sound recordings made in 1933. His voice did not alter with the onset of extreme old age, retaining its high-pitched and almost playful quality. Almost the most haunting song on the whole record is the one he called 'The Winged Horse'. Like all songs, it can only be appreciated fully when it is heard sung; the words on the page only convey half its magic, and nothing can equal his own rendering of it, exuberantly rhythmical, very faintly mad, at the same moment poignant and hilarious. It would be hard to write a prose paraphrase of the song; it tells of riding on a winged horse and flying up above the Berkshire downs, and catching sight of the channel, and of Michael the archangel, and of all the chivalrous heroes of French romance. But, in Belloc's voice, it is impossible not to catch in its tones an echo of his own defiant and joyful independence. The 'bloody dons' 'turned him out o' doors' in his early manhood, and it was a fact to which he

[1] Hesketh Pearson and Hugh Kingsmill: *Talking of Dick Whittington*, p. 213.

returned, obsessively, in his decrepitude. But his exile from the lost Paradise of Oxford, though he might have 'cut his feet on flinty lands', brought with it an extraordinary freedom.

> It's ten years ago today you turned me out o' doors
> To cut my feet on flinty lands and stumble down the shores,
> And I thought about the all-in-all, oh more than I can tell!
> But I caught a horse to ride upon and I rode him very well,
> He had flame behind the eyes of him and wings upon his side.
>   And I ride, and I ride!
>
> I rode him out of Wantage and I rode him up the hill,
> And there I saw the Beacon in the morning standing still,
> Inkpen and Kackpen and southward and away
> High through the middle airs in the strengthening of the day,
> And there I saw the channel-glint and England in her pride.
>   And I ride, and I ride!
>
> And once a-top of Lambourne down toward the hill of Clere
> I saw the Host of Heaven in rank and Michael with his spear,
> And Turpin out of Gascony and Charlemagne the Lord,
> And Roland of the marches with his hand upon his sword
> For the time he should have need of it, and forty more beside.
>   And I ride, and I ride!
>
> For you that took the all-in-all the things you left were three.
> A loud voice for singing and keen eyes to see,
> And a spouting well of joy within that never yet was dried!
>   And I ride.[1]

The mysterious 'you' who took the 'all-in-all' were of course the Fates, who dogged Belloc all his life, the old gods Baal and Ashtaroth for whom he always felt a sneaking pagan respect. But the defiance of the song was not ill-founded. All the things on which, as a young man he had set his heart, had been taken from him quite fiercely: the woman he loved, and with whom he hoped to spend his life; the prospects of academic success and of political advancement. It is only when we contemplate Belloc in extreme old age that we recognise how little the 'all-in-all' had to do with the figure on the winged horse; how little the controversial, political worldly Belloc had to do with his true genius. For he *was* a genius, and not merely a very clever writer. Indeed, his genius was only occasionally apparent in his writings, while being wholly apparent in himself, in the loud voice for

[1] *Complete Verse*, p. 67.

singing and the keen eyes to see; but above all in the 'spouting well of joy within which never yet was dried' and which could not be dried merely because he had stopped rambling and was no longer writing his books.

To this extent, we can be grateful for the long phase of pottering and shuffling, pathetic as many of his friends found it. For it emphasises that the greatness of Belloc is in the man. His total originality and uniqueness can only be assessed by contemplating the phenomenon known to his friends as Mr Belloc. It is not to be found in the frequently unsatisfactory 'hack work', nor wholly in the works where his genius flowered – *The Four Men*; the verse, but particularly the comic verse; almost all his essays, but particularly *Hills and the Sea* and the *Essays of a Catholic*; the fiction – particularly *Belinda* and *The Mercy of Allah*; the controversy – *The Servile State, The Jews* and *Survivals and New Arrivals*; the reconstructions of the past in *The Eye Witness*[1]; the brilliant mingling of topography and prejudice in *The Battleground*. The genius is there in the books. But when we turn away from the books to the letters and the memories of everyone who met him, whether they regarded him with love or hatred, we realise that his literary genius is only a shadow of his full greatness.

It was a greatness and a genius wholly at variance with the world. One of his grandsons once gazed at him with amazement as he staggered drunkenly out of the Black Horse at Horsham. 'I saw him tip and topple a small elastic banded bundle of notes – pound notes – along the gutter – his huge blackness concentrated on the cynical joke, as he edged it along with his blackthorn stick.'[2] If the cynicism of it shocked, and still shocks, the child, it remains a very good joke (Belloc was by now very poor) and provides a perfect counterbalance to the assertion, made at a very similar date to Hugh Kingsmill, that he had only written for money.

It is also a good joke, because in this silly gesture of pushing pound notes into the gutter, as in his political creeds; in the most brilliant of his fantasies, *The Mercy of Allah*, as in his profoundest readings of theology, he was completely and simply consistent. He believed that it was impossible to serve God and Mammon. That is not to say that he did not try to make money; nor even, on occasion, that he did not venture into the world of the Duke of Battersea and try to make himself very rich. But, with wonderful inevitability, he failed. The cynical old man. pushing pound notes along the gutter with his

[1] The accuracy of *The Eye Witness* does not match the charm of its prose manner, as can be judged by the sentence in which we read of King Charles I as 'the tall King'.
[2] Julian Jebb.

blackthorn stick, had long before made the decision, between Mammon and God, of whose servant he was.

Malcolm Muggeridge, brought down to see Belloc in extreme old age by his friend Auberon Herbert, thought him 'not a serene man. Although he has written about religion all his life, there seemed to be very little in him'.[1] This would certainly be true if by 'religion' is meant pious conversation, or an overt discussion of spirituality. It was contrary to Belloc's nature to be slushily pious; still less could he have boasted about the extent of his own spiritual enlightenment. But it is not wholly absurd to see in his last years the work of sanctification and grace in progress. That is not to say that he was turning into a saint in the full sense of the word. But there was an unquestionable growth in holiness. Night by night, morning by morning, he staggered in and out of the chapel and muttered his prayers, semi-audibly and rapidly. With much greater frequency than he had ever known in his active life, he received the sacraments. The time was when he would protest that, having been brought up before the days of Pius X, he could never get used to the idea of frequent communion. Now, he went to Holy Communion whenever mass was offered in the chapel at King's Land. A motley collection of priests were found to keep this going – an itinerant Italian sometimes came; sometimes, more rarely, the local parish priest. Now that Vincent McNabb was dead, Ronald Knox quite often came down to stay at King's Land for a few days. Belloc enjoyed his society very much. The two men shared a fastidious irony, which was all but inimical to religious feeling; combined with a firm sense of the truth of Catholicism to which they had consecrated their hearts as well as their intellects. In his funeral panegyric of Belloc, Knox was to preach,

> To be sure, he was prophet rather than apostle; he did not, as we say, 'make converts'. You do not often hear it said of Belloc, as you hear it said of Chesterton, 'I owe my conversion to him'. But the influence of a prophet is not to be measured by its impact on a single mind here and there; it exercises a kind of hydraulic pressure on the thought of his age. And when the day of wrath comes, and that book is brought out, written once for all, which contains all the material for a world's judgment, we shall perhaps see more of what Belloc was and did; how even his most irresponsible satire acted as a solvent force, to pierce the hard rind of self-satisfaction which, more than anything, kept Victorian England away from the Church; how the very overtones of his unostentatious piety

[1] Malcolm Muggeridge: *Like it was.*

H.B.—22

brought back to us memories of the faith, and of the Mass, and of our blessed Lady, to which English ears had grown unaccustomed.[1]

Whether or not it is proper to predict what we shall find in that aweful book, the evidence is that Belloc quietened down in old age. He was, in the first seventy years of his life, the most compulsively energetic person who could not bear to be in the same place for long. He was also irascible and selfish and unused to being checked. So one might have expected much railing and tempest when decrepitude bound him to King's Land. One can attribute the quietness of his latter days to many causes. He was tired and weak and senile before the age when it would be natural to use that adjective. He 'babbled o' green fields'; and there, among the green fields which he had celebrated with such strutting sentimentality in his verse, he was happy. The glorious thing about Belloc's verse is that it was almost all true; it sprang from the spouting well of joy which was his natural genius. Much to everyone's surprise, there therefore turned out to be more truth than could ever have been predicted in such verses as 'His own Country':

> When I get to my own country
> I shall lie down and sleep;
> I shall watch in the valleys
> The long flocks of sheep.
> And then I shall dream, for ever and all,
> A good dream and deep.[2]

But it would be false to dissociate this growing sense of peace from Belloc's religious faith. For the Faith, as well as providing a framework for his genius, was at its very core. And he was of his very essence a Catholic man that lived upon wine. His ancient prejudices against any Belloc joining religious orders were as strong as ever. When his beloved grand-daughter Marianne Jebb went to become a nun he thought it was 'damnable'; and a younger grandchild, Anthony Jebb, becoming a monk of Downside was 'a pretty good bore'.[3] After thirty years in a monastery, that grandson could perhaps be considered well qualified to judge the texture of Belloc's spirit in decrepitude. He recalls, with Bellocian certitude that, for all the limitations which old age and illness imposed upon him, Belloc was 'not imprisoned by these circumstances'.

[1] Speaight, p. 537.
[2] *Complete Verse*, p. 95.
[3] Speaight, p. 528 and Philip Jebb.

He would joke easily of his old age and decrepitude. He was never moody or sulky, but would accept with genuine outgoing responsiveness whoever or whatever was presented to him. He would sit in his study and make no demands to be amused or listened to, but would take up with you at once when you came into the room, and would accept it without a murmur when you upped and left him. As a monk I have lived with many old men and I can think of few who chafed less at the passing of their independence, the loss of their physical and mental powers, at the disappearance of their practical significance. Nor did he feel guilt over this dependence which was not his responsibility.[1]

*   *   *

For his eightieth birthday, it was decided to have a special party, as on his seventy-first and his sixtieth birthdays. It was a slightly pathetic affair now, for most of his old cronies were dead and, of close intimates, there were only left the handful of great ladies who made their periodic descent on King's Land to the excitement and amusement of the children: Katharine Asquith, Juliet Duff, Frances Phipps, Mary and Elizabeth Herbert. 'I have one foot in the grave,' he once muttered to Elizabeth Herbert, and then added – gesticulating with his short straight trouser-leg at the end of which was a knobbly hand-made boot – 'This foot.'

By now it was true, and even if King's Land had been large enough to contain all his friends, he would not have been able to receive them all at once. The party was therefore divided, with a small lunch-party on his birthday itself and a larger affair the next day. This division caused inevitable offence to his various acolytes and hangers-on. He was unaware of that. At moments, during both parties, it was not certain whether he knew what was going on. But he evidently did. 'I wish someone would give me something for my birthday,' he exclaimed with mischievous petulance, thoroughly enjoying the obsequious chorus which immediately went up, 'Oh! What can we get you, Mr Belloc? Do tell us.' There was a pause, and then they had their reply, 'A very large bag of money.'

The eightieth birthday was, inevitably, a time for semi-obituary 'assessments' of Belloc as a writer. Probably the most perceptive was a broadcast on the Home Service of the BBC by his old friend and sailing-companion Desmond MacCarthy, who as Literary Editor of *The New Statesman* had done so much to keep Belloc's reputation

---

[1] Anthony Jebb (Dom Philip Jebb, OSB).

alive. But, by 1950, MacCarthy was forced to concede that this reputation was already on the wane. He applied to Belloc Pope's lines

> The varying verse, the full resounding line
> The long majestic march and energy divine.

And the keynote of his tribute was Belloc's *variety*. 'I certainly cannot think of any other writer who has excelled or expressed himself in quite as many directions: drama is the only form he has never attempted ... Such versatility inspired distrust. The public loves labels; and there is no surer way of winning a safe reputation than to go on writing the same kind of book ...'[1]

But, although MacCarthy was a genuine admirer, the tone of his tribute is one of disappointment. He rightly praises the 'trenchancy' of Belloc's political and economic thought; the brilliance of his travel books; the wit of his satires, and the skill, as well as the variety, of his verse. There remains an unspoken 'but' in the encomium. And, with the passing of the years since Belloc's eightieth birthday, the 'but' has silenced all appreciation of his work. 'I have visited libraries,' MacCarthy wrote, 'where the works of Hilaire Belloc occupy several long shelves, but I doubt if even his ardent admirers possess them all.' Thirty years later, I have visited the same libraries and found that they have taken Belloc off the shelves and sold him to the second-hand bookshops.

There are two reasons for this. One is that Belloc is an offensive character to the majority of those who know about him. When, as a young publisher at Duckworths, Anthony Powell met him in 1928, he recalled, 'I can't imagine anyone more odiously bad mannered and charmless.'[2] This quality carries into Belloc's 'controversial' prose, his dealings with the heretics, his exposures of the corruptions of the rich. We live in a politer age than Belloc's. We dislike his bluster, his charmless rudeness, and we are nervous of anyone who could express such insensitively strong dislike of the Jews. This last, in my belief, is the chief reason for the obscurity of Belloc's reputation. In our century, for obvious and good reasons, anti-semitism is the unforgivable sin. One can laugh off almost any other psychological aberration in a man of genius. We allow writers to have flirted with Eugenics or Stalinism or the Occult. We forgive Yeats his silly adulation of frauds like Aleister Crowley and we forgive Shaw his unimaginatively blood-thirsty adulation of the Stalinist terror. But we cannot forgive Ezra Pound for snarling about the Jews. And we can forgive

[1] *The Listener*, July 27, 1950.
[2] Letter to the author.

Belloc even less, for in his book on the subject, published in 1922, he prophesied what would happen to European Jewry with such eery accuracy, as a direct consequence of liberal 'double-thinking' on the subject.

But the second reason why Belloc's reputation has not survived as well as those of some of his lesser contemporaries is his sheer carelessness as a craftsman. There was good reason for the librarians of the 1950s and 1960s to cart armfuls of Belloc's work into the lumber-room. He 'wrote' carelessly, and in later years he did not even bother to write: he merely strutted about his study dictating at a rapid pace to secretaries. Much of what he dictated in those years is remarkable if we consider it merely as *oratory*. It shows that he was extraordinarily eloquent, and that he thought, not in sentences, but in whole paragraphs. On the other hand, it is all very repetitive stuff. And there is not much in *Wolsey* that you cannot also find in *Cranmer*; little in *Cranmer* that is not to be found, often word for word, in *Cromwell* or *Milton*, or *Characters of the Reformation*.

But although Belloc's reputation has been tarnished by the second-rate things he wrote in a hurry, there is much of his work which will endure: the essays, the lyric poetry which he always modestly called his verse; *The Path to Rome*, *The Four Men* and almost all those passages in his books where he touches *Men* and almost all those passages in his books where he touches upon *place*. Perhaps he is best appreciated in anthologies, of which there are several. In his best work, moreover, we are always aware of him as a man, and not merely as a writer. There is a particular tone, a particular eye, which belongs to Belloc and to no other literary craftsman. It notices the beauty of the natural world. It feels a blend of anger and awe at the destruction of our past. Its note of tragedy is saved from sentimentality by irony. Its air of weary scorn is redeemed by piety.

Unfortunately Belloc left no Boswell, and we only catch half-echoes of his conversational manner in the letters which he dashed off, so voluminously but at such speed, to his friends and relations. His greatness really consisted not even so much in what he said as in what he was. There was no one else in the history of the world remotely like him. He was more strongly, more vigorously, more riotously, more intolerably *himself* than almost any other human being. Turn from almost any other biography to that of Belloc and it is what the palate would feel, having tasted a distinctive thing like coriander, only to be blasted by the hottest curry. The experience may be crude, but it is unforgettable.

Moreover, since his death, the world has become milder and

kinder. He found something 'horrible' in 'the Protestant ethos,' by which he meant, 'goodwill and peace and being kind to the cat and all that'.[1] This was partly because he thought that moral choice in a fallen universe was never as simple as the 'being kind to the cat' philosophy liked to imply. But it was also because he was temperamentally attracted to belligerence for its own sake. For instance, he was very fond of Luther, because 'he had that most valuable of the second-rate qualities, a passion for hatred which lent further drive to everything he did. His hatred was not directed against the Catholic Church nor against Italians nor against this or that but simply against anyone who put up the back of Martin Luther. It was a good straightforward honest human motive which we express in idiomatic English by the expression, "I'll larn you!" '[2] This admiration for Luther, and his reasons for it, are most revealing; and they should be borne in mind when we read his intemperate comments about the yids, or when he calls down 'the curse of the crucified God' upon the dons.[3] He curses from a demonic inner *energy*, 'the long majestic march and energy divine'.

★   ★   ★

It was the diminution of this energy which so shocked his friends when he grew old. The classic description of Belloc in old age is that of Evelyn Waugh in September 1952, when he and his wife paid their last visit to the great man.

> Sounds of shuffling. Enter old man, shaggy white beard . . . Thinner than I last saw him, with benevolent gleam. Like an old peasant or fisherman in a French film. We went to greet him at a door. Smell like fox. He kissed Laura's hand. I have known him quite well for nearly 20 years. It was slightly disconcerting to be greeted with a deep bow and the words: 'It is a great pleasure to make your acquaintance, sir'. Shuffled to chair by fire. During whole visit he was occupied with unsuccessful atempts to light an empty pipe.
>
> He wore black broad cloth garnished with garbage, enormous labourers' boots and an open collar. I in rather smart and conventional tweeds. He squinted at me for some time & said: 'We all wear exactly the same clothes nowadays . . .'
>
> He noticed my stick near the door and told the boys to put it away. Also a leaf that had blown in, which he had expelled. He looked hard at Laura and said: 'You are very like your mother, are you not'.

[1] JSN, September 23, 1940.
[2] BC, June 3, 1935.
[3] *The Diaries of Evelyn Waugh*, p. 572.

'She is taller'.

'English women are enormous. So are the men – giants'.

'I am short'.

'Are you sir I am no judge'. He could not follow anything said to him but enjoyed pronouncing the great truths which presumably he ponders . . .

There was now less than a year to pass before his death. Sunday, July 12, 1953, was an overcast day. Although summer had returned, Belloc had not resumed his normal custom, in the warmer months, of urinating on the lawn; instead, he made the journey down the dark corridor to the lavatory in preparation for luncheon. There were not many people in the house. Reginald Jebb was staying in London. There were only Eleanor Jebb, and her youngest child Julian, home from his first year at Cambridge with an old school friend, James Affleck. Frank Sheed's daughter Rosemary was also staying at King's Land; and that was all.

In all the years that Belloc had lived in that house, there had never been an accidental fire, though there was always an unspoken fear of it, based on the certainty that its wooden beams and panelled rooms could have gone up like a tinder-box with the greatest ease as someone with inebriated step carried a paraffin lamp down a darkened corridor, or turned over in bed and upset the candle on the table beside them. The smell of smoke on that Sunday before luncheon therefore awakened a very immediate response. Julian Jebb, who was with his mother in the kitchen, said at once, 'I think there's a fire in grandpapa's study', and they rushed to see what had happened.

The room was full of smoke. Julian Jebb made to open the window, but his mother told him not to, for if the fire was extensive, it would be encouraged by the draught.

Belloc was lying with his head on the fender. It would seem that a coal or log had fallen from the fire while he was out in the lavatory, and, stooping to pick it up, he had fallen into the grate. His head was not in the fire, and he was not disfigured, but his hair was a little scorched, and he was pale. As his grandson and his daughter propped him up with a pillow by the fender and covered him with a blanket, he murmured, 'This must be an awful bore for you.'

James Affleck and Rosemary Sheed, profoundly embarrassed to be attendant on this scene of intense family importance, hovered tactfully in the background. Julian Jebb knelt for a while and held his

[1] *The Diaries of Evelyn Waugh* p. 572.

grandfather's hand. Mrs Jebb dispatched James Affleck and Rosemary Sheed to ring for the ambulance. She gave them strict instructions not to summon the local hospital, but to take her father to the Mount Alvernia nursing-home of the Franciscan Missionaries in Guildford.

Belloc was peaceful and his eyes were closed while this was done. The only thing to do was to wait, and Julian Jebb went to join his mother in the drawing-room. She said, 'Poor darling: well, he has had a long and happy life.' There was no question but that this was the end, and when the ambulance came, she went with her father to Guildford.

With that exaggerated courtesy which seemed so anachronistic, Mr Belloc lingered three days in the nursing home at Guildford, giving his family and friends time to assemble for a conventional nineteenth-century death-bed scene. Even in the most slap-dash of his biographies, he was always good at describing his subject's death; and he was good at his own. His son Hilary arrived from California. Elizabeth Belloc materialised from nowhere, painfully thin, cigarette-stained and crowned in a blue cloche hat, thick with dust. Peter Belloc's widow Stella came, and her sister. James Hall came on the Wednesday and persuaded the Matron to allow Belloc to drink a glass of wine. On the next day, Thursday, July 16, 1953, he became unconscious, and some of his closest family and friends – J. B. Morton and his wife, Elizabeth Belloc, Reginald and Eleanor Jebb, Frances Phipps, and his old cook Edith Rance – knelt around the bed and recited the Rosary. Philip Jebb read prayers for a departing soul. Mr Belloc had already received last rites. It was a summer evening, still light, and upstairs in the chapel the nuns were singing 'O salutaris hostia', the Benediction hymn, whose final words moved him more than any other, with their prayer that we may enjoy eternal life in our true homeland with God. Outside the window, of that Franciscan house, the silence was broken with the song of a thrush.

INDEX